T0331546

Cyber–Physical Systems for Next–Generation Networks

Joel J. P. C. Rodrigues
National Institute of Telecommunications (Inatel), Brazil & Instituto de Telecomunicações, Portugal & University of Fortaleza (UNIFOR), Brazil

Amjad Gawanmeh
Khalifa University, UAE

A volume in the Advances in Computer and
Electrical Engineering (ACEE) Book Series

Published in the United States of America by
　　IGI Global
　　Engineering Science Reference (an imprint of IGI Global)
　　701 E. Chocolate Avenue
　　Hershey PA, USA 17033
　　Tel: 717-533-8845
　　Fax: 717-533-8661
　　E-mail: cust@igi-global.com
　　Web site: http://www.igi-global.com

Library of Congress Cataloging-in-Publication Data

Names: Rodrigues, Joel Jose P. C., editor. | Gawanmeh, Amjad, 1975- editor.
Title: Cyber-physical systems for next generation networks / Joel J.P.C.
　　Rodrigues and Amjad Gawanmeh, editors.
Description: Hershey, PA : Engineering Science Reference, [2018] | Includes
　　bibliographical references.
Identifiers: LCCN 2017045654| ISBN 9781522555100 (h/c) | ISBN 9781522555117
　　(eISBN)
Subjects: LCSH: Cooperating objects (Computer systems) | Automatic control.
Classification: LCC TK7895.E42 C94 2018 | DDC 006.2/2--dc23 LC record available at https://lccn.loc.gov/2017045654

This book is published in the IGI Global book series Advances in Computer and Electrical Engineering (ACEE) (ISSN: 2327-039X; eISSN: 2327-0403)

British Cataloguing in Publication Data
A Cataloguing in Publication record for this book is available from the British Library.

For electronic access to this publication, please contact: eresources@igi-global.com.

Advances in Computer and Electrical Engineering (ACEE) Book Series

Srikanta Patnaik
SOA University, India

ISSN:2327-039X
EISSN:2327-0403

MISSION

The fields of computer engineering and electrical engineering encompass a broad range of interdisciplinary topics allowing for expansive research developments across multiple fields. Research in these areas continues to develop and become increasingly important as computer and electrical systems have become an integral part of everyday life.

The **Advances in Computer and Electrical Engineering (ACEE) Book Series** aims to publish research on diverse topics pertaining to computer engineering and electrical engineering. **ACEE** encourages scholarly discourse on the latest applications, tools, and methodologies being implemented in the field for the design and development of computer and electrical systems.

COVERAGE

- Algorithms
- VLSI Fabrication
- Microprocessor Design
- Analog Electronics
- Programming
- Optical Electronics
- Computer science
- Computer Architecture
- Electrical Power Conversion
- Circuit Analysis

IGI Global is currently accepting manuscripts for publication within this series. To submit a proposal for a volume in this series, please contact our Acquisition Editors at Acquisitions@igi-global.com or visit: http://www.igi-global.com/publish/.

Titles in this Series

For a list of additional titles in this series, please visit: www.igi-global.com/book-series

Handbook of Research on Power and Energy System Optimization
Pawan Kumar (Thapar University, India) Surjit Singh (National Institute of Technology Kurukshetra, India) Ikbal Ali (Jamia Millia Islamia, India) and Taha Selim Ustun (Carnegie Mellon University, USA)
Engineering Science Reference • copyright 2018 • 500pp • H/C (ISBN: 9781522539353) • US $325.00 (our price)

Big Data Analytics for Satellite Image Processing and Remote Sensing
P. Swarnalatha (VIT University, India) and Prabu Sevugan (VIT University, India)
Engineering Science Reference • copyright 2018 • 253pp • H/C (ISBN: 9781522536437) • US $215.00 (our price)

Modeling and Simulations for Metamaterials Emerging Research and Opportunities
Ammar Armghan (Aljouf University, Saudi Arabia) Xinguang Hu (HuangShan University, China) and Muhammad Younus Javed (HITEC University, Pakistan)
Engineering Science Reference • copyright 2018 • 171pp • H/C (ISBN: 9781522541806) • US $155.00 (our price)

Electromagnetic Compatibility for Space Systems Design
Christos D. Nikolopoulos (National Technical University of Athens, Greece)
Engineering Science Reference • copyright 2018 • 346pp • H/C (ISBN: 9781522554158) • US $225.00 (our price)

Soft-Computing-Based Nonlinear Control Systems Design
Uday Pratap Singh (Madhav Institute of Technology and Science, India) Akhilesh Tiwari (Madhav Institute of Technology and Science, India) and Rajeev Kumar Singh (Madhav Institute of Technology and Science, India)
Engineering Science Reference • copyright 2018 • 388pp • H/C (ISBN: 9781522535317) • US $245.00 (our price)

EHT Transmission Performance Evaluation Emerging Research and Opportunities
K. Srinivas (Transmission Corporation of Andhra Pradesh Limited, India) and R.V.S. Satyanarayana (Sri Venkateswara University College of Engineering, India)
Engineering Science Reference • copyright 2018 • 160pp • H/C (ISBN: 9781522549413) • US $145.00 (our price)

Fuzzy Logic Dynamics and Machine Prediction for Failure Analysis
Tawanda Mushiri (University of Johannesburg, South Africa) and Charles Mbowhwa (University of Johannesburg, South Africa)
Engineering Science Reference • copyright 2018 • 301pp • H/C (ISBN: 9781522532446) • US $225.00 (our price)

IGI Global
DISSEMINATOR OF KNOWLEDGE

701 East Chocolate Avenue, Hershey, PA 17033, USA
Tel: 717-533-8845 x100 • Fax: 717-533-8661
E-Mail: cust@igi-global.com • www.igi-global.com

Table of Contents

Detailed Table of Contents

    Sa'ed Abed, Kuwait University, Kuwait
    Areej Abdelaal, Kuwait University, Kuwait
    Amjad Gawanmeh, Khalifa University, UAE

Energy demand has increased significantly in the recent years due to the emerging of new technologies and industries, in particular in the developing countries. This increase requires much more developed power grid system than the existing traditional ones. Smart grid (SG) offers a potential solution to this problem. Being one of the most needed and complex cyber-physical systems (CPS), SG has been addressed exhaustively by researchers, from different views and aspects. However, energy optimization yet needs much more studying and examination. Therefore, this chapter presents a comprehensive investigation and analysis of the state-of-the-art developments in SG as a CPS with emphasis on energy optimization techniques and challenges. It also surveys the main challenges facing the SG considering CPS factors and the remarkable accomplishments and techniques in addressing these challenges. In addition, the document contrasts between different techniques according to their efficiency, usage, and feasibility. Moreover, this work explores the most effective applications of the SG as a CPS.

    Jiwa Abdullah, University of Tun Hussein Onn Malaysia, Malaysia
    Nayef Abdulwahab Alduais, Hodeidah University, Yemen

Within the last 20 years, wireless communication and network has been one of the fastest-growing research areas. Significant progress has been made in the fields of mobile ad hoc network (MANET) and wireless sensor networks (WSN). Very recently, the cyber-physical system (CPS) has emerged as a promising direction to enrich human-to-human, human to-object, and object-to-object interactions in the physical world as well as in the virtual world. The possibilities are enormous, such that CPS would adopt, and even nurture, the areas of MANET and WSN because more sensor inputs and richer network connectivity are required. The chapter reviews what has been developed in these fields, outlines the projection of what may happen in the field of CPS, and identifies further works. The authors identify the unique features of WSN, raising some CPS critical examples, and then directing the future challenges of CPS. In order to fully comprehend the connection of WSN to CPS, the authors provide some preliminaries of WSN and establish their necessary connections.

Chapter 3

Cyber-physical systems (CPSs) are co-engineered integrating with physical and computational components networks. Additionally, a CPS is a mechanism controlled or monitored by computer-based algorithms, tightly interacting with the internet and its users. This chapter presents the definitions relating to dependability, safety-critical and fault-tolerance of CPSs. These definitions are supplemented by other definitions like reliability, availability, safety, maintainability, integrity. Threats to dependability and security like faults, errors, failures are also discussed. Taxonomy of different faults and attacks in CPSs are also presented in this chapter. The main objective of this chapter is to give the general information about secure CPS to the learners for the further enhancement in the field of CPSs.

Chapter 4

Software-defined networking (SDN) provides flexibility in controlling, managing, and dynamically reconfiguring the distributed heterogeneous smart grid networks. Considerably less attention has been received to provide security in SDN-enabled smart grids. Centralized SDN controller protects smart grid networks against outside attacks only. Furthermore, centralized SDN controller suffers from a single point of compromise and failure which is detrimental to security and reliability. This chapter presents a framework with multiple SDN controllers and security controllers that provides a secure and robust smart grid architecture. The proposed framework deploys a local IDS to provide security in a substation. Whereas a global IDS is deployed to provide security in control center and overall smart grid network, it further verifies the consequences of control-commands issued by SDN controller and SCADA master. Performance comparison and simulation result show that the proposed framework is efficient as compared to existing security frameworks for SDN-enabled smart grids.

Secured cyber-physical systems (CPS) requires reliable handling of a high volume of sensitive data, which is in many cases integrated from several distributed sources. This data can usually be interconnected with physical applications, such as power grids or SCADA systems. As most of these datasets store records using numerical values, many of the microaggregation techniques are developed and tested on numerical data. These algorithms are not suitable when the data is stored as it is containing both numerical and categorical data are stored. In this chapter, the available microaggregation techniques are explored and assessed with a new microaggregation technique which can provide data anonymity regardless of its type. In this method, records are clustered into several groups using an evolutionary attribute grouping algorithm and groups are aggregated using a new operator.

Chapter 6
Basman M. Alhafidh, Florida Institute of Technology, USA
William H. Allen, Florida Institute of Technology, USA

The process used to build an autonomous smart home system based on cyber-physical systems (CPS) principles has recently received increased attention from researchers and developers. However, there are many challenges to be resolved before designing and implementing such a system. In this chapter, the authors present a high-level design approach that simulates a smart home system by implementing three levels of the 5C architecture used in CPS modeling and uses well-known machine learning algorithms to predict future user actions. The simulation demonstrates how users will interact with the smart home system to make more efficient use of resources. The authors also present results from analyzing real-world user data to validate the accuracy of prediction of user actions. This research illustrates the benefits of considering CPS principles when designing a home autonomous system that reliably predicts a user's needs.

Chapter 7
Valentina Franzoni, La Sapienza University of Rome, Italy

The robot gAItano is an intelligent hexapod robot, able to move in an environment of unknown size and perform some autonomous actions. It uses the RoboRealm software in order to filter and recognize color blobs in its artificial vision stream, activate a script (VBScript in our case, or C or Python scripts) to compute decisions based on perception, and send the output to actuators using the PIP protocol. gAItano is thus a rational computerized agent: autonomous, or semi-autonomous when remote controlled; reactive; based on model (e.g., the line). gAItano moves in an environment which is partially observable, stochastic, semi-episodic, static, or semi-dynamic in case of human intervention, continuous both on perceptions and actions, multi-agent, because of human intervention that can have collaborative nature (e.g., when the human moves a block or the robot to increase his performance), or competitive (e.g., when the human moves a block or the robot to inhibit his performance).

Chapter 8
Antonio Marcos Alberti, Inatel, Brazil

Smart cities encompass a complex, diverse, and rich ecosystem with the potential to address humanity's biggest challenges. To fully support society demands, many emerging technologies should be gracefully integrated. Current architectures and platforms frequently address specific topics, requiring intricate coordination of partial solutions. In this context, interoperability of technological solutions is mandatory. Examples include interoperability of IETF standards (e.g., 6LowPAN, RPL, CoAP to other IEEE standards, such as 802.15.4, and Bluetooth). Designs based on these protocols are being largely employed worldwide. However, they have some limitations that deserve our attention. Recent examples, such as ramsomware and DDoS attacks, are concerning many people on the suitability of our current stacks. NovaGenesis (NG) is an alternative architecture for TCP/IP that has been already proofed. In this chapter, the NG model for smart cities is explored, presenting its benefits. Recent results in NG are summarized and discussed on the proposed scope.

Chapter 9

Mahmoud Meribout, Khalifa University, UAE
Imran Saied, University of Edinburgh, UK
Esra Al Hosani, Adco Corporation, UAE

Online and reliable monitoring of steam quality in power plants is of great importance in smart grids today since it can mitigate eventual erosions and buildups which may occur in associated metal equipment such as pipes and steam turbine. This in turn causes a substantial reduction in the amount of energy produced by the steam generator. This chapter presents state of the art online and offline sensing techniques used for steam quality monitoring in power plants. This includes optical, orifice, swirling, vortex, conductive, and PH meters. While offline monitoring techniques, such as isokinetic sampling technique are still widely deployed for steam monitoring mainly because of the relative simplicity, online monitoring techniques offer the possible to identify transient steam purity conditions. It also allows the prediction of future states of either the steam turbine or the steam quality and hence offers the possibility of effective preventive actions.

Chapter 10

Ali Ahmadinia, California State University – San Marcos, USA
Ahmed Saeed, COMSATS Institute of Information Technology, Pakistan

As computing devices have become an almost integral part of our lives, security of systems and protection of the sensitive data are emerging as very important issues. This is particularly evident for embedded systems which are often deployed in unprotected environments and at the same time being constrained by limited resources. Security and trust have also become important considerations in the design of virtually all modern embedded systems as they are utilized in critical and sensitive applications such as in transportation, national infrastructure, military equipment, banking systems, and medical devices. The increase in software content and network connectivity has made them vulnerable to fast spreading software-based attacks such as viruses and worms, which were hitherto primarily the concern of personal computers, servers, and the internet. This chapter discusses the basic concepts, security attacks types, and existing preventive measures in the field of embedded systems and multi-core systems.

Chapter 11

Yuri P. Pavlov, Institute of Information and Communication Technologies, Bulgarian
    Academy of Sciences, Bulgaria
Evgeniy Ivanov Marinov, Institute of Biophysics and Biomedical Engineering, Bulgarian
    Academy of Sciences, Bulgaria

Modeling of complex processes with human participations causes difficulties due to the lack of precise measurement coming from the qualitative nature of the human notions. This provokes the need of utilization of empirical knowledge expressed cardinally. An approach for solution of these problems is utility theory. As cyber-physical systems are integrations of computation, networking, and physical processes in interaction with the user is needed feedback loops, the aim of the chapter is to demonstrate the possibility to describe quantitatively complex processes with human participation. This approach permits analytical representations of the users' preferences as objective utility functions and modeling of the complex system "human-process." The mathematical technique allows CPS users dialog and is demonstrated by two case studies, portfolio allocation, and modeling of a competitive trade by a finite game and utility preference representation of the trader. The presented formulations could serve as foundation of development of decision support tools and decision control.

Preface

Cyber-physical systems (CPS) integrate real world applications with new computing, communication and networking technologies. This resulted in several advancement in the deployment and usage of such systems. Examples include the Smart Grid, SCADA, UAV, and several others. This book will introduce several state of the art on challenges in the techniques pertaining all aspects of CPS. It will provides a deep analyzes for different techniques and methodologies in the design and analysis of various types of CPS.

The new paradigms and tremendous advances in computing, communications and control have provided and supported wide range of applications in all domains of live, in particular, bridging the physical components and the cyber space leading to the Cyber Physical Systems (CPS). The notion of CPS is to use recent computing, communication, and control methods to design and operate intelligent and autonomous systems that can provide using cutting edge technologies. This require the use of computing resources for sensing, processing, analysis, predicting, understanding of data, and then communication resources for interaction, intervene, and interface management, and finally provide control for systems so that they can inter-operate, evolve, and run in a stable evidence-based environment. CPS has extraordinary significance for the future of several industrial domains and hence, it is expected that the complexity in CPS will continue to increase due to the integration of cyber components with physical and industrial systems.

Chapter 1 presents a comprehensive investigation and analysis of the state-of-the-art developments in the Smart Grid as a CPS with emphasis on the energy optimization techniques and challenges. It also surveys the main challenges facing the Smart Grid considering CPS factors and the remarkable accomplishments and techniques in addressing these challenges. In addition, the document analyzes and contrasts between different techniques and methodologies according to their efficiency, usage, algorithms and feasibility. Moreover, this work explores the most effective applications of the Smart Grid as a CPS; hopefully, this work contributes in energy optimization within the smart grid and encourages research efforts in this area.

Chapter 2 will address several applications of WSN in the area of CPS. The chapter addresses applications in CPS where wireless networks can be efficiently deployed, in particular, issues in mobile ad hoc networks (MANET) and WSN. The authors then identifies how wireless networks can help in enabling applications and platforms for Cyber Physical Sensor Networks.

Chapter 3 provides a brief introduction about safety-critical CPSs, dependable CPSs and fault-tolerant CPS. The chapter highlights current challenges in system safety, dependable and fault-tolerant. The authors identifies on state-of-the-art solutions that make CPS reliable.

Next, Chapter 4 tackles security issues in Software defined networking (SDN), an emerging paradigm that provides flexibility in controlling, managing, and dynamically reconfiguring the distributed heterogeneous smart grid networks. The chapter presents a framework with multiple SDN controllers and security controllers that provides a secure and robust smart grid architecture. The proposed framework deploys a local intrusion detection systems to provide security in a substation. Whereas a global intrusion detection systems is deployed to provide security in control center and overall smart grid network. It further verifies the consequences of control-commands issued by SDN controller and SCADA master. Performance comparison and simulation result show that the proposed framework is efficient as compared to existing security frameworks for SDN-enabled smart grids

Secured Cyber-Physical Systems is also addressed in Chapter 5, in particular, when dealing with a high volume of sensitive data, which is in many cases, integrated from several distributed sources. This data can usually be interconnected with physical applications, such as power grids or SCADA systems. The chapter proposed to extend microaggregation methods that are originally developed and tested on numerical data and apply it on CPS. The available microaggregation techniques are first explored and assessed, and then extended so that it can provide data anonymity regardless of its type. The technique is based on clustering records into several groups using an evolutionary attribute grouping algorithm and groups are aggregated using a new operator.

Chapter 6 presents a high-level design approach that simulates a smart home system by implementing three levels of the 5C architecture used in CPS modeling. The authors propose to use a well-known machine learning algorithms to predict future user actions. The simulation demonstrates how users will interact with the smart home system to make more efficient use of resources. The authors also present results from analyzing real-world user data to validate the accuracy of prediction of user actions. This research illustrates the benefits of considering CPS principles when designing a home autonomous system that reliably predicts a users' needs.

A CPS projected called *gAltano* is presented in Chapter 7, which is robot with real-time implementation of basic concepts for visual recognition of colored objects. The system is a combination of hardware and software components. The hardware includes a robot as well as other supporting equipment such as camera and sensors. On the other hand, the software part includes the design and implementation of an autonomous system that supports the artificial vision, color and camera management, colored-object recognition, object relocation, motion control, providing pros and cons considerations on the proposed solution.

Chapter 8 presents a novel smart city architecture based on the Nova Genesis project. It starts with an overview of the NovaGenesis proposal, its main concepts and current implementation. NovaGenesis concept that is presented in this chapter is an alternative architecture for the current TCP/IP architecture, applied in the context of smart cities. It is a project with continues development. Scalability and performance tests are being done at ICT Lab, Inatel, Brazil. A scenario closer to a real one is being deployed at Inatel smart campus (ISCampus) project.

Chapter 9 presents state of the art online and offline sensing techniques used for steam quality monitoring in power plants. This includes optical, orifice, swirling, vortex, conductive, and PH meters. While offline monitoring techniques, such as isokinetic sampling technique are still widely deployed for steam monitoring mainly because of the relative simplicity, online monitoring techniques offer the possible to identify transient steam purity conditions. It also allows the prediction of future states of either the steam turbine or the steam quality and hence offers the possibility of effective preventive actions. The chapter also presents a recent hybrid imaging system that uses both NIR (i.e. Near-infared) sensor to determine the type of contaminants and a THz imaging camera which measures the amount of contaminants as well as its flow rate.

Chapter 10 discusses the basic concepts, security attacks types and existing preventive measures in the field of embedded systems and multi-core systems. The issue of security and trust has become important in the design of embedded systems as they are utilized in critical and sensitive applications such as in transportation, national infrastructure, military equipment, banking systems and medical devices. The increase in software content and network connectivity has made them vulnerable to fast-spreading software-based attacks such as viruses and worms, which were hitherto primarily the concern of personal computers, servers, and the Internet. This chapter tackles embedded systems security.

Finally, Chapter 11 in this book demonstrates an analytical mathematical technique and the possibility to describe quantitatively complex social, ecological, biological and other processes. Such an approach provides analytical representations of the user's preferences as objective utility functions and mathematical description of the complex system „human-process". The suggested approach can be regarded as a realization of the prescriptive decision making and allows practitioners to take advantage of individual application of the achievements of decision making theory in various fields of human activities and CPS users dialog integrated in different networks and even with the internet. The approach is demonstrated by two case studies. The first one is portfolio allocation with Wiener process and portfolio allocation in the case of financial process with colored noise both modeled by Black-Scholes stochastic differential equation. The second case study is modeling of a competitive trade of small store by a finite game and *minmax* determination of the „saddle-point" as equilibrium of the trade. The presented formulations could serve as foundation of development of decision support tools for design of management/control in Cyber-Physical Systems. This value-oriented modeling leads to the development of preferences-based decision support in machine learning environment and control/management value based design.

This book highlights several challenging aspects in modern cyber physical systems. The contributors of this chapter come from various backgrounds with several real life applications. We hope this book will shed a light recent advancements in Cyber-Physical Systems for next generation networks.

Joel J. P. C. Rodrigues
National Institute of Telecommunications (Inatel), Brazil & Instituto de Telecomunicações, Portugal
& University of Fortaleza (UNIFOR), Brazil

Amjad Gawanmeh
Khalifa University, UAE

Chapter 1
DSM for Energy Optimization and Communications Within Smart Grid CPSs:
Investigation and Analysis

Sa'ed Abed
Kuwait University, Kuwait

Areej Abdelaal
Kuwait University, Kuwait

Amjad Gawanmeh
Khalifa University, UAE

ABSTRACT

Energy demand has increased significantly in the recent years due to the emerging of new technologies and industries, in particular in the developing countries. This increase requires much more developed power grid system than the existing traditional ones. Smart grid (SG) offers a potential solution to this problem. Being one of the most needed and complex cyber-physical systems (CPS), SG has been addressed exhaustively by researchers, from different views and aspects. However, energy optimization yet needs much more studying and examination. Therefore, this chapter presents a comprehensive investigation and analysis of the state-of-the-art developments in SG as a CPS with emphasis on energy optimization techniques and challenges. It also surveys the main challenges facing the SG considering CPS factors and the remarkable accomplishments and techniques in addressing these challenges. In addition, the document contrasts between different techniques according to their efficiency, usage, and feasibility. Moreover, this work explores the most effective applications of the SG as a CPS.

DOI: 10.4018/978-1-5225-5510-0.ch001

INTRODUCTION

Since electricity was discovered and utilized in the 19th century, impressive developments in the field of energy generation and transmission have occurred. Electric grids became a part of the infrastructure. These grids are essentially massive, interconnected physical networks. In addition, Renewable Energy (RE) resources like wind, geothermal, hydro and others are receiving more attention from the energy industry day by day. This is because energy demands are increasing as populations are increasing worldwide. The 2014 world energy outlook report (Energy Agency, n.d.) says that energy demand will raise by 37% by 2040 so the energy efficiency is required to utilize the energy supplies with the least environmental damage. As a result, the need for revolutionary improvements to the electric energy supply chain has increased dramatically. This need has led to the smart grid as an intelligent electric generation, transmission and distribution grid that integrates all the involved stakeholders in the process.

The smart grid can be viewed as the seamless integration of the physical power network infrastructure and the cyber systems of sensing, processing, communication and control. Adopting the emerging technologies of Cyber-Physical Systems (CPS) is vital for this integration to be properly deployed and utilized. This chapter provides an overview of the smart grid as a cyber-physical system and investigates the architecture of the grid accordingly.

Moreover, we focus on operation and transmission through the grid since this topic varies greatly from the traditional electric power grid. We also review the customer's side and how their role is different in this new envisioned future smart grid as "prosumers", producers and consumers of energy. In addition, the Demand-Side Management (DSM) part of this chapter is meant to provide the reader with clear, comprehensive view of the DSM concept and the different methods by which it is applied. These methods typically follow well-known approaches, such as heuristics and multi-agent systems. Consecutively, the widely used approaches are covered in the context of DSM.

An important difference between the traditional and smart grid is the later adopting two-way communication model instead of the typical one-way model, from the utility to the customer. This adds significant complexity to the communications through the smart grid, which communicates data, measurements and control information continuously and accurately in all the networks it includes. We find it is essential to examine the smart grid communications in detail. We support this part with security overview, security challenges and techniques.

The remainder of this chapter is organized as follows. Section 2 provides an overview of smart grid and Cyber-Physical System (CPS) concepts. Demand-Side Management (DSM) surveyed the various applicable methods such as heuristics and multi-agent systems is presented in Section 3. Furthermore, the smart grid communications is discussed in detail in Section 4 supported by comparisons. Section 5 presents important trends on smart grid CPS and provides an open discussion on the research areas. Finally, conclusions are presented in Section 6 with some future trends.

SMART GRID AS A CYBER-PHYSICAL SYSTEM

Smart Grid (SG) refers to a two-way flows of both electricity and information that creates an advanced, automated energy distribution network (Fang, Misra, Xue, & Yang, 2012). The smart grid is meant to solve many issues that face the traditional electric grid which has been almost unchanged for the last century (Karnouskos, 2011). Some of these issues are the delivery constraints due to limited transmission, limited control, centralized generation and manual restoration upon failures and blackouts (Fang et al., 2012). In order for the smart grid to replace the traditional one, it has to obtain specific features, documented by the National Energy Technology Laboratory for the U.S. Department of Energy as the seven principle characteristics for the grid; including self-healing, accommodation for all generation and storage options and optimization for assets and efficient operation (The NETL Modern Grid Initiative, 2007).

According to the National Institute of Standards and Technology (NIST) smart grid conceptual model (Nist, Publication, & National Institute of Standards and Technology, 2010), the smart grid has main seven domains, customers, markets, service providers, operations, bulk generation, transmission and distribution as shown in Figure 1. We use this architecture of different, interacting domains from (NIST) as a basis for the smart grid discussion. Customers in the smart grid architecture are not only consumers of energy; they have control on their energy usages and distribution. In addition, customers may generate energy as the Renewable Energy Systems (RESs) are improving, i.e., using solar, wind and hydro generators for micro generation of energy makes the customer a producer of energy, which makes the smart grid's two-way flows more efficient. Hence, the term "prosumers" has been introduced (Karnouskos, 2011).

Regarding the operation domain, the Energy Management Systems (EMSs) are used within the transmission operations to analyze and operate the transmission power system efficiently. In addition, Distribution Management Systems (DMSs) are used for operations of the distribution system. The operation domain focuses on managing and controlling the network, this control may be in monitoring and fault-management frames (Nist et al., 2010).

It is critical to view the generation and transmission domains within the smart grid. Generation is getting electricity from other energy forms. This includes bulk generation, managing its resources and measurements of the power flow. The generation domain communicates performance information with the transmission domain that links generation to distribution domain. The distribution domain has the

Figure 1. NIST smart grid framework
Source: Nist et al., 2010

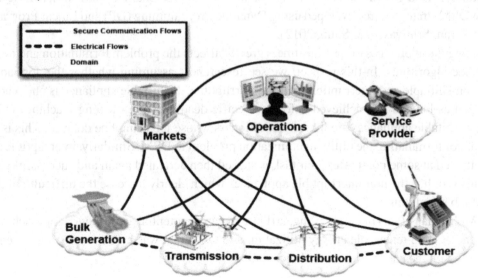

Remote Terminal Units (RTUs) and the distributed generation points as well as energy storage, control and measurements operations.

Looking more into the operation of the smart grid, the EMSs, from the operation domain, are placed in control centers to monitor and manage the transmission of electricity from generation domain to customers in the distribution domain. This is performed through Supervisory Control And Data Acquisition (SCADA) systems. These SCADA systems consist of networked sensors which obtain energy measurements, e.g. voltage and currents. This data is then dent to the control systems through RTUs within the SCADA system. Transmission lines and substations connect the physical generation, transmission and distribution systems (He & Yan, 2016).

Cyber-Physical Systems (SPSs) refer to physical systems with computational power, which are connected to web and may access specific services on the web (Thakur, Chaudhary, Tilokani, & Machado, 2017). CPSs are essential in the smart grid, especially the smart meters which manage the measurement of the energy consumption, transmit diagnosis to the service provider and receive signals from it (Zipperer et al., 1743).

Smart Grid is certainly an evolving technology in many ways. With various possibilities and considerations, including the demand-side management and renewable energy sources optimization, smart grid receives great attention in the research field. Even the vehicle-to-grid capability is addressed with algorithm designs and optimization approaches (Lopez, De La Torre, Martin, & Aguado, 2015).

DEMAND-SIDE MANAGEMENT

Demand-Side Management (DSM) is an important function of the smart grid as it aims to reduce the peak load demands for electricity with balance between utility and customers' needs. DSM methods are designed to schedule and shape the load profile which effectively increases the smart grid's viability and reduces costs of operation.

There are 6 main categories for DSM techniques: peak clipping and valley filling which are direct load-control methods, load shifting – from peak load to off-peak load using the time factor, strategic conservation, strategic load growth, and flexible load shape (Gellings & Chamberlin, 1987), (MAHARJAN, 2010). Most DSM strategies are developed using Dynamic Programming (DP) and Linear Programming (LP) (Logenthiran, Srinivasan, & Shun, 2012).

Categorizing the appliances of the consumers greatly affects the problem formulation and algorithm results in game algorithms. In this respect, we see researchers assuming whether the appliances are shifable or non-shiftable and interruptible or non-interruptible. A shiftable appliance is one whose task can be delayed as long as it is achieved before a specific deadline, i.e., washing machines or dryers, while the non-shifable appliances are like air conditioners whose job cannot be delayed. This is a basic consideration for formulating the utility maximization problem in DSM. Similarly, interruptible devices can be deactivated at some point after their task is started then activated again and successfully resume that task. This is unlike the non-interruptible appliances which clearly increase the difficulty of the load shifting and job scheduling.

In (Wu, Mohsenian-Rad, Huang, & Wang, 2011), a dynamic potential game theory approach was used propose a scheme with renewable energy utilization and DSM that was proven to save 38% generation cost compared with the case without DSM by simulation.

Heuristic-Based Methods

In Logenthiran et al., (2012), the authors proposed an Evolutionary Algorithm (EA) following the "load-shifting" technique, treating the scheduling issue as a minimization problem by a heuristics-based EA. The algorithm is generalized so it is independent from the load criteria which the given load curve represents, it shifts is to the desired load scheme. Clearly, this does not give a clear feedback on the effects the shifting produces on the other properties of the load. They raised some issues for most DSM strategies like system specific, which is not applicable to practical systems that have large controllable loads of a wide variety of independent devices because of the DP and LP used for developing them.

The authors in Ansar et al., (2017) and Javaid et al., (2017) implemented and compared different meta-heuristic techniques for load scheduling of House Energy Management System (HEMS). In Ansar et al., (2017), the techniques used are the Enhanced Differential Evolution (EDE), Harmony Search Algorithm (HSA), Bacterial Foraging Algorithm (BFA), and Genetic Algorithm (GA). EDE performed best considering the total cost, Peak-to-Average Ratio (PAR) and waiting time which reflects the user's comfort. However, it is important to note that meta-heuristic techniques do not reach optimization (Javaid et al., 2017). Furthermore, (Javaid et al., 2017) proposed a Genetic Wind-Driven (GWD) algorithm which outperformed GA and the other techniques in terms of electricity cost. The user comfort, represented by the waiting time was not considered in GWD. It is notable that heuristic-based solutions demonstrated a greater performance compared to exact solutions in (Goudarzi, Hatami, & Pedram, 2011) which addressed the problem of minimizing the electricity bills for the a single user by scheduling policies.

Authors in H. N. Khan et al., (2017) developed two heuristic algorithms, one is a BFA and the other is a StrawBerry Algorithm (SBA) with the goal of minimizing energy costs and PAR. BFA achieved better results in minimizing energy costs while SBA outperformed BF in terms of PAR minimization. The user comfort was traded-off for achieving the goal. The Binary Particle Swarm Optimization (BPSO), Ant Colony Optimization (ACO), two heuristic algorithms, along with GA, were used in (Rahim et al., 2016) to design a DSM system focused on PAR and electricity bill reduction and maximization of user-comfort. GA outperformed both BPSO and ACO in this regard. The work in (Meng & Zeng, 2016) used GA-based approach to develop an optimal pricing model for Demand Response (DR) considering shiftable and non-shiftable appliances. In Zhuang Zhao, Won Cheol Lee, Yoan Shin, & Kyung-Bin Song, (2013), GA was used to reduces electricity cost and PAR through the proposed architecture. It combined Real-Time Pricing (RTP) and Inclined Block Rate (IBR) pricing model to achieve the desired cost and PAR reduction.

Multi-Agents Methods

Multi-agents technology, MAS, has been taking an active role in power engineering applications as examined in (Kulasekera, Gopura, Hemapala, & Perera, 2011). We will focus here on MAS in microgrids which consists of distributed small power facilities.

Authors in Logenthiran, Srinivasan, & Shun, (2011) proposed a MAS approach for DSM which uses energy market for resource allocation. The system contains load agents, generator agents along with a DSM agent. An electronic auction platform is available through the DSM agent. The bidding behavior is managed by an intelligent system that dynamically reacts to market changes. Though not highly realistic, the system simulations demonstrate sustainable cost savings with reduction of peak load demand through load shifting.

MAS has been used extensively in market model analysis, i.e., electricity trading within microgrids, as we see in the literature. Maximizing revenue from the microgrid was addressed in (Funabashi, Tanabe, Nagata, & Yokoyama, 2008), where an approach of a single microgrid control agent and several load and generation agents was proposed. The simulation shows it is a promising method, by applying it to a model system. In H.-M. Kim & Kinoshita, (2009), a power market model is presented for the effective operation of the microgrid. This work considered the particular characteristics of microgrids as being eco-friendly and commercialization in a complex environment where ownership of each participant is different. The work in Basu et al., (2007) proposed a pricing mechanism for the microgrid energy using a case study where bidding strategies depend on demand and supply side.

Power restoration is another objective of MAS in microgrids. An interesting load restoration algorithm was proposed in Yinliang Xu & Liu, (2011) that consists of agents which learn information from their direct neighbors to make decisions of synchronized load restoration. Global information is also realized through Average-Consensus Theorem. This information is then modeled constructing a 0-1 knapsack problem and solved accordingly using existing algorithms. Through simulation studies, authors have demonstrated that this proposed algorithm can be applied effectively to systems of any structure or size.

Figure 2 illustrates a conceptual, single-layered architecture of MAS that includes a distributed generation agent, a control agent and a user agent. It also has a secondary database agent. These individual agents are important to allow distributed control for the microgrid system. However, it is noteworthy to point-out the importance of multi-layer architecture to achieve a robust distributed control model.

Figure 2. Conceptual architecture for MAS
Source: Kulasekera et al., (2011)

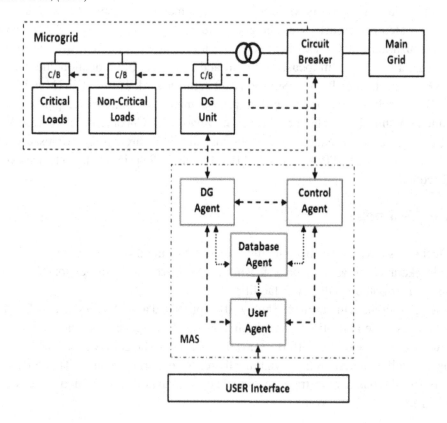

Along with MAS systems, game theory is effectively invested in DSM. In the following section, we examine it and see many approaches that used it to model different systems and effectively achieve high performance.

Game Theory in DSM

Game theory is an important mathematical modelling tool of situations in which multiple participants, i.e., players, affect each other's outcomes, with or without communication between these participants (Noam Nisan, Tim Roughgarden, ´C Eva Tardos, 2007). For the games in which participants are independent and do not perform communication or coordination of strategic decisions, the term "noncooperative game theory" is used in literature (Başar, Olsder, & Society for Industrial and Applied Mathematics., 1999). The other class of game theory, "cooperative game theory" implies the coordination between the players over the decisions they make to reach the outcomes. Researchers have addressed various applications of both classes in the smart grid over the recent years and we will go over their work in this section.

Another area of games that have major applications in smart grids is the "learning algorithms". A learning scheme has basically three steps each participant applies in order: observing the current state of the game, estimating the forthcoming utility and updating the strategy accordingly (Fudenberg & Levine, 1998).

It is fundamental to realize that game approaches in DSM aim to shape the load to achieve utility maximization for the players, i.e., minimizing electricity expenses for consumers and shifting the load from on-peak hours to off-peak hours for the utility or the electricity provider. Communication is typically available between a user and the utility through the smart meter, however, multiple users are assumed not to communicate over the consumption decisions. That is why most game algorithms that we will mention shortly are considered non-cooperative approaches (Saad, Han, Poor, & Basar, 2012).

Looking into work done under the assumption of interruptible appliances, the authors in Mohsenian-Rad, Wong, Jatskevich, Schober, & Leon-Garcia, (2010) proposed an algorithmic game approach. The method minimizes the PAR of the total energy demand and cost as well as individual's electricity expenses. This optimization is carried out in the scenario of a single utility serving the end users in an autonomous distributed DSM system taking the advantage of the two-way communication property in the envisioned smart grid to exchange information between the users and between the users and the utility company. The work in (Mohsenian-Rad et al., 2010) achieved the global optimal equilibrium of minimizing energy costs in the common scenario of a single utility company. To benefit from the storage possibility, (Nguyen, Song, & Han, 2012) proposed a theoretical game approach in which users can store energy during low-demand, and thus low-cost, periods and use that stored energy at the high-demand time slots. This minimizes the energy costs further and reduces PAR as well. The utility in such scenarios change the energy costs during the day according to users' profiles and load status. Continuing with the work done under the assumption of interruptible appliances with consideration of energy storage ability of users, Thanh Dang et al. in (Thanh Dang & Ringland, 2012) expanded to include the active users who can sell the energy they have back to the grid. By formulating a linear optimization problem with efficient solution, they show through simulation that the proposed approach can reduce the energy cost by 20% with comparison to other approaches mentioned in Thanh Dang & Ringland, (2012).

Moving to the more realistic, non-interruptible appliances assumption, an approximation algorithm was proposed and proven more effective than greedy and randomized algorithms in Tang, Huang, Li, & Wu, (2013) for reducing the peak demand or delay by a set of schedules. The main two factors considered in Tang et al., (2013) were the peak demand under fixed delay and the opposite, delay under fixed peak constraint, forming two problems solved effectively by their approximation methods. The authors in Goudarzi et al., (2011) also went for the non-interruptible appliances in their branch-and-bound approach to minimizing energy expenses from the single user perspective.

The assumption of both interruptible and non-interruptible appliances is heavily considered in the research work as well. For instance, Samadi et al. in (Samadi, Mohsenian-Rad, Wong, & Schober, 2014) addressed the problem of the utility's uncertainty of the energy prices effect on the users' profiles under the aforementioned assumption. The two designed two real-time pricing algorithms are based on simultaneous perturbation and finite-difference methods. The authors in R.-S. Liu & Ren-Shiou, (2016) addressed a more complex scenario in which the non-interruptible appliances can be delayed, meaning that they can be scheduled to be set active in later slots after the earliest slot in which they are allowed to. Considering the emerging use of renewable energy, the authors assume all users are equipped with solar-plus-battery system which reduces the overall system load. In N. Li, Chen, & Low, (2011), the authors considered the cases of the working times of some non-interruptible appliances were given while others considered shiftable appliances, like the hybrid electric vehicles.

COMMUNICATION IN THE SMART GRID

As we mentioned earlier, a main characteristic of the Smart Grid over the traditional grid is its bidirectional flow of energy and information. This flow occurs through transmission and distribution (T&D) systems. T&D include measurement and management technologies, which require specific communication requirements. These requirements are the quality of service (QoS), sustainability, reliability, coverage and security (Kabalci, 2016). Note that smart control and intelligent, adaptive communication within the smart grid is essential in providing these requirements (Fangxing (Fran) Li et al., 2010). We will investigate the different communication technologies in smart grid, their advantages and disadvantages and their security aspect as well.

Communication Overview

The traditional grid has the automated meter reading (AMR) and the automatic meter management (AMM) systems were used for metering and management, but in the smart grid, these two are subsystems of the advanced metering infrastructure (AMI). The AMI is a system that measures, saves and analyzes energy usage, upon request or a pre-defined schedule. AMI performs its tasks by receiving information from related devices, like smart meters (Hadi Safari Farmad & Saeedeh Biglar, 2012). Components of AMI include the AMR, AMM, smart meters, meter data management systems (MDMS), home and wide area networks (HAN & WAN), neighborhood area networks (NAN) and operational gateways and systems for data integration into software application platforms (Siano, 2014). Looking into MDMS as viewed by NELT in (NETL Modern Grid Strategy, 2008) gives an insight to the importance of AMI in the envisioned smart grid. MDMS is a database that performs validation, editing and estimation on the AMI data to ensure its accuracy regardless of the disruptions in the communications network or at customer premises. MDMS enables interaction between different information systems such as consumer information system, outage management system, geographic information system and the transformer load management. Figure 3 illustrates the communication networks in the smart grid.

Figure 3. Smart grid communications networks

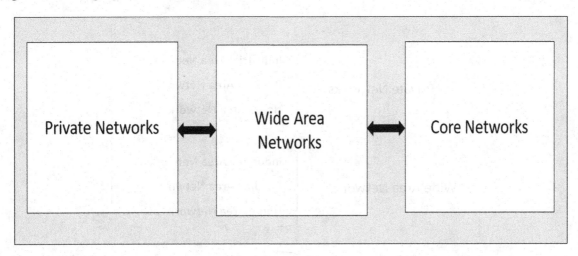

IEEE 2030-2011 standard defines the communication architecture of the smart grid ("IEEE SA -2030-2011- IEEE Guide for Smart Grid Interoperability of Energy Technology and Information Technology Operation with the Electric Power System (EPS), End-Use Applications, and Loads," n.d.). It defines a logical structure of three sub-networks. These are the core network for the utility, the distribution layer network and the private networks. Starting with the core network, it consists of broadband communication architectures, e.g., local area network (LAN), virtual private network (VPN) and voice over internet protocol (VoIP) (Ancillotti, Bruno, & Conti, 2013)(W. Li & Zhang, 2014)(Khalifa, Naik, & Nayak, 2011) (Fan et al., 2013). Moving to the network located at the distribution layer, a wide area network (WAN), we see it is constructed of the neighborhood area network (NAN) and field area network (FAN). Being at the distribution layer, NAN and FAN include various control and monitoring blocks like AMIs and remote terminal units (Kuzlu, Pipattanasomporn, & Rahman, 2014). The last network is related to customer side and it is made up of the home area network (HAN), building area network (BAN) and the industrial area network (IAN).

Figure 4 illustrates the main components of the structure (R. H. Khan & Khan, 2013). Communication within WAN network requires wide coverage range, low latency, high data throughputs and capacity. For customer premises network, low cost, low power consumption, simplicity and security are the main requirements (Kuzlu & Pipattanasomporn, 2013). Communication in smart grid networks utilizes both wired and wireless technologies. In the following section, we examine these technologies and discuss their fit within the communication requirements.

Wired Communication Technologies in the Smart Grid

The wireline technologies are basically the power-line communication (PLC), digital subscriber line (DSL) and the fiber optic. PLC is already constructed and widely used, this is a great advantage for suppliers who consider the low maintenance cost as basic decision criteria. There are two types of PLC, the narrowband PLC (NB-PLC) and the more recent broadband PLC (BB-PLC). PLC provides means for carrying signals over the existing power lines with consideration of its low data rates compared to DSL or fiber optic. NB-PLC operating range is between 3 to 500 kHz with data rates beyond 1 Mbps. There

Figure 4. Main components of the communication networks structure of the smart grid

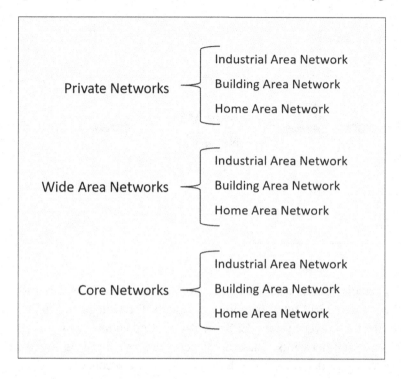

are low-frequency NB-PLC signals and high-frequency NB-PLC signals and each is more suitable for specific applications. On the other hand, BB-PLC has data rates of hundreds of Mpbs and an operating range of 2 – 250 MHz. the main drawback of BB-PLC is the short distance it covers compared to NB-PLC. Power line communication technology has key applications in the smart grid, including the automation of medium voltage grids and substations which require low data rates with focus on location and fault restoration as heavily examined in (Cataliotti, Cosentino, Di Cara, Russotto, & Tine, 2012). Another application of PLC in the smart grid is the PLC-based smart meters. AMI is another application for NB-PLC, especially the low frequency NB-PLC signals as they pass easily through the MV transformers (Galli, Scaglione, & Wang, 2010). Generally, NB-PLC technology has an effective role in sensing and communication tasks in the smart grid while BB-PLC is more suitable for end-user internet applications and smart grid applications (Usman & Shami, 2013). However, PLC has its limitations including its high signal losses, electromagnetic interference issues and complex routing. Also, PLC is not suitable for communication in areas involving switches and reclosers as in (Gungor & Lambert, 2006). Considering their characteristics, NB-PLC is used for communications within the NAN, FAN and WAN while BB-PLC is fit for HAN, BAN, IAN and small scale AMI as discussed in (R. H. Khan & Khan, 2013).

Another wireline communication technology used in the smart grid is the DSL. It is a digital data transmission technology, using the typical telephone lines. Since the DSL infrastructure is already established and provided at many customer premises, it is a cost-effective communication technology for smart grid applications. However, DSL efficiency degrades over distance, making it unreliable for customers far away from energy provider. There are three types of DSL, asymmetric DSL (ADSL) that provides 8 Mbps downstream of data, ADSL2+ that reaches downstream of 24 Mbps, and Very-high bit rate DSL (VDSL) transmitting up to 52 Mbps downstream data transmission over the copper wires.

It is noteworthy that communication operators may charge utilities for using their DSL infrastructure, decreasing the financial advantage of this communication technology. DSL finds fit for use in the AMI, NAN and FAN considering the distance it covers.

The last wireline technology used for communication within the smart grid that we discuss in this chapter is the fiber optic. Optical networks provide ultra-high bandwidth, long distance communication and robustness against electromagnetic interference which are the requirements for communication within WAN considering that WAN applications efficiency correlates with the most stringent communication network characteristics in terms of bandwidth, latency, and reliability (Kuzlu et al., 2014). Although fiber optic may appear suitable for all networks in the smart grid, it is not. Optic fiber networks require high installation cost and are not efficient for upgrading nor metering applications (Kabalci, 2016). Table 1 summarizes our discussion of wired communication technologies of the smart grid.

Wireless Communication Technologies in the Smart Grid

Wireless technologies utilization in the smart grid has been researched heavily, since these technologies offer advantageous installation and coverage features. However, they have limited bandwidth and are sensitive to interference (Yi Xu & Wang, 2013). LAN networks like NAN and FAN are thus the most suitable areas for wireless technologies deployment, communicating with the smart grid devices. Starting with the IEEE 802.15.4 standard, named WPAN, we find it has low deployment cost and very low power consumption. It also follows the ZigBee and ZigBee Pro standards which reach up to 100 m and 1600 m, respectively. IEEE 802.15.4 has data rate of 256 kbps, so WPAN has low bandwidth. On the other hand, WPAN is fully compatible with IPv6-based networks, making it a good choice for HAN, NAN, FAN, IAN and AMI. Wi-Fi is another technology, following standards IEEE 802.11 e/s/n and p

Table 1. Wireline technologies for smart grid communication

Technology	Characteristics (Distance and Data Rates)	Advantages	Disadvantages	Network(s)
PLC	NP-BLC: 150 Km or more, 1-10 kbps for low data rate, 10-500 kbps for high data rate. BB-PLC: 1.5 Km, 1-10 Mpbs typically.	• Low operation and maintenance cost. • Already constructed infrastructure.	High signal losses. Considerable disruptive effects by electromagnetic interference. Complex routing.	NP-PLC: NAN, FAN, WAN. BB-PLC: HAN, BAN, IAN, small scale AMI.
DSL	ADSL: 5 Km, 8 Mbps d/ 1.3 Mbps u ADSL2: 7 Km, 12 Mbps d/ 3.5 Mbps u ADSL2+: 7 Km, 24 Mbps d / 3.3 Mbps u VDSL: 1.2 Km, 52-85 Mbps d/ 16-85 Mbps u VDSL2: 300- 1.5 Km, 200 Mbps d/ 200 Mbps u	Already constructed infrastructure Widely distributed broadband	Possible high cost for using the infrastructure. Unsuitable for long distances	AMI, NAN, FAN.
Fiber Optic	AON: 10 Km, 100 Mbps u/ 100 Mbps d BPON: 20-60 Km, 155 – 622 Mbps EPON: 20 Km, 1 Gbps	Ultra-high data rates Long-distance coverage Robustness against electromagnetic interference.	High installation cost Not efficient for upgrading High cost for terminal equipment	WAN

(WAVE), provides much higher bandwidth, reaching up to 600 Mbps for IEEE 802.11n and a distance of 1 Km for IEEE 802.11 p. Although Wi-Fi has higher power consumption and a higher interference spectrum, it is more flexible and suitable for various use cases unlike WPAN which face limitation with building large networks (Ziming Zhu, Lambotharan, Woon Hau Chin, & Zhong Fan, 2012).

Cellular technologies that are based on global system for mobile communications (GSM) provide high coverage compared to other wireless technologies. For example, UMTS, a widely-used 3G technology provides a coverage distance up to 5 Km and uplink data rate of 22 Mbps in its HSPA+ standard. The (4G) technology, which follows LTE and LTE Advanced standards, is even a more improved choice with coverage up to 30 Km, 1 Gbps downlink, 500 Mbps uplink data rates and wider spectrum (R. H. Khan & Khan, 2013). However, higher cost comes with the more licensed spectrum. Utilities may be obligated to pay expensively for communication service providers as well. Concluding GSM, we point-out its flexibility and support of millions of devices, a major advantage.

Out of cellular coverage, comes the satellite technology fit. It provides high reliability even for long distance communication. Satellites are located at orbits named Low Earth Orbits (LEO), Medium Earth Orbits (MEO) and Geostationary Earth Orbits (GEO), each has its characteristics. LEO provides 2.4-28 kbps data rate, while GEO reaches 1 Mbps, with BGAN technology. Clearly, these are low transmission rates compared to cellular technologies, but satellite covers up to 6000 Km which is its notable advantage. With the expected lower costs of smaller satellite stations, there is a chance to integrate this technology into smart grid applications and AMI networks (Ancillotti et al., 2013). Table 2 lists the aforementioned wireless technologies along with others.

A topic that is extensively addressed by researchers regarding the smart grid is its security, with focus on traffic management and data accuracy. In the following section, we discuss the security aspect of smart grid communication as studied in the literature.

Table 2. Wireless technologies for smart grid communication

Technology	Characteristics (distance, data rates)	Advantages	Disadvantages	Network(s)
WPAN	ZigBee Pro: 1600 m IEEE 802.15.4: 256 kbps	Very low power consumption Low deployment cost Fully-compatible with IPv6-based networks	Low bandwidth Limitations to building large networks	HAN, BAN, IAN, FAN, NAN, AMI
Wi-Fi	IEEE 802.11n: 300 m, 600 Mbps	Low deployment cost Cheap equipment Flexibility	High power consumption High interference spectrum Simple QoS support	HAN, BAN, IAN, FAN, NAN, AMI
GSM	3G (HSPA+): 5 Km, 84 Mbps d/ 22 Mbps u 4G (LTE Advanced): 30 Km (acceptable performance), 1 Gbps d/ 500 Mbps u	Supports millions of devices. Low terminal-equipment power consumption High flexibility Open-industry standards	High use charges (to service providers) High cost for the licensed spectrum	HAN, BAN, IAN, FAN, NAN, AMI
Satellite	100 – 6000 Km. LEO: 2.4 – 28 Kbps GEO: to 1 Mbps	High reliability Long distance	High latency High Cost (terminal equipment)	WAN, AMI

Source: R. H. Khan & Khan, 2013

Communication Security of the Smart Grid

As the envisioned smart grid will be connecting millions of devices through communication networks, critical security issues arise. These issues include the software-level security, i.e., privacy and protection of the communication systems and the collected and processed information throughout the grid. Also, physical security requirements are studied for the physical components of the grid, e.g., smart meters, devices and power systems (Wang & Lu, 2013). Security requirements of the smart grid are discussed extensively in (Yan, Qian, Sharif, & Tipper, 2012). In short, these requirements include privacy, integrity, availability, authentication, authorization, auditability, non-repudiability, third-party protection and trust.

Privacy is concerned with the power consumption data of the customers. This behavioral information becomes especially worthy when financial or political motivations align (McDaniel & McLaughlin, 2009). Data integrity attacks attempt to illegitimately, deliberately modify the information in the smart grid system by unauthorized persons or systems. The main target for such attacks is the critical information exchanged through the grid's communication system including the customer's pricing details or utility's voltage readings. In (Y. Liu, Reiter, & Ning, 2009), the authors presented a false data injection attack (FDIA), and proved it can be used by attackers to bypass the existing bad-measurements detection techniques.

A survey was conducted in Liang, Zhao, Luo, Weller, & Dong, (2017) covering FDIA in power systems. Multiple FDIA schemes have been developed, mainly fulfilling the objective of finding the least-effort attack, the least-information attack or the specific-target attack. Each objective of the aforementioned three objective has been addressed by developing schemes for achieving it. For instance, the first objective, i.e., finding the least-effort attack, schemes have been developed to identify it, based on heuristic (Y. Liu et al., 2009), sparse (L. Liu, Esmalifalak, Ding, Emesih, & Han, 2014), greedy (Hao, Piechocki, Kaleshi, Chin, & Fan, 2015; T. T. Kim & Poor, 2011) and graph theoretic optimization (Kosut, Jia, Thomas, & Tong, 2011). For the least-information FDIA, graph method has been used to develop effective schemes as (Rahman & Mohsenian-Rad, 2012). An even more complicated scenario, with basically no knowledge of the system topology, was studied (Esmalifalak, Nguyen, Zheng, & Zhu Han, 2011; Yu & Chin, 2015) and FDIA schemes were developed depending on historic measurements. Regarding the third objective, we find in the literature that target-specific FDIA techniques were developed. An interesting utilization of such FDIA schemes causes load re-distribution in the transmission systems and induces transmission congestion in power markets to increase operational costs and financial issues (He & Yan, 2016).

When intruders attempt to deny, delay or even corrupt the information transmission through the system between authorized users and nodes, this attempt is an availability attack, or a Denial-of-Service (DoS) attack. Since most part of the smart grid will be IP-based components (Sidhu & Yin, 2007) that follow IP/TCP protocols which are vulnerable to DoS attacks (Schuba et al., n.d.; Yaar, Perrig, & Song, n.d.), research work has been conducted heavily in this regard as in (Shichao Liu, Liu, & El Saddik, 2013) in which a careful study was conducted and proved that the existence of DoS attacks make the dynamics of a power system unstable. In wireless-based communication networks, launching DoS attacks can be very easy for intruders, since these networks are prone to jamming attacks (Y. Liu, Ning, Dai, & Liu, 2010; Strasser, Popper, Capkun, & Cagalj, 2008).

Authentication is the ability to correctly determine the identity of a communication system participator and matches this identity with the corresponding system-defined user account. Authorization usually utilizes the authentication result to control the access of each user, or system, to other systems. Another significant security requirement of the smart grid is the ability to reconstruct all the relevant system actions from its historic records, after a malfunction or an attack. This is auditability, which is needed to determine the malfunction reasons and the attack consequences. This is essential for the effective operation of a large-scale system, such as the envisioned smart grid. Non-repudability means providing an irrefutable proof of specific actions taken by a third party within the system, even when that party is refusing to take responsibility for these actions. This is related to legal issues and regulations. The third-party protection is concerned with the ability to protect and compensate a harmed third party for any damages that resulted from security attacks on the grid. Finally, the security architecture of the future grid is not a completely new system; it is rather an expansion to existing technologies, in many aspects. Only some of this architecture is newly and specifically developed for the grid. Both the old and new layers of the architecture must be compatible with all the software applications and protocols used within the grid and acquire the flexibility of securely updating or interchanging parts of the system later, according to new laws and requirements (Kuntze, Rudolph, Cupelli, Liu, & Monti, 2010).

After we looked into the main security concerns of the future smart grid, we move on to examine some possibilities and determine their suitability in the scope of the aforementioned requirements. The first choice one may have is to isolate the communication networks from the public, i.e., do not use existing internet and keep the grid network private within the utility access. This certainly limits the threats that typically use the internet to reach to victims, including worm attacks. We find more sense in such isolation by recalling a distributed DoS attack that disrupted the directory name servers (DNSs). That attack blocked users from accessing all resources through these DNSs (Carl, Kesidis, Brooks, & Suresh Rai, 2006). However, making a completely separate network in the highly-connected world of today, is not feasible nor reasonable from a business point of view (Yan et al., 2012). Instead, investing the effort and technology in securing all network connections with focus on Internet connections is efficient and more convenient for customers and utilities. One of the solutions proposed in the literature is the compressed reading for smart metering in the smart grid communication (H. Li, Mao, Lai, & Qiu, 2010). As the smart meters are required to wirelessly transmit their readings to an access point (AP) and these meters are numerous, a simultaneous access is needed to avoid the large delay that would arise if carrier sensing multiple access (CSMA) were used. The proposed compressed reading allows this simultaneous transmission and the AP is able to distinguish the information from different smart meters. This is meant to protect the privacy of customers' data. Another solution serving the same purpose, i.e., ensuring privacy, was proposed in (Efthymiou & Kalogridis, 2010) where authors presented an anonymization process for the frequent electrical metering data transmitted by a smart meter. This method provides authenticated anonymous metering data to the utility that is difficult to associate with a specific meter or consumer, but attributable to a specific location within the electricity distribution network. Authors in (Kalogridis, Efthymiou, Denic, Lewis, & Cepeda, 2010) suggested that routing scheme for home electrical power can be used to protect the consumer's privacy by moderating the home's load signature. This hides appliance load information. This work proposed a power-mixing algorithm with a power management model with a rechargeable battery. The authors then evaluated the protection level according to three different privacy metrics: information theoretic privacy matrix, correlation/regression matrix and a clustering classification matrix.

Stored data encryption received proper research attention as stated in (Kühn, Selhorst, & Stüble, 2007), (Cesena, Ramunno, & Vernizzi, 2008) and (Kühn & Stüble, 2009). These efforts proposed mechanisms for encrypting stored data with storage key shielded. Individual storage keys include private part that is unknown to the host system, the storage root key (SRK) encrypts these keys to develop a key chain. Then, these individual keys can be used to secure potentially unlimited data with no restrictions on the medium. Privacy management software tools made available to consumers to manage their data privacy was discusses in (Simo Fhom et al., 2010) as well.

Bad data is one of the cyber-attacks modeled and investigated in the literature as well. These cyber-attacks need to be overcome in the condition of being multiple and simultaneous. The work in (Bretas, Bretas, Carvalho, Baeyens, & Khargonekar, 2017) modeled and investigated such attacks on SCADA system and network database then proposed a method that detects, identifies and corrects this bad data. The method is built on Weighted Least Square state estimator formula. Simulations of the proposed method were conducted in different scenarios where the attacks targeted measurements, parameters and topology. One notable advantage of this approach is it does not require a previous knowledge of how the attack was performed, as far as it is restricted to a change of measurements, parameters or topology. This correction does not discard data from the measurements set and thus avoids the possibility of local or global unnoticeable conditions.

DISCUSSION AND OPEN ISSUES

In this section, we identify possible future trends on applications of Cyber-Physical Systems in the Smart Grid. These areas are suggested based on ongoing and earlier research efforts. To the best of our knowledge, the following topics can be considered open for potential new contributions in the area:

WSN for Power Grid

Wireless Sensor Networks (WSNs) are very popular in several CPS applications. Given their low cost, availability of technology, and popularity in both industry and academia, WSNs will provide a very cost-effective sensing and communication platform for remote system monitoring and diagnosis. In addition, the existing support, such as dedicated operating systems, and efficient protocols, will make it feasible to efficiently design and implement such platform. It has been reported that WSN can help reduce system-wide breakdowns. Specifically, for the breakdowns emerging from a single-system contingency in the grid, which leads to damages through the whole system, detecting and isolating this contingency is feasible by WSN (Gungor & Lambert, 2006). This concept can be further enhanced by considering smart communication protocols within WSN where such contingency can be detected and communicated faster. Finally, WSN can be helpful in power optimization in urban areas by making use of the environmental conditions and providing feedback to a smart grid distribution system.

DSM Scheduling Algorithms

The deployment of Demand Side Management (DSM) schemes based on demand response in the smart grid is becoming very popular. A distributed algorithm can be used in order to organize the operation of several types of electrical appliances. The objective is to encourage consumers to reduce the peak demand in order to lower electricity costs. In order to design and implement such system, first, it must meet the grid operation conditions; second, it must consider isolation conditions under faults and disturbance. Finally, it must be able to identify and handle operation situations such as islanding (S & Ramesh, 2015).

Finding the proper schedule for appliances operating in order to minimize power consumption is very interesting topic. The problem is reported as NP hard one (Zhu, Lambotharan, Chin, & Fan, 2015). In addition, due to the ability of contributing power to the gird, locally-generated power sources become available to consumers, besides the utility's grid. Consequently, efficiency of demand management algorithms is vital for optimizing energy demand and supply (Zhu et al., 2015).

In order to make efficient use of power resources while at the same time meeting the required demand, it is required to design proper optimization algorithms for energy consumption taking into consideration contemporary issues, such as contributing to the gird. Such method must be able to provide a systematic schedule for daily energy consumption of appliances at household level. It should aim at reducing peak-accumulated consumption. As a result, consumers will get their energy needs fulfilled for less cost. In particular, energy reaches households from the utility grid and from the local generation of renewable energy sources. Through optimization, usage of the utility energy, i.e., the main grid, is reduced to be a second option while the locally-generated energy is maximized as stated in (Zhu et al., 2015).

Software Defined Networks

The recently emerged Software Defined Networking (SDN) paradigm can be used in order to address issues in smart grid such as resilient data collection, data protection, and management of data flow operations. SDN can help in providing global view of the smart grid and identify major modifications without the need to access each part of the grid. In addition, data communication in smart grid architectures can be achieved through SDN-enabled devices, this will eliminate the need to upgrade the infrastructure or install a new one. This issue requires further investigations and it is believed that SDNs will provide reasonable solutions for several arising issues in the grid.

Data Interoperability

Interoperability is the ability of two or more devices to exchange information and work together in a system. Any integration of new system to the power grid must consider the technical domains of the smart grid. Therefore, this should be taken into consideration before expanding existing protocols or implementing new ones. In addition, standardization should be following for information models and information exchange requirements.

Interconnection of Scheduling Algorithms

If scheduling algorithms for DSM are designed and implemented at small areas, then it might be useful to design a hyper level of distributed system that connects several algorithms. This will help in the prediction of the trends of power consumption and distribution in the grid and as a result, enhance utilization. This, however, may require elaboration of the design of distributed control methods for the smart grid.

Distributed Control

Centralized control methods of operation are greatly prone to single point of failure reliability issue. Also, they control various operations continuously thus they require a high performance central processing unit. In addition, managing big data that is generated within the smart grid becomes infeasible. In fact, the emerging smart grid systems tend to use distributed methods. This is due to the dynamic behavior of the power grid system. In order to design and implement distributed control in smart grid, several technologies can be adapted, such as multi-agent frameworks.

CONCLUSION

In this chapter, various, but connected topics of the smart grid were surveyed and examined. Firstly, it was viewed as a Cyber-Physical System (CPS) and discussed accordingly. The work continued with details on the DSM of the smart grid: what it means and how it applies. Multiple approaches of DSM implementation were discussed as well, including heuristic, multi-agent and game theory based methods. We viewed these methods as a big picture then we went through many examples from the literature and analyzed them. After the DSM discussion, communication in the smart grid received detailed investigation. An overview was provided at first, and then we examined communication technologies in the two branches of wired and wireless distinction. The document also provided a clear sight on the networks in the grid, the functions of each network and how the different technologies achieve or fail in fulfilling these functions. We concluded with the communication security, considering both physical and cyber challenges and defenses.

REFERENCES

Ancillotti, E., Bruno, R., & Conti, M. (2013). The role of communication systems in smart grids: Architectures, technical solutions and research challenges. *Computer Communications, 36*(17–18), 1665–1697. doi:10.1016/j.comcom.2013.09.004

Ansar, S., Ansar, W., Ansar, K., Mehmood, M. H., Raja, M. Z. U., & Javaid, N. (2017). Demand side management using meta-heuristic techniques and ToU in smart grid. In L. Barolli, T. Enokido, & M. Takizawa (Eds.), *Advances in Network-Based Information Systems. NBiS 2017. Lecture Notes on Data Engineering and Communications Technologies* (Vol. 7, pp. 203–217). Cham: Springer.

Başar, T., & Olsder, G. J. (1999). *Dynamic noncooperative game theory*. Society for Industrial and Applied Mathematics, Classics in Applied Mathematics.

Basu, A. K., Panigrahi, T. K., Chowdhury, S., Chowdhury, S. P., Chakraborty, N., Sinha, A., & Song, Y. H. (2007). Key energy management issues of setting market clearing price (MCP) in micro-grid scenario. In *2007 42nd International Universities Power Engineering Conference* (pp. 854–860). Academic Press.

Bretas, A. S., Bretas, N. G., Carvalho, B., Baeyens, E., & Khargonekar, P. P. (2017). Smart grids cyberphysical security as a malicious data attack: An innovation approach. *Electric Power Systems Research*, *149*(August), 210–219. doi:10.1016/j.epsr.2017.04.018

Carl, G., Kesidis, G., Brooks, R. R., & Suresh Rai. (2006). Denial-of-service attack-detection techniques. *IEEE Internet Computing*, *10*(1), 82–89. doi:10.1109/MIC.2006.5

Cataliotti, A., Cosentino, V., Di Cara, D., Russotto, P., & Tine, G. (2012). On the use of narrow band power line as communication technology for medium and low voltage smart grids. In *2012 IEEE International Instrumentation and Measurement Technology Conference Proceedings* (pp. 619–623). IEEE. 10.1109/I2MTC.2012.6229503

Cesena, E., Ramunno, G., & Vernizzi, D. (2008). Secure storage using a sealing proxy. In *Proceedings of the 1st European workshop on system security - EUROSEC '08* (p. 27). New York: ACM Press. 10.1145/1355284.1355290

Dang, T., & Ringland, K. (2012). Optimal load scheduling for residential renewable energy integration. In *2012 IEEE Third International Conference on Smart Grid Communications (SmartGridComm)* (pp. 516–521). IEEE. 10.1109/SmartGridComm.2012.6486037

Efthymiou, C., & Kalogridis, G. (2010). Smart Grid Privacy via Anonymization of Smart Metering Data. In *2010 First IEEE International Conference on Smart Grid Communications* (pp. 238–243). IEEE. 10.1109/SMARTGRID.2010.5622050

Energy Agency, I. (n.d.). *International Energy Agency: Executive Summary, An energy system under stress*. Author.

Esmalifalak, M., Nguyen, H., Zheng, R., & Han, Z. (2011). Stealth false data injection using independent component analysis in smart grid. In *2011 IEEE International Conference on Smart Grid Communications (SmartGridComm)* (pp. 244–248). IEEE. 10.1109/SmartGridComm.2011.6102326

Fan, Z., Kulkarni, P., Gormus, S., Efthymiou, C., Kalogridis, G., Sooriyabandara, M., & Chin, W. H. (2013). Smart Grid Communications: Overview of Research Challenges, Solutions, and Standardization Activities. *IEEE Communications Surveys and Tutorials*, *15*(1), 21–38. doi:10.1109/SURV.2011.122211.00021

Fang, X., Misra, S., Xue, G., & Yang, D. (2012). Smart Grid – The New and Improved Power Grid. *IEEE Communications Surveys and Tutorials*, *14*(4), 944–980. doi:10.1109/SURV.2011.101911.00087

Farmad, H. S., & Biglar, S. (2012). Integration of demand side management, distributed generation, renewable energy sources and energy storages. In *Integration of Renewables into the Distribution Grid, CIRED 2012 Workshop* (pp. 1–4). Academic Press. 10.1049/cp.2012.0784

Fudenberg, D., & Levine, D. K. (1998). *The theory of learning in games*. MIT Press.

Funabashi, T., Tanabe, T., Nagata, T., & Yokoyama, R. (2008). An autonomous agent for reliable operation of power market and systems including microgrids. In *2008 Third International Conference on Electric Utility Deregulation and Restructuring and Power Technologies* (pp. 173–177). Academic Press. 10.1109/DRPT.2008.4523397

Galli, S., Scaglione, A., & Wang, Z. (2010). Power Line Communications and the Smart Grid. In *2010 First IEEE International Conference on Smart Grid Communications* (pp. 303–308). IEEE. 10.1109/SMARTGRID.2010.5622060

Gellings, C. W., & Chamberlin, J. H. (1987). *Demand-Side Management: Concepts and Methods*. Academic Press.

Goudarzi, H., Hatami, S., & Pedram, M. (2011). Demand-side load scheduling incentivized by dynamic energy prices. In *2011 IEEE International Conference on Smart Grid Communications (SmartGridComm)* (pp. 351–356). IEEE. 10.1109/SmartGridComm.2011.6102346

Gungor, V. C., & Lambert, F. C. (2006). A survey on communication networks for electric system automation. *Computer Networks*, *50*(7), 877–897. doi:10.1016/j.comnet.2006.01.005

Hao, J., Piechocki, R. J., Kaleshi, D., Chin, W. H., & Fan, Z. (2015). Sparse Malicious False Data Injection Attacks and Defense Mechanisms in Smart Grids. *IEEE Transactions on Industrial Informatics*, *11*(5), 1–12. doi:10.1109/TII.2015.2475695

He, H., & Yan, J. (2016). Cyber-Physical Attacks and Defenses in the Smart Grid: A Survey. *IET Cyber-Physical Systems: Theory & Applications*, *1*, 13–27.

IEEE SA - 2030-2011 - IEEE Guide for Smart Grid Interoperability of Energy Technology and Information Technology Operation with the Electric Power System (EPS), End-Use Applications, and Loads. (n.d.).

Javaid, N., Javaid, S., Abdul, W., Ahmed, I., Almogren, A., Alamri, A., & Niaz, I. (2017). A Hybrid Genetic Wind Driven Heuristic Optimization Algorithm for Demand Side Management in Smart Grid. *Energies*, *10*(3), 319–363. doi:10.3390/en10030319

Kabalci, Y. (2016). A survey on smart metering and smart grid communication. *Renewable & Sustainable Energy Reviews*, *57*(May), 302–318. doi:10.1016/j.rser.2015.12.114

Kalogridis, G., Efthymiou, C., Denic, S. Z., Lewis, T. a., & Cepeda, R. (2010). Privacy for Smart Meters: Towards Undetectable Appliance Load Signatures. *Smart Grid Communications (SmartGridComm), 2010 First IEEE International Conference on*, 232–237.

Karnouskos, S. (2011). Cyber-physical systems in the SmartGrid. *IEEE International Conference on Industrial Informatics (INDIN)*, 20–23.

Khalifa, T., Naik, K., & Nayak, A. (2011). A Survey of Communication Protocols for Automatic Meter Reading Applications. *IEEE Communications Surveys and Tutorials*, *13*(2), 168–182. doi:10.1109/SURV.2011.041110.00058

Khan, H. N., Iftikhar, H., Asif, S., Javaid, N., Maroof, R., & Ambreen, K. (2017). Demand Side Management using Strawberry Algorithm and Bacterial Foraging Optimization Algorithm in Smart Grid. In L. Barolli, T. Enokido, & M. Takizawa (Eds.), *Advances in Network-Based Information Systems. NBiS 2017. Lecture Notes on Data Engineering and Communications Technologies* (Vol. 7, pp. 191–202). Cham: Springer.

Khan, R. H., & Khan, J. Y. (2013). A comprehensive review of the application characteristics and traffic requirements of a smart grid communications network. *Computer Networks*, *57*(3), 825–845. doi:10.1016/j.comnet.2012.11.002

Kim, H.-M., & Kinoshita, T. (2009). Multiagent system for Microgrid operation based on power market environment. In *INTELEC 2009 - 31st International Telecommunications Energy Conference* (pp. 1–5). Academic Press. 10.1109/INTLEC.2009.5351771

Kim, T. T., & Poor, H. V. (2011). Strategic Protection Against Data Injection Attacks on Power Grids. *IEEE Transactions on Smart Grid*, *2*(2), 326–333. doi:10.1109/TSG.2011.2119336

Kosut, O., Jia, L., Thomas, R. J., & Tong, L. (2011). Malicious Data Attacks on the Smart Grid. *IEEE Transactions on Smart Grid*, *2*(4), 645–658. doi:10.1109/TSG.2011.2163807

Kühn, U., Selhorst, M., & Stüble, C. (2007). Realizing property-based attestation and sealing with commonly available hard- and software. In *Proceedings of the 2007 ACM workshop on Scalable trusted computing - STC '07* (p. 50). New York: ACM Press. 10.1145/1314354.1314368

Kühn, U., & Stüble, C. (2009). User-Friendly and Secure TPM-based Hard Disk Key Management. In *Future of Trust in Computing* (pp. 171–177). Wiesbaden: Vieweg+Teubner. doi:10.1007/978-3-8348-9324-6_18

Kulasekera, A. L., Gopura, R. A. R. C., Hemapala, K. T. M. U., & Perera, N. (2011). A review on multi-agent systems in microgrid applications. *2011 IEEE PES International Conference on Innovative Smart Grid Technologies-India, ISGT India 2011*, 173–177. 10.1109/ISET-India.2011.6145377

Kuntze, N., Rudolph, C., Cupelli, M., Liu, J., & Monti, A. (2010). Trust infrastructures for future energy networks. In *IEEE PES General Meeting* (pp. 1–7). IEEE. 10.1109/PES.2010.5589609

Kuzlu, M., & Pipattanasomporn, M. (2013). Assessment of communication technologies and network requirements for different smart grid applications. In Innovative Smart Grid Technologies (ISGT), 2013 IEEE PES (pp. 1–6). IEEE. doi:10.1109/ISGT.2013.6497873

Kuzlu, M., Pipattanasomporn, M., & Rahman, S. (2014). Communication network requirements for major smart grid applications in HAN, NAN and WAN. *Computer Networks, 67*, 74–88. doi:10.1016/j.comnet.2014.03.029

Li, F., Qiao, W., Sun, H., Wan, H., Wang, J., Xia, Y., ... Zhang, P. (2010). Smart Transmission Grid: Vision and Framework. *IEEE Transactions on Smart Grid, 1*(2), 168–177. doi:10.1109/TSG.2010.2053726

Li, H., Mao, R., Lai, L., & Qiu, R. C. (2010). Compressed Meter Reading for Delay-Sensitive and Secure Load Report in Smart Grid. In *2010 First IEEE International Conference on Smart Grid Communications* (pp. 114–119). IEEE. 10.1109/SMARTGRID.2010.5622027

Li, N., Chen, L., & Low, S. H. (2011). *Optimal demand response based on utility maximization in power networks.* IEEE Power and Energy Society General Meeting.

Li, W., & Zhang, X. (2014). Simulation of the smart grid communications: Challenges, techniques, and future trends. *Computers & Electrical Engineering, 40*(1), 270–288. doi:10.1016/j.compeleceng.2013.11.022

Liang, G., Zhao, J., Luo, F., Weller, S. R., & Dong, Z. Y. (2017). A Review of False Data Injection Attacks Against Modern Power Systems. *IEEE Transactions on Smart Grid, 8*(4), 1630–1638. doi:10.1109/TSG.2015.2495133

Liu, L., Esmalifalak, M., Ding, Q., Emesih, V. A., & Han, Z. (2014). Detecting False Data Injection Attacks on Power Grid by Sparse Optimization. *IEEE Transactions on Smart Grid, 5*(2), 612–621. doi:10.1109/TSG.2013.2284438

Liu, R.-S. (2016). An Algorithmic Game Approach for Demand Side Management in Smart Grid with Distributed Renewable Power Generation and Storage. *Energies, 9*(8), 654.

Liu, S., Liu, X. P., & El Saddik, A. (2013). Denial-of-Service (dos) attacks on load frequency control in smart grids. In 2013 IEEE PES Innovative Smart Grid Technologies Conference (ISGT) (pp. 1–6). IEEE.

Liu, Y., Ning, P., Dai, H., & Liu, A. (2010). Randomized Differential DSSS: Jamming-Resistant Wireless Broadcast Communication. In 2010 Proceedings IEEE INFOCOM (pp. 1–9). IEEE.

Liu, Y., Reiter, M. K., & Ning, P. (2009). False data injection attacks against state estimation in electric power grids. In *Proceedings of the 16th ACM conference on Computer and communications security - CCS '09* (pp. 21-32). New York: ACM Press. 10.1145/1653662.1653666

Logenthiran, T., Srinivasan, D., & Shun, T. Z. (2011). Multi-Agent System for Demand Side Management in smart grid. *2011 IEEE Ninth International Conference on Power Electronics and Drive Systems*, 424–429. 10.1109/PEDS.2011.6147283

Logenthiran, T., Srinivasan, D., & Shun, T. Z. (2012). Demand Side Management in Smart Grid Using Heuristic Optimization. *Smart Grid. IEEE Transactions on, 3*(3), 1244–1252.

Lopez, M. A., De La Torre, S., Martin, S., & Aguado, J. A. (2015). Demand-side management in smart grid operation considering electric vehicles load shifting and vehicle-to-grid support. *International Journal of Electrical Power and Energy Systems, 64*, 689–698.

Maharjan, I. (2010). *Demand Side Management: Load Management, Load Profiling, Load Shifting, Residential And Industrial Consumer, Energy Audit, Reliability, Urban, Semi-urban And Rural Setting.* LAP LAMBERT Academic Publishing.

McDaniel, P., & McLaughlin, S. (2009). Security and Privacy Challenges in the Smart Grid. *IEEE Security & Privacy Magazine, 7*(3), 75–77. doi:10.1109/MSP.2009.76

Meng, F.-L., & Zeng, X.-J. (2016). A Profit Maximization Approach to Demand Response Management with Customers Behavior Learning in Smart Grid. *IEEE Transactions on Smart Grid, 7*(3), 1516–1529. doi:10.1109/TSG.2015.2462083

Mohsenian-Rad, A.-H., Wong, V. W. S., Jatskevich, J., Schober, R., & Leon-Garcia, A. (2010). Autonomous Demand Side Management Based on Game-Theoretic Energy Consumption Scheduling for the Future Smart Grid. *IEEE Transactions on Smart Grid, 1*(3), 320–331. doi:10.1109/TSG.2010.2089069

National Energy Technology Laboratory for the U.S. Department of Energy. (2008). *Advanced Metering Infrastructure. NETL Modern Grid Strategy.* Author.

National Institute of Standards and Technology. (2010). NIST Special Publication 1108 NIST Framework and Roadmap for Smart Grid Interoperability Standards. *NIST Special Publication*, 1–90.

Nguyen, H. K., Song, J., Bin, & Han, Z. (2012). Demand side management to reduce Peak-to-Average Ratio using game theory in smart grid. In *2012 Proceedings IEEE INFOCOM Workshops* (pp. 91–96). IEEE.

Nisan, N. (2007). *Tim Roughgarden, ´C Eva Tardos, V. V. V* (1st ed.). Algorithmic Game Theory.

Rahim, S., Javaid, N., Ahmad, A., Khan, S. A., Khan, Z. A., Alrajeh, N., & Qasim, U. (2016). Exploiting heuristic algorithms to efficiently utilize energy management controllers with renewable energy sources. *Energy and Building, 129*, 452–470. doi:10.1016/j.enbuild.2016.08.008

Rahman, M. A., & Mohsenian-Rad, H. (2012). False data injection attacks with incomplete information against smart power grids. In *2012 IEEE Global Communications Conference (GLOBECOM)* (pp. 3153–3158). IEEE. 10.1109/GLOCOM.2012.6503599

S, S. R., & Ramesh, V. (2015). A Novel Integrated Approach of Energy Consumption Scheduling in Smart Grid Environment With The Penetration of Renewable Energy. *International Journal of Renewable Energy Research, 5*(4), 1196–1205.

Saad, W., Han, Z., Poor, H. V., & Basar, T. (2012). Game-theoretic methods for the smart grid: An overview of microgrid systems, demand-side management, and smart grid communications. *IEEE Signal Processing Magazine, 29*(5), 86–105. doi:10.1109/MSP.2012.2186410

Samadi, P., Mohsenian-Rad, H., Wong, V. W. S., & Schober, R. (2014). Real-Time Pricing for Demand Response Based on Stochastic Approximation. *IEEE Transactions on Smart Grid, 5*(2), 789–798. doi:10.1109/TSG.2013.2293131

Schuba, C. L., Krsul, I. V., Kuhn, M. G., Spafford, E. H., Sundaram, A., & Zamboni, D. (n.d.). Analysis of a denial of service attack on TCP. In *Proceedings. 1997 IEEE Symposium on Security and Privacy (Cat. No.97CB36097)* (pp. 208–223). IEEE Comput. Soc. Press. 10.1109/SECPRI.1997.601338

Siano, P. (2014). Demand response and smart grids - A survey. *Renewable & Sustainable Energy Reviews, 30*, 461–478. doi:10.1016/j.rser.2013.10.022

Sidhu, T. S., & Yin, Y. (2007). Modelling and Simulation for Performance Evaluation of IEC61850-Based Substation Communication Systems. *IEEE Transactions on Power Delivery, 22*(3), 1482–1489. doi:10.1109/TPWRD.2006.886788

Simo Fhom, H., Kuntze, N., Rudolph, C., Cupelli, M., Liu, J., & Monti, A. (2010). A user-centric privacy manager for future energy systems. In *2010 International Conference on Power System Technology* (pp. 1–7). Academic Press. 10.1109/POWERCON.2010.5666447

Strasser, M., Popper, C., Capkun, S., & Cagalj, M. (2008). Jamming-resistant Key Establishment using Uncoordinated Frequency Hopping. In *2008 IEEE Symposium on Security and Privacy (sp 2008)* (pp. 64–78). IEEE. 10.1109/SP.2008.9

Tang, S., Huang, Q., Li, X.-Y., & Wu, D. (2013). *Smoothing the energy consumption: Peak demand reduction in smart grid.* Proceedings IEEE INFOCOM.

Thakur, A., Chaudhary, N., Tilokani, P., & Machado, J. (2017). A cyber-physical system based collaborative distributed manufacturing system architecture for intelligent manufacturing. In A cyber-physical system based collaborative distributed manufacturing system architecture for intelligent manufacturing. Academic Press.

The NETL Modern Grid Initiative. (2007, January). The NETL Modern Grid Initiative: A systems view of the modern grid. *Technology*.

Usman, A., & Shami, S. H. (2013). Evolution of communication technologies for smart grid applications. *Renewable & Sustainable Energy Reviews*, *19*(January), 191–199. doi:10.1016/j.rser.2012.11.002

Wang, W., & Lu, Z. (2013). Cyber security in the Smart Grid: Survey and challenges. *Computer Networks*, *57*(5), 1344–1371. doi:10.1016/j.comnet.2012.12.017

Wu, C., Mohsenian-Rad, H., Huang, J., & Wang, A. Y. (2011). Demand side management for Wind Power Integration in microgrid using dynamic potential game theory. In 2011 IEEE GLOBECOM Workshops (GC Wkshps) (pp. 1199–1204). IEEE. doi:10.1109/GLOCOMW.2011.6162371

Xu, Y., & Liu, W. (2011). Novel Multiagent Based Load Restoration Algorithm for Microgrids. *IEEE Transactions on Smart Grid*, *2*(1), 152–161. doi:10.1109/TSG.2010.2099675

Xu, Y., & Wang, W. (2013). Wireless Mesh Network in Smart Grid: Modeling and Analysis for Time Critical Communications. *IEEE Transactions on Wireless Communications*, *12*(7), 3360–3371. doi:10.1109/TWC.2013.061713.121545

Yaar, A., Perrig, A., & Song, D. (n.d.). Pi: a path identification mechanism to defend against DDoS attacks. In *Proceedings 19th International Conference on Data Engineering (Cat. No.03CH37405)* (pp. 93–107). IEEE Comput. Soc.

Yan, Y., Qian, Y., Sharif, H., & Tipper, D. (2012). A Survey on Cyber Security for Smart Grid Communications. *IEEE Communications Surveys and Tutorials*, *14*(4), 998–1010. doi:10.1109/SURV.2012.010912.00035

Yu, Z.-H., & Chin, W.-L. (2015). Blind False Data Injection Attack Using PCA Approximation Method in Smart Grid. *IEEE Transactions on Smart Grid*, *6*(3), 1219–1226. doi:10.1109/TSG.2014.2382714

Zhao, Z., Lee, W. C., Shin, Y., & Song, K.-B. (2013). An Optimal Power Scheduling Method for Demand Response in Home Energy Management System. *IEEE Transactions on Smart Grid*, *4*(3), 1391–1400. doi:10.1109/TSG.2013.2251018

Zhu, Z., & Lambotharan, S. (2012). Overview of demand management in smart grid and enabling wireless communication technologies. *IEEE Wireless Communications*, *19*(3), 48–56. doi:10.1109/MWC.2012.6231159

Zhu, Z., Lambotharan, S., Chin, W. H., & Fan, Z. (2015). A Game Theoretic Optimization Framework for Home Demand Management Incorporating Local Energy Resources. *IEEE Transactions on Industrial Informatics*, *11*(2), 353–362.

Zipperer, A., Aloise-Young, P. A., Suryanarayanan, S., Zimmerle, D., Roche, R., Earle, L., ... Zimmerle, D. (2013). Electric Energy Management in the Smart Home: Perspectives on Enabling Technologies and Consumer Behavior. *Proceedings of the IEEE*, *101*(11), 2397–2408. doi:10.1109/JPROC.2013.2270172

Chapter 2
Wireless Sensor Network as Enabling Technology for Cyber–Physical System

Jiwa Abdullah
University of Tun Hussein Onn Malaysia, Malaysia

Nayef Abdulwahab Alduais
Hodeidah University, Yemen

ABSTRACT

Within the last 20 years, wireless communication and network has been one of the fastest-growing research areas. Significant progress has been made in the fields of mobile ad hoc network (MANET) and wireless sensor networks (WSN). Very recently, the cyber-physical system (CPS) has emerged as a promising direction to enrich human-to-human, human to-object, and object-to-object interactions in the physical world as well as in the virtual world. The possibilities are enormous, such that CPS would adopt, and even nurture, the areas of MANET and WSN because more sensor inputs and richer network connectivity are required. The chapter reviews what has been developed in these fields, outlines the projection of what may happen in the field of CPS, and identifies further works. The authors identify the unique features of WSN, raising some CPS critical examples, and then directing the future challenges of CPS. In order to fully comprehend the connection of WSN to CPS, the authors provide some preliminaries of WSN and establish their necessary connections.

INTRODUCTION

Advanced design in microelectronics, material sciences and networking capability are driving the deployment of large scale WSN and Wireless Actuator Network (WAcNet). These technologies actually enabled the low cost WSN, low power, micro devices with multifunctional characteristics connected to multiple sensors (Dargie & Poellabauer, 2010). These micro devices accumulate sensed data from the environment and transmitted it over certain distance and further routed by multi hopping to a typical gateway. The data can then be aggregated and streamed over the region through the cloud. Nowadays

DOI: 10.4018/978-1-5225-5510-0.ch002

WSN can be seen almost everywhere, where data need to actually being monitored and managed. Significant research contributions have made WSN communications more reliable for realtime applications (Akyildiz et. al., 2002). With the maturity of WSN, networks require the extended functionality and formal interaction with other networked system, with additional reliability. Hence the Cyber Physical Systems (CPS) paradigm comes into the sensing applications as a platform to provide extended interactive functionality, thus bridging real time and virtual environments. With an additional WAcNet scenario, it will produce a very comprehensive system.

Wireless sensor networks (WSN), and actuator networks (WAcNet), are spatially distributed autonomous sensors to monitor physical or environmental conditions, such as temperature, sound, pressure, gaseous, electricity usage, sensing people, and so on. The nodes cooperatively pass their data through the network to other locations. Currently the networks are bi-directional, also enabling control of sensor activity, resulting what we may called as WAcNet, such networks are used in many industrial and consumer applications. WSN is built of nodes, from a few in numbers to thousands, where each node is connected to one or several sensors. Each node has typically several parts: a radio transceiver with an internal antenna, a microcontroller, an interfacing with the sensors and an energy source, usually a battery or an embedded form of energy harvesting mechanism. A sensor node might vary in size from that of a matchbox down to the size of a grain of dust, although functioning motes of microscopic dimensions have yet to be manufactured. Size and cost constraints on sensor nodes result in corresponding constraints on resources such as energy, memory, computational speed and communications bandwidth. The WSN topology can vary from a simple star network to an advanced multi-hop wireless mesh network. The radio propagation technique between the hops of the network is accomplished by routing mechanism.

A mobile ad hoc network (MANET) is generally defined as a network that has many free or autonomous nodes, often composed of mobile devices, which can arranged themselves in various ways and operate without strict top-down network administration. The communication maybe achieved through multi hop mechanism. MANET, now a topic of commercial research, was originally used in military projects, including in tactical networks and defense projects. Some use 4G networks and other wireless systems as examples of a potential topology for a MANET, while others refer to a vehicular ad-hoc network (VANET), where the free network nodes are installed in cars and other vehicles. MANET has the potential but face various challenges, including signal protection and the reliability of mobile or dynamic nodes. In addition there's an issue of limited processing power, especially mobile nodes within MANET. Smart phones as an example of node within MANET may experience this power constraint.

Cyber-Physical Systems(CPS) is integrations of element of computations with some physical processes. Networked embedded computers are used to monitor and control physical processes based upon local network and remote computation (Akella & McMillin, 2009). The main features of CPS are that it is tightly coupled between physical and software components. CPS may operate on different spatial and temporal scales and exhibiting multiple and distinct behavior. Furthermore, CPS is continuously interacting with the physical world, causing the behavior of a CPS changes with the operational scheme. Hence, CPS actually is a system to provide a virtual environment that incorporates an interacting network of elements with physical inputs and outputs at both ends as shown in Figure 1. It provides an intuitive interconnection mechanism for human-to-human, human-to-machine and machine-to-machine interactions through seamless network connectivity (Edward A. Lee, 2006).

CHARACTERISTICS OF CYBER-PHYSICAL SYSTEMS

CPS is a collection of physical elements, firmware elements and generally speaking the humanism elements. The following items are the general characteristics of CPS.

1. **Heterogeneous:** CPS demonstrate a high level of heterogeneity which may includes; sensor nodes with small memory having low bandwidth less reliable connectivity; mobile devices such as smart phones depending on the cellular infrastructures; high end workstations and servers with high reliability wired networks.
2. **Unreliable Networking:** CPS typically interact with other elements in a distributed fashion connected wirelessly, may be unreliable; many operate within the paradigm of ad hoc wireless network; some in mobility environment; power constraint; incorporate wireless sensor networks with high packet loss and thus less predictable performances. Hence, any modeling approach for CPS design must therefore respect this uncertainty (IEEE Standard 802.15.4d, 2009).
3. **Mobility:** CPS with mobility, which is almost necessary, present additional complexity. In mobile environment, devices interact opportunistically; as example consider the vehicular network, interaction starts when two vehicles comes in within the transmission range, plus some unusual aspect of humanism, such as human behavior.
4. **Tight Environmental Coupling:** Statically deployed CPS there exists a tight coupling with the environment, means that external system requires greater consideration than in traditional networks. For example, in a wireless system, external interference sources may have a greater effect upon the reliability of distributed interactions than any of the internal system components. Hence these networking aspects must be modeled appropriately.

Generally, MANET, WSN and CPS seem quite similar in many networking aspects, but there are obvious differences. MANET supports ad hoc communications or extends the coverage of infrastructure networks. WSN is designed for delivering sensor related data. CPS typically involves multiple dimensions of data sensing, cross multiple sensor networks, internetworking, supporting more intelligent aspect of networking and also putting element of humanism within the interaction sphere. In the following paragraph, features of MANET, WSN and CPS are put to comparisons.

1. **Network Generation:** MANET network formation is random event and random location, supporting node mobility. For WSN, its formation is field specific, less mobility and deterministic nature (TEOS, 2010). CPS, on the other hand, may cross several fields. Connecting these fields usually depends on the Internet. Dynamic participation and departure of a sensor nodes is possible, causing hole formation.
2. **Communication Style:** A MANET usually supports variety of communication pattern, such as unicast, multicast, and broadcast, while a WSN involves a more collective communications (Upadhyayula et al., 2003; Intanagonwiwat et al., 2000), such as convergecast and query/response transactions. Hence, the requirements on routing capability are different. CPS may invoke WSN communications. Furthermore, cross-domain communications may happen quite frequently in CPS applications (Han et al., 2010).

Figure 1. Network elements in CPS architecture

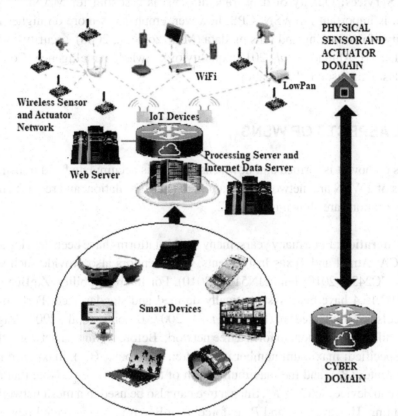

3. **Power Usage:** Both MANET and WSN emphasize on energy saving, but is critical for WSN, due to sensor nodes' remote location (Lee et al., 2010). Sleeping modes are preferred for WSN, whereas nodes' sleeping in MANET are normally by opportunity. Activation of sensors in CPS is likely mission oriented. Different modes may wake up different groups of sensors.

4. **Network Coverage:** While MANET needs to meet some connectivity requirements, WSN needs to meet both connectivity and some coverage criteria (Wang *et. al.*, 2003). This leads to a lot of studies on the co-design of coverage and connectivity in WSNs. CPS imposes the same requirements for WSN, but different levels of connectivity and coverage for different WSNs.

5. **Node Mobility:** Node mobility in a MANET is arbitrary, but vehicular manet, mobility is very important criteria. In WSN, little mobility has been assumed (Ma & Yang, 2007). With the emerging mobile sensing applications, both controllable and uncontrollable mobility has been studied widely. In CPS applications, sensing data may be collected from static and mobile sensor nodes (such as those in vehicles and smart phones) with both controllable and uncontrollable mobility.

6. **Knowledge Mining:** A MANET emphasizes only on networking issues. A WSN focuses more on collecting and managing sensing data. However, CPS emphasizes more on how to discover new knowledge across multiple sensing domains and to utilize intelligence properly. For example, a smart grid system (Lee *et. al.*, 2010), may involve power meters, micro-climate sensors, wind and solar energy metering sensors to make intelligent energy distribution decisions.

7. **Quality of Services:** Quality of data transmissions is essential for MANET, while quality of sensing data is important for WSN. CPS, however, emphasizes more on higher-level QoS, such as availability of networking and sensing data (Miluzzo *et al.*, 2008), security and confidentiality of sensing data (H. Ahmadi *et. al.*, 2010), quality of knowledge/intelligence (Constandache *et al.*, 2010), and lastly the user authentication.

FUNCTIONAL ASPECTS OF WSNS

WSN emphasizes on how it is formed and how sensing data is accumulated and transmitted. The three functional aspects of a WSN are: network generation, data accumulation, and request and reply. A summary of these descriptions are shown in Figure 2.

1. **Network Generation:** For a many years, many WSN platforms have been developed and marketed, such as MICA, Atmel and Texas Instruments. Chip vendors also provide such solutions (Texas Instruments CC2431, 2010; JennicJN5121, 2010). For interoperability, ZigBee (ZigBee, 2006), and IEEE 802.15.4 have been systematically defined and standardized. Performance studies of these protocols are conducted in, (Baronti *et. al.*, 2007; Baronti, et. al., 2007). ZigBee relies on a distributed address assignment to form a tree network. Before forming a network, three parameters need to be specified: maximum number of children of a router (C_m), maximum number of child routers of a router (R_m), and the maximum depth of the network (L_m). Note that a child can be a router or an end device, so $C_m \geq R_m$. Such a tree can also be used in a mesh network as a backbone for basic routing. However, C_m and R_m enforce a ZigBee tree as a bounded-degree tree. In graph theory, forming a degree-constrained spanning tree from an arbitrary graph is NP-complete (Garey & Johnson, 1990). There's also a polynomial-time graph algorithms when additional connectivity and maximum degree of a graph are given (Czumaj & Strothmann, 1997), without considering the depth constraint. An approximation algorithm can be utilized to find the spanning tree with a maximum degree of O(K + log |V|), where K is the degree constraint and *V* is the set of nodes in the graph (Konemann & Ravi, 2000; Konemann & Levin, 2004).

    In ZigBee tree formation, WSN may experience orphan problem, hence some nodes may be rejected from joining the tree (Pan *et. al.*, 2009). An orphan node is when it cannot associate with any parent router although there are still unused address spaces available. As previous reference, the orphan problem is formulated as two subproblems: (1) bounded-degree-and-depth tree formation (BDDTF) problem for router connection and (2) end-device maximum matching (EDMM) problem, for connecting end devices. However, when the n-cube is incomplete, orphans may still exist. In Ould-Ahmed-Vall *et. al.*, (2005), a distributed algorithm for ID assignment is proposed. It starts by assigning long unique IDs and organizes nodes in a tree structure. This preprocessing helps compute the size of the network. Then, unique IDs are assigned with the minimum number of bits, producing a long thin topology suitable for lengthy side of the building structure (Pan *et al.*, 2008).

2. **Data Accumulation:** The main function of a WSN is to accumulate information, thus operate in convergecast style. In convergecast, there are three categories of solutions: (a) schedule-based solutions, (b) clusterbased solutions, and (c) correlation-based solutions.

Figure 2. Functional aspects of WSN

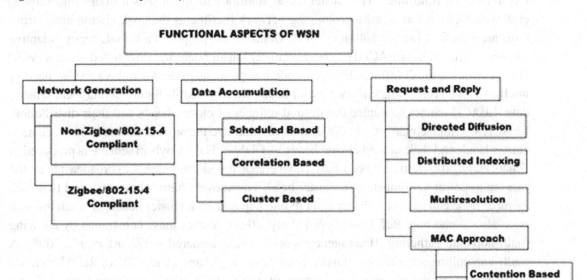

a.   **Schedule-Based Solutions:** The schedule-based solutions arrange communication timing with reducing latency and energy consumption as the goal. An inherent problem of data accumulation is the funneling effect (C. Wan, *et. al.*, 2005), where contentions occur more seriously as data reaches the sink area. Such solutions rearrange codes/channels/slots for sensor nodes along data collection trees to mitigate interference. Some suggested the used of multiple codes to reduce the contention problem (Y. Yu, *et. al.*, 2004). S.Upadhyayula (S. Upadhyayula, *at. el.*, 2003) shows how to connect sensors as a balanced reporting tree and how to assign CDMA codes to sensors to relieve interference among sensors. Others, try to minimize the overall energy consumption to a bounded data reporting interval (Y. Yu, *et. al.*, 2004). Here, dynamic programming algorithms are proposed by ensuring that the sensor nodes receive multiple packets simultaneously. Using CDMA is somewhat too much and heavy for WSN. Time-based scheduling has been widely studied with a staggered wake-up schedule. An energy-efficient and low-latency MAC, called DMAC, is proposed as in (G. Lu, *et. al.*, 2004), where sensors are connected by a tree and stay in a sleep state, most of the time. Nodes wake up in a staggered manner along the tree. However, since ZigBee enforces that a node can only wake up twice per superframe, the solutions in (H. Choi, *et. al.*, 2009; IEEE standard for IT, 2006), are not ZigBee-compatible. A beacon-enabled IEEE 802.15.4/ZigBee tree network is widely adopted, where a superframe structure is used for the power-saving purpose. Each superframe is composed of an active portion and an inaction portion. Routers have to choose different times for their active portions to avoid collisions. In the revised IEEE 802.15.4 (Tseng *et. al.*, 2008), a router can select one active portion as its outgoing superframe and, based on the active portion selected by its parent, its incoming superframe is decided. In the beginning of an outgoing /incoming superframe, a router is expected to transmit/receive a beacon to/from its child/parent router.

b. **Cluster-Based Solutions:** The cluster-based solutions partition sensor nodes into groups, each with a group leader, with prolonging network lifetime as the goal. Hierarchical structures are exploited in such solutions. W.R. Heinzelman, proposed a Low-Latency Adaptive Clustering Hierarchy (LEACH) protocol to cluster sensor nodes in a distributed manner (W.R. Heinzelman, et. al., 2000). Each sensor node independently decides to be a cluster head or not based on its remaining energy. Cluster heads are responsible for collecting local sensing data. LEACH cannot guarantee the desired number of cluster heads and their distribution. LEACH-C (Heinzelman, *et. al.*, 2002) tries to minimize the sum of distances between non-cluster heads and their nearest cluster heads. A CDMA/TDMA hybrid scheme is proposed in (Zhao, et. al., 2004), to enhance LEACH, where each node only needs to broadcast at its the maximum power to compete as a cluster head. The above schemes have assumed that each member node can reach its cluster head in one hop and each cluster head can reach the sink node also in one hop. Ref. (Younis & Fahmy, 2004), relaxes these constraints by allowing multi-hop data gathering. Heterogeneous nodes are considered in (Zhang *et. al.*, 2008). A multi-hop polling schedule for clusters is proposed in (Zhang *et. al.*, 2008). Ref. (Xu *et. al.*, 2010) points out the biased energy consumption rate (BECR) phenomenon among cluster heads in a heterogeneous WSN. In single-hop gathering, cluster heads farther away from the sink node will deplete energies faster. In multi-hop gathering, cluster heads closer to the sink node will deplete energies faster.

c. **Correlation-Based Solutions:** The correlation-based solutions exploit spatial and temporal redundancies of sensing data to reduce the transmission cost. Sensing data are usually spatially or temporally correlated. Exploiting data correlations can reduce data gathering cost (Cristescu *et. al.*, 2010). K.W. Fan on the other hand, proposed a structure-free aggregation based on spatial correlations of sensing data (Fan *et. al.*, 2007). Temporal correlations are also considered in this proposal, where a randomized waiting scheme is utilized.

3. **Request and Reply:** Request and reply interactions are fundamental issues in WSNs (Akkaya & Younis, 2005), and are categorized into three types: (a) directed diffusion, (b) distributed indexing, and (c) multi-resolution summary.

a. **Directed Diffusion:** Directed diffusion (Intanagonwiwat *et. al.*, 2000), is a popular paradigm as a result of much research work. Sources owning sensing data publish what they have, and sinks with interests in specific pieces of data subscribe to them. A request is routed to a specific location if it with geographic information embedded in it; otherwise, it may be flooded. However, the flooding overhead is extremely high due to periodic refreshing activity.

b. **Distributed Indexing:** Features of the dataset may be indexed to facilitate data search. The idea of geographic hashing is explored in Ratnasamy *et. al.*, (2002). A hash function is used to map event names to locations. Events may be further grouped spatially by their name types.

c. **Multi-Resolution Summary:** In some applications, accurate sensing data is not always needed. Users may request a rough overview periodically, low-resolution report, and query in-depth data occasionally, often with high-resolution report. Thus, it needs in-network multi-resolution query-and-reply solutions. In Ganesan *et. al.*, (2005), a lossy, gracefully degrading storage model is described to support progressive and long-term in-network query processing. Using a wavelet-based processing mechanism, it achieves low communication overhead for multi-resolution summarization, highly efficient drill-down search over such summaries, and use of network storage for load-balancing and progressive aging of data summaries.

COVERAGE AND DEPLOYMENT OF WSNS

In WSN, the coverage problem is how well a sensing field is monitored by sensors. The deployment problem would be to place sensor nodes to meet the constraints. Such solutions are classified into three types: (a) coverage and connectivity; (b) energy-conserving and scheduling strategies, and (c) mobile sensor solutions.

1. **Coverage Solutions:** Maintaining coverage of all nodes is essential for a WSN. Sensors are assumed to have fixed sensing and communication ranges. The coverage problem is formulated as a decision problem (Huang & Tseng, 2005). Given a set of sensors deployed in a field, the problem is to determine if the area is sufficiently k-covered, in the sense that every point in the field is covered by at least k sensors, where k is an integer. Rather than directly determining the coverage of each location, Ref. (Huang & Tseng, 2005) looks at how the perimeter of each sensor's sensing range is covered and proposes an efficient polynomial-time solution. Detail understanding of coverage issues can be obtained from Ref. (Wang *et al.* 2003). In determining the coverage level, it would be necessary to look at how intersection points between sensors' sensing ranges are covered. It claims that a region is k-covered by a set of sensors if all intersection points between sensors and between sensors and the boundary of this region is at least k-covered. Further, it proves that k covered implies k-connected when sensors' communication ranges are not less than twice their sensing ranges. Furthermore, protocols such as Coverage Configuration Protocol (CCP) (Wang *et al.*, 2003). can provide different coverage levels even when the communication ranges are more than twice their sensing ranges. Also, it allows some sensors to go to sleep when they are not needed.

2. **Connectivity Solutions:** When the communication ranges are less than twice the sensing ranges, a connectivity-maintaining protocol, ensure that all active nodes form a backbone and all inactive nodes are directly connected to at least one active node (Wang *et al.*, 2003). An improvement is further proposed in (X. Wang, *et. al.* 2003), such that protocols allowed an arbitrary relationship between sensing ranges and communication distances (Huang *et al.*, 2007). Not only putting sensors to sleep, the work also tunes nodes' transmission powers. Necessary and sufficient conditions for a WSN to be *k*-covered and *k*-connected and to be *k*-covered and *1*-connected are presented. It simultaneously addresses the issues of coverage, connectivity, power management, and power control under one framework. Ref. (H.M. Ammari, S.K. Das, 2008), analyzes the relationship between deploying density and coverage and connectivity by the percolation theory. It raises the sensing coverage phase transition (SCPT) and the network-connectivity phase transition (NCPT) problems. Imagining that sensor deployment is similar to rain drops falling on a field; SCPT asks the probability of the first occurrence of complete coverage that spans the entire network, while NCPT asks the probability of the first occurrence of a connected component that spans the entire network. Based on a Poisson process, this work gives some theoretical analyses (H.M. Ammari, S.K. Das, 2009)). Another solution provides a node connectivity index (*nci*) as a numerical value to show the strength of node pair connectivity from one node to the other especially if one of the node is moving (Abdullah & Parish, 2007).

3. **Energy-Conserving and Scheduling Strategies:** Sensors are usually deployed with redundancy. Therefore proper scheduling their on-duty time while maintaining the required coverage level is critical. It can be classified into two types: (a) cover set scheme and (b) opportunistic selection scheme.

a. **Cover Set Scheme:** How to find multiple mutually exclusive sets of sensor nodes such that each set completely covers the field has been proved to be NP-complete in (Slijepcevic & Potkonjak, 2001), where a greedy heuristic is proposed. Allowing nodes to have different sensing and transmission ranges, (Das *et. al.*, 2009) shows how to find a minimum connected subset that covers a region of interest.

b. **Opportunistic Selection Scheme:** The probe-based density control algorithm (Ye *et al.*, 2003), adopts this approach. Nodes are initially in sleep mode. When waking up, they broadcast a probing message within a certain range. If no reply is received within a pre-defined period, they have to remain active. The coverage degree is controlled by sensors' probing ranges and wake-up rates. However, this approach has no guarantee of complete coverage and thus may have blind holes. Ref. (Choi & Das, 2009) also randomly selects sensors to meet the required coverage. It forces a minimum distance between any pair of active sensors so as to maintain network connectivity.

4. **Mobile Sensor Solutions:** Generally, WSNs are assumed to be static, but mobility has now been introduced to WSNs. This improves network capability so that, there can be automatic node deployment, flexible topology adjustment, and rapid event reaction. It may be classified into two types: (i) tries to relocate nodes to help form/enhance a WSN in terms of coverage and connectivity; (ii) address the path-planning issues for data ferries to relay data and/or extend network lifetime. The first type can be further divided into three sub-types. The first sub-type is to help adjust the topology. For example, researchers have applied the virtual force concept and some graph approaches to achieve this goal. The second sub-type is to help enhance coverage and connectivity of a WSN. The third sub-type is to guide mobile sensor nodes to desired locations. The second type can be further divided into two sub-types. The first sub-type is to find paths for relaying messages for static/isolated nodes. Such paths may be adaptive or probabilistic ones. The second sub-type is to help prolong the network's lifetime (Choi & Das, 2009).

CYBER PHYSICAL SENSOR NETWORK DEPLOYMENT

What is described before is the physical sensing domain connected within the monitoring capabilities over the cloud. This could be one typical approach to promote the CPS deployment. The WSN platforms can replace the sensing domain of CPS without major changes; however, the gateway interface must be able to manipulate the commands from and to the Cloud seamlessly.

Considering WSN communication protocols, the IEEE 802.15.4 PHY and MAC has been the most widely used data-link standard in WSN deployments while the ZigBee protocol which is an extension of IEEE 802.15.4 further provides support for distributed addressing with tree topologies (Arampatzis *et al.*, 2005). The deployment of CPS enabled gateways for WSN can be further leveraged by use of internet-ready sensor gateway devices, where a recent trend is to even provide open source IPv6 compatible software extension with the devices (Misra *et. al.*, 2013). Data collection activities could be very extensive requirements in the CPSN physical domain, peer-to-peer communication may have higher overheads; hence, a low packet exchange mechanism may be used. The converge cast mechanism, where sink nodes are required to frequently gather sensing data from a set of nodes, might be considered a better mechanism for CPS considering there is an intelligent gateway residing at the CPS and WSN boundary. Communication in CPSN physical monitoring environments can take the form that contributes to the success of WSN mechanism, which is based on cluster, scheduling and correlation mechanism. Hence this should show that it can actually be modeled according to WSN setup.

Data dissemination in the sensor network domain of CPS is very important. To enable consistent communication reliability in CPS sensing plane throughout the monitoring period, a query-and-reply method between nodes is used frequently that may become difficult to handle in complex topologies with thousands of nodes. This step of data dissemination with communication reliability can thus be carried out in more intelligent ways all of which can be broadly categorized under query-and-response. Again it utilized the concept of WSN data transmission capability in terms of request and reply mechanism.

In the CPS sensing node, with plane layouts and theoretical design, sensors may be assumed to have fixed communication and sensing ranges initially. The coverage problem for CPS can be formulated as a decision problem where, given a number of sensors to be deployed in the field, the main target is to determine if the area is sufficiently covered. Sensing plane coverage solutions for CPS can be categorized into opportunistic sensor node selection mechanisms or covering-set methods that utilize graph theory. The sensor node localization can be done using Global Positioning System (GPS) related methods for outdoor deployments or through trilateration, proximity and other out-of-range methods including fixed anchor nodes. Figure 3, shows the network communication parameters for cyber physical sensor network architecture. The similarity to the WSN deployment means that WSN can be part of the whole architecture of CPS. Table 1 shows the similarity of the scopes of CPS and WSN.

One other important network parameter dealing with CPS deployment is the node mobility. It must be properly accounted for in the networking information for mobile nodes deployed within the monitoring area. Mobility normally improved the network capability, such as, the use of automatic node deployment, flexibility in the topology adjustment and possibility of rapid event detection. Overall, such mobility related solutions for CPS can be classified into two types where the first one would be to try relocating sensor nodes to improve network coverage and connectivity while the other solution would be to try addressing the path planning issues for data relaying nodes that would ultimately allow extended network lifetime (Wu *et al.*, 2014). Highlights of the mobility and reconfiguration related parameters, issues and research dimensions for CPSN are listed in Figure 4.

Figure 3. Network communication parameters for cyber physical sensor network architecture

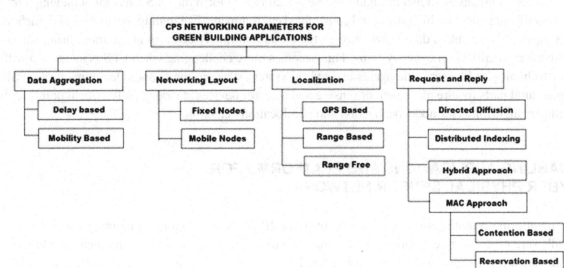

Figure 4. Wireless sensor network parameters and issues related to mobility and reconfiguration in a cyber-physical environment

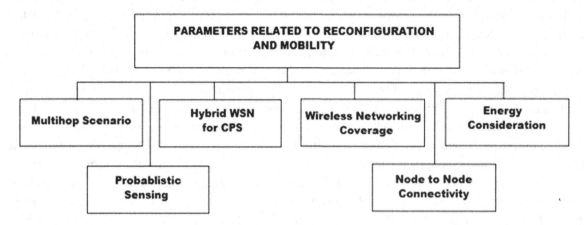

Table 1. Example implementation layers and protocols for a cyber-physical sensor network environment

IMPLEMENTATION LAYERS	PROTOCOL	SCOPE
Application	HTTP	End to End
Transport	UDP, TCP	End to End
Network	IP	End to End
Routing	RPL	Per Hop
Data Link	IEEE 802.15.4	Per Hop

Prediction of accurate output decisions and reliability of sensing information are considered critical for CPS. There is therefore a need to define strictly the network requirement factors in terms of cyber and physical domains as shown in Figure 5. These factors also form the QoS basis for achieving a real time intelligent system for high stress and constrained environments like mining, healthcare and warfare. QoS factors like seamless data flows through the cloud and timely delivery at the monitoring station are considered critical for cyber systems. This becomes more challenging when CPS is integrated with other technologies like semantic agents and hybrid system states in the Cloud. Deployment of CPSN architectural parts require placement of sensing and actuator devices at strategically critical points with intelligent algorithms for node localization and geo-location detection.

ENABLING APPLICATIONS AND PLATFORMS FOR CYBER PHYSICAL SENSOR NETWORK

For monitoring remote sensor applications over the IP framework, cloud computing can provide a middleware cost effective solution to CPS that provides a rich interactive communication platform. Since network communication costs a lot of bandwidth overhead for linking Virtual Machines (VMs)

Figure 5. A division of cyber-physical sensor network requirements

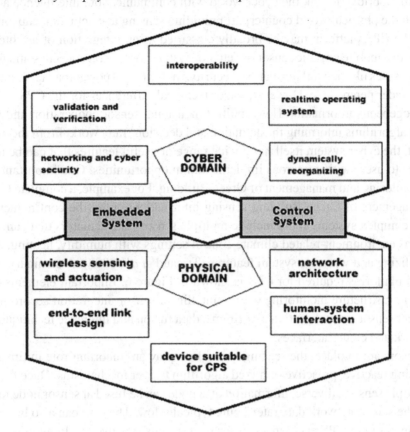

in data intensive environments, a decentralized approach, where migration of VM services is provided with monitoring of traffic fingerprints can relieve the wasted overhead. Also, in particular cases, faults can occur in the middle of a query from distributed databases. This can be fixed by dividing queries into sub-queries and mapping them in an intelligent way such that the results return on different nodes.

A global middleware concept can be a convenient way to provide flexibility integration and discovery of sensor networks and sensor data. Such a middleware would be required to provide fast deployment of testbeds with distributed querying, filtering and aggregation of sensor data with support for dynamic adaptation of the system configuration parameters. This would be linked to the use of virtual sensor abstraction that can enable users to declaratively specify deployment descriptions in an open standard human readable language like XML. Such an approach becomes more powerful for remote monitoring once there is a possibility of integration of sensor network data through querying language like SQL over local and remotely available sensor network resources. Sensor Modeling Language (SML) can be used to represent any of the physical sensor's metadata like their accuracy, type, physical location and similar measures. In addition to SML, XML encoding will be used for the measurement and description of the physical sensor specifications. The use of XML language allows encoding the sensors in a way that the implementation is available across several hardware platforms and operating systems through simple translation or use of a wrapper. A map for translating between physical and virtual sensor parameters can be used to translate commands (Wua *et al.*, 2011; Mottola & Picco, 2011).

CPS is actually a bridge to link the cyber world with communication, intelligence and information components with the physical world counterpart providing sensing and actuation capabilities (Elson & Estrin, 2004). The CPS platform may be broadly classified as an integration of an intelligent control design system with a mobile or static sensor or actuator system. When considering standalone individual sensor networks, issues like network formation, security, mobility and power management remain almost the same in a broader perspective. However, major technical differences for the CPS approach include the use of heterogeneous information flow, multi-dimensional sensor cooperation and a high level of intelligence and algorithms informing the actuation and decision framework. From the service applications' viewpoint, the cyber system itself has a wide range of useful features that can be used to provide elevated services to users with numerous implementation opportunities. One important application of CPS is in the monitoring and management of Green Building. For example, a complete CPS can be used to assist in management of Green Building sensing information within the confinement of this large structure. More complex systems could include multiple sensors and actuators that can be used for applications such as environment-related climate control settings with humidity, heating, carbon dioxide generation, fertilizing and watering system features (Tricaud *et al.*, 2009). A summary of the enabling applications and platforms required for CPS is shown in Figure 6. Important elements for CPS based Green Building infrastructure monitoring require intelligent sensor integration according to the building layout, correct sensor event detection algorithms, data fusion and inference techniques, data routing across the network and cloud interfaces.

Once the sensors are in place, the sensing algorithms play an important role in timely detection of sensor events using reactive, proactive or mixed algorithm trigger mechanisms. Once the events are detected from multiple sensors, diverse information on a node can be fused at sensor node for compressing data following the sensor network data rates being typically low. The data can also be fused at relay or gateway nodes in case the CPS encompasses several sub sensor networks. In addition to data fusion, data processing codes can be found in a distributed manner where one code instance runs on the sensor nodes and another runs on the remote control station. Overall, design of a CPS based wireless sensor network would require topology controlled infrastructure design, actuation mechanisms, an intelligent middleware lying in the Cloud and a data routing mechanism from the sensor node towards the remote monitoring station, as well as feedback from the controller to the actuation platform.

For example, a CPS can facilitate greenhouse asset management through the deployment of multiple WSNs (Melodia *et al.*, 2006). Each WSN is composed of multiple sensors and actuators to form a climate control system with lighting, cooling and heating, carbon dioxide generating, watering, and fertilizing subsystems. Thus, light intensity, temperature, humidity, and density of carbon dioxide need to be collected and reported. The decision system will transform these sensing data into high-level knowledge, to trigger actuators to maintain good environmental factors in the greenhouse. Note that multiple actuations may coexist, with an example of cooling subsystem may cowork with the carbon dioxide generating subsystem. Efforts on sensor–actuator and actuator–actuator coordinations can be found in Melodia *et al.*, (2006). Robotic actuators are introduced in Akyildiz and Kasimoglu, (2004) .

Cyber-physical systems bridge the cyber world to the physical world through lots of sensors and actuators. A CPS may consist of multiple static/mobile sensor and actuator networks integrated under an intelligent decision system. For each individual WSN, the issues such as network formation, network/ power/mobility management, security and other parameters would remain the same. However, CPS is featured by cross-domain sensor cooperation, heterogeneous information flow, and intelligent decision/ actuation. The concept is illustrated in Figure 7.

Figure 6. Summary of wireless sensor network-based CPS monitoring of green building

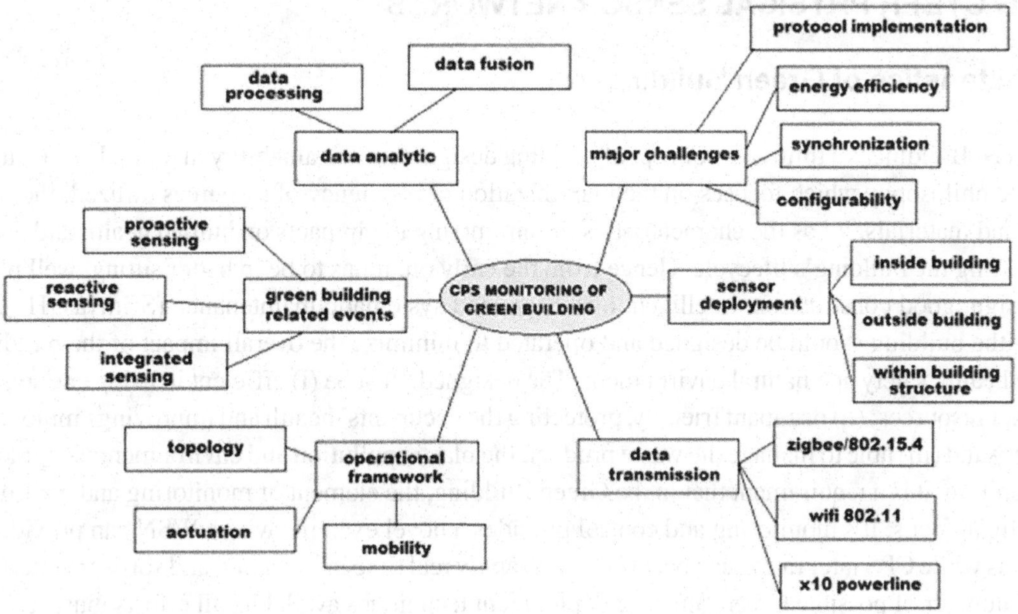

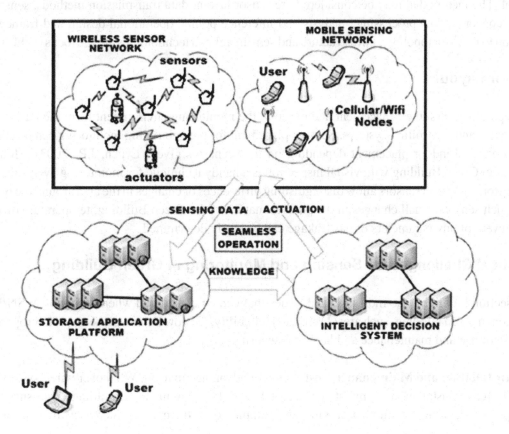

Figure 7. A CPS architecture model

A CASE STUDY ON GREEN BUILDING MONITORING USING CYBER PHYSICAL SENSOR NETWORKS

Characteristics of Green Building

The Green Building is a futuristic concept of building design with sustainability in mind. It is an outcome from the philosophy which focuses on the maximization of efficiency of resources utilized, the energy, water, and materials. It has the characteristics of minimizing the impacts on human health and environment during the building's lifecycle. Hence from the early on, it has to be in better sitting, well planned and design, good construction, intelligent operation, and systematic maintenance (Srinivas, H., 2017). Hence, the building should be designed and operated to minimize the overall impact of the building on human health, safety and natural environment. The designed must be (i) efficient in using energy, water, and other resources; (ii) occupant friendly, protecting the occupants' health and improving employee productivity and (iii) able to manage the waste product, the plastic pollution and environmental degradation.

Therefore, it is a requirement that in the Green Building, the element of monitoring and control must be the main focus. It's monitoring and control provides a novel example where WSN can provide these functions while CPS integration can be leveraged to apply real time information and software interfacing. With a number of possible Green Building deployment techniques available, all efforts must reflect the characteristics of the medium needed for data transmission that depends upon the environmental and built material. The design needs to provide intelligent, flexible and reliable CPS based monitoring and control. The factors that may be considered are sensor layout, data transmission methods, sensor node power concerns, data processing, analysis and inference points, operational design and framework in addition to network topology, infrastructure and sensing related technologies are the focus of this section.

Sensor Layout

The type of sensors, their placement and usage in the monitoring environment form the basis for CPS monitoring and controlling systems. Sensors placement for green building monitoring can be classified as outdoor and indoor placement depending on the scenarios given (Lynch, J.P., 2007). Monitoring changes in Green Building with visual inspection is a handy technique for monitoring events that occur above ground. Vision sensors allow distinguishing differences or changes in the area around the building. With such sensors, small changes in the physical nature of the Green Building, temperature difference or the event of any parameters or gas leakage can be easily determined.

Practical Challenges for Sensing and Monitoring in Green Building

This section highlights the most practical issues that can be considered when designing WSN/IoT application in green building, such are; (1) cost; (2) reliability; (3) power management; (4) interoperability; (5) ease of use and maintenance and lastly (6) security.

1. **Installation and Maintenance Cost:** A major advantage in using WSN over wired systems is the decreased installation and maintenance cost. In wired systems in a large building, cost issues become prominent when the number of wires and complexity of the network increases. In addition, it has

been reported that the typical wiring process accounts for 75% of the installation cost of sensor networks in a structural health monitoring system (Lynch, J.P., 2007). While the installation cost depends upon the type of construction, the size of the building, and the need for radio repeaters, the declines in the prices of the radio hardware. The number of nodes is the key factor in assessing the cost of a WSN/IoT in the system. The number of nodes will be based on the desired resolution in a particular application, while the building construction, size, and wireless transmission scheme will dictate the need for extra nodes for repeaters.

2. **Reliability:** Reliability of the WSN devices is one of the major concerns for potential users of wireless technology in buildings. It is expected that the same level of reliability with wireless system as to the wired systems. The different aspects of reliability are affecting the WSN in various ways such as; accuracy, signal coverage through the building materials, interference, latency and fault tolerance.

Accuracy

Accuracy in specific measurement to WSN is a concern with all sensor devices. The noise may affect sensor readings by modifying the analog signal generated by the transducer. Additionally, data corruption or distortion caused by environmental impact will typically result in values that are in error. One positive characteristic of wireless sensor networks with respect to accuracy is node redundancy. High node density may compensate for overall uncertainty caused by the noise and non-ideal conditions, and can increase the overall accuracy of the measurement in a particular areas. For instance, a cluster-based topology can be employed to collect sensory data at the same local area. Densely distributed WSN nodes, could help increase the overall accuracy by allowing redundant measurements.

Signal Coverage Through Building Materials

The coverage area of WSN and variety of construction types couple with propagation of the wireless signal in building are significant factors for the reliability of a wireless link. The maximum allowable distance between the transmitter and the receiver is specified when there are no obstructions between the two radios. However, the actual prediction of signal propagation is much more complicated because walls, floors, ceilings, and furnishings are often present in the indoor environment. Different construction materials also attenuate the signal to varying degrees, and even tend to stop propagation of radio-frequency (RF) waves. Also, different frequencies and transmission power levels may respond in different manners in different buildings or the same building with variety of internal arrangement (J. Abdullah, 2014).

Interference

A low-power wireless device is potentially vulnerable to interference from other wireless technologies that have much higher power within the same industrial, scientific, and medical (ISM) band. Typically, many of the devices being constructed as part of wireless sensor networks operate in the 2.4 GHz band because of its worldwide usage. While the risk of interference is minimized by various techniques of signal communication, there still exists the potential for interference from other equipment considering the large number of devices emitting at similar frequencies.

Latency

Acquiring data in real-time is considered an application-specific issue in wireless sensor network. Inherent features of WSNs, such as dynamic topology, lossy links, limited bandwidth, and channel variations, often limit the real-time performancě. Different demands on end-to-end latency are required because most applications have different expectations that data acquired from a wireless sensor should be made available to a receiver within a reasonable period of time.

Fault Tolerance

In the design of sensor networks for building application, it is important to identify the failures that will affect the overall performance of the system and that will degrade the confidence level in the measurements. In building applications, a fault can be classified by three categories; (1) node faults, (2) network faults, and (3) sink faults. First, various sources of node faults can be identified under harsh environmental conditions. A variety of extreme conditions can cause antenna failures, circuit failures, and battery leakage, which will lead to poor performance of WSNs. Second, a network fault is another common fault in a WSN since the high density of deployed nodes will increase the chance of individual communication failures. Third, sinks, the points where data are collected, are subject to faults.

Received Signal Strength Indication (RSSI)

Received Signal Strength Indication (RSSI) is a term used to describe a measurement of the power present in a received radio signal. RSSI is calculated at the radio chip on the receiver and provides useful implication of network link quality.

Link Quality Indication (LQI)

The use of a Link Quality Indication (LQI) is specified by IEEE802.15.4 to assess the quality of the communication link between a receiver and transmitter (IEEE 802.15.4, 2006). LQI is based on signal-to-noise ratio or energy density of the signal in the frequency band used by the standard and provides average correlation values for each incoming packet over at least 8 symbol periods. As with RSSI, LQI allows users to assess the communication link considering the environmental effects on a single transmitter/receiver pair.

Packet Error Rate

Packet error rate (PER) is defined as the ratio of the number of packets unsuccessfully received to the total number of packets transmitted over certain period of time. In a reliable system, it is simply expected that each data packet transmitted is received correctly by the receiver. One way to measure reliability in this manner is to keep track of the number of messages sent by the transmitter and compare the number of messages successfully received at the base station. The reliability can then be expressed as the percentage of dropped packets of data over the total number of transmissions, or as a packet error rate.

3. **Power Management:** In wireless sensor networks, the energy source is generally limited, often being comprised of small battery. This limitation becomes critical when hundreds of nodes are placed in a network for long-term monitoring applications. For power management, minimal energy should be consumed by going to sleep-mode when not reading the data, transmitting data packets for very short periods, and minimizing the amount of transmitted data. Typically, signal transmission constitutes a very larger source of energy consumption compared to data acquisition and processing. Thus any efforts to minimize radio transmission will help prolong battery life. While a mesh network offers a potential to increase communication reliability, each node in that network serves as a repeater that must consume significantly more energy relaying messages than if it were only required to send its own data. One advantage of sensor use in buildings is that line power is often available, and therefore, sensors can transmit data wirelessly yet get their power from a wire (Roth, K. & Brodrick, J., 2008).

4. **Interoperability:** Familiarity with IEEE 802.11/WiFi for wireless networking access has provided confidence for the relatively rapid adoption of wireless sensing technology in buildings. Interoperability with 802.15.4/Zigbee has made WiFi attractive. By adopting the IEEE 802.15.4 standard for the physical layer of wireless communications, ZigBee has added standards that will increase interoperability in both the networking protocol and data exchange.

5. **Ease of Use and Maintenance:** Easy deployment and minimal maintenance are also key factors that potential end users seek. Most civil and building engineers who use the wireless sensors will have little expertise in the electrical engineering and radio physics that are critical to the operation of wireless sensor networks.

6. **Security:** With wireless data transmission, there is recurring concern that hackers will tweak the measured data or access building automation systems to use the wireless sensor network as a tunnel into other critical information infrastructure.

Data Transmission and Delivery

There must be a suitable mechanism for data transmission after the parameters from sensors are successfully measured and recorded. For this purpose, various network architecture and topologies have been proposed (Ye *et al.*, 2003; Choi & Das, 2009). Factors such as real time sensing node design, building and network infrastructure, connectivity of nodes to base station and battery life or duty cycle directly affect data transmission (Arampatzis, 2005). Several wireless networking standards such as ZigBee are frequently used in integration for sensor network implementation. For building situated in remote areas, it is desirable to make use of long range networks like GSM and GPRS to transmit data collected on the backhaul network. For infrastructure monitoring of linear and hierarchical designs, different wireless standards of transmission may be employed at different hierarchy levels. The choice of the transmission standard will depend on the cost and the desired range. Wireless signals get severely attenuated in the closed buildings, underground and underwater transmission resulting in data unreliability. The effect of extreme path loss, reflection/refraction, multi-path fading, reduced propagation velocity, and noise on the propagation of electromagnetic waves in underground networks has been described in Younis & Fahmy, (2004). Several alternatives to underground problems have been provided in Misra *et. al.*, (2013) that make use of electro-magnetic induction for transmitting signals. Hence applications in place like basement parking can emulate this kind of wireless installation.

Figure 8. Interacting elements of cyber physical sensor network for green building monitoring and actuating

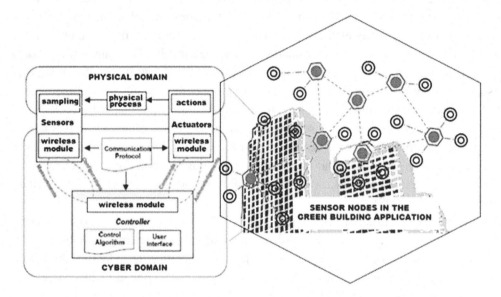

ARCHITECTURE FOR REMOTE GREEN BUILDING MONITORING

The structured WSN deployment on green building simplifies the routing protocols and increases efficiency and cost-effectiveness of the network. A hierarchical structure for green building monitoring based on sensor networks has been described in (Zhang *et al.*, 2008), wherein the functionalities are distributed among the nodes. The nodes at the lowest level are the sensing nodes that sense the parameters from the environment (Tricaud *et al.*, 2009). Relay nodes closer to sensing nodes collect sensed data and pass it on to data dissemination nodes which finally transmit the data over long haul communication links to the control center. The advantage of such a topology is that it adds redundancy to the whole architecture while reducing the range of each node that ultimately induces low energy consumption (Melodia *et al.*, 2006). The functionalities of nodes on each level can be made distinctively diverse so as to make the data collecting system more intelligent as shown in Figure 8.

ENERGY EFFICIENCY AND LIFETIME CONCERNS OF THE WSN NODES

Continuous condition monitoring requires a continuous, uninterrupted power supply. Wireless transceivers utilize most of the battery in a sensor node. Hence, increased battery life and optimal utilization of the power is of critical value especially for location that is less accessible, for example, the roof top, outside the building, lift tower, sewage disposal pipes and wiring duct, especially true for high rise building. The commercially available sensor nodes usually provide a discrete, limited set of tunable power levels making dynamic adaptation less beneficial. The communication itself carried out by the sensor nodes can be either periodic or event-based. More intelligent monitoring schemes use aggregated sensing (Y. Yu, *et. al.*, 2004) where the only primary sensing mechanism runs periodically, triggering other mechanisms and waking up nodes from sleep only when anomalies are detected. Some schemes incorporate intelligent node algorithms which perform correlation of the recently sensed data with the previous reading and transmit the reading only when the readings differ from the normal measurements (Akyildiz & Kasimoglu, 2004). A vibration energy harvester utilizes the energy available in kinetic form and converts it into electrical energy, usable for the sensor nodes.

REMOTE INFRASTRUCTURE SECURITY CONCERNS

At early stages, there were no way the WSN can determine whether the message belonged to their own network, other networks or from network hacker. The failure was due to the requirement of an authentication mechanism, which led the system to interpret any type of message that was intrinsically relevant to the sensor domain. When deploying wireless sensor networks in industry, particularly related to industrial automation applications, the consequence of architectural failures will be more than a mere loss of sensing information. With faulty, inaccurate or altered information being delivered to the control station, the system is potentially vulnerable to physical damage. For example, a sensor transmitting data to the valve controller or a direct motor informing it about the system speed requirements or component processing levels being too high could cause reversible damage to the whole industrial setup. Even in practical terms, a failed security aspect in the developed system or a revelation of weakness in the deployed sensor network could result in a loss of engineering power. For a standalone secure network, security requirements need to be fulfilled at the protocol as well as system implementation and deployment level. The ZigBee Smart Energy related protocols have also undergone extensive review by security experts and numerous implantation tests. In particular, the WirelessHART protocol is the key enabling technology for most of the sensor network deployments around the world that are potential candidates for security concerns. The end users of the securely deployed networks put trust in the application in terms of provisioning processing control information reliably and in confidence between two authenticated sensor nodes. In CPS Green Building applications, as new protocols emerge, particularly related to Internet of Things, the security measures need to be compatible with the IPv6 communication procedures. Once CPS is set up, the realm of security concerns changes drastically. All such concerns need to be addressed with thorough understanding and assessment.

FUTURE CHALLENGES FOR WSN/CPS INTEGRATION

The energy efficiency in CPSN is one of the prime issues researchers have been working on for years. In order for sensing planes to perform their monitoring tasks for longer periods of time and due to the nature of their sensing in harsh environments, battery replacement is not an easy task and sometimes even impossible (Roth & Brodrick, 2008). For extending network lifetime, much research work has been done on MAC protocols and routing in addition to energy harvesting.

MAC protocols provide efficient resource sharing and contribute in saving power by utilizing the node's hardware only when it is needed. Major causes for energy consumption in wireless nodes are due to collision of transmitted packets, overhearing of transmitted packets, packet overheads and idle listening of the radios (Intanagonwiwat *et al.*, 2000). Numerous MAC protocols have been proposed but only a few manage to bear the harsh physical environment for sensing applications. Some of the widely used MAC protocols for WSN are SMAC, TMAC and BMAC (Akyildiz *et al.*, 2002), however, the need for efficient MACs for Green Building applications with linear and hierarchical layouts is still an open issue. An optimum and well-designed antenna use can not only improve the energy efficiency of the system and transmission range but also provide reliable communication making the sensing node small enough to fit inside the sensing environment (Wang *et al.*, 2003).

Wireless sensor nodes consume power in data sharing, processing, transmission/reception and in data routing. Routing protocol needs to be simple by reducing computational complexity and power efficiency in order to help increase the network lifetime (Dargie & Poellabauer, 2010). There is a need for such cross layer efficient routing algorithms, particularly in different pipeline monitoring applications. Some initial work has been done in determining an optimum routing protocol but still extensive efforts are required in this field. Reliability and robustness complements each other, reliability being the most desired aspect of the sensor system in order to perform and maintain its functions in normal as well as hostile environments, while robustness enables the system to handle errors during execution. Middleware offers the ability to assimilate and reprocess software components on demand and help abstract the dissemination and heterogeneity of the underlying computing environment and services. It also supports the addition of non-functional values such as interoperability, load balancing, scalability, reliability, availability, usability, extensibility, manageability, reusability, services discovery, Quality of Service (QoS), stability, efficiency and security (Cuomo *et al.*, 2009).

To address the design and implementation issues related to CPS applications, a new approach to integrate the middleware layer has been proposed. The middleware is present between an operating system and the application layer in a sensor node. It can be divided into many sub-middleware functions some of which include time synchronization, location detection, battery-power control and networking. In traditional computing devices, operating systems are well established, but for sensor nodes the applications are executed on bare hardware without a separate operating system. Hence, the identification and implementation of appropriate operating systems and middleware in CPS is still a research focus. Research could be initiated on developing different reliable and robust sensor nodes for diverse types of building monitoring as summarized in Table 2.

CONCLUSION

CPS have taken their roots from mergers between computational and physical components of systems. CPS has played a critical role in a number of underlying domains namely healthcare, manufacturing, energy, transportation, aerospace and industrial infrastructure based conditional monitoring. A complete transformation of human-to-human, human-to-machine and machine-to-machine interactions is thus expected. While previously, much of the research activities focused on Mobile Ad Hoc Networks and Wireless Sensor Networks (WSN), more recently, a changing trend has been to benefit from the physical and virtual environment synergy provided by CPS to perform the conventional activities of WSN more reliably and with ease. In this work, we have reviewed the applications of a Cyber Physical Sensor Network (CPS) environment from a reliability perspective and demonstrate how the physical information collected from different sensing planes be exploited to abridge the cyber space and real world. We also identified the challenges and architecture design issues of CPSN. The techniques and parameters that still need to be addressed for seamless integration of cyber and sensing domains with QoS and the current measures adopted have also been summarized. While the sensing plane focuses more on the designs for sensing, data-retrieving, event-handling, communication, and coverage problems, the cyber plane focuses on the development of cross-layered and cross domain intelligence from multiple sensing

Table 2. Popular WSN platforms available for industrial and academic use

RESOURCE	SUPPLIER / MANUFACTURER / DISTRIBUTOR
Sensor Nodes	Argo Systems, WisMote, BTnode, IMote, KMote, TinyMote, EPIC Mote. EyesIFX, FlatMesh, Mica, Telos, Iris, NeoMote, Waspmote, RedBee, Ubimote, Shimmer, WizziMote, FireFly, Bitsym Bitsense
Gateway Node	AdvanticSys, Dwara, Shimmer Span, Stargate, FlatMesh,VEmesh, DigiMesh, Bitsym Bithaul
Microcontrollers	Texas Instruments, Atmel ATmega, ARM Cortex, Thumb Microcontroller Renesas, Marvell, PIC
Transceivers	Chipcon, ATmega, ZigBit, himmer,RFM
Operating Systems	Contiki, ERIKA Enterprise,Nano-RK, TinyOS, LiteOS, OpenTag, NanoQplus
Programming Languages	C, LabVIEW, nesC
Software	Arduino API, TinyDB, TOSSIM, NS-2, NS-3, NetSim, LinuxMCE, QualNet
Industry Standard Protocols	ANT 6LoWPAN, DASH7, ONE-NET, ZigBee, Z-Wave, Wibree, WirelessHART, 802.15.4, MiWi

environments and the interactions between the virtual world and the physical world. A CPS application is expected to provide a bridge between multiple remote WSNs and invoke actuation based on inference from the sensed information. A lot of successful vehicle- and mobile phone-based CPSN services have been developed over time. Data from such applications may be expected to be of continuous form at a very large volume, so storing, processing, and then intelligent interpretation of it in real-time is essential. Important factors for the success of CPS include management of cross-domain sensor related data, embedded and mobile sensing technologies and applications, elastic computing and storage related technologies with integrated privacy and security designs. This summary of CPS is expected to stimulate an interested reader with current technological developments and the expected features of future sensing networks over the Cloud.

The possibility to develop a CPS enabled sensor network has arisen through the accelerated development of wireless technology and embedded computing with applications like micro sensing MEMS, inertial motion detection, bio-signal sensing, environment parameter sensing, location and vehicular movement detection. While a single platform is being sought for defining common parameters, the major technical differences need to be emphasized. WSN has been designed and implemented mainly with the idea of communicating sensing related data with coordination over some limited geographical environment. CPS, on the other hand, utilizes a broader definition and dimension of sensing data over multiple wireless sensor networks with a Cloud specific link to the Internet with the aim of providing flexible control and intelligence. The CPS architecture resembles traditional embedded systems that aim to integrate abstract computations with physical processes. Contrary to traditional embedded systems, CPS provides an interconnected interaction with outputs and inputs that pertain to physical existence and are standalone devices. The main layers of CPS are the virtual layer and physical layer. For the physical layer, an intelligently deployed network of actuators and sensors collects information and actually controls the physical world. By converting the analog information into a digital format, the information is sent to a virtual layer input which serves as the decision-making setup. This information is further used to calculate abstract computations that feed into the real world actuation system to drive and control physical world outputs or objects.

REFERENCES

Abdullah, J. (2014). *Chapter: Radio Propagation Model For Wireless Sensor Network Simulation. In Advances in wireless Network Research*. Nova Publisher.

Abdullah, J., & Parish, D. J. (2007). Node connectivity index as mobility metric for GA based QoS routing in MANET. *Proceedings of the 4th international Conference on Mobile Technology, Applications, and Systems*, 104-111. 10.1145/1378063.1378082

Ahmadi, H., Pham, N., Ganti, R., Abdelzaher, T., Nath, S., & Han, J. (2010). Privacy-aware regression modeling of participatory sensing data. *Int'l Conf. Embedded Networked Sensor Systems*, 99–112. 10.1145/1869983.1869994

Akella, R., & McMillin, B. M. (2009). Model-Checking BNDC Properties in Cyber-Physical Systems. *Proceedings of the 33rd Annual IEEE International Computer Software and Applications Conference.*

Akkaya, K., & Younis, M. (2005). A survey on routing protocols for wireless sensor networks. *Ad Hoc Networks*, *3*(3), 325–349. doi:10.1016/j.adhoc.2003.09.010

Akyildiz, I. F., & Kasimoglu, I. H. (2004). Wireless sensor and actor networks: Research challenges. *Ad Hoc Networks*, *2*(4), 351–367. doi:10.1016/j.adhoc.2004.04.003

Akyildiz, I. F., Su, W., Sankarasubramaniam, Y., & Cayirci, E. (2002). Wireless Sensor Networks: A Survey. *IEEE Comput. J.*, *38*, 393–422.

Ammari, H. M., & Das, S. K. (2008). Integrated coverage and connectivity in wireless sensor networks: A two-dimensional percolation problem. *IEEE Transactions on Computers*, *57*(10), 1423–1433. doi:10.1109/TC.2008.68

Ammari, H. M., & Das, S. K. (2009). Critical density for coverage and connectivity in three-dimensional wireless sensor networks using continuum percolation. *IEEE Transactions on Parallel and Distributed Systems*, *20*(6), 872–885. doi:10.1109/TPDS.2008.146

Arampatzis, T., Lygeros, J., & Manesis, S. (2005). A survey of applications of wireless sensors and wireless sensor networks. *Proceedings of the 20th IEEE International Symposium on Intelligent Control*, 719–724. 10.1109/.2005.1467103

Baronti, P., Pillai, P., Chook, V. W., Chessa, S., Gotta, A., & Hu, Y. F. (2007). Wireless sensor networks: A survey on the state of the art and the 802.15.4 and ZigBee standards. *Computer Communications*, *30*(7), 1655–1695. doi:10.1016/j.comcom.2006.12.020

Choi, H., Wang, J., & Hughes, E. A. (2009). Scheduling for information gathering on sensor network. *Wireless Networks*, *15*(1), 127–140. doi:10.100711276-007-0050-9

Choi, W., & Das, S. K. (2009). CROSS: A probabilistic constrained random sensor selection scheme in wireless sensor networks. *Performance Evaluation, 66*(12), 754–772. doi:10.1016/j.peva.2009.08.004

Constandache, I., Bao, X., Azizyan, M., & Choudhury, R. R. (2010). Did you see Bob?: Human localization using mobile phones. *MobiCom, 2010*, 149–160.

Cristescu, R., Beferull-Lozano, B., Vetterli, M., & Wattenhofer, R. (2010). Network correlated data gathering with explicit communication: NP-completeness and algorithms. *IEEE/ACM Transactions on Networking, 14*(1), 41–54. doi:10.1109/TNET.2005.863711

Cuomo, F., Cipollone, E., & Abbagnale, A. (2009). Performance analysis of IEEE 802.15.4 wireless sensor networks: An insight into the topology formation process. *Computer Networks, 53*(18), 3057–3075. doi:10.1016/j.comnet.2009.07.016

Dargie, W., & Poellabauer, C. (2010). *Fundamentals of Wireless Sensor Networks: Theory and Practice* (Vol. 191). New York: John Wiley & Sons, Ltd. doi:10.1002/9780470666388

Das, S. K., Datta, A. K., Potop-Butucaru, M. G., Patel, R., & Yamazaki, A. (2009). Self-stabilizing minimum connected covers of query regions in sensor networks. *Wireless Communications and Mobile Computing*.

Elson, J., & Estrin, D. (2004). Sensor Networks: A bridge to the Physical World. *Wireless Sensor Network*, 3–20.

Fan, K. W., Liu, S., & Sinha, P. (2007). Structure-free data aggregation in sensor networks. *IEEE Transactions on Mobile Computing, 6*(8), 929–942. doi:10.1109/TMC.2007.1011

Fasolo, E., Rossi, M., Widmer, J., & Zorzi, M. (2007). In-network aggregation techniques for wireless sensor networks: A survey. *IEEE Wireless Communications, 14*(2), 70–87. doi:10.1109/MWC.2007.358967

Ganesan, D., Greenstein, B., Estrin, D., Heidemann, J., & Govindan, R. (2005). Multiresolution storage and search in sensor networks. *ACM Transactions on Storage, 1*(3), 277–315. doi:10.1145/1084779.1084780

Han, L., Potter, S., Beckett, G., Pringle, G., Welch, S., Koo, S.-H., ... Tate, A. (2010). FireGrid: An e-infrastructure for next-generation emergency response support. *Journal of Parallel and Distributed Computing, 70*(11), 1128–1141. doi:10.1016/j.jpdc.2010.06.005

Heinzelman, W. B., Chandrakasan, A. P., & Balakrishnan, H. (2002). An application-specific protocol architecture for wireless microsensor networks. *IEEE Wireless Communications, 1*(4), 660–670. doi:10.1109/TWC.2002.804190

Heinzelman, W. R., Chandrakasan, A. P., & Balakrishnan, H. (2000). *Energy-efficient communication protocol for wireless microsensor networks*. Hawaii Intl Conf. on System Sciences. doi:10.1109/HICSS.2000.926982

Huang, C. F., & Tseng, Y. C. (2005). The coverage problem in a wireless sensor network. *Mobile Networks and Applications*, *10*(4), 519–528. doi:10.100711036-005-1564-y

Huang, C. F., Tseng, Y. C., & Wu, H. L. (2007). Distributed protocols for ensuring both coverage and connectivity of a wireless sensor network. *ACM Transactions on Sensor Networks*, *3*(1), 5, es. doi:10.1145/1210669.1210674

IEEE 802.15.4-2006. (2006). *Wireless MAC and PHY Specifications for Low Rate Wireless Personal Area Networks (WPANs).* IEEE Computer Society.

IEEE Standard 802.15.4d. (2009). *Low-power Wireless Network technology.* IEEE Computer Society.

IEEE standard for IT. (2006), *Telecommunication and information exchange between systems; local and metropolitan area networks specific requirements part 15.4: wireless MAC and PHY layer specifications for low-rate wireless personal area networks (LR-WPANs) (rev. of IEEE Std 802.15.4-2003), 2006.* IEEE.

Intanagonwiwat, C., Govindan, R., & Estrin, D. (2000). Directed diffusion: A scalable and robust communication paradigm for sensor networks. *MobiCom*, *2000*, 56–67. doi:10.1145/345910.345920

Intanagonwiwat, C., Govindan, R., & Estrin, D. (2000). Directed diffusion: A scalable and robust communication paradigm for sensor networks. *MobiCom*, *2000*, 56–67. doi:10.1145/345910.345920

Jennic JN5121. (2010). Retrieved from http://www.jennic.com/

Konemann, J., Levin, A., & Sinha, A. (2004). A. Sinha, Approximating the degree-bounded minimum diameter spanning tree problem. *Algorithmica*, *41*(2), 117–129. doi:10.100700453-004-1121-2

Lee, H. C., Banerjee, A., Fang, Y. M., Lee, B. J., & King, C. T. (2010). Design of a multifunctional wireless sensor for in-situ monitoring of debris flows. *IEEE Transactions on Mobile Computing*, *59*(11), 2958–2967.

Lee, J., Jung, D.-K., Kim, Y., Lee, Y.-W., & Kim, Y.-M. (2010). Smart grid solutions, services, and business models focused on telco. IEEE/IFIP Network Operations and Management Symp. Workshops, 323–326.

Lee. (2006). *Cyber-Physical Systems - Are Computing Foundations Adequate?* Position Paper for NSF Workshop On Cyber-Physical Systems: Research Motivation, Techniques and Roadmap, Austin, TX.

Lu, G., Krishnamachari, B., & Raghavendra, C. S. (2004). An adaptive energy-efficient and low-latency MAC for data gathering in wireless sensor networks. *Intl. Parallel and Distributed Processing Symp.*

Lynch, J.P. (2007). *An Overview of Wireless Structural Health Monitoring for Civil Structures.* Academic Press.

Ma, M., & Yang, Y. (2007). SenCar: An energy-efficient data gathering mechanism for large-scale multihop sensor networks. *IEEE Transactions on Parallel and Distributed Systems*, *18*(10), 1476–1488. doi:10.1109/TPDS.2007.1070

Melodia, T., Pompili, D., & Akyildiz, I. F. (2006). A communication architecture for mobile wireless sensor and actor networks. *Sensor and Ad Hoc Communications and Networks Conf.*, 109–118. 10.1109/SAHCN.2006.288415

Melodia, T., Pompili, D., Gungor, V. C., & Akyildiz, I. F. (2005). *A distributed coordination framework for wireless sensor and actor networks*. Intl Symp. Mobile Ad Hoc Networking and Computing. doi:10.1145/1062689.1062704

Miluzzo, E., Lane, N. D., Fodor, K., Peterson, R., Lu, H., Musolesi, M., ... Campbell, A. T. (2008). Sensing meets mobile social networks: the design, implementation and evaluation of the CenceMe application. *Int'l Conf. Embedded Networked Sensor Systems*, 337–350. 10.1145/1460412.1460445

Misra, P. K., Mottola, L., Raza, S., Duquennoy, S., Tsiftes, N., Hoglund, J., & Voigt, T. (2013). Supporting cyber-physical systems with wireless sensor networks: An outlook of software and services. *Journal of the Indian Institute of Science*, *93*, 441–462.

Mottola, L., & Picco, G.P. (2011). Programming wireless sensor networks: Fundamental concepts and state of the art. *ACM Comput. Survey, 43.*

Ould-Ahmed-Vall, E., Blough, D. M., Heck, B. S., & Riley, G. F. (2005). Intl Conf. Mobile Ad Hoc and Sensor Systems. Academic Press.

Pan, M. S., Fang, H. W., Liu, Y. C., & Tseng, Y. C. (2008). Address assignment and routing schemes for ZigBee-based long-thin wireless sensor networks. *Vehicular Tech. Conf.*, 173–177. 10.1109/VETECS.2008.48

Pan, M. S., Tsai, C. H., & Tseng, Y. C. (2009). The orphan problem in ZigBee wireless networks. *IEEE Transactions on Mobile Computing*, *8*(11), 1573–1584. doi:10.1109/TMC.2009.60

Ratnasamy, S., Karp, B., Yin, L., Yu, F., Estrin, D., Govindan, R., & Shenker, S. (2002). GHT; a geographic hash-table for data-centric storage. *ACM 2002 Intl Workshop on WSN and their Applications*, 78–87.

Roth, K., & Brodrick, J. (2008). Energy Harvesting for Wireless Sensors. *ASHRAE Journal*, *50*(5), 84–90.

Slijepcevic, S., & Potkonjak, M. (2001). *Power efficient organization of wireless sensor networks*. Intl Conf. Communications. doi:10.1109/ICC.2001.936985

Srinivas, H. (2017). *What is a green or sustainable building?* GDRC Research Output E-029. Kobe, Japan: Global Development Research Center. Retrieved from http://www.gdrc.org/uem/green-const/1-whatis.html

TEOS. (2010). *Terrestrial ecology observing systems, center for embedded networked sensing*. UCLA. Retrieved from http://research.cens.ucla.edu/

Texas Instruments CC2431. (2010). Retrieved from http://www.ti.com/

Tricaud, C.,& Chen, Y.Q. (2009). Optimal mobile actuator/sensor network motion strategy for parameter estimation in a class of CPS. *Proc of the American Control Conference*, 367–372.

Tseng, Y. C., & Pan, M. S. (2008). Quick convergecast in ZigBee beacon-enabled tree-based wireless sensor networks. *Computer Communications*, *31*(5), 999–1011. doi:10.1016/j.comcom.2007.12.015

Upadhyayula, S., Annamalai, V., & Gupta, S. K. S. (2003). A low-latency and energy-efficient algorithm for convergecast in wireless sensor networks. *Global Telecommunications Conf.*, 3525–3530. 10.1109/GLOCOM.2003.1258890

Wan, C., Eisenman, S., Campbell, A., & Crowcroft, J. (2005). *Siphon: overload traffic management using multi-radio virtual sinks in sensor networks*. Intl Conf. Embedded Networked Sensor Systems. doi:10.1145/1098918.1098931

Wang, X., Xing, G., Zhang, Y., Lu, C., Pless, R., & Gill, C. (2003). *Integrated coverage and connectivity configuration in wireless sensor networks*. Intl Conf. Embedded Networked Sensor Systems. doi:10.1145/958491.958496

Wang, X., Xing, G., Zhang, Y., Lu, C., Pless, R., & Gill, C. (2003). Integrated coverage and connectivity configuration in wireless sensor networks. *Intl Conf. Embedded Networked Sensor Systems*, 28–39.

Wu, D., Chatzigeorgiou, D., Youcef-Toumi, K., Mekid, S., & Ben-Mansour, R. (2014). Channel-aware relay node placement in wireless sensor networks for pipeline inspection. *IEEE Transactions on Wireless Communications*, *13*(7), 3510–3523. doi:10.1109/TWC.2014.2314120

Wua, F. J., Koab, Y. F., & Tseng, Y. C. (2011). From WSN towards cyber physical systems. *Pervasive and Mobile Computing*, 7, 397–413. doi:10.1016/j.pmcj.2011.03.003

Xia, F., Tian, Y. C., Li, Y., & Sung, Y. (2007). Wireless Sensor/Actuator Network Design for Mobile Control Applications. *IEEE Sensor*, *7*(10), 2157–2173. doi:10.33907102157 PMID:28903220

Xu, K., Hassanein, H., Takahara, G., & Wang, Q. (2010). Relay node deployment strategies in heterogeneous wireless sensor networks. *IEEE Transactions on Mobile Computing*, *9*(2), 145–159. doi:10.1109/TMC.2009.105

Ye, F., Zhong, G., Cheng, J., Lu, S., & Zhang, L. (2003). *PEAS: a robust energy conserving protocol for long-lived sensor networks*. Intl Conf. Distributed Computing Systems.

Younis, O., & Fahmy, S. (2004). HEED: A hybrid, energy-efficient, distributed clustering approach for ad hoc sensor networks. *IEEE Transactions on Mobile Computing*, *3*(4), 366–379. doi:10.1109/TMC.2004.41

Yu, Krishnamachari, & Prasanna. (2004). Energy-latency tradeoffs for data gathering in wireless sensor networks. *INFOCOM2004*.

Zhang, Z., Ma, M., & Yang, Y. (2008). Energy-efficient multihop polling in clusters of two-layered heterogeneous sensor networks. *IEEE Transactions on Computers*, *57*(2), 231–245. doi:10.1109/TC.2007.70774

Zhao, L., Hong, X., & Liang, Q. (2004). Energy-efficient self-organization for wireless sensor networks: a fully distributed approach. *Global Telecommunications Conf.*, 2728–2732.

ZigBee. (2006). *ZigBee document 064112. IEEE standard for IT(2003), Telecommunications and information exchange between systems; local and metropolitan area networks specific requirements part; 15.4: wireless medium access control (MAC) and physical layer (PHY) specifications for low-rate wireless personal area networks (LR-WPANs)*, Zigbee Alliance 2003. Author.

Chapter 3
Safety–Critical, Dependable, and Fault–Tolerant Cyber–Physical Systems

Guru Prasad Bhandari
Banaras Hindu University, India

Ratneshwer Gupta
Jawaharlal Nehru University, India

ABSTRACT

Cyber-physical systems (CPSs) are co-engineering integrating with physical and computational components networks. Additionally, a CPS is a mechanism controlled or monitored by computer-based algorithms, tightly interacting with the internet and its users. This chapter presents the definitions relating to dependability, safety-critical and fault-tolerance of CPSs. These definitions are supplemented by other definitions like reliability, availability, safety, maintainability, integrity. Threats to dependability and security like faults, errors, failures are also discussed. Taxonomy of different faults and attacks in CPSs are also presented in this chapter. The main objective of this chapter is to give the general information about secure CPS to the learners for the further enhancement in the field of CPSs.

1. INTRODUCTION

Cyber-Physical System (CPS) is computer-enabled mechanism interacting networks of physical and computational components with feedback loops where physical processes affect computations and vice versa. CPS will provide the basics of our critical infrastructure, in terms of emerging and future smart services, and improve our quality of life in many aspects (Wolf, 2009; Alho, 2017). Basically, CPS is a mechanism controlled or monitored by computer-based algorithms, tightly integrated with the Internet and its users functioning on different spatial and temporal scales, exhibiting multiple and distinct behavioral modalities, and interacting with each other in a numerously that change with context (Foundation, 2008).

DOI: 10.4018/978-1-5225-5510-0.ch003

CPS is also known as a special class of embedded systems that use embedded computers and networking infrastructure to control physical workflow processes. CPS uses multiple sensing and actuation units that gather, process, exchange and use information as a team is the next generation of co-engineered systems. Such collection of units that bridge the cyber- world of computing and communications with the physical and biological worlds are called Cyber-Physical Systems (Antsaklis, 2014). CPS has been applied in many areas specially in automotive robotics, aerospace, defense, medical devices (pacemakers, insulin pumps), in critical infrastructure (supervision and direct control of power plants, oil and gas distribution networks, refineries), transportation (airplanes and air-traffic control, rail), in consumer products (camcorders, cameras, mobile phones), in chemical process industries, manufacturing and automobiles (anti-lock braking system (ABS), electronic stability control, fuel injection, emission control) etc.

The major problem of achieving dependable operations for CPS's open and networked control systems is approached using a systems engineering process to gain an understanding of the problem domain, since fault tolerance cannot be solved only as a software problem due to the nature of CPSs, which includes close coordination among hardware, software and physical objects (Alho, 2017). Challenges for software architecture of CPSs includes - sharing of huge amounts of data to optimize processes, utilization and predictive maintenance levels while having predictable timing for end-to-end latencies, V&V, especially security and safety, of evolving systems, scale increase from closed network to integrated system of systems, flexible allocation of resources needed for scalability, stakeholders want systems to be easy to use, build, maintain and repurpose, wide range of timing requirements, stakeholders want to use whatever communication network best meets application specific requirements, support for evolvability, including modifiability and maintainability, product variation for mass-produced systems etc.

In this chapter, we will give a brief introduction about CPSs with its background information. Safety-critical CPSs, dependable CPSs and fault-tolerant CPS will be introduced and their composite explanation will also be emphasized in this chapter. Current challenges in CPSs to make the system safety, dependable and fault-tolerant will be explained with their associated issues. State-of-the-art of the proposed solution to make CPS reliable will also be provided through the chapter. Finally, future direction and conclusion will be provided. Figure 1 presents a Cyber-Physical Systems- a concept map (as in (Asare et al., 2017)).

The structure of this chapter is as follows. Introduction section briefly overviews the chapter, its theme, and purpose. Background of the cyber-physical systems is given in the second section followed by the literature review section. Safety-critical, dependable cyber-physical systems are briefly explained in third section. After that, some current challenges of cyber-physical systems are also presented. State-of-the-art on the solutions for current challenges is also discussed followed. The final section concludes the chapter.

2. BACKGROUND

CPS (Cyber-Physical System) integrates with computing and communication capabilities, monitoring and control of entities in the physical world through a network system that works so dependability, safely, securely, efficiently and in real-time (NSF, 2006). Based on such a broad definition, CPSs are almost synonymous with networked digital control systems and embedded systems. Moreover, CPS means large, complex physical systems that are interacting with a considerable number of distributed computing

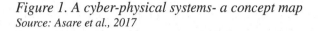

Figure 1. A cyber-physical systems- a concept map
Source: Asare et al., 2017

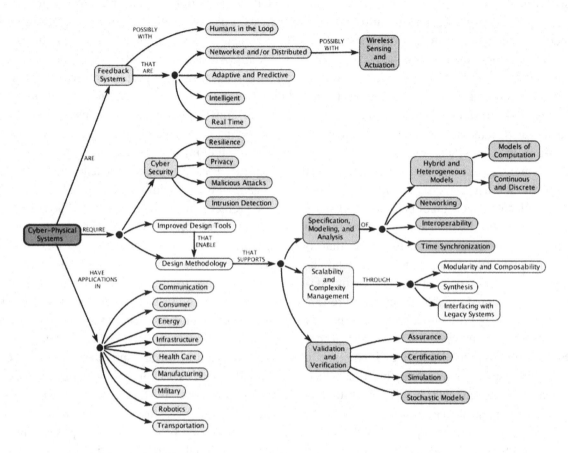

elements for monitoring, control and management which can exchange information between them and with human users (Engell & TU Dortmund, 2014). CPS integrates the dynamic nature of the physical processes with those of the software and networking, facilitating abstractions and modeling, design, and analysis (Asare et al., 2017). The economic and societal impact of CPSs is vastly greater than what has been realized and major investments and efforts are being made worldwide to enhance the technology.

3. THE LITERATURE REVIEW

CPS (Cyber-Physical System) is expected to play a major role in the development of next-generation smart energy systems and data centers. Innovative computational methodologies such as green CPS and energy efficient CPS design have become critical to enable the sustainable development of such systems (Kabashkin & Kundler, 2017). Many researchers have been emphasized in safety-critical, dependable and fault-tolerant CPS observed in the literature. Some of the works are as follows.

Kabashkin and Kunder (2017) have proposed a Markov model for reliability analyses of a sensor node in CPS. It has been observed that the reliability of the sensor node depends on the strategy of its monitoring and is a unimodal function of the test period. CPS is by nature self-adaptive. It is necessary to use feedback loop mechanisms to deal with the various sources of uncertainty, control their emergent behavior, and be resilient to changes.

To explore the self-adaptivity natures of CPS, Muccini and Weyns (2016) have conducted a review on self-adaptation for CPS. In their review, a number of studies have been using self-adaptation features in the engineering of CPS. In the paper, Liu et al. (2017) have reviewed on CPS issues and challenges. They have noticed safety control, system security, uncertainty processing as major research challenges in CPS. Alho (2015) has proposed an architecture for CPSs towards resilient and dependable systems in his thesis. Remote handling control system for CPS is also developed. He has presented dependability issues and challenges in CPS.

Basic definitions relating to dependability, safety-critical and fault-tolerance of CPS (Cyber-Physical Systems) are represented in this chapter. These definitions are supplemented by other definitions like as reliability, availability, safety, maintainability, integrity. The main objective of this chapter is to give the general information about secure CPS to the learners for the further enhancement in the field of CPS. This is an emerging field, other platforms like the Internet of Things, Smart Cities, Smart Grids, Cloud Computing are also currently present associated with CPS.

4. SAFETY CRITICAL CYBER-PHYSICAL SYSTEMS

Software and control systems usually can be classified in the following way. For example vehicle application (Herrmann, 1999) as follows:

- *Safety-critical* software (e.g., brake control).
- *Safety-related* software, intended to maintain safe conditions or prevent risks (e.g., seatbelt pre-tensioning and airbag control).
- *Non-safety-related* software (e.g., air conditioning control).

As we can see from the example, not all control software is safety-critical. The scope of what is considered safety-critical depends on the context; for example, it can cover the whole control system software if a fault can cause economic losses (e.g., losing a satellite) or endanger human lives (e.g., through nonfunctional mobile machinery). Moreover, a non-critical component that can influence the safety-critical candidate components become safety-critical itself (NASA, 2004). *Mission-critical systems* may have a combination of the aforementioned software modules; therefore, partitioning (i.e., the separating of different software units) is usually used so that a failure in a multimedia system does not cause a crash in brake control software (Herrmann, 1999).

Alho's Ph.D. thesis (2017) has mentioned some of the power standards for safety-critical cyber-physical systems. Standards can be used to show compliance with legal requirements, which in the case of the ITER, may include the European Union machinery directive, French nuclear laws, etc.

- IEC 61508 is a standard for developing software-based safety-related systems. It sets out the requirements for ensuring that these systems are designed, implemented, operated and maintained to provide the required safety integrity level (SIL), which ranges from 1 to 4 (highest reliability). The standard also has domain-specific variants, such as IEC 62061 for machinery.
- In the United States, the "DO- 178C Software Considerations in Airborne Systems and Equipment Certification" document and the "MIL-STD-882E Standard Practice for System Safety" military standard are commonly used references.
- According to a report completed for U.S. National Academies (Jackson et al., 2007), certification of the dependability of software-based systems is considered to typically rely more on assessments of the development processes than on properties of the system itself, due to the difficulty of assessing the dependability of software.

Restrictions set by the safety standards can conflict with the vision of creating CPSs that can function in dynamic computing and physical environments perform autonomously or in cooperation with humans, etc. It is still unclear how software-based safety functions could be implemented cost-efficiently; current approaches rely on separating safety and control systems (Douglass, 2010), but this approach prevents the utilization of the increasingly larger amounts data available in the control systems of the machines to support the safety systems. Currently, such reuse of information in the safety system is avoided in order to prove that the safety system is independent of other systems and not affected by fault propagation. However, this kind of information could provide an improved level of safety as part of a layered safety approach (Alho, 2017).

5. DEPENDABLE CYBER-PHYSICAL SYSTEMS

This chapter uses the definition of dependability, given by Avizienis et al. (2004), in which dependability is defined as the ability to deliver service that can be justifiably trusted. Dependability encompasses attributes of reliability, availability, maintainability, integrity and safety, and it is closely connected to reliability, availability, maintainability and safety (RAMS) requirements in systems engineering. A fault is a defect in a system, whereas a failure is an instance in time during which a system displays behavior that is contrary to its specifications (Avižienis et al., 2004). A fault, when activated, can lead to an error (i.e., an invalid state), and the invalid state generated by an error may lead to another error or a failure. Means for achieving dependability can be categorized into four groups: fault prevention, fault tolerance, fault removal and fault forecasting (Avižienis et al., 2004). While the key results in the publications of this thesis focus on fault tolerance, an inclusive system engineering approach to dependability are necessary.

5.1 CPSs and Dependability

It is possible to verify or extensively test the code of closed control systems with limited connectivity. For example, the automotive industry uses an approach in which each function of a the vehicle has its own electronic control unit (ECU), which can be developed and tested separately. This is necessary in order to manage the large amounts of software coming from multiple vendors that are required in modern cars to control safety, emissions, communications, convenience and entertainment functions, among others. Retaining test coverage over growing functionalities of new ECUs leads to longer test periods (Caliebe et al., 2011) and the complexity of integrating tens of ECUs means that the system integration phase becomes the major source of challenges. The downsides of increasing the number of ECUs include also the increased component costs, weight, heat and power consumption. Therefore, it is unclear how well the historical approach of using separate hardware modules to isolate safety-certified applications scales to the need for integrating more networked and complex functionalities in CPSs. To manage software and hardware complexity in vehicles, the automotive industry has developed the open AUTomotive Open System ARchitecture (AUTOSAR) standard, which can be used to 10 integrate a high amount of functionality into a single ECU in a controlled way; however, the migration process to adopt it is still underway. Other proposed approaches in the industry include using language-, location- and platform-independent middleware (e.g., Common Object Request Broker Architecture (CORBA)), to connect and manage tasks (Medrano et al., 2017).

However, the added intelligence and advanced features, such as x-by-wire applications and machine-to-machine (M2M) communications, mean that CPSs become more vulnerable to software faults caused by, for example, timing or integration issues that have potential to cause severe damage or economic losses; in such cases, the smart car could just as well be a forest harvester or an ITER RH robot. The networked CPSs require new approaches to real-time fault tolerance and reasoning about consequences of faults because the fault tolerance of CPSs cannot be solved solely as a software problem—since, by their nature, these systems function on the tight coordination among hardware, software and physical elements. Further challenges (Alho, 2017) faced in the development of CPSs are introduced by their cross-disciplinary natures since engineers must define requirements, interfaces and error management for components that bridge engineering disciplines both horizontally (subsystems and functions) and vertically (software, computers, physical platform). For a hydraulic diverter cassette mover, these sub-systems would include, at a minimum, electrical, pneumatic, hydraulic, mechanical, power unit and user interface subsystems. Components and subsystems are likely coming from multiple vendors from diverse engineering disciplines with specific domain expertise (Alho, 2017); thus, they must be somehow integrated into an effective and dependable system.

CPSs are networked computing units that monitor and control physical processes (often in feedback loops). This is a particularly cogent issue when considering that, compared to classical control theory, these systems include dynamics introduced by networks and software (e.g., the timing jitter in com-munications and computation, packet losses in networks and resource contention) that may affect the stability and dynamics of the physical subsystems. If timing effects the system, small changes in the environment, software or hardware can cause unexpected changes in the timing for a brittle design. As a consequence, manufacturers of embedded systems with long lifecycles need to stockpile components. They cannot take advantage of improvements in computing capabilities because the testing costs for new hardware would be too high. This can lead to an outdated system architecture, obsolete hardware and unsupported software.

The claim that software does not decay is a fallacy, as pointed out by the 1st law of Lehman (Lehman, 1980) which states that, since the environment of the real world is constantly changing, in order for a system that performs a real-world activity to continue to be relevant, it must adapt and evolve as the world as well. The alternative is for the system to become progressively less applicable and useful.

The 2nd law of Lehman states that, as an evolving program is continually changed, its complexity increases unless work is done to maintain or reduce it. These laws are highly relevant for automation systems with long expected lifetimes, especially when moving to increasingly distributed designs. Since the systems will need to be maintained (changed) in order to retain functionality and security, the system dependability may degrade. Therefore, the evolvability of the architecture, which can be supported through a high level of decoupling between subsystems and components is needed to facilitate the capability to maintain software (Alho, 2017). Figure 2 shows the dependability and security attributes of the CPS systems.

6. FAULT TOLERANT CYBER-PHYSICAL SYSTEMS

Before coming to the understanding of fault-tolerant CPSs. We need to be familiar with some preliminary definitions. IFAC Technical Committee SAFE-PROCESS (Parisini, 2016) has defined some unified preliminary definitions towards in terms of fault diagnosis. Some of the relevant terminologies are presented here as a way to introduce the field. List of definitions are as follows:

6.1 Basic Terminologies

- **Fault:** It can be defined as "an unpermitted deviation of at least one characteristic property or variable of the system from acceptable/usual/standard behavior".
- **Failure:** It is defined as "a permanent interruption of system's ability to perform a required function under specified operating conditions".
- **Fault Detection:** It resembles with the determination of faults present in a system and time of detection.
- **Fault Isolation:** It deals with the determination of kind, location, and time of detection of a fault. It takes place after fault detection.
- **Fault Identification:** It associates with the determination of the size and time-variant behavior of a fault. It follows fault isolation.

Figure 2. Dependability and security attributes
Source: Avižienis et al., 2004

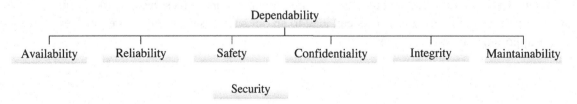

- **Fault Diagnosis:** It can be defined as the determination of kind, size, location, and time of detection of a fault. Generally, it is defined as an act of identifying a problem from its signs and symptoms. It follows fault detection and includes fault isolation and identification. It also covers fault detection.

- **Fault Tolerant:** Fault tolerance is used to make systems more resilient to unanticipated faults, such as residual software faults (i.e., bugs). A fault tolerance solution consists of error detection and recovery (Avižienis et al., 2004), although some techniques address only one of these phases. According to Somani and Vaidya (1997), the hardware is getting more reliable and fault-tolerant but there is an increasing demand for tolerance of design, operator, environmental and reconfiguration faults. This development is hardly surprising, since hardware faults are mostly physical faults whereas software faults are typically design faults, which are harder to visualize, classify, detect, and correct (Lyu, 1996).

6.2 Threats to Dependability

Correct service is delivered when the service implements the system function. A failure is an event that occurs when the delivered service deviates from correct service (Avižienis et al., 2004). A failure may either occurs because it does not comply with the functional requirements, or because this specification did not satisfactorily describe the system function. A failure is a transformation of a service from correct to incorrect, i.e., to not implementing the system function. Moreover, a service is a sequence of the system's functional states, a service failure means that at least one (or more) external state of the system deviates from the correct state (Avižienis et al., 2004). The deviation is meant by an error. The cause of an error is called a fault. Figure 3 depicts the basic fault propagation model in CPS systems (as in (Avižienis et al., 2004)).

Figure 3. Error propagation
Source: Avižienis et al., 2004

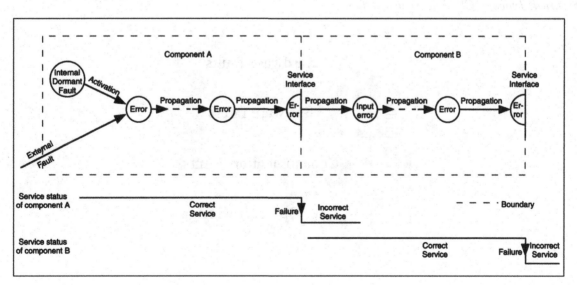

The period of delivery of incorrect service is a service outage. The transition from incorrect service to correct service is a service restoration. The deviation from correct service may assume different forms that are called service failure modes and are ranked according to failure severities.

6.3 Classification of Faults

Faults can be classified as an internal or external. The prior presence of vulnerability, i.e., an internal fault that enables an external fault to harm the system, is necessary for an external fault to cause an error and possibly subsequent failure(s). In most cases, a fault first causes an error in the service state of a component that is a part of the internal state of the system and the external state is not immediately affected. For this reason, the definition of an error is the part of the total state of the system that may lead to its subsequent service failure. It is important to note that many errors do not reach the system's external state and cause a failure. A fault is active when it causes an error, otherwise, it is dormant. CPS fault can also be categorized as other general system faults into three categories; hardware fault, software faults, communications faults and user/operator wrongs. Figure 4 shows the CPS faults which are related to the infrastructure faults. Fault taxonomy of dependable distributed system can be found in (Avižienis et al., 2004) and (Bhandari & Gupta, 2018). Here, we have briefly classified CPS faults into four categories.

- *Hardware faults* in a system can be the root cause of faults in a system as the may cause either crashes or execution faults while the system is running.
- *Software faults* may arise due to the problem in requirements, features, input data, system structure, interfaces, software coding, association integration and testing.
- *Communication faults* associated with routing problem, missing or abandoned packets, wrong routing to authorization conflicts, congestion problem, packet overflow etc.

Figure 4. Types of CPS infrastructure faults

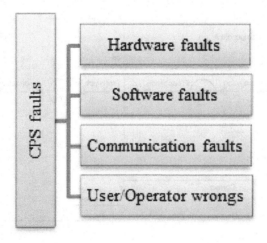

- *User/Operator wrongs* are related to the errors made by the user while inserting the input or due to not following the validation of the system. There are basically four types (Shwartz et al., 2010) of wrongs noticed in a distributed system that lead to the erroneous execution of change and release operations: wrong request, wrong target, wrong time, and wrong command.

6.4 Dependability

The original definition of dependability is the ability to deliver service that can justifiably be trusted. The alternate definition that provides the criterion for deciding if the service is dependable is the dependability of a system is the ability to avoid service failures that are more frequent and more severe than is acceptable. It is usual to say that the dependability of a system should suffice for the dependence being placed on that system. The dependence of system A on system B, thus, represents the extent to which system A's dependability is (or would be) affected by that of System B. The concept of dependence leads to that of trust, which can very conveniently be defined as accepted dependence. As developed over the past three decades, dependability is an integrating concept that encompasses the following attributes:

- *Availability* refers to the readiness for correct service.
- *Reliability* means the continuity of correct service.
- *Safety* refers absence of catastrophic consequences on the user(s) and the environment.
- Integrity states absence of improper system alterations.
- *Maintainability* mentions the ability to undergo modifications and repairs.

When addressing security, an additional attribute has great prominence, confidentiality, i.e., the absence of unauthorized disclosure of information. Security is a composite of the attributes of confidentiality, integrity, and availability, requiring the concurrent existence of 1) availability for authorized actions only, 2) confidentiality, and 3) integrity with "improper" meaning "unauthorized." Figure 5 summarizes the relationship between dependability and security in terms of their principal attributes (as shown in (Avižienis et al., 2004)). The picture should not be interpreted as indicating that, for example, security developers have no interest in maintainability, or that there has been no research at all in the dependability field related to confidentiality- rather it indicates where the main balance of interest and activity lies in each case. The dependability and security specification of a system must include the requirements for the attributes in terms of the acceptable frequency and severity of service failures for specified classes of faults and a given use environment. One or more attributes may not be required at all for a given system.

Fault prevention means to prevent the occurrence or introduction of faults. *Fault tolerance* means to avoid service failures in the presence of faults. *Fault removal* means to reduce the number and severity of faults. *Fault forecasting* means to estimate the present number, the future incidence, and the likely consequences.

There are many reasons for faults in the system that may be of any facets which are listed as bellow.

1. Human factor
2. Communication failure/miscommunication
3. Insufficient energy

Figure 5. Dependability and security tree
Source: Avižienis et al., 2004

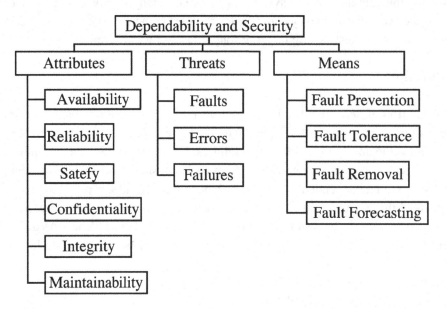

4.   Unrealistic development timeframe
5.   Poor design logic
6.   Poor coding practices (noted inefficient or missing error/exception handling and lack of proper validations)
7.   Lack of version control
8.   Buggy third-party tools
9.   Lack of skilled testing
10. Last minute changes and so on.

7. APPROACHES TO ACHIEVING FAULT TOLERANCE (CURRENT OR PROPOSED SOLUTIONS)

Architecture and system structure have key roles in how the final system fulfills the qualityattribute requirements, such as dependability and its sub-attributes. Examples of architecturaldesign approaches that can be used to improve dependability include redundancy and modularity (IEC, 2005) (Bass et al., 2012). There is a fault tolerant system paradigm proposed by Suri (Bakken, 2002) while developing any fault tolerant system. The steps to follow to construct a fault tolerant system are as follows.

1.   Identify the classes of faults expected over the life of the system.
2.   Specify goals for the system dependability
3.   Partition the system into subsystems, both hardware and software, taking both performance and fault tolerance into account.

4. Select error detection and fault diagnosis algorithms for every sub-system.
5. Device state recovery and fault removal techniques for every subsystem.
6. Integrate subsystem fault tolerance on a global scale.
7. Evaluate the effectiveness of fault tolerance and its relationship with performance.
8. Repeat the steps 3 through 7 to refine the design.

There are some popular fault-tolerant architectures which are listed below.

7.1 Redundancy

Fault tolerance techniques applied at the architectural level make use of redundancy in one form or another, to the extent that redundancy is almost synonymous to fault tolerance. In order to make the system able to tolerate faults, it needs to be able to detect and react to errors and implementing these features adds redundancy to the system (e.g., code to detect faults). Redundancy refers to forward recovery techniques based on multiple versions (e.g., NVP (Pullum, 2001)) or active/passive node redundancy (Bass et al., 2012).

The effectiveness of software redundancy techniques requires that redundant modules must be diverse otherwise the software faults are replicated in all of the modules. This is typically avoided by using design diversity. NVP is an example of a well-known fault tolerance approach based on design diversity, in which two or more functionally equivalent programs are independently created from the same initial specifications and run on separate hardware channels (Avizienis & Chen, 1977). This form of redundancy can be especially effective at tolerating intermittent faults. However, most of the software faults are design faults (Capers Jones, 2012) and NVP does not solve the problems related to incorrect specifications. NVP has been criticized, for example, in (Knight & Leveson, 1986) because programmers tend to make same kinds of mistakes. This may result in the different versions having the same types of faults, regardless of independent development. Faults do not need to be identical, it is sufficient that they are coexistent to cause a failure. Diverse software redundancy can create further problems due to slightly different behaviors between versions, especially when an abnormal input occurs into the system. Although Laprie et al. (1990) show that an N-variant software module is less costly than N times a non-fault-tolerant software module, the costs of using design diversity are often hard to justify, unless necessitated by a fail-operate application (e.g., flight controller) or required by the functional safety standards. There are several types of redundancy mechanism for fault handling (Torres-pomales & Langley, 2000). Some of them are mentioned as follows.

1. Passive redundancy (as shown in Figure 6)
2. Passive redundancy with input voting (as shown in Figure 7)
3. Active redundancy with comparison (as shown in Figure 8)
4. Dynamic redundancy with self-checking pairs (as shown in Figure 9)
5. Hybrid redundancy using N-Modular redundancy with spares (as shown in Figure 10)

Figure 6. Passive redundancy
Source: Torres-pomales & Langley, 2000

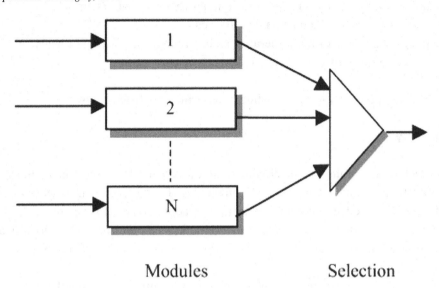

Modules   Selection

Figure 7. Passive redundancy with input voting
Source: Torres-pomales & Langley, 2000

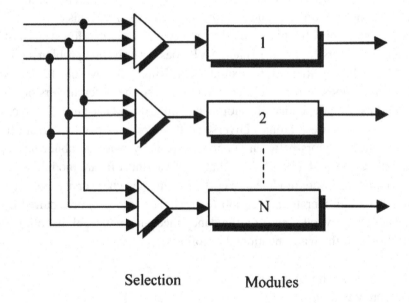

Selection   Modules

Each of them is briefly described as follows,

1. Passive Redundancy

In passive redundancy, the modules are replicated several times depending on the desired fault tolerance capability. Figure 6 presents a basic example of passive redundancy in case of hardware.

2. Passive Redundancy With Input Voting

A selection mechanism usually a voter, is used to mask errors that reach the outputs of the modules (Torres-pomales & Langley, 2000). Figure 7 shows an approach where the voters are moved to the input of the modules to eliminate the single point of failure that is the single voter (as in Figure 6). This configuration guards the computations performed by the replicated components nonetheless requires that redundant components reading the outputs use the identical approach to avoid the propagation of errors and single point of failure.

3. Active Redundancy With Comparison

In an active redundancy with the comparison, error detection is achieved by comparing the outputs of two modules performing the same function (Torres-pomales & Langley, 2000). Figure 8 displays an active redundancy approach with the comparison. If the outputs of the modules disagree, an error condition is raised followed by diagnosis and repair actions to return the system to operate smoothly. In a similar approach, only one module would actually perform the intended function with the other component being a dissimilar monitor that checks the outputs looking for errors (Torres-pomales & Langley, 2000).

Figure 8. Active redundancy with comparison
Source: Torres-pomales & Langley, 2000

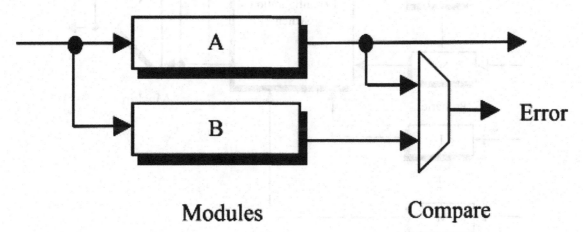

Figure 9. Dynamic redundancy with self-checking pairs
Source: Torres-pomales & Langley, 2000

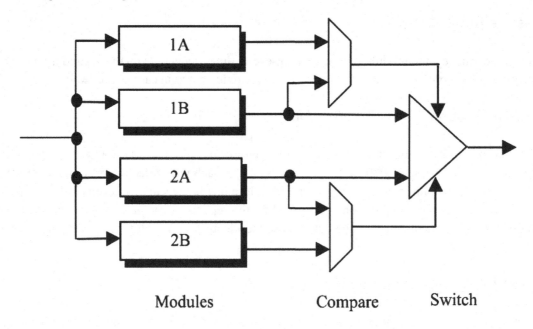

Modules   Compare   Switch

Figure 10. Hybrid redundancy using N-Modular redundancy with spares
Source: Torres-pomales & Langley, 2000

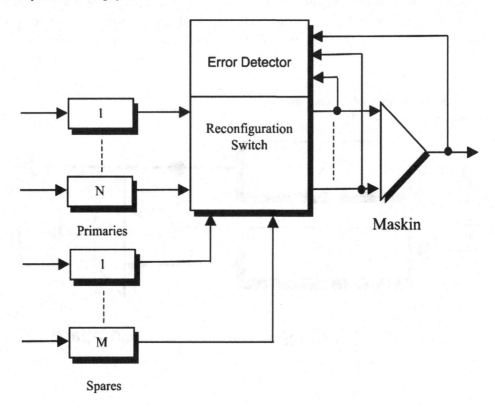

4. Dynamic Redundancy With Self-Checking Pairs

In this approach, the comparators perform the error detection function. Normally the output is taken from one of the pairs known as the primary pair, with the other pair acting as a spare or backup. When an error on the primary is detected, the spare is brought online and the primary is taken offline for diagnosis and maintenance if any necessary (Torres-pomales & Langley, 2000). Figure 9 shows four modules arranged in a self-checking pair configuration or dual-dual configuration.

5. Hybrid Redundancy Using N-Modular Redundancy With Spares

In this type of redundancy configuration, we are combining the masking approach used in passive redundancy with the error detection, diagnosis, and reconfiguration used in dynamic approaches. The system (as in Figure 10) utilizes a set of primary modules to deliver inputs to the voter to implement error masking. Simultaneously an error detection component monitors the outputs of the active modules observing for errors. When an error is detected, the faulty module is taken offline for diagnosis and a spare module is brought online to participate in the error-masking configuration. Implemented properly, it has better dependability properties than purely passive or active configurations. However, the cost and complexity are higher for this approach. The selection of one of the three approaches is highly dependent on the application (Torres-pomales & Langley, 2000). Figure 10 shows an example of hybrid redundancy using an N-modular masking configuration with spares.

7.2 Modular Approach

The modular approach entails design principles to implement information hiding, well-defined interfaces, loose coupling and strong cohesion, and to limit module size and structural complexity. Highly decoupled architectural styles and patterns (e.g., SOA and publish-subscribe) could improve dependability in control systems, since the designers of the consumer services cannot make the assumption that a service provider is available all the time, thus forcing them to take this situation into account in the design and implementation (Hargrave & Kriens, 2007). Decoupling limits fault propagation and also increases the simplicity of the system, thus improving dependability (Jackson, 2009).

Triple modular redundancy, NVP and other redundant systems also need a voting algorithm. The voter acts as an adjudicator that determines the correct output. This part of the system, implemented either in software or hardware, needs to be as simple as possible in order to avoid the need for introducing fault detection for the voter. Dunn (2003) presents a practical approach to implementing fail-safe systems without extensive redundancy. If a fault is detected, the system can be guided to a known non-operating safe state. The fail-safe system can be implemented, for example, with the monitor-actuator pattern, in which a separate sensor channel watches over the actuator channel, looking for an indication that the system should be commended into its fail-safe state (Douglass, 2002). NASA calls this type of systems failure-tolerant (Herrmann, 1999). Even though the fail-safe approach can improve safety, the system reliability may decrease compared to fault masking techniques. Another threat to reliability with the fail-safe approach is false positive errors.

7.3 Recovery Blocks (Forward Recovery)

Recovery blocks scheme, another commonly used form of design diversity, is based on backward recovery instead of forward recovery. Recovery blocks have better overall performance than NVP (Chiaradonna et al., 1994). This is because NVP has to always wait for the slowest variant, whereas recovery block-based solution causes execution time overhead only when the system is recovering from an error. In hard real-time systems, it should be noted that this overhead can cause the system to miss execution deadlines, whereas NVP has more consistent performance. Another similar solution to recovery blocks is retry blocks in which the fault tolerance is based on re-expressing input data on error detection. Unlike NVP, recovery blocks and retry blocks do not use multiple hardware channels for redundancy and they are recommended as cost-efficient fault tolerance schemes in (Hiller, 1998). Figure 11 shows recovery block model.

7.4 NVP (N-Version Programming)

N-version programming is a multi-version technique (as defined by Avizienis in (1985)) in which all the versions are designed to satisfy the same basic requirements and the decision of output correctness is based on the comparison of all the outputs. Figure 12 presents the basic N-Version programming model.

Figure 11. Recovery block model
Source: Torres-pomales & Langley, 2000

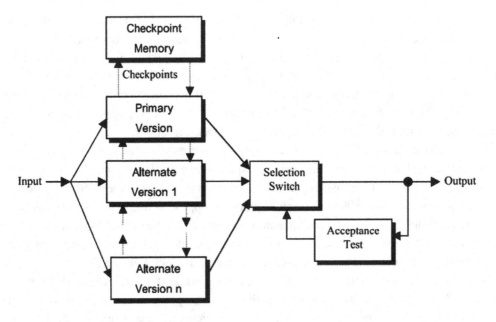

Figure 12. N-Version programming model
Source: Torres-pomales & Langley, 2000

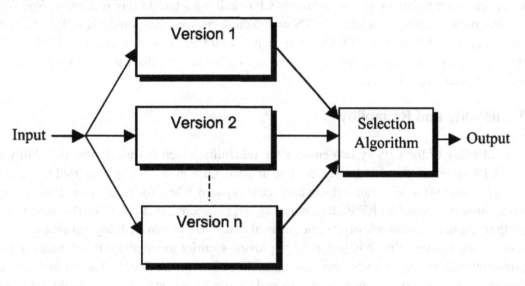

7.5 Erlang

Erlang (Armstrong, 2003) programming language/runtime system uses a low-cost process-based model toimplement loosely coupled communication for processes, supporting a large number of smallprocesses to carry out tasks. Initially developed for telecommunication systems, it has been used to achieve high system-level availability. Even if a single process terminates, it does not affect the availability of the whole system. For example, Erlang-based implementation in web server has been shown to be more resilient and to have better availability than a similar C++ implementation. Erlang has been used for mobile robot control (Szominski et al., 2013), to provide separation of processes and ability to recover crashed drivers. However, this research does not give information about system real-time or dependability performance. Sotirovksi (2001) uses object-oriented design approach based on encapsulation and exception mechanism for developing a fault-tolerant software architecture. The downside of using objects as units for fault containment is that a failure affects the execution of the whole application, including other objects.

8. CHALLENGES OF CYBER-PHYSICAL SYSTEMS

There are many issues and challenges identified in CPS systems. Some participant component of CPS might be black-box whose structure in does not permit in nature, therefore obtaining probabilistic data need for fault analysis. It is required to be measured by sampling the input space to obtain the probabilistic data. Breivold et al. (2015) have categorized some distributed systems' challenges on the basis of industrial automation perspective. CPS is decentralized distributed system so one challenge may affect the overall CPS system rather than just one module. Reliability and availability could be challenges for domain-specific constraints as well as industrial CPS challenges too. In this section, we specify CPS fault management challenges in overall CPS architecture perspective. Antsaklis (2014) has noticed some of the goals and challenges of CPSs in his paper. There are so many challenges while CPS fault handling but some of the major challenges related to CPS systems are discussed in this chapter. Figure 13 presents the challenges of CPS.

8.1 Availability and Reliability

24 x 7 availability of the CPS system ensures the reliability which is trustworthy. Reliability is the ability of CPS system to do its task in given time interval. Qian et al. (2017) have tried to formulate a practical transmission model for an ambient backscatter system, where the reader can get some low-rate messages, through an ambient RF(Radio Frequency) signal source, that enhances the availability and reduces the computational complexity. Service unavailability or data unavailability can have severe effect on the customer business, thus it is important to provide security mechanisms to increase the level of data protection and security for messages communications between devices to devices such as sensors, actuators etc. to ensure service continuity and indeed Quality of Service (QoS) (Breivold & Sandstrom, 2015). Through responsiveness, we can measure the success of an environment calculating a probable value against response time.

Figure 13. Challenges on handling fault in CPS

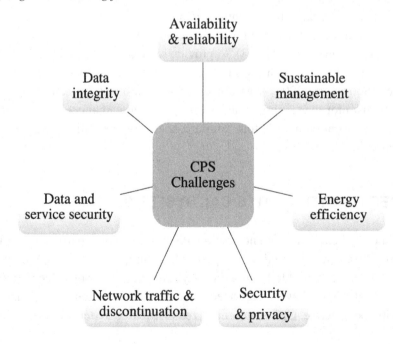

8.2 Sustainable Management

Millions of devices are attached each other in CPS by means of smart industries, smart cities, smart homes etc. (Sajid, Abbas, & Saleem, 2016) and it is very complex to manage such large-scale systems. Energy-driven management is desirable to promise more efficient and optimised usage of global resources. Many researchers (Jeon et al., 2016) have focused in the sustainable management of CPS for fault handling.

8.3 Security and Privacy

Involving a large number of devices, systems, components and technologies together leads to more decentralized entry points for security disruptions (Vermesan & Friess, 2014). Securities, safety, verification of properties need to be reassessed regularly, because of the expected behavior of the system.

8.4 Data Integrity

Network resources and users of the CPS system need to have a trustworthy environment to the information and services being exchanged. Building a trustworthy fault tolerant system in the CPS environment needs taking care of how to protect communications, how to ensure integrity and confidentiality, authenticity, access control, authorization etc. to the CPS resources. The fault may occur in CPS system due to lack of data integrity and lack of information privacy.

8.5 Scalability

Scalability is the ability of the system that allows the system process more user requests in the prescribed time interval. Many researchers (Guo et al., 2017) (Khan et al., 2017) (Jeon et al., 2016) have highlighted in scalability as challenges while handling fault in CPS applications. Run-time security monitors for CPS applications either generate high false alarm rates or limit application performance that insists scalability limitations. So, many researchers have addressed this issues like Khan et al. (2017) using run-time security monitor. Various transmission channels (GPRS, 3G, WLAN, WiMax) seriously affect the always-on connectivity on-demand scalability of wireless connectivity (Ayari et al., 2008). Many researchers (Guo et al., 2017) have emphasized in mobility issues of CPS devices in handling faults (Bhandari & Gupta, 2017).

8.6 Dynamism

Dynamic changes should be predicted, especially when the whole life cycle of the system is considered. The physical part of the system may cause the CPS system to vary; links may disappear, modules may stop operating. The objective is to achieve a fault-tolerant system with decreasing cost of computation, networking, and sensing. We should keep noticing that a variety of social and economic forces will necessitate the more efficient use of infrastructures; also, environmental stresses will mandate the rapid introduction of technologies to improve energy efficiency and reduce pollution (Antsaklis, 2014). For instance, for more efficient use of healthcare systems, ranging CPS design considerations should be concerned.

9. CONCLUSION

This chapter presents the definitions relating to dependability, safety-critical and fault-tolerance of CPS (Cyber-Physical Systems). These definitions are supplemented by other definitions like as reliability, availability, safety, maintainability, integrity. Threats to dependability and security like faults, errors, failures are also discussed. Taxonomy of different faults in CPS is also presented in this chapter. The main objective of this chapter is to give the general information about secure CPS to the learners for the further enhancement in the field of CPS. This is an emerging field, other platforms like the Internet of Things, Smart Cities, Smart Grids, Cloud Computing are also currently present associated with CPS. CPS as the dependable system only ensures the reliability if the system is fault-tolerant.

ACKNOWLEDGMENT

The authors would like to thank ICCR, Ministry of Foreign Affairs, India (Silver Jubilee Scholarship Scheme) for providing funds and DST-CIMS, Institute of Science, BHU, India for providing necessary infrastructure and facilities for undertaking this research work.

REFERENCES

Alho, P. (2015). *Service-Based Fault Tolerance for Cyber-Physical Systems : A Systems Engineering Approach*. Tampere University of Technology. Retrieved from http://www.tut.fi/tutcris

Alho, P. (2017). *Service-based Fault Tolerance for Cyber-Physical Systems*. Tampere University of Technology.

Antsaklis, P. (2014). Goals and Challenges in Cyber-Physical Systems Research Editorial of the Editor in Chief. *IEEE Transactions on Automatic Control*, *59*(12), 3117–3119. doi:10.1109/TAC.2014.2363897

Armstrong, J. (2003). *Making reliable distributed systems in the presence of sodware errors*. Mikroelektronik och informationsteknik. Retrieved from http://citeseerx.ist.psu.edu/viewdoc/download?doi=10.1.1.3.408&rep=rep1&type=pdf

Asare, P., Broman, D., Lee, E. A., Prinsloo, G., Torngren, M., & Sunder, S. S. (2017). *A Cyber Physical Systems- a concept map*. Retrieved September 5, 2017, from http://cyberphysicalsystems.org

Avizienis, A. (1985). The N-version approach to fault-tolerant software. *IEEE Transactions on Software Engineering*, *SE-11*(12), 1491–1501. doi:10.1109/TSE.1985.231893

Avizienis, A., & Chen, L. (1977). On the Implementation of N-Version programming for software fault tolerance during execution. *Ieee Compsac*, *77*, 149–155.

Avižienis, A., Laprie, J. C., Randell, B., & Landwehr, C. (2004). Basic concepts and taxonomy of dependable and secure computing. *IEEE Transactions on Dependable and Secure Computing*, *1*(1), 11–33. doi:10.1109/TDSC.2004.2

Ayari, N., Barbaron, D., Lefevre, L., & Primet, P. (2008). Fault tolerance for highly available internet services: Concepts, approaches, and issues. *IEEE Communications Surveys and Tutorials*, *10*(2), 34–46. doi:10.1109/COMST.2008.4564478

Bakken, D. (2002). Paradigms for Distributed Fault Tolerance. *Verssimo & Rodrigues Book*, 1–57.

Bass, L., Clements, P., & Kazman, R. (2012). *Software Architecture in Practice*. Pearson Education India. doi:10.1024/0301-1526.32.1.54

Bhandari, G. P., & Gupta, R. (2017). Fault Repairing Strategy Selector for Service-Oriented Architecture. *I.J. Modern Education and Computer Science Modern Education and Computer Science*, *6*(6), 32–39. doi:10.5815/ijmecs.2017.06.05

Bhandari, G. P., & Gupta, R. (2018). Extended Fault Taxonomy of SOA-Based Systems. *CIT. Journal of Computing and Information Technology*, *25*(4), 237–257. doi:10.20532/cit.2017.1003569

Breivold, H. P., & Sandstrom, K. (2015). Internet of Things for Industrial Automation-Challenges and Technical Solutions. *Proceedings - 2015 IEEE International Conference on Data Science and Data Intensive Systems; 8th IEEE International Conference Cyber, Physical and Social Computing; 11th IEEE International Conference on Green Computing and Communications and 8th IEEE Inte*. 10.1109/DSDIS.2015.11

Caliebe, P., Lauer, C., & German, R. (2011). Flexible integration testing of automotive ECUs by combining AUTOSAR and XCP. In *ICCAIE 2011 - 2011 IEEE Conference on Computer Applications and Industrial Electronics* (pp. 67–72). IEEE. 10.1109/ICCAIE.2011.6162106

Capers Jones. (2012). Software Quality in 2012: a Survey of the State of the Art. *White Paper, Software Productivity Research*, 1–25. Retrieved from http://sqgne.org/presentations/2012-13/Jones-Sep-2012.pdf

Chiaradonna, S., Bondavalli, A., & Strigini, L. (1994). On Performability Modeling and Evaluation of Software Fault Tolerant Structures. *Proceedings of the First European Dependable Computing Conference on Dependable Computing*, 97–114. Retrieved from http://0-dl.acm.org.wam.city.ac.uk/citation.cfm?id=645330.650098

Douglass, B. P. (2002). *Real-Time Design Patterns: Robust Scalable Architecture for Real-Time Systems* (Vol. 1). Addison-Wesley Professional.

Douglass, B. P. (2010). Design Patterns for Embedded Systems in C. *Embedded*, *384*. doi:10.1016/B978-1-85617-707-8.00006-6

Dunn, W. R. (2003). Designing safety-critical computer systems. *Computer*, *36*(11), 40–46. doi:10.1109/MC.2003.1244533

Engell, S. (2014). *Cyber-physical Systems of Systems Definition and core research and innovation areas Systems of Systems.* TU Dortmund.

Guo, J., Chen, I. R., Tsai, J. J. P., & Al-Hamadi, H. (2017). A hierarchical cloud architecture for integrated mobility, service, and trust management of service-oriented IoT systems. In *2016 6th International Conference on Innovative Computing Technology, INTECH 2016* (pp. 72–77). Academic Press. 10.1109/INTECH.2016.7845021

Hargrave, B. J., & Kriens, P. (2007). *OSGi Best Practices! IBM Lotus OSGi Best Practices.* London: Event.

Herrmann, D. (1999). *Software Safety and Reliability.* Institute of Electrical & Electronics Engineers.

Hiller, M. (1998). *Software Fault-Tolerance Techniques from a Real-Time Systems Point of View.* Technical Report No.98-16, Department of Computer Engineering, Chalmers University of Technology.

IEC. (2005). IEC 61508:2005 Functional safety of electrical-electronic-programmable electronic safety related systems. *IEC 61508.*

Jackson, D. (2009). A direct path to dependable software. *Communications of the ACM, 52*(4), 78. doi:10.1145/1498765.1498787

Jackson, D., Thomas, M., & Millett, L. (2007). *Software for Dependable Systems.* National Academies Press; doi:10.17226/11923

Jeon, S. Y., Ahn, J. H., & Lee, T. J. (2016). Data distribution in IoT networks with estimation of packet error rate. In *International Conference on Next Generation Mobile Applications, Services, and Technologies* (pp. 94–98). Academic Press. 10.1109/NGMAST.2016.25

Kabashkin, I., & Kundler, J. (2017). *Reliability of Sensor Nodes in Wireless Sensor Networks of Cyber Physical Systems.* Academic Press. 10.1016/j.procs.2017.01.149

Khan, M. T., Serpanos, D., & Shrobe, H. (2017). A rigorous and efficient run-time security monitor for real-time critical embedded system applications. In *2016 IEEE 3rd World Forum on Internet of Things, WF-IoT 2016* (pp. 100–105). IEEE. 10.1109/WF-IoT.2016.7845510

Knight, J. C., & Leveson, N. G. (1986). An Experimental Evaluation of the Assumption of Independence in Multiversion Programming. *IEEE Transactions on Software Engineering, SE, 12*(1), 96–109. doi:10.1109/TSE.1986.6312924

Laprie, J.-C., Arlat, J., Beounes, C., & Kanoun, K. (1990). Definition and analysis of hardware-and software-fault-tolerant architectures. *Computer, 23*(7), 39–51. doi:10.1109/2.56851

Lehman, M. M. (1980). Programs, Life Cycles, and Laws of Software Evolution. *Proceedings of the IEEE, 68*(9), 1060–1076. doi:10.1109/PROC.1980.11805

Liu, Y., Peng, Y., Wang, B., Yao, S., Liu, Z., & Concept, A. (2017). Review on Cyber-physical Systems. *IEEE/CAA Journal of Automatica Sinica, 4*(1), 27–40.

Lyu, M. R. (1996). Handbook of software reliability engineering. Academic Press.

Medrano-E'Vers, A., Morales-Hernández, A. E., Valencia-López, R., & Hernández-Salcedo, D. R. (2017). *Enfermedad granulomatosa crónica* (Vol. 33). Medicina Interna de Mexico. doi:10.100713398-014-0173-7.2

Muccini, H., & Weyns, D. (2016). *Self-Adaptation for Cyber-Physical Systems: A Systematic Literature Review*. Academic Press. 10.1145/1235

NASA. (2004). *NASA Software Safety Guidebook. National Aeronautics and Space Administration.* Retrieved from http://www.hq.nasa.gov/office/codeq/doctree/871913.pdf

NSF. (2006). *National Science Foundation- Call for Position Papers.* Retrieved August 2, 2017, from http://varma.ece.cmu.edu/CPS/

Parisini, T. (2016). *TC6.4. Fault Detection.* Supervision & Safety of Technical Processes-SAFEPROCESS.

Pullum, L. L. (2001). *Software Fault Tolerance - Techniques and Implementation.* Artech House. Retrieved from http://books.google.com/books?hl=en&lr=&id=hqXvxsO5xz8C&oi=fnd&pg=PR11&dq=Software+Fault+Tolerance+Techniques+and+Implementation&ots=Db4NT-35tv&sig=HP7s49bjFlS9YQF3Q5DUSO7p2rQ

Qian, J., Gao, F., Wang, G., Jin, S., & Zhu, H. (2017). Noncoherent Detections for Ambient Backscatter System. *IEEE Transactions on Wireless Communications, 16*(3), 1412–1422. doi:10.1109/TWC.2016.2635654

Sajid, A., Abbas, H., & Saleem, K. (2016). Cloud-Assisted IoT-Based SCADA Systems Security: A Review of the State of the Art and Future Challenges. *IEEE Access: Practical Innovations, Open Solutions, 4*, 1375–1384. doi:10.1109/ACCESS.2016.2549047

Shwartz, L., Rosu, D., Loewenstern, D., Buco, M. J., Guo, S., Lavrado, R., ... Singh, J. K. (2010). Quality of IT service delivery #x2014; Analysis and framework for human error prevention. *Service-Oriented Computing and Applications (SOCA), 2010 IEEE International Conference on*, 1–8. 10.1109/SOCA.2010.5707161

Somani, A. K., & Vaidya, N. H. (1997). Understanding Fault Tolerance And Reliability - Guest Editors' Indroduction. *Computer, 30*(4), 45–50. doi:10.1109/MC.1997.585153

Sotirovski, D. (2001). Towards fault-tolerant software architectures. In *Software Architecture, 2001. Proceedings. Working IEEE/IFIP Conference on* (pp. 7–13). IEEE. 10.1109/WICSA.2001.948399

Szominski, S., Gadek, K., Konarski, M., Blaszczyk, B., Anielski, P., & Turek, W., ... Intel. (2013). Development of a cyber-physical system for mobile robot control using Erlang. In *2013 Federated Conference on Computer Science and Information Systems, FedCSIS 2013* (pp. 1441–1448). IEEE. 10.1109/DeSE.2015.33

Torres-pomales, W., & Langley, W. (2000). Software Fault Tolerance : A Tutorial. *October*.

USNS Foundation. (2008). *Cyber-Physical Systems (CPS)*. Retrieved from https://www.nsf.gov/pubs/2014/nsf14542/nsf14542.htm

Vermesan, O., & Friess, P. (2014). Internet of Things Applications - From Research and Innovation to Market Deployment (O. Vermesan & P. Friess, Eds.). Academic Press. doi:10.100711036-012-0415-x

Wolf, W. (2009). *Cyber-physical systems*. Academic Press. 10.1109/MC.2009.81

Chapter 4
Securing SDN–Enabled Smart Power Grids:
SDN–Enabled Smart Grid Security

Uttam Ghosh
Tennessee State University, USA

Pushpita Chatterjee
Old Dominion University, USA

Sachin Shetty
Old Dominion University, USA

ABSTRACT

Software-defined networking (SDN) provides flexibility in controlling, managing, and dynamically reconfiguring the distributed heterogeneous smart grid networks. Considerably less attention has been received to provide security in SDN-enabled smart grids. Centralized SDN controller protects smart grid networks against outside attacks only. Furthermore, centralized SDN controller suffers from a single point of compromise and failure which is detrimental to security and reliability. This chapter presents a framework with multiple SDN controllers and security controllers that provides a secure and robust smart grid architecture. The proposed framework deploys a local IDS to provide security in a substation. Whereas a global IDS is deployed to provide security in control center and overall smart grid network, it further verifies the consequences of control-commands issued by SDN controller and SCADA master. Performance comparison and simulation result show that the proposed framework is efficient as compared to existing security frameworks for SDN-enabled smart grids.

DOI: 10.4018/978-1-5225-5510-0.ch004

INTRODUCTION

Smart grid is a large-scale heterogeneous complex networking between a several number of sensors, actuators, smart meters, supervisory control and data acquisition (SCADA) systems, and also end-user devices and appliances located on residential and commercial premises in order to facilitate the generation, transmission and distribution of power. The communication infrastructure must be scalable, reliable, secure and efficient to sustain the transmission of a massive amount of real-time data generated by the deployed sensors in smart grid. Software defined networking (SDN) can be integrated in smart grid to achieve such communication infrastructure. It allows to manage and verify the correctness of network operations at run time. The globalized view of the SDN controller allows fault (due to accidental failures and malicious attacks) detection, isolation of affected components, and remediates of abnormal operation in the SDN-enabled smart grid networks more efficiently as compared to legacy based networks.

The proliferation of the smart grid technologies brings the promise of an era of easy and optimal use of power delivery systems as well as intelligence and efficiency. Recently, a number of research papers have been proposed in the literature (A.Goodney, Kumar, Ravi, & Cho, 2013) (Aydeger, Akkaya, & Uluagac, 2015) (Dorsch, Kurtz, Georg, Hagerling, & Wietfeld, 2014) (Ghosh, Dong, Tan, Kalbarczyk, Yau, & Iyer, 2016) (K. Akkaya, 2015; J. Zhao, 2016) (D. Gyllstrom, 2014) to introduce the concept of SDN in smart grid networks. Most of these proposals mainly focus on (i) the advantages and potential risks of using SDN in smart grid and (ii) investigation how SDN can fulfill communication requirements of smart grid communication networks regarding properties like quality of service (QoS), latency and link failover time (recovery time from a link failure). However, considerably less attention has been given to provide security in SDN-enabled smart grid networks (Cahn, Hoyos, Hulse, & Keller, 2013) (Dong, Lin, Tan, Iyer, & Kalbarczyk) (Dorsch, Kurtz, Georg, Hagerling, & Wietfeld, 2014). Most of the researchers assume that SCADA master, SDN controller and their applications are non-compromised. They further consider that SDN can offer security in smart grid by providing consistent access control, applying efficient and effective security policies, and managing and controlling the network centrally. Their main focus on protecting the smart grid networks against various forms of outsider attacks and providing security assurance within the cyber (or SDN) domain only. They significantly overlook the insider attacks that may harm the smart grid system as a whole (Zhang, Wang, Sun, II, & Alam, 2011). It further suffers from possible reliability and security issues due to use of a centralized SDN controller.

This Chapter propose a security framework with multiple SDN controllers and intrusion detection systems (IDS) to provide a secure and robust smart grid architecture. A light- weight identity based cryptography (Akkaya, 2015) has been used to protect the smart grid network from outside attacks. A local IDS is deployed in a substation to collect the measurement data periodically and to monitor the control-commands that are executed on SCADA slaves. Whereas a global IDS runs at control center and collects the measurement data from the substations and estimates the state of the smart grid system by utilizing the theory of differential evolution (Akkaya, Uluagac, & Aydeger, 2015). It further verifies the consequences of control-commands issued by either SDN controller or SCADA master. The global IDS generates an alarm and notifies to the intrusion elimination system (IES) if it detects unsteady state of smart grids.

Chapter Objectives: The objectives of this Chapter are as follows: The Chapter gives a brief overview of SDN and smart power grid. The state-of-the-art study in SDN-enabled smart power grid is presented which is followed by the attack scenario and system model. The Chapter proposes a security framework for SDN-enabled smart grid. It compares the proposed framework with existing security frameworks and discusses simulation environment and result.

BACKGROUND

An Overview of SDN

Figure 1 shows major components and interfaces of the SDN architecture. The SDN architecture has three layers: data plane, control plane and application plane.

- **Data Plane:** The data plane comprises a set of one or more network elements, each of which contains a set of traffic forwarding devices. These forwarding devices are known as OpenFlow (OF) switches. OF switches receive instructions (flow rules) and forward the data from source to destination in a SDN network accordingly.
- **Control Plane:** The control plane comprises a set of SDN controllers. The SDN controller is a logical entity (or software known as network operating system) that receives instructions or requirements from the SDN application layer and relays them to the data plane components. The controller further extracts information about the network topology (global view of the network) and the statistics of the network traffic and communicates back to the application plane with an abstract view of the network.
- **Application Plane:** The application plane comprises of one or more applications. These applications are pro- grams and control network resources with the SDN controller via application programming interface (APIs). The applications collect information from the controller for decision-making purposes. These applications include routing, quality-of-services (QoS) and network management. For instance, an application can be built to monitor the network traffic for detecting malicious nodes in SDN network.

Northbound API defines the communication between application plane and control plane whereas southbound API defines the connection between the control plane and data plane. OpenFlow is a popular protocol that can be used as an southbound API. The SDN controller sends flow rules into the OpenFlow switches using OpenFlow protocol as the protocol is secure (uses secure socket layer) and reliable (uses TCP).

Figure 2 presents an SDN operation where a device A (source) sends packets of a flow to a device B (destination):

Figure 1. SDN architecture

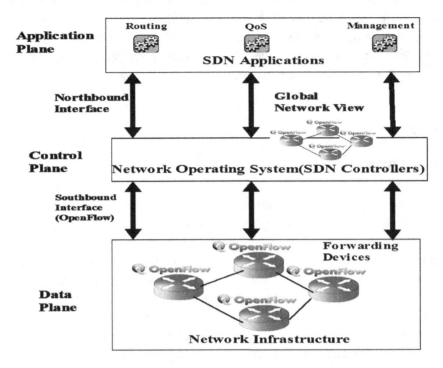

Figure 2. SDN operation

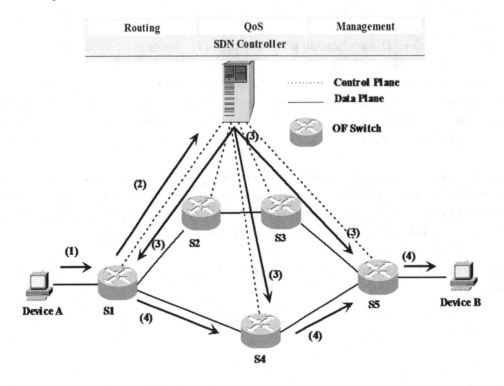

1. Device A sends packet to SDN OpenFlow (OF) switch S1.
2. OF switch S1 forwards the first packet from the flow to SDN controller as S1 does not know how to forward the packet.
3. SDN controller has the global view of the network topology and hence it computes the shortest path between devices A and B. In this example, the shortest path is A-S1-S4-S5-B. In response, SDN controller sends flow rules to the corresponding OF switches S1, S4 and S5.
4. OF switch S1 forwards the packet to S4, S4 forwards the packet to S5 as per flow table (received from SDN controller in previous step).
5. Thereafter, device A sends all the packets of the flow to device B through OF switches S1-S4-S5.

Legacy versus SDN: The forwarding devices (switches) in traditional or legacy networks are vendor dependent and complicated. It is difficult to add a new functionality (application) to these forwarding devices as the devices are strongly coupled between control and data planes. The fact is illustrated in Figure 3. The coupling of the control and data planes makes the development and deployment of new networking functionalities (e.g., routing, load balancing algorithms) very difficult since it would imply a modification of the control plane of all forwarding devices it needs installation of new firmware and, in some cases, up-gradation of hardware. The forwarding devices are distributed in a large area that makes it even harder to later change the network topology, configuration, and functionality. In contrast, SDN decouples the control plane from the forwarding devices and becomes a separate entity: the network operating system or SDN controller. It has several advantages:

*   SDN controller is programmable. It is easier to add new network functionalities through programs (as applications) at the top of SDN controller.

Figure 3. Legacy networking versus SDN

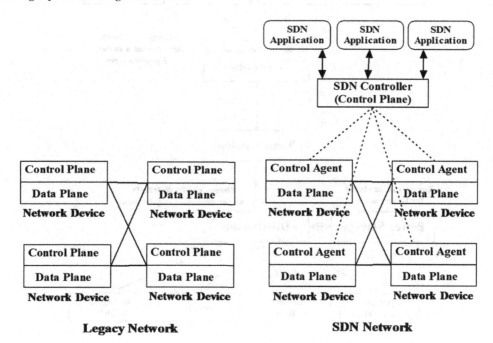

- SDN controller is logically centralized. It has global view of the network and statistics of the network traffic. The controller can take consistent and effective decisions for routing, QoS and load balancing.
- Logically central SDN controller can control, configure and monitor the distributed forwarding devices.
- As SDN controller is programmable it can provide security over the distributed forwarding devices. It monitors the all the devices and their traffic in data plane. The controller can detect the malicious device if the device injects false data into the network or behaves abnormally. It can further eliminates the malicious device from the network on-fly by writing a policy (flow rule).

An Overview of Smart Power Grid

A power grid is mainly used for an electricity system that supports electricity generation, transmission, distribution, and control. It is being used to carry power from a few centralized generators to a large number of users. Whereas smart grid is an up-gradation of existing power grid with advanced information and communications technologies (ICT) technologies, intelligent smart devices and computing systems. In order to facilitate the generation, transmission and distribution of power, smart grid forms a large-scale heterogeneous complex network between a several number of sensors, actuators, smart meters, supervisory control and data acquisition (SCADA) systems, and also end-user devices and appliances located on residential and commercial premises. Figure 4 shows an architecture of smart grid. It creates

Figure 4. Architecture of smart power grid

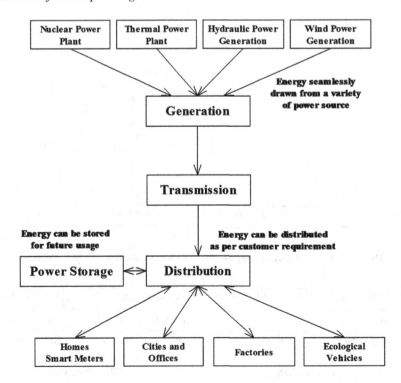

an automated, self-healing and distributed advanced energy delivery network by using the smart devices (such as sensors, switches) and two-way flows of electricity and information. It can improve reliability, quality and resilience to disruption of power, and also enhance the capacity and efficiency of existing power grids. Smart grid effectively delivers high quality of electricity to the users with information of consumers about their electricity consumption in real time. It further enables integration and inter-operability of alternative energy sources (such as wind, solar, nuclear) in power grid. Smart grid enables self-healing in case of disturbances, natural disasters or security threats. In summary, ICT in smart grid includes the following features with power grid:

- Two-way communication of electricity and information
- Interaction between users and the electricity market
- Monitoring power network in real time
- Flexibility to changing situations
- Optimal use of resources and equipment
- Management and prediction of electrical energy consumption
- Integration, monitoring, control, security and maintenance
- Security against attacks and threats

RELATED WORKS

In (A.Goodney S. K., 2013), Goodney et al. proposed to use SDN for controlling communication between PMUs. The authors developed a SDN-based network application to facilitate the management of PMUs and implemented multicast and data rate filtering functionalities using OpenFlow rules installed on SDN switches. Dorsch et al. (Dorsch, Kurtz, Georg, Hagerling, & Wietfeld, 2014) demonstrated the use of SDN for controlling and managing the transmission and distribution in power grids. The authors introduced algorithms for fast recovery from a link failure and load management. They developed a SDN testbed to measure the communication delays for IEC 61850 traffic. They further demonstrated the QoS enforcement for grid data traffic with different priorities. Kim et al. proposed in (Kim, He, Thottan, & Deshpande, 2014) to use OpenFlow switches to form virtual local area networks (VLANs) for multiple grid applications with different QoS requirements. In (Gyllstrom, Braga, & Kurose, 2014), Gyllstrom et al. also developed and evaluated fast recovery from a link failure algorithm in SDN-based smart grid networks.

In (A. Aydeger, 2015), Aydeger et al. demonstrated the usefulness of SDN to achieve resilience in smart grid networks. They introduced multiple connection interfaces among distributed substations and investigated the effect of failures of the wired connection. Zhao et al. discussed in (Zhao, Hammad, & Farraj, 2016) the efficacy of SDN to improve the quality of service (QoS) routing for smart grids. The authors designed a framework to enable an efficient decoupled implementation of dynamic routing protocols. Akkaya et al. (A. Aydeger, 2015) presented different SDN deployment scenarios in local networks of smart grid to substantiate the potential utilization of the SDN technology. Ghosh et al. in (Ghosh, Dong, Tan, Kalbarczyk, Yau, & Iyer, 2016) proposed a simulation based analysis to demonstrate the effect of controller faults (single-point-of-failure) in a SDN-enabled smart grid infrastructure.

Molina et al., presented a SDN based architecture in (Molina, Jacob, Matias, Moreira, & Astarloa, 2015) for a substation that follows the IEC 61850 standard. The authors included automation techniques for performing a flow-based resource management that enable features such as routing, traffic filtering, QoS, load balancing, monitoring, or security. Cahn et al. (Cahn, Hoyos, Hulse, & Keller, 2013) proposed a SDN-based power grid architecture, called Software-Defined Energy Communication Network (SDECN). This architecture mainly provides substation automation that allows the network to auto-configure, secure and reliable against possible incorrect configured systems. The authors developed the SDECN prototype using Ryu OpenFlow controller and tested with real intelligent electronic devices (IEDs). Dong et al. presented a position research study (Dong, Lin, Tan, Iyer, & Kalbarczyk) to show how SDN can improve the resilience of smart grid networks to malicious attacks. The authors further discussed additional risks introduced by SDN in smart grids and how to manage them.

ATTACK SCENARIO

A SDN-enabled smart grid mainly consists of three parts: a control center; (2) communication networks and (3) smart power grid devices. Figure 5 illustrates the attacks in smart grid. Control center runs the SDN controller and SCADA master commodity computers and servers. The SCADA master performs various grid control applications, e.g., grid status monitoring, under-frequency load shedding, frequency and voltage controls, and so forth. It collects measurement data periodically from the SCADA slaves (sensors, actuators) through the use of OpenFlow (OF) switches and SDN controller. The SCADA master processes the received data and sends the control-command (such as read, write or execute (Lin, Slagell, Kalbarczyk, Sauer, & Iyer, 2016) to the SCADA slaves.

Figure 5. Architecture of smart power grid

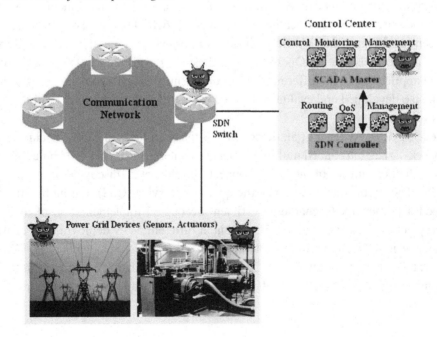

In *first attack scenario*, an application of SCADA master or SCADA master itself can be compromised. Similarly, an application of SDN controller or SDN controller itself can be compromised. The compromised SDN controller may issue malicious control-commands (such as Add_Flow, Del_Flow, Mod_Flow) to degrade the performance of the network and subsequently smart grid. Table 1 summarizes the control- commands in SDN-enabled smart grid networks.

In *second attack scenario*, the OF switches may be com- promised. These OF switches may drop, inject false packets and delayed the packets that carry measurement data/control- commands from SCADA slaves/master to SCADA master/slaves. For example, a packet that carries a critical control- command like open a breaker of a relay. This packet can be dropped or delayed by an intermediate malicious switch. It may cause a potential risk to physical infrastructure of a substation.

The detection and identification of bad data in measurements are important phases for state estimation of a smart grid. The poor calibration of SCADA slaves, the failure communication between SCADA slaves and SCADA master, and also inject malicious measurements by SCADA slaves (Liu, Ning, & Reiter, 2009) are the main sources of bad data. These bad data can influence the quality of results obtained from state estimation algorithm. In *third and final attack scenario*, we consider compromised SCADA slaves that can inject malicious measurements (Ghosh & Datta, A secure addressing scheme for large-scale managed manets, 2015) into smart grid network.

SYSTEM MODEL

We consider an SDN-enabled smart power grid network that has several substations with a control center. We assume that all the smart grid and communication devices have unique *ID*s and registered to either their corresponding substation or control center. In addition, the public (*KPA*) /private (*KSA*) key pair of a device A is generated using the following technique [13]: $G1$ and $G2$ be the two groups of a prime order q, $Q1$ and $Q2$ be the generators of $G1$, and a bilinear pairing is a map $e: G1 \times G1 \rightarrow G2$ having the following properties:

- **Bilinear:** $e(uQ1, vQ2) = e(Q1, Q2)uv$, $\forall u, v \in Zq$;
- **Non-Degenerate:** There exist $Q1, Q2 \in G1$ such that $e(Q1, Q2) \neq 1$;
- **Computable:** $\forall Q1, Q2 \in G1$, there is an efficient algorithm to compute $e(Q1, Q2)$.

Table 1. Control-commands in SDN-enabled smart grids

SCADA Control Commands	Functionalities	SDN Controller Commands	Functionalities
Read	Retrieve measurements from substations	Add _Flow	Add a new flow in OF switches
Write	Configure Smart grid devices	Del_Flow	Remove a flow from OF switches
Execute	Operate smart grid devices	Mod _Flow	Edit a flow in OF switches

All the devices in smart grid network keep the security parameters *G1, G2, e, H1, H2, Q1, Ppub =
sQ1*, where *s* is the master key and it is kept secret by control center. Here, *H1* and *H2* are two cryptographic hash functions such that *H1*: {0, 1}* → *G1* and *H2*: {0, 1}* × *G1* → *Zq* . For a device *A* with
identifier *IDA*, there will be a public key *KPA = H1(IDA)* and a private key *KSA = sKPA*. The device
identifiers *IDs* are type specific. For example, the meter number is the *ID* for a smart meter whereas
hardware/IP address is the *ID* for a sensor.

In order to generate a secret session key *KAB* between devices *A* and *B*, they exchange random numbers *r1* and *r2* to each other. Device *A* generates the secret session key using *KAB = e(r1KSA, r2KPB)*,
whereas device *B* also generates the secret session key using *KBA = e(r1KPA, r2KSB)*. The following
equation shows that both devices *A* and *B* generate the same secret session key (Ghosh & Datta, A secure
addressing scheme for large-scale managed manets, 2015):

$$K_{AB} = e(r_1KS_A, r_2KP_B) = e(KS_A, KP_B)^{r1r2} = e(sKP_A, KP_B)^{r1r2}$$

$$= e(KP_A, KP_B)^{sr1r2} = e(r_1KP_A, r_2sKP_B) = e(r_1KP_A, r_2KS_B) = K_{BA}$$

THE PROPOSED SECURITY FRAMEWORK FOR SDN-
ENABLED SMART POWER GRIDS

Figure 6 presents the propose secure framework for SDN- enabled smart grids. Our framework mainly
includes a control center and a several number of substations and all of them connected in a wide area
network. Control center comprises of three components: (1) a global SDN controller which is respon-

Figure 6. Secure SDN-enabled smart grid architecture

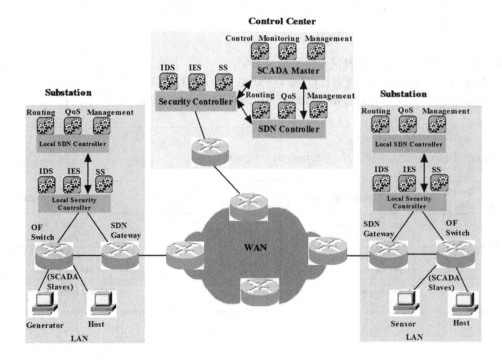

sible for communication between control center to substations and a substation to other substations; (2) a SCADA master which is mainly responsible for controlling, monitoring and managing smart grid devices such as sensors, actuators (in general SCADA slaves in substations); and (3) a global security controller which is responsible for providing security in both smart grid and communication devices. A substation contains: (1) a local SDN controller that controls the communication between devices inside the substation; (2) a local security controller that provides security inside the substation; and (3) openflow (OF) switches, a gateway and SCADA slaves.

With respect to SDN layers, the propose secure SDN-enabled smart grid layering architecture is shown in Figure 7. It has infrastructure, control and application layers. Infrastructure layer contains OF switches, SCADA master and slaves. We divide control layer into security and network sub- layers. Security sub-layer includes a global security controller (for control center) and a local security controller (for a substation). Network sub-layer involves with a global SDN controller (for control center) and a local SDN controller (for a substation). Application layer runs the application programs at SDN controller, security controller and SCADA master. SDN controller runs the application programs to manage devices and provide routing and QoS in infrastructure layer. SCADA master runs the application programs to control, configure and manage the smart grid devices (SCADA slaves).

Security controller runs three application programs: (1) a security system (SS) that generates and manages the cryptographic keys (public/private or shared keys as discussed in Section SYSTEM MODEL) and provides message authentication and integrity for each device; (2) an intrusion elimination system (IES) that eliminates the attackers (detected by IDS) from smart grid network through the use of SDN controller; and (3) an intrusion detection system (IDS) that monitors all the devices and their activities in a substation/control center and generates an alarm and notifies to IES once attacks detected.

Figure 7. Secure SDN-enabled smart grid layers

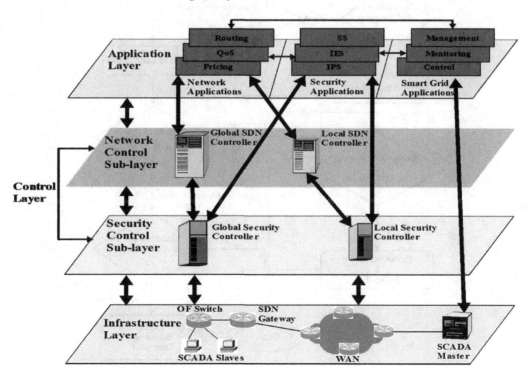

In order to provide message authentication and integrity in smart grid communication, we use digital signature for broadcasting/multicasting messages and MAC for unicasting messages. Device *A* generates the digital signature using its private key *KSA* to the broadcast/multicast messages and sends the signed messages along with its *IDA*. On receiving the signed message, device *B* can verify the signature by using the public key *KPA* of *A*. For unicast communication, device *A* generates a MAC tag using the secret session key *KAB* to the message and sends the message along with the MAC tag to device *B*. Device *B* also generates a MAC tag using the secret key *KBA* on the received message from *A*. It then compares both generated MAC tag and received MAC tag from *A*. Device *A* is authenticated to *B* if both tags are same.

A global security controller runs in control center whereas a local security controller runs in a substation. The workflow diagrams of the local security controller and the global security controller are presented in Figure 8 and Figure 9 respectively. Both security controllers discard the packet if they receive it without the authentication tag (signature or MAC). The security controllers further verify authentication and integrity of the packet. If verification successful, the local security controller sends the packet to local the IDS whereas the global security controller sends the packet to the global IDS.

The local IDS collects the measurement data periodically from SCADA slaves and verifies for suspicious data. It generates an alarm and notifies to IES if suspicious data detected. Otherwise the local

Figure 8. Workflow at local security controller

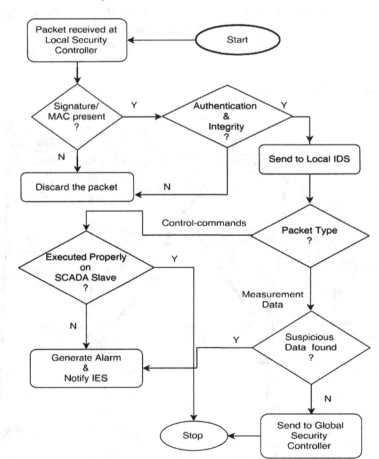

Figure 9. Workflow at global security controller

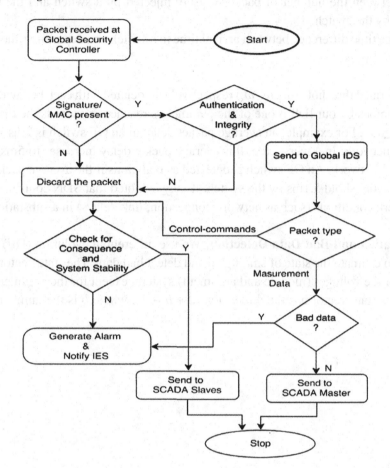

IDS allows to send the measurement data from the substation to control center. It further monitors the control-commands (sent by SCADA master) that are executed on SCADA slaves. The global IDS collects the measurement data from the substations. It verifies the measurement data for bad data detection and identification and estimates the state of the smart grid system by utilizing the theory of differential evolution (Storn & Price, Dec. 1997) (discussed below). The global IDS further measures the consequences of control-commands issued by either SDN controller or SCADA master. It generates an alarm message and notifies the intrusion elimination system (IES) if an unsteady state of smart grid system found.

Our proposed IDS allows to insert flows (defined by IP/hardware/port address, VLAN) into the network and monitors each of them. A predefined threshold has been set by IDS for each flow in order to detect DoS attack. Our IDS further monitors the OF switches and computes the packet drop ratio (β), packet false injection ratio (γ), and an average packet delay (δ) for each OF switch. The parameters are defined as follows:

- β: A ratio between the number of packets drop by a switch and the total number of packets received by the switch.

- **γ:** A ratio between the number of packets falsely injected by a switch and the total number of packets sent by the switch.
- **δ:** The average time difference between arrival time to a switch and departure time from the switch for n number of packets.

There is a predefined threshold (ω_β, ω_γ, ω_δ) respectively associated with each behavior. An OF switch is detected as malicious by our IDS if one of the parameters reaches or exceeds the threshold e.g., $\beta \geq \omega_\beta$ or $\gamma \geq \omega_\gamma$ or $\delta \geq \omega_\delta$. For example, an average packet delay in an OF switch is 2ms when there is no congestion in the network. In a worst case, this average packet delay increases to 5ms due to increase of congestion in the network. An OF switch is detected as malicious if the average packet delay for 100 packets exceeds the threshold 5.1ms by the switch. It may be noted that SDN controller has the global view on the network conditions (such as network congestion, link delays) in a substation.

- **State Estimation and Bad Data Detection:** We use differential evolution (DE) (Storn & Price, Dec. 1997) to estimate the state of smart grid and detect bad data. The state vector is composed of all or most of the voltages (module and argument) system, except for the argument bus reference. Therefore this state vector has the dimension ($2 * b - 1$), where b is the number of buses in the system.

$$
\begin{pmatrix}
|V_1| \\
|V_2| \\
\vdots \\
|V_h| \\
|\theta_1| \\
|\theta_2| \\
\vdots \\
|\theta_{b-1}|
\end{pmatrix}
$$

In DE, in order to get a new population at each iteration it is necessary to optimize the problem by using mutation, crossover and selection.

- **Mutation:** For each vector belonging to the population, a new mutated vector is created using Equation 1.

$$
k_{i,G+1} = x_{u1,G} + F \times (x_{u2,G} - x_{u3,G}) \tag{1}
$$

where the indices $v1$, $v2$, $v3 \in \{1, 2, ..., NP\}$ are all mutually different and random. These are different from the index i. G corresponds to the current iteration of the simulation. F is a constant real value, $F \in [0, 2]$ and controls the amplification of the differential variation($x_{v2,G} - x_{v3,G}$).

- **Crossover:** To introduce a wider range of results from several generations of populations, crossover is used to create a new vector y using the following Equation,

$$
y_{ji};_{G+1} = \begin{cases} k_{ji;G+1}; if \left(r \ and \ b\left(j \right) \leq CR \right) \ or \ j = rnbr(i) \\ \overline{x_{ji;G}; if \left(r \ and \ b\left(j \right) > CR \right) \ or \ j \neq rnbr\left(i \right)} \end{cases} \tag{2}
$$

Here, *randb(j)* is the jth evaluation of a uniform random number generator with outcome $\in$ [0, 1] where CR is the crossover constant, a real and constant value chosen from $\in$ [0,2], given by the user. *rnbr(i)* is a randomly chosen index$\in$ [1,2,...D] to ensure that $y_{i;G+1}$ gets at least one parameter from $k_{i;G+1}$.

- **Selection:** In order to verify whether the new test vector y may be inserted into the new population of values, it is necessary to check if this function has a lower cost compared to the same position as the previous generation (vector x). If the cost function of the test vector is less than the amount reported by the vector x, it is replacing, otherwise the previous value is kept unaltered. Once the selection process is done using DE method, the measured data is selected if there is no bad data. If bad data is detected by the IDS, it generates an alarm and notifies IES.

PERFORMANCE COMPARISON

Table 2 presents the comparison of proposed framework with existing security frameworks for SDN-enabled smart grids. It can be seen that our propose framework only consider the security of all the attack scenarios discussed in Section ATTACK SCENARIO. We use distributed IDS to provide security in substations and control center. The propose framework further deploys multiple SDN controllers in substations and control center. The global SDN controller at control center can be used as the backup controller in case a SDN controller fails in a substation. Hence the propose framework is robust.

Table 2. Comparison with existing frameworks

Framework Architecture	First Attack Scenario		Second Attack Scenario (OF Switch Security)	Third Attack Scenario (SCADA Slave Security)	Security Tool Used	Robustness
	SCADA Master Security	SDN Controller Security				
Cahn et al. (Cahn, Hoyos, Hulse, & Keller, 2013)	Not Considered	Not Considered	Considered	Not Considered	SDN Controller Policies	Robust
Molina et al. (Molina, Jacob, Matias, Moreira, & Astarloa, 2015)	Not Considered	Not Considered	Considered	Not Considered	sFlow Collector	Robust
Dong et al (Dong, Lin, Tan, Iyer, & Kalbarczyk).	Considered	Not Considered	Considered	Not Considered	Centralized IDS	Not Robust
Proposed	Considered	Considered	Considered	Considered	Distributed IDS	Robust

Figure 10. Network topology for IEEE 37-buses

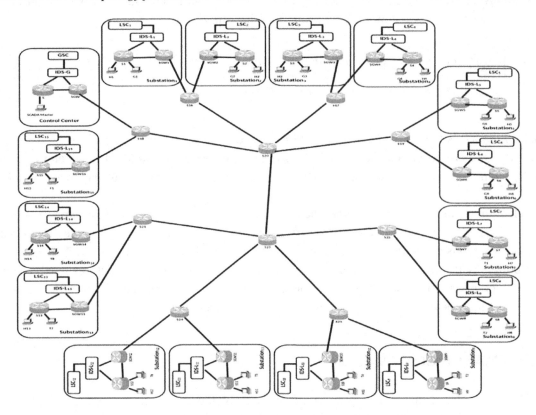

Figure 11. DoS attack detection and elimination

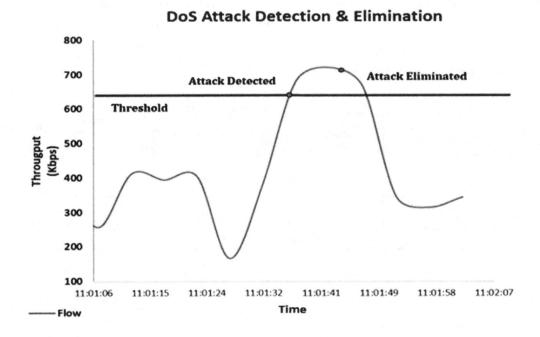

SIMULATION

In simulation, Mininet (Mininet: An instant virtual network on your laptop (or other pc)) is used to simulate an IEEE 37-buses smart grid network as shown in Figure 10. The network connects 15 substations with a control center over a wide-area network. Control center has (1) a global SDN controller *GSC*, (2) a virtual host that runs our IDS (*IDS– G*), and (3) a virtual host that runs as DNP3 server. Each substation, say i, consists of: (1) a local SDN controller (LSC_i), (2) an open flow (OF) switch (S_i), (3) a SDN-enabled gateway (SGW_i), (4) an IDS ($IDS -L_i$), (4) a sensor/actuator (T_i) that runs DNP3 clients to mimic communications between control center (with DNP3 server) and electronic devices in the substation, and (5) a virtual host (H_i) to generate back- ground traffic. The SDN has a data plane with 26 OpenFlow (v1.3) (Openflow switch specification)enabled switches and 16 gateways. A Ryu (Ryu sdn framework) controller is running remotely on Linux (Ubuntu 3.16.0-38- generic kernel) from the switches.

Figure 11 shows DoS attack detection and elimination using our proposed IDS and IES respectively. In this DoS attack, an attacker (H_1) that floods ICMP Echo Request packets. We set a threshold of 100 packets per second in our IDS.

CONCLUSION

This Chapter presented a framework with multiple SDN controllers and security controllers to provide a secure and robust smart grid architecture. The proposed framework has used a light-weight identity-based cryptography to protect the smart grid network from outside attacks. In order to provide security in a substation, a local IDS is deployed to collect the measurement data periodically and monitors the control-commands that are executed on SCADA slaves. Whereas a global IDS is deployed in control center to collect the measurement data from the substations and estimate the state of the smart grid system by utilizing the theory of differential evolution. It can further verify the consequences of control-commands issued by SDN controller and SCADA master. The Chapter presented a comparison of the proposed framework with existing security frameworks to show that the proposed framework is more efficient against attacks related to SDN- enabled smart grids.

ACKNOWLEDGMENT

This material is based upon work supported by the Department of Energy under award number DE-OE0000780 and DHS Award 2014-ST-062-000059. The views and opinions of authors expressed herein do not necessarily state or reflect those of the United States Government or any agency thereof.

REFERENCES

Akkaya, K. A. S. (2015). Software defined net- working for wireless local networks in smart grid. SoftwarLocal Computer Networks Conference Workshops (LCN Workshops), 2015 IEEE 40th, 826–831.

Aydeger, A. K. A. (2015). Sdn-based resilience for smart grid communication. *Network Function Virtualization and Software Defined Network (NFV-SDN), 2015 IEEE Conference on*, 31-33.

Aydeger, A., Akkaya, K., & Uluagac, A. S. (2015). Sdn-based resilience for smart grid communication. *Network Function Virtualization and Software Defined Network (NFV-SDN), 2015 IEEE Conference on*, 31-33.

Cahn, A., Hoyos, J., Hulse, M., & Keller, E. (2013). Software-defined energy communication networks: From substation automation to future smart grids. IEEE SmartGridComm, 558–563.

Dong, X., Lin, H., Tan, R., Iyer, R. K., & Kalbarczyk, Z. Software- defined networking for smart grid resilience: Opportunities and challenges. *1st ACM Workshop on CPSS 2015.*

Dorsch, N., Kurtz, F., Georg, H., Hagerling, C., & Wietfeld, C. (2014). Software- defined networking for smart grid communications: Applications, challenges and advantages. *IEEE SmartGridComm, 2014.*

Ghosh, U., & Datta, R. (2015). A secure addressing scheme for large-scale managed manets. *IEEE eTransactions on Network and Service Management, 12*(3), 483–495. doi:10.1109/TNSM.2015.2452292

Ghosh, U., Dong, X., Tan, R., Kalbarczyk, Z., Yau, D. K., & Iyer, R. K. (2016). A simulation study on smart grid resilience under software- defined networking controller failures. *Proceedings of the 2nd ACM International Workshop on Cyber-Physical System Security, CPSS 2016*, 52-58. 10.1145/2899015.2899020

Goodney, A., Kumar, S., Ravi, A., & Cho, Y. H. (2013). Efficient pmu networking with software defined networks. *IEEE SmartGridComm, 2013.*

Goodney, S. K. (2013). Efficient pmu networking with software defined networks. *IEEE SmartGridComm, 2013.*

Gyllstrom, D. N. B. (2014). Recovery from link failures in a smart grid communication network using openflow. IEEE SmartGridComm, 254–259.

Gyllstrom, D., Braga, N., & Kurose, J. (2014). Recovery from link failures in a smart grid communication network using openflow. IEEE SmartGridComm, 254–259.

Kim, Y.-J., He, K., Thottan, M., & Deshpande, J. G. (2014). Virtualized and self-configurable utility communications enabled by software-defined networks. IEEE SmartGridComm, 416–421.

Lin, H., Slagell, A., Kalbarczyk, Z., Sauer, P., & Iyer, R. (2016). Runtime semantic security analysis to detect and mitigate control-related attacks in power grids. *IEEE Transactions on Smart Grid*.

Liu, Y., Ning, P., & Reiter, M. K. (2009). False data injection attacks against state estimation in electric power grid. *16th ACM Conference on Computer and Communications Security ccs. Mininet: An instant virtual network on your laptop (or other pc)*. Retrieved from http://mininet.org/

Molina, E., Jacob, E., Matias, J., Moreira, N., & Astarloa, A. (2015). Using software defined networking to manage and control iec 61850-based systems. *Computers & Electrical Engineering, 43*, 142–154. doi:10.1016/j.compeleceng.2014.10.016

Openflow switch specification. (n.d.). Retrieved from http://www.openflow.org/documents/ openflow-spec-v1.0.0.pdf

Ryu sdn framework. (n.d.). Retrieved from https://osrg.github.io/ryu/

Storn, R., & Price, K. (1997, December). Differential evolution; a simple and efficient heuristic for global optimization over continuous spaces. *Journal of Global Optimization, 11*(4), 341–359. doi:10.1023/A:1008202821328

Zhang, Y., Wang, L., Sun, W. II, Green, R. C. II, & Alam, M. (2011). Distributed intrusion detection system in a multi-layer network architecture of smart grids. *IEEE Transactions on Smart Grid, 2*(4), 796–808. doi:10.1109/TSG.2011.2159818

Zhao, E. H. (2016). *Network-Aware QoS Routing for Smart Grids Using Software Defined Networks*. Academic Press.

Zhao, J., Hammad, E., & Farraj, A. (2016). *Network-Aware QoS Routing for Smart Grids Using Software Defined Networks*. Academic Press.

KEY TERMS AND DEFINITIONS

Control Center: Control center controls, monitors, and manages all the substations in a smart grid network.

Intrusion Detection System (IDS): An IDS is a device or software that monitors a network or systems for malicious activity or policy violations. Network based IDS (NIDS) monitors the network whereas host-based IDS (HIDS) monitors the host.

Openflow: Openflow is a communication protocol in SDN that enables the SDN controller to directly interact with the data plane. It provides reliable and secure communication between the SDN controller and all the switches in data plane.

Smart Power Grid: A smart power grid broadly refers to the power grid that adopts modern information and communications technologies (ICT).

Software-Defined Networking (SDN): SDN is an emerging area in computer networking that allows network administrators to programmatically control, configure and manage the network dynamically via open interfaces and provide abstraction of lower-level functionality.

Substation: A substation is a part of smart power grid that generates, transmits, and distributes electricity in a local area.

Supervisory Control and Data Acquisition (SCADA): SCADA generally refers to an industrial computer system that monitors and controls a process. It has two types of devices: master and slave. In smart power grid, SCADA master controls and monitors substations, transformers and other electrical devices.

Chapter 5
Protecting Big Data Through Microaggregation Technique for Secured Cyber–Physical Systems

Shakila Mahjabin Tonni
East West University, Bangladesh

Sazia Parvin
Melbourne Polytechnic, Australia

Amjad Gawanmeh
Khalifa University, UAE

Joanna Jackson
Melbourne Polytechnic, Australia

ABSTRACT

Secured cyber-physical systems (CPS) requires reliable handling of a high volume of sensitive data, which is in many cases integrated from several distributed sources. This data can usually be interconnected with physical applications, such as power grids or SCADA systems. As most of these datasets store records using numerical values, many of the microaggregation techniques are developed and tested on numerical data. These algorithms are not suitable when the data is stored as it is containing both numerical and categorical data are stored. In this chapter, the available microaggregation techniques are explored and assessed with a new microaggregation technique which can provide data anonymity regardless of its type. In this method, records are clustered into several groups using an evolutionary attribute grouping algorithm and groups are aggregated using a new operator.

DOI: 10.4018/978-1-5225-5510-0.ch005

INTRODUCTION

With the growing use of cloud computing technology, a new generation of SCADA systems (Wikipedia. org, SCADA, 2017) is emerging that is incorporating new technologies. Many CPS require continuous communications accessing big data. In addition, several CPS applications, such as power grid, and SCADA systems impose high reliability, security and availability. Moreover, possibilities of physical or cyberspace intrusions may lead to exposure of sensitive data. Therefore, protecting data in critical CPS applications should be considered a priority.

Increasing utilization of cyber-physical systems is opening new possibilities of enormous impact on the society and economy. Many CPSs are now trying to enhance its capability using evolving cloud (Zhang, Qiu, Tsai, Hassan, & Alamri, 2017) and distributed technology (Jaskolka & Villasenor, 2017), where different types of sensitive data are collected. Although, it can be said from the past experiences, most of the attacks on CPSs are physical or environmental in nature (Frey, Rashid, Zanutto, Busby, & Follis, 2016), there are evidences of cyber-attacks on ICS (Industrial Control System). For instance, Stuxnet (Wikipedia.org, Stuxnet, 2017) is a worm that caused considerable damage to Iran's nuclear program by intercepting both sensor and actuator data, and tampering the centrifuge. According to (Martínez, Sánchez, & Valls, 2012), the wide use of CPSs from medical devices to smart cars, CPS security is crucial due to the vulnerabilities of the legacy systems that are used to build them. So, in such contexts, securing control data produced by the systems is highly needed. Secured controlled data can be protected by using widely used data microaggregation techniques. Microaggregation is a technique massively used as a mean of statistical disclosure control (Domingo-Ferrer J. &.-S., 2002). The main idea is to group and then apply an aggregation operator on microdata (Kabir & Wang, 2011), (Martínez, Sánchez, & Valls, 2012) to produce a confined record. In this chapter, we discuss different microaggregation techniques and assess the usefulness of our new microaggregation algorithm proposed in (Tonni, Rahman, Parvin, & Gawanmeh, 2017) for CPSs.

To serve the purpose of protecting data privacy, numerous techniques are introduced for privacy in statistical databases that are collectively known as Statistical Disclosure Control (SDC). Data protection methods can be divided into two categories:

- **Perturbative:** In these methods, the actual data set is altered using some technique like noise addition, and the deformed new data set might have some fake information. Naturally, it introduces new sets of attribute values while losing a few. The generated data set cannot be matched with the real data set. Therefore, it protects the dataset by preventing external intrusion. Among all the other methods k-anonymity and microaggregation techniques are highly studied.
- **Non-Perturbative:** Protection is achieved through replacing an original value by another one that is not incorrect but less specific. For example, we replace a real number by an interval. In general, non-perturbative methods reduce the level of detail of the data set. This detail reduction causes different records to have the same combinations of values, which makes disclosure difficult to intruders.

Either way, the target of SDC is to produce a dataset in such a way so that the risk of re-identification of some sensitive data is low and produces same or close results when statistical techniques are applied on the newly generated data set.

K-ANONYMITY

The possibility of identifying an individual by linking two or more datasets is growing spectacularly with the trend of recording huge amount of data in diversified areas like storing user web browsing behavior, or consumer trend for market analysis etc. Thus, it has become imperative to find out an optimal way to protect user data privacy that are being stored or published. Sweeney (Sweeney, 2002) shows that, for example, ZIP code, gender and date of birth can uniquely identify 87% of the individuals in the U.S. To resolve this problem, Sweeny proposes the concept of k-anonymization. K-anonymization assures that, for an attribute in the data set there will be at least k-1 similar data, which makes it difficult to link with other data sets to reveal any protected user data.

A data set V is a collection of records where each record r represents a point in a multidimensional space defined by the number of attributes. The attributes a_i can be classified in three categories: identifiers(id) which directly identify an object/entity (example attribute is the car license no.), quasi-identifiers which can identify an entity/object when some of those attributes are combined (e.g. age or postal code) and confidential attributes which contain sensitive information about the entity/object on which the data is collected (e.g. injected dose of drug). Generally, the last types of attributes contain information of statistical value. So, a dataset V is defined as:

$$V = a_{id} \left\| a_q \right\| a_c$$

where a_{id} are the identifier attributes, a_q are the non-confidential quasi-identifier attributes, and a_c are the confidential attributes.

In k-anonymization, not all attributes are anonymized. Only the quasi-identifier attributes that are considered to be a possible threat for data linkage are modified using k-anonymization technique. Once k-anonymization is applied, the probability of an individual's identity disclosure becomes 1/k. The process of k-anonymization is straightforward and is illustrated in Figure 1. Typically, before releasing

Figure 1. Data anonymization process using k-anonymization

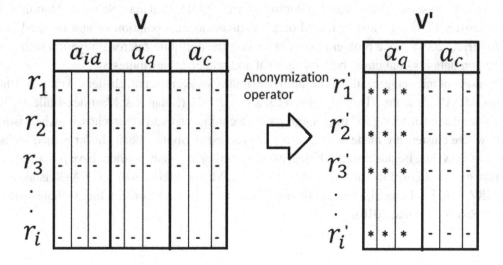

a data set V with confidential attributes, a protection method is applied on it. It produces a protected data set V', where, identifier attributes in V are either removed or encrypted and confidential attributes are untouched. Only non-confidential attributes are perturbed in order to generate a protected dataset. Therefore,

On the other hand, many criticisms of k-anonymity are raised in past years. In contrast to its efficiency in privacy preservation, it creates increased rate of possibilities of a dataset to lose its statistical value with the increase of anonymization level. One other problem with k-anonymity is, if an unaltered attribute value is the same for all the k records in k-anonymization, it can be easily concluded that any individual among those records possesses that attribute value. To illustrate this, assume a dataset that has individual medical records, where there is a confidential attribute that has yes or no value for having AIDS (Soria-Comas J. D.-F., 2014). After anonymizing this data set, if all the anonymized records in some group has 'yes' as the value of this attribute, and an intruder can identify an individual's record to be in that group based on other attributes (Age, gender, race), then, he can easily make a conclusion that, the individual is diagnosed with AIDS. To minimize the issues, many adjustments of k-anonymity combining the idea of data set splitting is proposed like, l-diversity (Machanavajjhala, 2007), t-closeness (Li, 2007, April) etc. However, these techniques also have their own limitations (Domingo-Ferrer J. &., 2008, March).

MICROAGGREGATION

k-anonymization (Sweeney, 2002) (Bredereck, Nichterlein, Niederm, & Philip, 2011) produces a protected dataset by ensuring k-1 number of similar records in the dataset. But, this may cause a huge amount of information loss, which results in decrease in statistical utility of the dataset. To minimize the amount of data loss caused by anonymization, microaggregation concept was developed. Microaggregation can be used to produced k-anonymized dataset. For instance, consider a dataset R with m individual records and n attributes. For each attribute, there are several attribute values. In fixed-size microaggregation, k number of attribute values are clustered and then replaced by the value of the cluster centroid (Kabir & Wang, 2011), generating a protected dataset R'.

However, microaggregation problem is known to be NP-hard for multivariate data sets. So, heuristic methods are used to solve it (Oganian & Domingo-ferrer, 2001), (Solanas, Seb´e, & Domingo-Ferrer, 2008). Moreover, for categorical or mixed data, arithmetical manipulation cannot be used (Torra & Domingo-Ferrer, 2001). So, a problem exists in finding the optimum microaggregation technique that can be used on datasets containing both categorical and numerical attributes.

The first step of microaggregation is grouping attributes in several small clusters. Among all the other algorithms, MDAV algorithm (Domingo-Ferrer J. &.-S., 2002), (Solanas & Martinez-Balleste, 2006) is extensively used as a clustering and microaggregation technique in many researches. It's a heuristic based approach, where clusters are made with k number of closest attributes. Each cluster is then replaced by cluster's average value. Beside distance based attribute clustering, many authors have proposed methods based on the genetic algorithm, such as GOMM (Balasch, Munts, & Nin, 2014), GKA (Krishna & Murty, 1999), FGKA (Lu, Lu, Fotouhi, Deng, & Brown, 2004) and genetic algorithm for attributes with mixed data types (Roy & Sharma, 2010).

The fundamental idea of grouping attributes using genetic algorithm was proposed in Grouping Genetic Algorithm (GGA) (Falkenauer, 1998). It groups attributes based on randomly generated chromosomes. Chromosome fitness's are evaluated over each generation using a cost function and only best fitted chromosomes remain active in next generations. Also, to introduce new characteristics, a number of genetic operators are applied on the chromosomes. The final grouping of attributes is done according to the best fitted chromosome evaluated at the last generation. This idea is also implemented in (Tonni, Rahman, Parvin, & Gawanmeh, 2017), where a new microaggregation operator is used based on Huffman encoding.

Quality of Anonymization

To determine the information loss due to anonymization, the difference between the masked and actual data set is needed to be assessed. Sum of the Square Error (SSE) is a common way to estimate this deviation of a protected data set. SSE means the sum of squared distances from the centroid of each cluster to every record in the cluster (Kabir & Wang, 2011), and is defined as:

$$SSE = \sum_{i=0}^{n} \sum_{r_j=0}^{n_i} \left(r_j - \overline{r_i} \right)^T \left(r_j - \overline{r_i} \right)$$

where, n is the number of groups in the k-partition and n_i is the number of records in the i-th group. As attribute grouping is an essential part of total anonymization process, the target of these algorithms is to minimize this SSE.

Although, there are several ways of measuring quality of anonymization, SCORE (Torra & Domingo-Ferrer, 2001) is extensively used as a measure of anonymization quality among other methods. It measures effectiveness of the anonymized dataset based on the average of information loss (IL) and disclosure risk (DR):

$$Score\left(V,V'\right) = \frac{IL\left(V,V'\right) + DR\left(V,V'\right)}{2}$$

where, V is the original dataset and V' is the anonymized dataset.

Many ways have been used in the literature in order to calculate the information loss such as the average vectors, covariance matrices, variance vectors or correlation matrices. Since the goal of microaggregation is to minimize the SSE, which is a specific information loss measure for any k-anonymity model, it was used as an IL measure in (Balasch, Munts, & Nin, 2014), (Domingo-Ferrer J. &.-S., 2002).

When measuring the quality of a protected dataset, measuring only the amount of information loss is not enough. It is also necessary to measure how many values can be re-identified by linking with other datasets. There are two ways to calculate the DR (Domingo-Ferrer J. a., 2001):

- **Distance-Based Record Linkage:** To get sensitive data an intruder may use record-linkage method (Domingo-Ferrer V. T., 2003). In such cases, the worst scenario is always presumed that, an intruder already has knowledge of the used key variables as in the created altered dataset. The disclosure risk is measured by counting the number of attribute values same as the previous one. That means DR is the number of disclosed attribute values that becomes available to an intruder, if he tries to establish a connection between the protected dataset with the external dataset. In distance based record linkage method, Euclidean distance between the actual and the masked value is measured to identify the disclosure risk.

In (Balasch, Munts, & Nin, 2014), DR is calculated as below:

$$DR = \left(0.5ID + 0.5DLD\right)$$

where, ID is the Interval Disclosure Risk (ID) and DLD is Distance Linkage disclosure. If intervals are created around actual attribute values, then, the average percentage of protected values that falls into such intervals is called ID. According to (Agrawal, 2000), ID is calculated as:

$$ID = \left[\left(r_{ij} - r_{ij} \cdot 10\%\right), \left(r_{ij} - r_{ij} \cdot 10\%\right)\right]$$

To measure DLD, below method is used in (Balasch, Munts, & Nin, 2014):

$$DLD = \frac{no.\ of\ identified\ links}{|V|} \times 100$$

where, |V| is the total number of records

- **Probabilistic Record Linkage:** Protection is achieved through replacing an original value by another one that is not incorrect but less specific. For example, we replace a real number by an interval. In general, non-perturbative methods reduce the level of detail of the data set. This detail reduction causes different records to have the same combinations of values, which makes disclosure difficult to intruders.

In (Jaro, 1989), a matching algorithm was proposed that uses the linear sum assignment model to 'pair' records in the two files, for example, one is the original file and the other is the protected dataset. The percentage of exactly paired records is then considered to be the disclosure risk. Although this method is more complex than calculating the Euclidean distance and (Balasch, Munts, & Nin, 2014) suggest this measure to be inappropriate for evolutionary microaggregation algorithms.

MDAV ALGORITHM

In (Domingo-Ferrer J. &.-S., 2002), the Maximum Distance method (MD) was proposed as multivariate microaggregation technique, where clusters are formed around two most distant elements of the data. But complication arises in case of large scale data due computational overhead of finding the most distant records on every iteration. To minimize these drawbacks the Maximum Distant Average Vector (MDAV) was proposed as a part of the Mu-Argus software. MDAV and V-MDAV (Solanas & Martinez-Balleste, 2006) both algorithm's complexity is O(n^2).

MDAV algorithm starts by computing the average $\bar{x}$ of Xrecords. Then the most distant record r from x and most distant record s from r are determined. Around r and s, two clusters areformed with $(k-1)$ closest members to them. This clustering process is continued while there are at least $2k$ members yet to be grouped. However, a new group of records is formed if there are a remaining number of ungrouped members between k and $2k-1$. Similarly, if there are less than k remaining members that donot belong to any of the groups, they are added to the already formed group with the closest average value to the average of the remaining points (Martínez, Sánchez, & Valls, 2012).

(Domingo-Ferrer, Mart´ınez-Ballest´e, Mateo-Sanz, & Seb´e, 2006) suggested MDAV to be the most appropriate heuristic for grouping huge number of data. Figure 2 shows the information loss of MDAV and V-MDAV algorithms using the "Tarragona", "Census" and "EIA" datasets. (Chettri, Paul, & Dutta, 2013) proposes a new adaptation of V-MDAV algorithm called Centroid based Variable size Maximum Distance to Average Vector (CV-MDAV), where in case of group size expansion, they used a gain factor γ to reduce the information loss.

Figure 2. Difference between information losses (IL)for k=3,4, 5 and 10 after applying MDAV and V-MDAV on three datasets
Source: (Chettri, Paul, & Dutta, 2013)

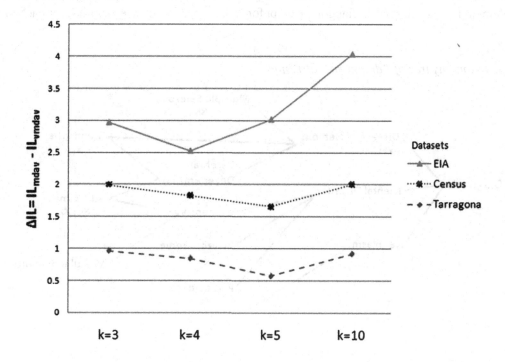

SEMANTICMARGINALITY FOR NOMINAL DATA

In (Domingo-Ferrer J. a.-T., 2013), a comparatively new concept is proposed, where semantics of data is also considered for anonymizing nominal data. In the method, an attribute is first ontologically organized based on a knowledge-based numerical mapping of the attribute. Then, the attribute semantics are modeled as an ontological order. After calculating the semantic distances of each attribute, the attribute's marginality can be measured. Count of the number of taxonomic ancestors (TA) is used to calculate the distance between two attribute values. Below equation is used to measure the distant between two attribute values:

$$D\left(x_1, x_2\right) = \log_2\left(1 + \frac{\#\ of\ all\ TA\ of\ x_1, x_2 - \#of\ common\ TA\ of\ x_1, x_2}{\#of\ all\ TA\ of\ x_1, x_2}\right)$$

So, the marginality of an attribute can be measured as:

$$M\left(x_i\right) = \sum_{j=1}^{n} D\left(x_i, x_j\right)$$

where, n is the number of total taxonomic elements. Marginal value measures the centrality of the attribute values, which is the minimum value obtained from the list of marginalities. Once the marginal value is identified, all the other attribute values are then replaced by this numerical value. Thus, this may enable any other numerical analysis to be performed on the data.

For example, for a health dataset, consider a nominal attribute "Diagnosis", for which available values can be taxonomically arranged as showed in Figure 3. Consider, according to the data sample there are *n* element for each diagnosis category, except for "Alzheimer" and "Meningitis", for each of which

Figure 3. Taxonomy tree of "diagnosis" attribute

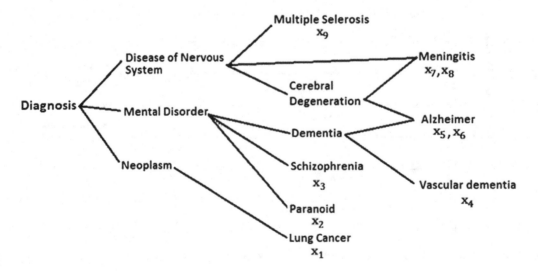

there are two elements. These elements are denoted by x_1, x_2, x_3, x_4, x_5, x_6, x_7, x_8 and x_9. So, the matrix representation of the distances between each element $d(x_i, x_j)$ can be created from the taxonomy tree. For instance,

The marginality of an element can be obtained by adding the distances from all other elements. Marginalities for all elements are shown in Table 1. It turns out that $x1$ (lung cancer) is the most marginal element, which is consistent with the layout of the taxonomy in Figure 3, since it is the most outlying element. On the other hand, $x5$ and $x6$ (Alzheimer) are the least marginal elements, due to both their central position in the hierarchy (given that they belong to both the mental disorder and the disease of nervous system taxonomic branches) and the fact that there are two Alzheimer elements. This technique makes it possible to compute different statistical and mathematical operations like mean, variance and covariance functions on nominal data.

For microaggregation, this algorithm ensures reduced information loss by replacing the nominal attributes using synthetic data instead of replacing with group mean/centroid value. Records are compared and averaged according to the marginality-based definitions of variance, S-distance and mean. The formula for computing variance of a taxonomy tree (TX) is:

$$var = \frac{\sum_{x_j \in TX} M\left(x_j\right)}{n}$$

where, n is the number of element of possible attribute value. So, for "Diagnosis" attribute, the variance is,

Table 1. Marginality matrix and marginality values of "Diagnosis" attribute

	x_1	x_2	x_3	x_4	x_5	x_6	x_7	x_8	x_9	$M\left(x_i\right)$
x_1	0	0.85	0.85	0.87	0.91	0.91	0.85	0.85	0.85	6.94
x_2	0.85	0	0.58	0.68	0.78	0.78	0.85	0.85	0.85	6.22
x_3	0.85	0.58	0	0.68	0.78	0.78	0.85	0.85	0.85	6.22
x_4	0.87	0.68	0.68	0	0.65	0.65	0.87	0.87	0.87	6.14
x_5	0.91	0.78	0.78	0.65	0	0	0.65	0.65	0.65	5.07
x_6	0.91	0.78	0.78	0.65	0	0	0.65	0.65	0.65	5.07
x_7	0.85	0.85	0.85	0.87	0.65	0.65	0	0	0.58	5.3
x_8	0.85	0.85	0.85	0.87	0.65	0.65	0	0	0.58	5.3
x_9	0.85	0.85	0.85	0.87	0.65	0.65	0.58	0.58	0	5.88

$$\left(6.94 + 6.22 + 6.22 + 6.14 + 5.07 + 5.07 + 5.3 + 5.3 + 5.88\right) / 9 = 5.79$$

After the attribute grouping, for each group the S-distance between two records in the group is calculated. The S-distance between two records is the root-squared sum of each attribute's variance for that group. However, these variances are normalized by dividing each of them by their attribute variance over the entire dataset. The formula for computing S-distance for two records x_1 *and* x_2 is:

$$S\left(x_1, x_2\right) = \sqrt{\left(\frac{var_{12}^1}{var^1}\right)^2 + \left(\frac{var_{12}^2}{var^2}\right)^2 + \ldots + \left(\frac{var_{12}^m}{var^m}\right)^2}$$

where, m is the total number of attributes to microaggregate. So, for a group, we will have a set of S-distance between any two records in a group. After that, using this value, a synthetic data is generated and replaces attribute values for each record. For each attribute of a record, randomly select a permitted value for the attribute so that,

$$S\left(x_{jl}, x_{jl}'\right) \leq S_{max}\left(x_{jl}\right)$$

GENETIC OPTIMIZER FOR MULTIVARIATE MICROAGGREGATION

The concept of using evolutionary algorithms for attribute grouping is used in several algorithms. The main idea is to evaluate a set of chromosomes to find the best possible grouping of attributes. Then the grouped attributes are normalized using their group mean.

In Genetic Optimizer for Multivariate Microaggregation (GOMM) (Balasch, Munts, & Nin, 2014), chromosomes are encoded using alphabets that is the group names to form a population. This idea was illustrated earlier in Grouping Genetic Algorithm (GGA) (Falkenauer, 1998). Each chromosome is GOMM has an object part c_{ag}, where each gene represents the corresponding attribute's association in a group, and a group part c_g, which contains the group names used in the chromosome. Figure 4 illustrates the chromosome encoding used in GOMM.

A good anonymization method always tries to minimize the trade-off between information loss and disclosure risk. So, in this technique, the fitness function considered both information loss and disclosure risk. Below equation is used fitness function for evaluating chromosomes:

$$f\left(c_i\right) = Score_i = \left(IL + DR\right) / 2$$

where, i is the number of chromosomes.

For DR calculation, Distance-Based Record Linkage method is used (discussed earlier in this chapter). The IL component in the fitness function is computed as below that ensures value of IL to be in a range of 0 and 100-

Figure 4. Chromosome encoding used in evolutionary algorithm

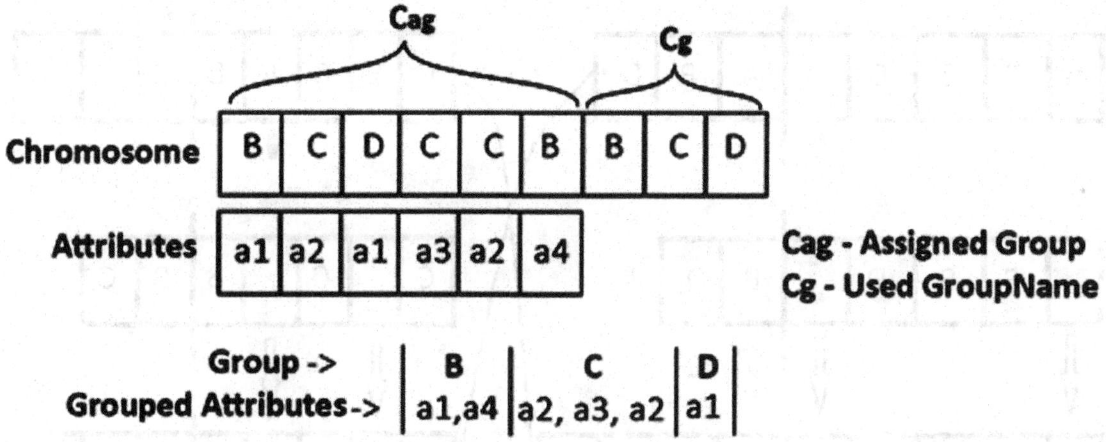

$$IL = \frac{SSE}{SST} \times 100$$

The evolution of the best solution is achieved by applying several genetic operators on a population of chromosomes. Crossover and mutation are most commonly used genetic operators. The crossover operation in GOMM is achieved by combining two random chromosomes and exchanging genes between them to produce two new chromosomes (offspring). In crossover, from two chromosomes, a crossover point is selected. Then, all instances of the selected gene at the crossover point are removed from the chromosomes (in this case A & E are removed from the chromosomes). Finally, all the empty spots of each chromosome are replaced by gene(s) from the other chromosome. Figure 5 depicts the crossover operation.

Figure 6 illustrates the mutation operations used to select next generation chromosomes. Mutation is used in GA to bring diversity in chromosomes. It alters one or more genes in a chromosome from its initial state. This operation introduces new gene values preventing the evaluation process from being trapped on a local optimum. Mutation operation can be of several types like new group creation, group elimination, element swap etc.

After each iteration, the best fit chromosomes are selected to create new population. The selection is done by evaluating each chromosomes fitness value. So, the target of this method is to identify most suitable grouping of attributes that ensures low information loss and disclosure risk.

MICROAGGREGATION BASED ON HUFFMAN ENCODING

Most SDC methods deals with numerical data as it is possible to apply different arithmetical functions like comparisons and transformation operation on numerical values. Microaggregation methods are not easy to implement on datasets containing both numerical and categorical data. To find an optimal microaggregation algorithm (Tonni, Rahman, Parvin, & Gawanmeh, 2017) used encoding generated by Huffman compression algorithm to normalize a group's attribute values. This method anonymizes

Figure 5. Crossover operation in GOMM

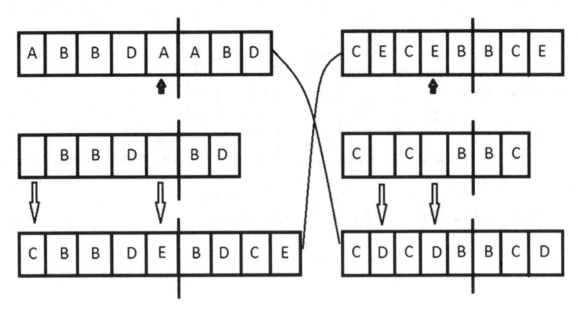

attributes regardless of their data type. In the generated protected data set, the quasi-identifier variables are masked by binary numbers.

In this method, each attribute is processed individually. The first step of the method is grouping attribute values using an evolutionary grouping algorithm. Once the attributes are grouped optimally, they are normalized or microaggregated by the encoded value generated using Huffman compression algorithm. As, datasets of most of CPSs stores huge amount of data, attribute grouping becomes easier if we split the target attribute into several segments beforehand. Attribute grouping and microaggregation operator are then applied individually on each segment.

Attribute Grouping

This is the first step of the microaggregation. As in GOMM, an initial population of chromosomes is created randomly using alphabetic characters (genes) that represent the group names for the purpose of grouping the attributes. On each stage of attribute grouping, only the best fitted chromosomes are selected to perform grouping in next stage. Below is the equation used to calculate the cost of a chromosome in an interval between (0,100]:

$$F\left(C\right) = \frac{1}{\left(SSE + 1\right)} * 100$$

For each chromosome, the group names are extracted from it and the attribute values are grouped under them accordingly for attribute grouping. This mechanism can be illustrated as below:

1.   For each chromosome C in the population perform following steps

Figure 6. Mutation operation in GOMM

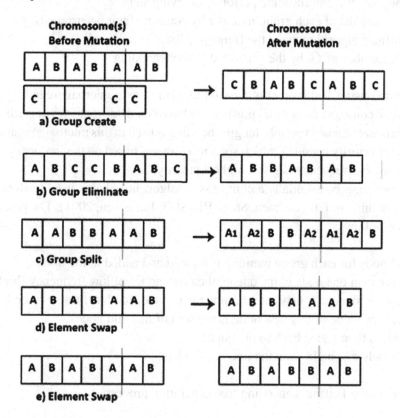

2. Extract the group names from the chromosome into $group[\ ]$
3. For each character in C, do
4. If $C[i] = group[j]$ then, add $attr\_val[i]$ to the attribute list of $group[j]$

After each iteration, a set of chromosomes are selected based on their fitness value for creating next generation. Different genetic operators like crossover and mutations are also applied on the chromosomes to introduce new characteristics in the population. For mutation, the Group Create mutation operator is used as in (Balasch, Munts, & Nin, 2014), it is observed that, this operator introduces very interesting properties, with average maximum efficiency values around 10%.

Microaggregation

Once grouped, attributes of each group are microaggregated and then the fitness function is calculated for that chromosome. This process is applied on every selected chromosome of each generation. Microaggregation process starts by generating binary strings for each attribute values of a group. Then each member of that group is replaced by the generated binary strings. Once all the group members are microaggregated, then the fitness function for the chromosome under process is computed. The microaggregation process is done using below steps-

1. For each group G of a chromosome perform following steps
2. Create a frequency list of each group member by counting their occurrences
3. Generate Huffman algorithm using the frequency list.
4. Replace each member of G by the generated binary encoding

The reason behind using Huffman compression algorithm as a microaggregation operator is, this greedy algorithm can construct an optimal prefix code based on data frequency regardless of the actual data value. To improve efficiency variable-length encoding is used in this microaggregation method. The algorithm uses a min-priority queue Q, which sorts its elements based on the frequency of the attributes and the node with lowest frequency is given highest priority.

The Huffman encoding is essentially a compression algorithm, that is used to store each character of a text using less number of bits (Cormen, Stein, Rivest, & Leiserson, 2001). The process of Huffman tree generation is as follows:

1. At first a leaf node for each group member is created and added to the queue.
2. If there is more than one node in the queue, then two nodes of low frequency (highest priority) is removed from the queue. A new internal node is created that has these two nodes as child node and the frequency value of this new node is the sum of its child nodes.
3. This new node is then added back to the queue.
4. Once there is only one node, then the tree is complete.

Figure 7 illustrates the Huffman encoding tree generation process.

Figure 7. Huffman encoding tree generation process

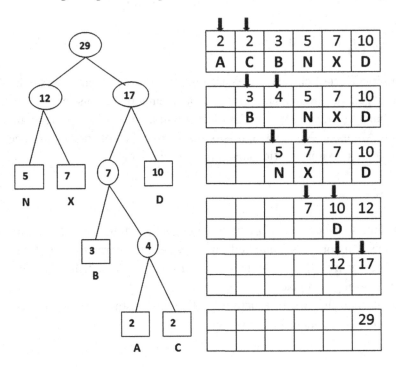

Using a priority queue improves algorithm performance in finding two lowest frequency values for merging. The number of merging step to build the Huffman tree is equal to the number of distinct attribute values in a group. The final tree represents the optimal prefix code. The codeword for an attribute is the sequence of edge labels on the simple path from the root to the letter. Figure 8 shows how Huffman coding is generated for each node of the tree. So, during microaggregation, after each iteration, final outcome is a dataset that has quasi-identifier attribute values replaced by binary strings.

Quality of the Protected Dataset

Below equation is used to calculate the information loss as used in (Domingo-Ferrer J. &.-S., 2002) keeping the IL value within the range of 0 to 100 interval:

$$IL = \frac{SSE}{SST} * 100$$

DR can be measured by counting the number of attributes that are disclosed. So, it can be simply calculated by identifying the attributes that has the same encoding as before. For this, Huffman encoded attribute set is generated beforehand and matched with the dataset generated after microaggregation. A binary XOR operation is performed on each attribute set. For example, if v_{enc} is the initial binary encoding of a variable and v'_{enc} is the encoding in protected dataset, then $v_{enc} \oplus v'_{enc}$ operation is performed to check whether this value is re-identifiable or not. Exclusive Disjunction or XOR is a logical operation that outputs true only when inputs are different from each other (one is true, the other is false).

So, for each attribute value v_i in an attribute a, DR will be calculated as below:

$$DR_a = \left| \left\{ 1, if \; v_{enc} \oplus v'_{enc} = false \right\} \right|$$

RESULT AND DISCUSSION

For analysis purpose, we used the Air Quality Dataset from UCI repository (Vito, 2016) that contains 9357 records of the responses collected from Air Quality Chemical Multi-Sensor Device. From the dataset, microaggregation techniques are applied on two variables, one is "Relative Humidity(RH)", which contains numerical(continuous) data and another is "CO_level", that contains categorical data. These variables are evaluated for k=10, 20 &25.

To evaluate microaggregation based on Huffman encoding algorithm, the dataset is encoded in binary using Huffman encoding beforehand for calculating SSE and DR, so that the distance of the generated value from the original binary value can be counted easily. As, the RH attribute values are continuous type, the Huffman encoding is generated considering the range of attribute values. Figure 9 and 10 illustrates the generated Huffman encoding for the attributes Co_Level and RH respectively.

During attribute grouping, the initial population contained 100 chromosomes. They were evaluated in 20 generations applying crossover (10) and mutation (10) operations. In (Tonni, Rahman, Parvin, & Gawanmeh, 2017), we performed 50 generations of chromosome evaluation. But, it is observed that, the improvement of grouping is very insignificant in higher generations. So, for simplicity, we have reduced the evaluation process to 20 generations. As mutation operator, Group Creator (GC) was used.

Because, it was observed in (Balasch, Munts, & Nin, 2014) that, the GC mutation operator introduces very interesting properties, with average maximum efficiency values around 10%.

In case of "RH" variable, as it contains only numerical data, MDAV and our proposed algorithm is applied on it. In contrast, for "CO_Level" variable, the anonymization technique based on semantic marginality is applied beside our proposed method.

While applying semantic marginality based anonymization, Figure 11 shows the ontological structure that we created based on the attribute values. After using the equations for distance and marginality calculation, the marginality matrix and marginality values for each attribute are depicted in Table 2.

Each k no. of records is grouped together (k=5, 10 & 25). The S-distance for each two records in a group is measured as follows:

Figure 8. Huffman encoding for each node

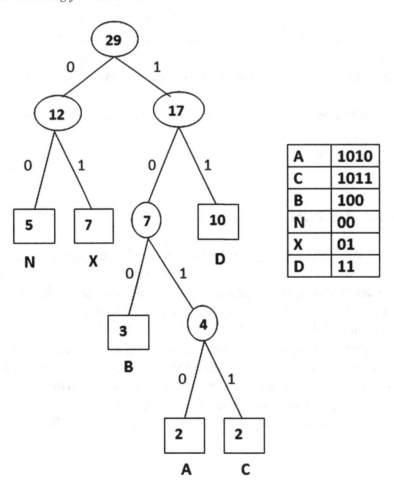

A	1010
C	1011
B	100
N	00
X	01
D	11

Figure 9. Huffman encoding of "CO-Level" attribute

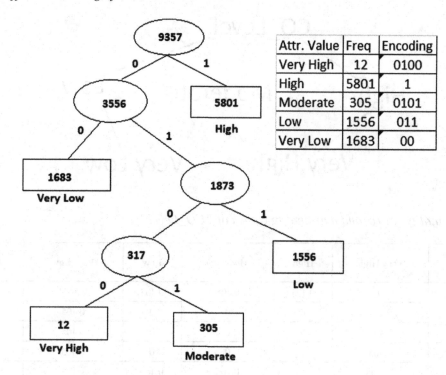

Attr. Value	Freq	Encoding
Very High	12	0100
High	5801	1
Moderate	305	0101
Low	1556	011
Very Low	1683	00

Figure 10. Huffman encoding of "RH" attribute

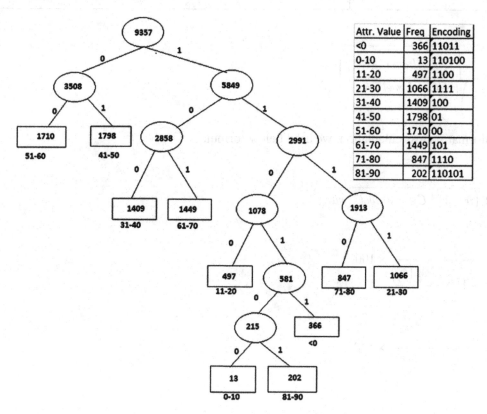

Attr. Value	Freq	Encoding
<0	366	11011
0-10	13	110100
11-20	497	1100
21-30	1066	1111
31-40	1409	100
41-50	1798	01
51-60	1710	00
61-70	1449	101
71-80	847	1110
81-90	202	110101

Figure 11. Taxonomy of "CO-Level" variable

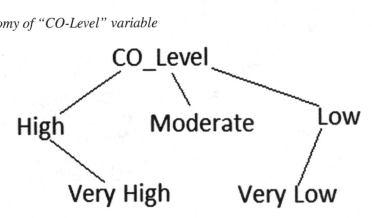

Table 2. Marginality matrix and marginality values of "CO_Level"

x_i	Very High	High	Moderate	Low	Very Low	$M(x_i)$
Very High	0	0.405	0.405	0.405	0.5108	1.7258
High	0.405	0	0	0	0.405	0.81
Moderate	0.405	0	0	0	0.405	0.81
Low	0.405	0	0	0	0.405	0.81
Very Low	0.5108	0.405	0.405	0.405	0	1.7258
					$\sum M(x_i)$	85.2616

$$S\left(x_i, x_j\right) = \sqrt{\left(\frac{CO\_Level\_var_{ij}}{CO\_Level\_var}\right)^2}$$

For information loss calculation, we used below formula:

$$IL = \frac{1}{1 + (n-1) * CO\_Level\_var} \times 100$$

$$= \frac{1}{1 + (n-1) * \dfrac{\sum M(x_i)}{n}} \times 100$$

$$= \frac{n}{n + (n-1) * \sum M(x_i)} \times 100$$

Table 3. Information Loss(IL) after microaggregation "RH" & "CO_Level" using different algorithms

	RH			CO_Level		
	K=10	K=20	K=25	K=10	K=20	K=25
MDAV	0.007145	0.007152	0.007155	-	-	-
Semantic Marginality	-	-	-	7.868992	15.350644	12.434239
Proposed Algorithm	0.000207	0.000163	0.000183	0.109943	0.095814	0.107312

Table 3 shows IL values after applying microaggregation operations on both "RH" and "CO_Level" attribute. It is observed from the table that, using the Huffman encoding based microaggregation produces better result with low IL value. This is because, on each iteration of attribute grouping, SSE is measured as the fitness function. It is also observed that, when semantic marginality is applied for anonymizing the attribute, it may increase intra-group homogeneity, that may increase data disclosure risk (Soria-Comas & Domingo-Ferrer, 2012). Also, it may not always be possible to create taxonomy tree for any variable independently. In such situations, the tree will have height of 1, with the attribute name as the parent node and the attribute values as direct children nodes of it. This may produce zero marginality.

CONCLUSION

This chapter discusses the necessity of microaggregation or protecting data in different CPSs. Microaggregation techniques are also discussed and assed on a real dataset containing a device's response. Our proposed microaggregation algorithm (Tonni, Rahman, Parvin, & Gawanmeh, 2017) produced optimized result on CPS data regardless of its type. The proposed approach can be applied on big data processed in new generation ICS or SCADA systems. Therefore, the method can be applied in order to secure data in applications that require real time data access, while providing different data-centric applications with a mean of microaggregation.

As future work, we intend to minimize the computational complexity associated with fitness calculation at each iteration of the attribute grouping, especially for continuous attributes. Also, performance analysis of this algorithm could be carried out on real-time datasets. It is also possible to consider

REFERENCES

Agrawal, R. a. (2000). *Privacy-preserving data mining* (Vol. 29). ACM.

Balasch, J., Munts, V., & Nin, J. (2014). Using genetic algorithms for attribute grouping in multivariate microaggregation. *Intelligent Data Analysis, 18*(5), 819–836.

Bredereck, R., Nichterlein, A., Niederm, R., & Philip, G. (2011). The effect of homogeneity on the complexity of kanonymity. *18th international conference on Fundamentals of computation theory* (pp. 53-64). Berlin: Springer-Verlag.

Chettri, S. K., Paul, B., & Dutta, A. K. (2013). Statistical Disclosure Control for Data Privacy Preservation. *International Journal of Computers and Applications*, *80*(10).

Cormen, T. H., Stein, C., Rivest, R. L., & Leiserson, C. E. (2001). *Introduction to Algorithms* (2nd ed.). McGraw-Hill Higher Education.

Domingo-Ferrer, J. a. (2001). A quantitative comparison of disclosure control methods for microdata. *Confidentiality, disclosure and data access: theory and practical applications for statistical agencies*, 111-134.

Domingo-Ferrer, J. (2005). Microaggregation for protecting individual data. *Proceso de Toma de Decisiones, Modelado y Agregaci´on de*, 171–178.

Domingo-Ferrer, J. (2008, March). A critique of k-anonymity and some of its enhancements. In *Availability, Reliability and Security, 2008. ARES 08. Third International Conference on* (pp. 990-993). IEEE.

Domingo-Ferrer, J., Mart'ınez-Ballest'e, A., Mateo-Sanz, J., & Seb'e, F. (2006). Efficient multivariate data-oriented microaggregation. *The VLDB Journal*, *15*(4), 355–369. doi:10.100700778-006-0007-0

Domingo-Ferrer, J., & Mateo-Sanz, J. M. (2002). Practical data-oriented microaggregation for statistical disclosure control. *IEEE Transactions on Knowledge and Data Engineering*, *14*(1), 189–201. doi:10.1109/69.979982

Domingo-Ferrer, J., Sánchez, D., & Rufian-Torrell, G. (2013). Anonymization of nominal data based on semantic marginality. *Information Sciences*, *242*, 35–48. doi:10.1016/j.ins.2013.04.021

Domingo-Ferrer, J., Solanas, A., & Martinez-Balleste, A. (2006). Privacy in statistical databases: k-anonymity through microaggregation. *GrC*, 774-777.

Domingo-Ferrer, J., & Torra, V. (2005). Ordinal, continuous and heterogeneous k-anonymity through microaggregation. *Data Mining and Knowledge Discovery*, *11*(2), 195–212. doi:10.100710618-005-0007-5

Domingo-Ferrer, J. T., Sánchez, D., & Rufian-Torrell, G. (2013). Anonymization of Nominal Data Based on Semantic Marginality. *Information Sciences*, *242*, 35–48. doi:10.1016/j.ins.2013.04.021

Domingo-Ferrer, V. T. (2003). Record linkage methods for multidatabase data mining. Information Fusion in Data Mining, 101-132.

Falkenauer, E. (1998). *Genetic Algorithms and Grouping Problems*. New York: John Wiley & Sons, Inc.

Frey, S., Rashid, A., Zanutto, A., Busby, J., & Follis, K. (2016). On the role of latent design conditions in cyber-physical systems security. In *Software Engineering for Smart Cyber-Physical Systems (SEsCPS), 2016 IEEE/ACM 2nd International Workshop on* (pp. 43-46). IEEE.

Jaro, M. A. (1989). Advances in record-linkage methodology as applied to matching the 1985 census of Tampa, Florida. *Journal of the American Statistical Association*, *84*(406), 414–420. doi:10.1080/01621459.1989.10478785

Jaskolka, J., & Villasenor, J. (2017). *Identifying implicit component interactions in distributed cyber-physical systems*. Academic Press.

Kabir, M. E., & Wang, H. (2011). Microdata protection method through microaggregation: A median-based approach. *Inf. Sec. J.: A Global Perspective, 20*(1), 1-8.

Krishna, K., & Murty, M. N. (1999). Genetic k-means algorithm. *Trans. Sys. Man Cyber. Part B, 29*(3), 433–439. doi:10.1109/3477.764879 PMID:18252317

Li, N. L. (2007, April). t-closeness: Privacy beyond k-anonymity and l-diversity. In *ICDE 2007. IEEE 23rd International Conference on* (pp. 106-115). IEEE.

Lu, Y., Lu, S., Fotouhi, F., Deng, Y., & Brown, S. J. (2004). Fgka: a fast genetic k-means clustering algorithm. In *Proceedings of the 2004 ACM symposium on Applied computing* (pp. 622-623). New York, NY: ACM.

Machanavajjhala, A. G., Kifer, D., Gehrke, J., & Venkitasubramaniam, M. (2007). l-diversity: Privacy beyond k-anonymity. *ACM Transactions on Knowledge Discovery from Data, 1*(1), 3, es. doi:10.1145/1217299.1217302

Martínez, S., Sánchez, D., & Valls, A. (2012). Semantic adaptive microaggregation of categorical microdata. *Computers & Security, 31*(5), 653–672. doi:10.1016/j.cose.2012.04.003

Oganian, A., & Domingo-ferrer, J. (2001). On the complexity of optimal microaggregation for statistical disclosure control. *Statistical Journal of the United Nations Economic Commission for Europe, 18*, 345–354.

Roy, D. K., & Sharma, L. K. (2010). Genetic k-means clustering algorithm for mixed numeric and categorical data sets. *International Journal of Artificial Intelligence & Applications, 1*(2), 23–28. doi:10.5121/ijaia.2010.1203

Solanas, A., & Martinez-Balleste, A. (2006). V-mdav: a multivariate microaggregation with variable group size. *17th COMPSTAT Symposium of the IASC.*

Solanas, A., Seb'e, F., & Domingo-Ferrer, J. (2008). *Microaggregation-based heuristics for p-sensitive k-anonymity: one step beyond. In 2008 international workshop on Privacy* (pp. 61–69). New York: ACM.

Soria-Comas, J., & Domingo-Ferrer, J. (2012). Probabilistic k-anonymity through microaggregation and data swapping. *2012 IEEE International Conference on Fuzzy Systems,* (pp. 1-8). Brisbane, QLD: IEEE. 10.1109/FUZZ-IEEE.2012.6251280

Soria-Comas, J. D.-F., Domingo-Ferrer, J., Sánchez, D., & Martínez, S. (2014). Enhancing data utility in differential privacy via microaggregation-based k-anonymity. *The VLDB Journal, 23*(5), 771–794. doi:10.100700778-014-0351-4

Sweeney, L. (2002). k-anonymity: A model for protecting privacy. *International Journal of Uncertainty, Fuzziness and Knowledge-based Systems, 10*(5), 557–570. doi:10.1142/S0218488502001648

Tonni, S. M., Rahman, M. Z., Parvin, S., & Gawanmeh, A. (2017). Securing Big Data Efficiently through Microaggregation Technique. In *Distributed Computing Systems Workshops (ICDCSW), 2017 IEEE 37th International Conference on* (pp. 125-130). IEEE.

Torra, V., & Domingo-Ferrer, J. (2001). *Disclosure control methods and information loss for microdata.* Elsevier.

Vito, S. D. (2016, March 23). Retrieved September 10, 2017, from UCI Machine Learning Repository: https://archive.ics.uci.edu/ml/datasets/Air+Quality

Wikipedia.org. (n.d.a). *SCADA.* Retrieved September 10, 2017, from https://en.wikipedia.org/wiki/SCADA

Wikipedia.org. (n.d.b). *Stuxnet.* Retrieved September 10, 2017, from https://en.wikipedia.org/wiki/Stuxnet

Zhang, Y., Qiu, M., Tsai, C., Hassan, M. M., & Alamri, A. (2017). Health-CPS: Healthcare cyber-physical system assisted by cloud and big data. *IEEE Systems Journal, 11*(1), 88–95. doi:10.1109/JSYST.2015.2460747

KEY TERMS AND DEFINITIONS

Categorical Data: Categorical data is a type of data that may be divided into categories or groups.

DR: Disclosure risk, used to assess the quality of data anonymization, by identifying the number of re-identifiable data from the dataset.

Huffman Encoding: Using the greedy Huffman compression algorithm generates binary encoding for each value for a set of values.

K-Anonymization: K-anonymization is a technique for data privacy protection that ensures at least K-1 similar records in a dataset, in order to decrease data disclosure risk by linking with other datasets.

MDAV: Maximum distant average vector is an algorithm that groups values based on their distances.

Microaggregation: A perturbative statistical disclosure control method that clusters attribute values in groups containing between K to 2K-1 members and replaces each original data by the centroid of the corresponding cluster.

SSE: Sum of squared error, is a measure of dissimilarity between a group's value and the group centroid.

Chapter 6

High–Level Design and Implementation of a Home Autonomous System Based on CPS Modeling

Basman M. Alhafidh
Florida Institute of Technology, USA

William H. Allen
Florida Institute of Technology, USA

ABSTRACT

The process used to build an autonomous smart home system based on cyber-physical systems (CPS) principles has recently received increased attention from researchers and developers. However, there are many challenges to be resolved before designing and implementing such a system. In this chapter, the authors present a high-level design approach that simulates a smart home system by implementing three levels of the 5C architecture used in CPS modeling and uses well-known machine learning algorithms to predict future user actions. The simulation demonstrates how users will interact with the smart home system to make more efficient use of resources. The authors also present results from analyzing real-world user data to validate the accuracy of prediction of user actions. This research illustrates the benefits of considering CPS principles when designing a home autonomous system that reliably predicts a user's needs.

INTRODUCTION

In general, CPS tries to represent the real world as a virtual phenomenon (Cyber Mode) by producing cyber components which are intended to match the design and purpose of a physical device. One goal is to gain a better understanding of the physical world and to improve the system intelligence and mitigate limitations that could occur in the physical world. Therefore, networked, embedded components and network control systems must be connected to the physical world to address the CPS's requirements.

DOI: 10.4018/978-1-5225-5510-0.ch006

Such a CPS should embed all essential capabilities to satisfy the overall system requirements. These may include a feedback loop either from another component or humans, adaptability to any changes, and the ability to be reconfigured to satisfy the dynamic changes in real time processes. (Lee, 2008).

This chapter focuses on an application of the principles of CPS design by presenting a high-level design pattern for smart homes. The proposed system, as shown in Figure 1, tries to enhance the design of the smart home environment based on Cyber-Physical principles by an approach that uses a smart agent for each subsystem, a storage agent-based cloud for backup data with an enterprise-level analysis, and a centralized intelligent agent that connects all the components of the proposed system in a unique design that authors call the BUTLER. The purpose of the proposed design is to present a new structure for the high-level design of a personal assistant in the home environment that is implemented under CPS design principles.

BACKGROUND

Cyber-Physical System (CPS) has become a very interesting field for many researchers, and the United States government labeled CPS as one of its strategic developments in 2007 (Kao, Jin, Siegel, & Lee, 2015). CPS have been defined as" engineered systems that are built from, and depend upon, the seamless integration of computational and physical components" (Horvath & Gerritsen, 2012). Other researchers present CPS as software and hardware elements which are connected together for a certain purpose by saying:" A Cyber-physical system can be viewed as an advanced collaborative collection of both software and physical entities which share data, information, and knowledge to achieve a function (which can be technical, service, or social in nature)" (Lu & Cecil, 2016). CPS can be applied to many research topics including, but not limited to, Swarm Robotics, Sensor Networks, Automotive, Aviation, Internet of Things (IoT), and the Smart Home, which can represent the basic unit in a Smart City (Alhafidh & Allen, 2016; Kao et al., 2015; Hu, 2013).

Cyber-Physical Systems Challenges

There are many challenges in the implementation of a Cyber-Physical System and several of them impact the design of a Smart Home. Prior research has identified the following issues:

- **Portability:** Portability issues take much of the developer's time due to the large variety of CPS hardware platforms for different real-life applications and compatibility issue between devices in one application also (Koçak, 2014). In Sztipanovits et al., (2012), the researchers labeled the heterogeneity as one of the biggest problems that the developer face during the designing of cyber-physical system in the real world by saying," Heterogeneity demands cross-domain modeling of interactions between physical and cyber (computational) components and ultimately results in the requirement of a framework that is model-based, precise and predictable for acceptable behavior of CPS.".

- **Time:** Time constraints are critical problems for CPS software developers or even for a programmer. This constraint exists in both the design phase and the implementation phase. Every tiny detail in systems requirements must be calculated to ensure proper design. If not, then even the best software developer with evolutionary methodologies cannot ensure that these initial requirements can be exploited during the implementation phase in real life (Koçak, 2014). Therefore, a proper timing analysis must be computed for using static analysis methods and dynamic analysis methods. The first one will calculate the static time needed to analyze both source code and machine codes without implementing them on physical or software (simulator) environment; the second one is related to calculating the actual runtime for that piece of code or CPS's system software. However, there is an acceptable range of limited time that is affected by the requirements of CPS systems. Some research indicates that a 1-s delay could produce a catastrophic result (Hu, 2013). Another paper indicates that some systems accept (500 ms) as a maximum delay, such as an ihome system in the home. However, this delay is not acceptable in a real-time application such as health monitoring systems or alarm and monitoring systems of a nuclear power plant (Koçak, 2014).

- **Connection Problems (Predictability and Integrity):** Predictability is one of the main connection dilemmas between CPS framework, the jitter that happens in almost all the communication links is significant, and undesired factor. These dilemmas need to be eliminated especially in applications that demand a real-time communication phenomenon (Stone & Jeffay, 1995). The second problem is the integrity of heterogeneous hardware and software components in one system which is difficult to be assured in cyber-physical systems. The communication in CPS is a very important element for learning, adapting, and even teaching (Suh, Tanik, Carbone, & Eroglu, 2014). An example is a temperature sensor for HVAC that gets the information from a weather channel or a home micro-grid weather station to close the shutter in case of a hurricane or emergency. The autonomous reaction for this process has become essential today to increase usability and interoperability of such systems.

PROPOSED SMART HOME DESIGN FOR CYBER-PHYSICAL SYSTEMS

Delegating most of the user's needs to the automated system is an essential part of a Smart Home. Therefore, providing an environment that can detect burglary, fire and smoke, gas or water leaks, and other threats is essential to protect residents. In addition, it should be capable of monitoring and control the lighting system, appliances, multimedia devices, energy resource system and the home power grid. Awareness of these requirements gives developers insight when they try to develop such a system that fits each resident's specific needs.

This means that the first three software layers in the 5C architecture, shown in Figure 1, should present an advanced analytical and flexible functionality over other layers. Therefore, having the ability to be autonomous, intelligent, and adaptable are mandatory when designing such a system. These capabilities make the cyber version of a system understand the home environment and the resident's needs to enable it to create an ecosystem which makes the resident's life easier and more comfortable than before. The following paragraphs discuss the necessary steps to present the authors' intelligent CPS system design.

The Overall System Design

To satisfy the resident and system requirements, the design of proposed system consists of eight subsystems, in addition to the centralized Intelligent Agent (IA) shown in Figure 2. Each subsystem has the appropriate types of sensors, actuators, and devices which authors call "NODES". For each subsystem, all the nodes should be connected to the subunit of that subsystem. For example, the multimedia subunit

Figure 1. CPS 5C architectural design
Source: Bagheri, Yang, Kao, & Lee, 2015

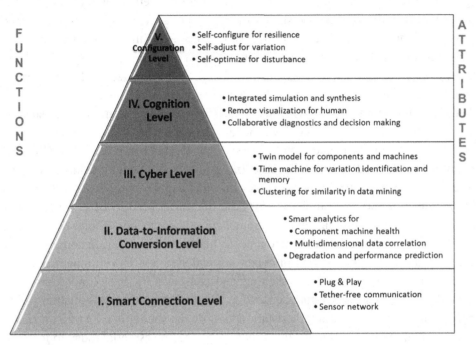

connects all the multimedia devices in the home. By comparing these components to 5C CPS architecture, these connected components represent the smart connection level in the 5C pyramid architecture that includes data collecting, buffering and streamlining.

Since a row of collected data may be generated from different subsystems or even different devices in one subsystem, data must be filtered to remove noise and redundancy by the subsystem agent to convert it to more meaningful information for upper layers. The subsystem agents map to the Data-to-Information layer in CPS architecture design to ensure real-time data streamlining and feedback from the cyberspace (Lee, Ardakani, Yang, & Bagheri, 2015). In addition to data filtration and noise reduction, the subsystem agents play an important role in communication between the subunits and the central agent (IA). The subsystem agents and the central IA communicate using the same communication protocols, whether the communication medium is wired or wireless. Thus, subsystem agents were used to ensuring integrity between heterogeneous components and solve the portability issues that were mentioned in cyber-physical systems challenges section.

The central IA represents the second main element in the CPS architecture, which is described as "The intelligent machine computing for the collected data which represents the cyberspace." (Lee et al., 2015). Thus, the second level (IA) is the knowledge and prediction level that provides advanced computing algorithms and resilience (Kao et al., 2015; Hu, 2013). It is positioned in the center of the proposed CPS system and connects all other subsystems as one interconnected system. It is actually representing the brain (Cyber level) of the automated system that continuously works to track the user's behavior. Therefore, all information, after minimizing and analyzing data, will be saved in a short-term database and long-term backup memory. After extracting specific information about the preferences of the users, the next important stage is to predict each user's needs and act on behalf of the user to perform the expected actions.

Figure 2. The intelligent home system design (Project BUTLER)

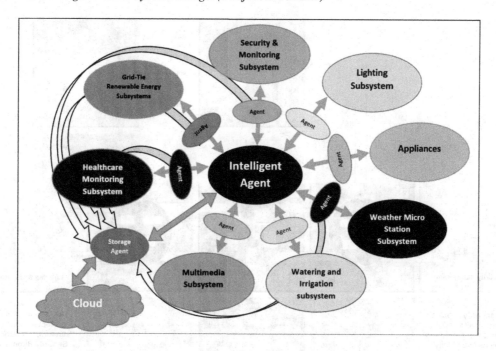

In the proposed design, both the cognition and the configuration levels of the CPS architecture are provided via a third-party company, such as Amazon, Google, or Microsoft via their cloud-based analytics tools. This cloud-based logging and data analysis will provide the system with online monitoring and will diagnose and predict potential failures. These analytic services can help to extend the configuration level of this Smart Home to interface with an associated Smart City.

To illustrate how the specific design that was discussed above meets the system's overall requirements, Figure 3 shows the architectural design of the communications between two of the subsystem agents and the IA to control and manage the message flows for those subsystems.

Figure 3 shows that each subsystem has its own specific nodes which are distinct from the other subsystems; hence, the security subsystem has many types of nodes, such as motion, smoke, door lock, window break, or CCTV, while the lighting subsystem has different kinds of nodes, such as illuminance sensors, light bulbs, and LED. All security nodes are connected to a security subunit which connects all security sensors, actuators, and devices to a security subsystem agent, using either wired or wireless standard communication protocols. It is important to mention that there are many tasks assigned to each subsystem agent which differ from one agent to another. These tasks may include monitoring and controlling all security nodes, buffering, sending the current status to the intelligent agent, running predefined commands from the IA, or data mining and context-aware processing.

The lighting subsystem agent is implemented to deal with different kinds of lighting nodes. The subsystem's agents, as seen in Figure 3, take the block numbers 2 and 4. These agents are located between the subsystem and the IA. The agents here try to read the nodes' status from the subsystem's subunit by polling an operation process and saving the data in its local memory. After that, it filters and analyzes the data and sends it to the IA. In some cases, selected data may be sent directly to the storage agent (block number 6) to be saved in the cloud (block number 7) as backup data for the system and for further

Figure 3. The communication and information flow between the IA, two subsystems, and cloud

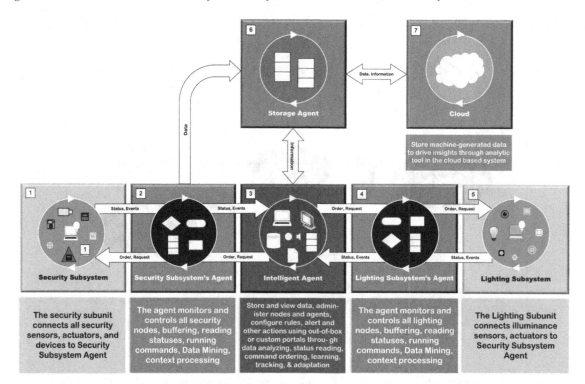

analyses. When a lighting node's status changes, it is sent directly via the agent to the brain of the entire system (the IA) to determine the action to take. The lighting subsystem agent will continuously read and implement any new commands from the IA.

The centralized Intelligent Agent plays the most important role in the system because it acts as the brain of the designed system and represents the cyber level in CPS's 5C architecture. The IA will perform long and short-term learning and optimization to predict user behavior and adapt to changes in that behavior over time. The storage agent is the only component that interacts with the Internet and, therefore, will be provided with firewall capabilities to isolate components of Smart Home environment from the cloud system.

System Modes of Operation

The modes of operation that the BUTLER adopts are divided into two modes, Manual Mode, and Automatic Mode. The manual mode here means the direct interface between the user and the node itself, or what people do in their daily life; in other words, it uses the regular nodes and electrical outlets that people use every day without using the smart environment, such as a tungsten lamp plugged into a simple electrical outlet or any appliances like regular HVAC systems because the BUTLER functionalities are disabled. The Automatic mode represents the mode where all the functionalities in BUTLER are being used in the same environment to do any job which has been delegated to the BUTLER by any stakeholder. Doing the job in an efficient way demands using some type of artificial intelligence. To reach this level of intelligence, this mode requires two steps that must be implemented before reaching the current level. The following section discusses these steps in detail.

The Automatic Mode of Operation

When the system runs in automatic mode, the IA takes control of a home environment to do all the tasks that have been delegated to it by the resident. To reach this level of processing, which presents the cyber level in 5C Architecture, there are three proposed phases of the automatic mode of operation that must be implemented, as discussed in the following paragraph.

System Development Phases for Automatic Mode of Operation

The automatic mode of operation represents a more complex system than the simple Smart Home controllers which are used today. Figure 4 shows a three-phase approach, which includes the Initialization Phase, the Learning Phase, and the Action Phase.

Phase One: Initialization Phase

This phase configures the initialization parameters for the nodes and related subsystem agent software programs for each agent, in addition to the IA's initial configuration. The initial parameters and software programs are necessary when any part of the system needs to be restarted or rebooted. Many of the parameters and pre-configured rules that are presented as initial rules for operation from the starting point are actually present in the default rules that any system begins with. Adding to that, there are several predefined procedures that will be included in the initial state. These procedures are pre-programmed steps that the Intelligent Agent will use to handle certain events which can occur at any time, such as detecting potentially dangerous events or certain weather conditions. Since these events will be processed in a standard way, such as closing windows during rain or sounding an alarm during a fire, they do not require learning user behavior.

Phase Two: Learning Phase

This represents the second phase of the automatic mode of operation. It consists of four essential steps that begin with collecting the status for each physical node from all the subsystem agents in the IA local memory. The next step is to analyze and aggregate the information that comes from the agents using some feature extraction and context processing. The decision step makes use of decision theory to generate a hypothesis from the set of current inputs. The hypothesis represents the target function that the IA wants to model for that set of input information. If this hypothesis is new for the IA, then the IA should wait for the user to take an action. After this step, the IA can build or generate a new rule to use in the future for the same hypothesis. If the current hypothesis is similar to a hypothesis that exists in the local memory, then the IA will act in the way it has already learned to from those earlier inputs.

This phase is very important because it tries to build a new rule that consists of gathering input variables coming from node's status and producing the correct output, which is based on predicting the user's actions when that input occurs. The strategy used to build new rules comes from tracking the user behaviors against different nodes' status in the surrounding environment and to implement these rules in the last phase of automatic mode. The new rule is used, along with the initial rules, to control the system on behalf of the user during the next phase.

Phase Three: Action Phase

In this phase, the IA tries to take the right action by using the applicable rule for the current state or node status. This action is represented by the Act block in Figure 4. The last block is labeled Adapt which means that the IA should have the capability to update the learned rules from the previous phase due to an unexpected change that has been done by the resident manually. In other words, the system could change the rules produced in the learning phase based on changes in user behavior (i.e., changing the output variable for the target function) for the same input node status (the target function's inputs variables). This phase is necessary to allow the system to adjust when the user changes his mind, or has a guest, or responds to changes in weather. This requires that the IA continuously monitor and update to track these changes to satisfy the resident's needs and to perform the tasks that have been assigned to the BUTLER.

The Configurations in the Automatic Mode of Operation

Many human activities, which happen while the resident inside a home, are different from other actions when the user is absent. Therefore, the proposed system designed to work in a different mode when the resident is not at home. The authors refer to the *Active Mode* as that time when at least one of the residents is at home, and the *Standby Mode* describes the time when the residents are all away for more than a short time. Each mode has its own configuration and pre-defined working rules assigned during the software design phase as follows:

The Configurations for Active Mode: The configuration for the active mode here means the needed steps to set up predefined parameters and rules that the system must follow as an initial behavior. These parameters are selected by the resident along with the preferred values for each occupant in the home. There are also some simple rules for normal operations. For example, turning the front-yard light ON at sunset is a very basic rule that could be predefined rather than learned. Of course, both the predefined rules and the learned rules can be modified when the BUTLER is running in the active mode.

The following paragraphs describe predefined algorithms and procedures for two subsystems as an example of how subsystems will operate differently.

- **Security and Monitoring Subsystem:** The configuration for this subsystem consists of five important algorithms. Figure 5 shows a flowchart of one of five algorithms. The flowchart shows how the security agent reacts when monitoring any changes that could happen in any of its nodes.
- **Lighting Subsystem:** Usually, the time of day and the weather in this subsystem play an important role but after analyzing the working scenario, the authors decided to depend on the illuminance level in a home due to better performance and efficient use of energy consumption. Several algorithms have been chosen also to make use of predefined rules, as summarized in Figure 6.

The Configurations for Standby Mode: This mode will be activated by a resident when he leaves the house for a vacation or long trip. In this case, the IA (which represents the cyber layer) becomes the manager of every electronic device in the home. Therefore, there are several important steps that must be

Figure 4. The development phases for the automatic mode during the active mode of operation

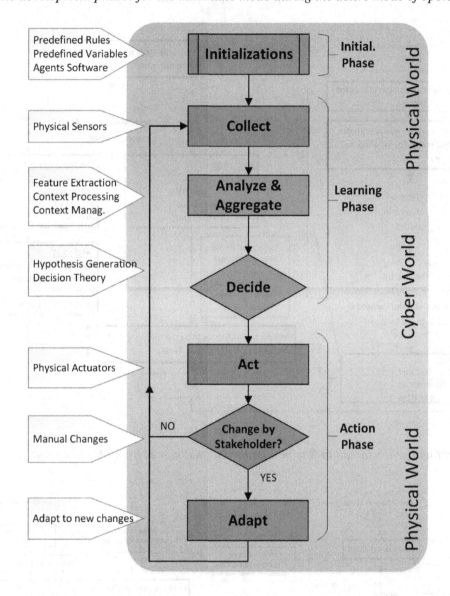

done by the IA when this mode is activated. The IA will look for any changes that could have happened in any node or subsystem. For instance, the IA could receive a status message from the security agent that reports some abnormal activity in some security nodes. If the IA finds the current state is critical, then the IA instantly could follow a set of predefined steps, such as sending a notification message to the owner, turning all lights ON, recording any activity using CCTV, activating the panic button, or calling 911.

In another example, the IA could detect that an outside door is unlocked. The IA could wait for a period of time to sense if there is a person inside the home. If motion is detected, it could follow the emergency steps described above, or if the IA cannot sense any motion inside the home, then it could assume that the door was left unlocked by accident and send a command message to the security agent to lock the door and notify the resident that a door was left unlocked.

Figure 5. Security agent's thread to monitor and notify any change in security sensor status to the intelligent agent

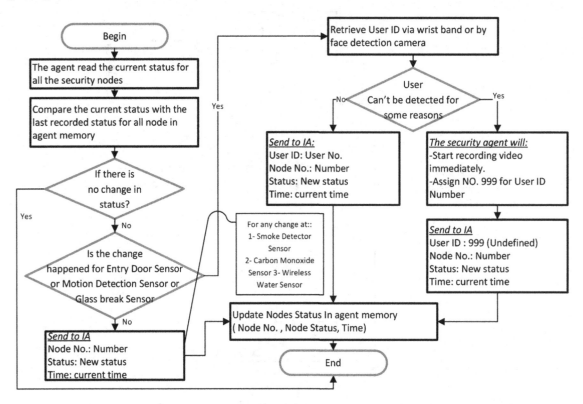

Figure 6. Lighting agent's thread to Run new command that comes from IA and Report the new status

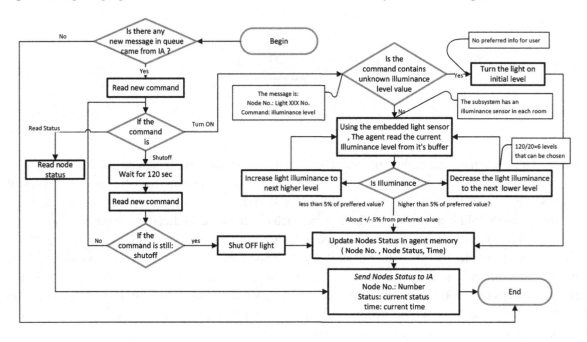

SYSTEM SIMULATION

After assigning all the requirements and necessary design for all the needed components of the proposed system, a NetLogo 5.2.0 simulation program was used to simulate the home environment and necessary hardware components. Figure 7 shows a map as an example of a simple home plan. The home consists of one bedroom, one bathroom, a living room, a kitchen, and a garage. In addition to the home map, there are many components marked with numbers 1 to 11. These components are used to manually control and monitor the status of different node types, labeled 6, 7, and 8 as shown in Figure 7. In addition, the two power plots labeled with numbers 9 and 10, show the instant and average power consumption of the home nodes, and the real-time status of some of the lighting nodes is labeled 11.

The *setup* button, which is labeled with number 1, is used to reset the nodes in the home environment to the initial state, while the *run* button, labeled with number 2, is used to execute the software program in a continuous loop. The *standby mode* button, labeled with number 3, allows operators to choose between two types of configurations, the active mode, and the standby mode. Because of the different procedures between each mode, the first mode must be chosen when the user at home, otherwise, standby mode must be chosen when the user is out of the home. By operating the manual mode button, a selection between the manual mode of operation and the automatic mode of operation can be implemented.

The *manual mode* button represents what people have in their homes today and how they control the nodes in their daily life. In other words, this mode doesn't have any agents for each subsystem or an Intelligent Agent. Therefore, the control process for any node must be done by the user himself through a direct interface. This allows the simulator to represent the status of the home when there is no Smart Home controller.

The *auto mode* button represents the existence of an agent for each subsystem, the central Intelligent Agent as the brain of the automated system and the cloud as a storage backup for the entire system. In this mode, the BUTLER would take control of the nodes and make changes according to the predefined and learned rules. However, it is important to mention here that if the user tries to change the status for any nodes in the environment for some reason, the BUTLER should give the user the privilege to execute what the user needs and record that new behavior. Since the BUTLER is tracking the user's behavior, if the BUTLER sees that the same action happens several times upon the same set of input states or sensor values, then the BUTLER would adapt by building or editing the current rule for that status in the database that exists inside the IA. Section 4.1, discusses in more detail what the BUTLER does during a certain time of a weekday when choosing the automatic mode of operation.

The manual control for any node during both manual or auto modes are done via the buttons labeled 5, 6, 7, and 8 as shown in Figure 7. Some of the nodes have a status represented by Boolean values, which mean the nodes are either in an 'ON' state or an 'OFF' state. This represents devices such as a TV, a voice mail device, a coffee maker, a smoke detector sensor, or windows break sensor. Other types of nodes present analog values such as dimmer switches for the lighting in each of bedroom, bathroom, kitchen, and so on.

The landscape has the *sprinkler motor* button labeled number 6. This button turns the sprinkler motor ON in four areas around the home. Each area has two sprinklers in addition to one soil moisture sensor. The soil moisture sensors are only used in the auto mode. This means the sprinklers in the manual mode work according to a fixed time schedule, much like the standard watering system found in many homes. Sections 4.1 and 4.2 give two daily scenarios as follows:

Figure 7. The designed home plan using NetLogo

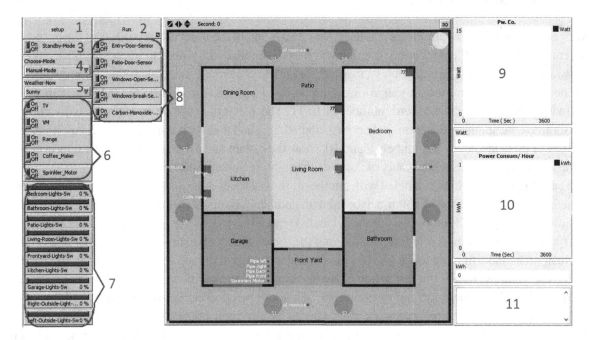

Morning Scenario

To show how the user will use the home facilities, the authors explain the morning scenario, which the user probably will do every weekday. This morning scenario begins at 6 AM. At this time, the home will be dark because the sun has not yet risen. As the alarm clock goes on, the person wakes up and tries to physically interface with the surrounding devices or nodes, so the first interface will be to turn on the bedroom lights. After that, the person may spend 10 to 15 minutes in the bathroom, also turn the lights on and take a shower. Then he leaves the bathroom and goes toward the kitchen at 6:15 AM to make his breakfast. On his way, the person would like to turn on the TV to listen to the latest news while eating his breakfast. In the kitchen, the user also would turn the light on and try to make fresh coffee and some light meals using the range or oven. After finishing the breakfast at 6:45, the user goes back to his bedroom again to change his clothes. Finally, he leaves the house for work at 7 AM.

Dealing with this simple scenario makes the power resource calculation clear and easy to understand because the same steps are used to explain how the automatic mode works to predict the user behavior and try to work on behalf of the user to execute the delegated tasks.

Standby Mode Scenario

This scenario shows how the BUTLER is going to react to any normal conditions that may happen at any time when the user is away from home during the standby mode of operation. The BUTLER must act autonomously according to any change in security nodes statuses like an open access door, a broken window, and smoke detected by sensors. If a window breaks, the sensor detects broken glass, and then the IA instantly should do take the following steps. These steps include sending a notification message to the owner, turning all lights ON, recording video from the CCTV, activating the alarm, and then calling 911.

Since one of the benefits of the Smart Home is the more efficient use of resources such as electricity and water, the following paragraph discusses how the simulation calculates the use of water and electrical power.

Energy Monitoring for Electrical Consumption and Water Usage

This section describes how the authors calculate the electrical power consumption and water resource usage. Every node has a different rate of power consumption measured in watt-hour (Wh) or kilowatt-hour (kWh) and this display helps the user understand the impact of energy use on the monthly electric bills. The power consumption will be calculated using a software program function to check every working device in the home continuously.

$$E\left(\frac{kWh}{day}\right) = P(W) * t\left(\frac{h}{day}\right) / 1000\left(\frac{W}{kW}\right) \tag{1}$$

To calculate the energy consumption for nodes that the user may use every day, the authors use Equation 1. Therefore, as the system is working in the manual mode, the authors calculate the average power consumption for daily usage during the morning scenario period only from 6 AM to 7 AM. The authors find the electrical power consumption to be about 0.630 kWh in the weekday. So, the electrical power consumption for one month, based on this scenario only, will be 18.9 kW and for one year will be about 226.8 kWh for the morning scenario only.

To calculate water consumption for the four landscape zones, a water pump motor (what people normally have in their house) assumed to be scheduled to run for 30 minutes per cycle, 3 days a week as follows:

$$Nc = Nm * Tz \tag{2}$$

where Nc represents the number of gallons per cycle, while Nm represents the number of water gallon consumed per one minute for each zone, and Tz is the time for each zone. After applying Equation 2, there are 360 gallons per cycle which are consumed in (30 min) periods as shown in Equation 3.

$$360\left(\frac{Gallon}{Cycle}\right) = \frac{12\left(\frac{Gallons}{Min}\right)}{Zone} * 30\left(\frac{Min}{Zone}\right) \tag{3}$$

For four zones, the water consumption is 1,440 gallons per cycle which produce 5,760 gallons per week. Therefore, the monthly water consumption is 23,040 gallons a month, which represents a large number that reflects a large utility bill each month. So, when the simulation runs in automatic mode, authors can determine how well the BUTLER's prediction of the user's behavior may help in reducing power consumption during different scenarios.

SYSTEM IMPLEMENTATION

Currently, the modernized technology, which advances quickly, leads people to assign most of their essential needs to smart devices. These devices are created with the anticipating capabilities trying to predict the users' future actions in a specific environment like a smart home. In Marufuzzaman and Reaz, (2013), the authors noted that" The more complex the operating system is, the more it is expected to do on behalf of its users." Therefore, the use of an artificial intelligence is an essential solution for such demand. This solution may contain an estimation of next stakeholder actions from the database, followed by extra stochastic calculations to predict the next user action using machine learning algorithms.

For that reason, the smart home system must be an adaptable and dynamic intelligent system, which means it needs to adapt to the stakeholder's lifestyle and to anticipate their next activities to optimize the direct interface between the user and the home appliances. Knowing the lifestyle of a certain user in a home requires precise knowledge about the history of appliance usage for each state in the entire environment. This leads to the use of an intelligent agent as shown back in Figure 1. Therefore, the following section will discuss more details about the basic requirements from that IA.

Intelligent Agent Requirements

As brought up in the previous paragraph, the IA represents the brain of the entire system and plays an important role in the design. Many functionalities have been delegated to this agent, such as performing reasoning process over predefined rules, in addition to the decision-making process to generate new rules according to context information and related output action for current status; therefore, several tasks have been distributed to several points as follows:

Communication With IA/Subsystems

Since the IA is noted as a central unit in the designed smart home system, then the IA should:

- Oversee both users' behaviors and external effects, such as weather behavior.
- The communication between the IA and subsystems must be implemented through a dedicated agent for each subsystem. Therefore, each subsystem has an attached agent that is entirely hidden from other agents of other subsystems.
- The IA must assign its effects to other components. In other words, the subsystem's agents must filter the row of data that comes from nodes based on the IA needs. For example, the IA needs to know the status when there is a change in the event (event change) of any node. So, IA does not need to know about the unchanged status of the oven in the kitchen, as an example.
- Be connected to all the subsystems via the agents using an individual standard communication protocol for each line of connection.
- Use Private/ Public Keys to ensure the anonymous data transfer between the IA and each agent.
- The IA should use a standard language protocol in all connections with each subsystem's agent (The same context messaging protocol).

Learning User's Behavior Patterns

The capabilities of self-learning and adaptation must be embedded in IA operation. These features are mandatory and highly promising for a tuned interaction between the stakeholders and the IA (Man-to-Machine) in one direction, and between the IA and the subsystem (Machine-to-Machine) technique in the other direction. The M2M technique presents an integral part of the Internet of Things and Smart Cities (Alhafidh, Khzaali, Mahmood, & Allen, 2016). Therefore, to keep updating the current rules or to create a new one relies on the up-to-date status. If the latest status was not found in the log file, then a new rule will be created by the IA and saved in the log file. If the latest status is found in the log file, then there is no need to modify any rule. Creating a rule is relying on stakeholder behavior or an external behavior. In both cases, it means that the IA must keep track of any perversion in the event (Event Tracking). The adaptation in rules is obligatory for the whole systems design to manufacture an intelligent system that can predict both the explicit and tacit knowledge from both short-term and long-term learning stages. Therefore, the IA needs to be able to expose the following demands:

- Manipulate stakeholder activities in specific log files for extended computations, such as generating new rules or modifying old ones.
- Equip context awareness capabilities.
- Generate decisions and prediction depending on past behaviors and new inputs/outputs.
- Provide ascending stakeholders' privileges for each status. For instance, some stakeholders have a higher granted right than others or some occurrences are essential than others changes.

User Interface

Supplying the IA with several interface techniques ensures the ability for that smart product to gain a wide acceptance by people for both Machine-to-Human/Human-to-Machine communication ends. Therefore, the interface may embed several techniques such as audio, visual, gesture, authentication, and configuration by the stakeholder himself. For instance, the IA will execute any voice command made by a defined stakeholder or by a touchable keypad that existed in IA 's display unit.

Database Storage

A huge row of data in such a system which is configured by many data generating devices needs to be saved in a secure place inside the system itself. Therefore, a storage memory that existed in IA has enough space to log long-term and short-term actions. In addition, the local data storage actually presents an important backup database that the IA can retrieve anytime when it is needed, in case of normal and abnormal operation states.

Prediction Process and Experimental Results

The prediction process will follow many essential steps as primary steps to reach this level of intelligence. In other words, collecting the status, analyzing, and aggregating the information are mandatory steps before using decision theory. The decision theory here is represented by using Machine Learning Algorithms (MLAs) to generate a hypothesis before predicting new commands depending on that hypothesis. Therefore, the authors' experimental design includes the use of Support Vector Machine (SVM) and Random Forest (RF) decision tree logarithms which are applied to a MavPad dataset (Youngblood & Cook, 2007).

The MavPad data was congregated by monitoring an individual living in an apartment, so it consists of observations of human activities in a real-world environment. A sum of 127 nodes that include sensors and actuators were collected in the environment for 49 days. A filtering preprocesses for a row of data was applied using MATLAB simulation code to retrieve the information by removing the noise. Consequently, the number of rows in this dataset after filtration is more than 3 million observations for five weeks. Each row has a status value for each node type which represents a predictor value or an attribute at a certain time. In other words, the dataset contains 86 columns that represent the status of the sensors, referred to as predictors or Input Vector X. Moreover, there were 41 columns which represent the actuator's values or the Output Vector Y. The authors factorize an input vector as $Xt = (x_1t, x_2t, \ldots, x_{86}t)$ for the sensors while actuators were represented by the status of each one at a certain time t, so they were denoted with $Yt \in \{1,\ldots, N\}$ for N possible states.

The authors decided to investigate the accuracy performance of two different MLAs approaches that have been used in two separate experiments. The first experiment deals with a living room zone, while the second experiment deals with a restroom zone. The training set consists of the first four weeks. At the same time, the test data was taken from the last week (fifth week) which followed the training set period to predict the delegated action day by day. For instance, to predict the action last Monday, the authors take a four-week period before that Monday as a training dataset and so on for other days last week. The following subsections discuss the two experiments in more detail.

Living Room Zone Experiment

In this experiment, the living room zone was the authors' focus of attention. Two different cases were applied to predict the next user action on ceiling light actuator: Case 1 deals with thirty-four input variables (predictors) which represent all the nodes inside the local (living room) zone itself. Case 2 deals with all nodes inside all zones in the apartment which are a sum of eighty-six nodes as input variables (predictors). Comparing the prediction accuracies results as shown in Figure 8 between case 1 and 2 for both SVM and RF, shows that both models give a rate of success for more than 90% to predict next user action on that actuator.

More precisely, SVM model gives accuracy about 93.6%, while RF gives 96.5% in Case1, but with a big gap in system performance (Prediction Time) as shown in Figure 9.

In Case 2, the SVM shows a wider range of accuracies scores than the RF model if readers do not consider Friday's result in RF approach in Figure 8. As a result, RF gives better accuracy result (90%) compared with (84%) using SVM.

Since these accuracies reflect a good rate of success to predict the next user action, readers should not forget that this type of experiment is not like other researchers' experiments. In other words, this experiment is implemented to work in a real-time environment that requires a fast response time during the prediction process; Therefore, a prediction process for more than (1 sec) response time does not represent a real-time process. Consequently, much attention neds to be given in such an application. This leads the researcher to find a good balance between accuracy and time consumption for each case. Thus, Figure 9

Figure 8. Daily accuracy values due to using SVM and RF MLAs in living room zone

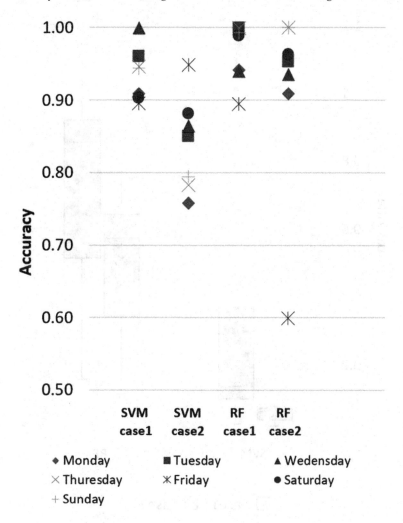

shows that RF consumes more than 10 times of prediction time (508 ms) needed compared with SVM which consumed only (50 ms) on average. Thus, the authors decided to choose SVM over RF in Case1.

In Case 2, since SVM gives a poor performance with 84% accuracy result, as mentioned in the previous paragraph, the authors choose the RF model with a better accuracy score despite the fact that RF needs more time to predict. In other words, a (0.74 ms) is still under the (1 sec) threshold level for real-time applications.

Restroom Zone Experiment

In this experiment, the authors decided to take the same strategy as in the previous experiment by studying two different cases to predict the action on the ceiling light actuator as an experiment observer. The number of input predictors in this zone is a sum of seven sensors which were used for the first case to

Figure 9. Daily execution time values due to using SVM and RF in living room zone

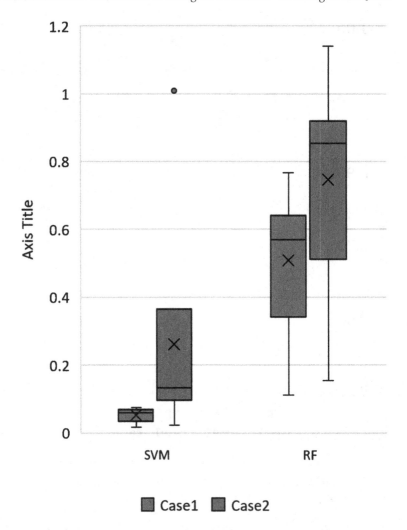

predict the action of that actuator. On the other hand, a sum of the same eighty-six sensors, which were used in living room experiment and distributed in all zones at the apartment, were used for prediction process in the second case. Figure 10 shows the daily accuracy values due to using SVM and RF MLAs for both cases. At the same time, Figure 11 presents the performance for each MLAs approach for both cases.

Comparing the current results with the previous results of the living room zone, the authors notice a very poor performance (32.4%) of accuracy score result for SVM-Case 2, but a better accuracy result (98.6%) in SVM-Case 1. The authors conclude that depending on a small number of predictors using SVM, as in Case 1, for both zones leads to the best results with the minimum time (response time) needed for prediction process.

A controversial result that leads to a different conclusion was figured out after looking carefully at RF results. A better accuracy (97.3%) was produced using a higher number of input predictors (86 predictors) but within lower speed performance (0.812 ms) to predict the next user action.

Figure 10. Daily accuracy values due to using SVM and RF MLAs in restroom zone

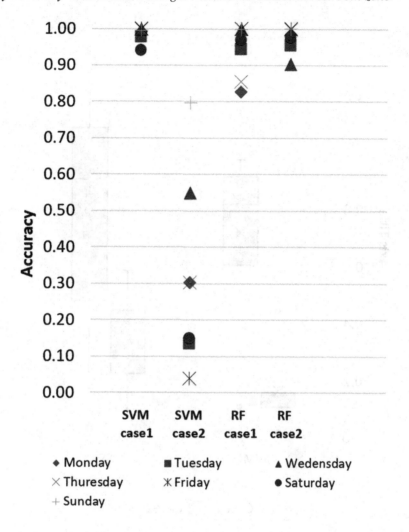

Finally, the target function that is produced using an approach of MLAs should ensure one consistent principle. This principle is basically "A maximum accuracy score with a minimum performance time." So, from the mentioned two experiments in previous paragraphs, SVM-Case 1 achieves this principle and surpasses the RF model.

FUTURE RESEARCH DIRECTIONS

The next phase of this research may utilize different kinds of feature selection approaches to select the important features (input predictors) that construct tuned MLA prediction models. Feature Selection technique is an important strategy to enhance not only the accuracy of MLA but also to improve model performance (Prediction Time). In other words, the authors try to maximize the accuracy and minimize the time needed to predict next user action simultaneously to get a better MLAs' performance. In addi-

Figure 11. Daily execution time values due to using SVM and RF in restroom zone

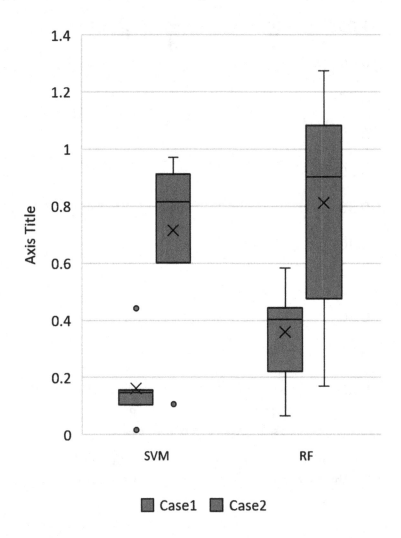

tion, prediction process may extend to include multi-user interface instead of a single user in the same environment, then determine the more effective machine learning approaches to use for prediction of the users' behaviors.

CONCLUSION

The increasing need to implement CPS for heterogeneous large scale complex applications, such as smart city, smart grid, and smart manufacturing, has resulted in more focus on CPS by both researchers and providers. However, the large scale of these systems creates several problems that need to be solved, such as portability, Time, predictability, and integration. This chapter presents a synergistic high-level design approach for a Cyber-Physical System (CPS) in a home environment that tries to overcome the several of these problems. In addition, this chapter proposed a novel modeling methodology of an intelligent home automation system-based CPS that the authors call "The BUTLER". The design of the BUTLER shows how each physical element from a tiny sensor to a smart agent device that occurs in the physical world can be interfaced to the cyber world and how they can be interconnected and configured to represent the first three levels of a system based on the 5C architecture. Finally, implementing the designed system to work autonomously using different approaches of MLAs is applicable and produces a high performance in prediction process using the SVM model for different experimental zones in the real-time environment.

REFERENCES

Alhafidh, B., Khzaali, H., Mahmood, A., & Allen, W. (2016). *Smart homes based on smart cities design patterns*. United Scholars Publishing.

Alhafidh, B. M., & Allen, W. (2016). Design and simulation of a smart home managed by an intelligent self-adaptive system. *International Journal of Engineering Research and Applications*, *6*(8), 64–90.

Bagheri, B., Yang, S., Kao, H. A., & Lee, J. (2015). Cyber-physical systems architecture for self-aware machines in industry 4.0 environment. *IFAC-PapersOnLine*, *48*(3), 1622–1627. doi:10.1016/j.ifacol.2015.06.318

Horvath, I., & Gerritsen, B. H. (2012). Cyber-physical systems: Concepts, technologies and implementation principles. In Proceedings of tmce (Vol. 1, pp. 7–11). Academic Press.

Hu, F. (2013). *Cyber-physical systems: Integrated computing and engineering design*. CRC Press. doi:10.1201/b15552

Kao, H.-A., Jin, W., Siegel, D., & Lee, J. (2015). A cyber physical interface for automation systems—methodology and examples. *Machines*, *3*(2), 93–106. doi:10.3390/machines3020093

Koçak, D. (2014). Thinking Embedded, Designing Cyber-Physical: Is it Possible? In *Applied Cyber-Physical Systems* (pp. 241–253). New York, NY: Springer. doi:10.1007/978-1-4614-7336-7_18

Lee, E. A. (2008, May). Cyber physical systems: Design challenges. In *Object oriented real-time distributed computing (isorc), 2008 11th ieee international symposium on* (pp. 363-369). IEEE.

Lee, J., Ardakani, H. D., Yang, S., & Bagheri, B. (2015). Industrial big data analytics and cyber-physical systems for future maintenance & service innovation. *Procedia CIRP*, *38*, 3–7. doi:10.1016/j.procir.2015.08.026

Lu, Y., & Cecil, J. (2016). An internet of things (IoT)-based collaborative framework for advanced manufacturing. *International Journal of Advanced Manufacturing Technology*, *84*(5-8), 1141–1152.

Marufuzzaman, M., & Reaz, M. B. I. (2013). Hardware simulation of pattern matching and reinforcement learning to predict the user next action of smart home device usage. *World Applied Sciences Journal*, *22*(9), 1302–1309.

Stone, D. L., & Jeffay, K. (1995). An empirical study of delay jitter management policies. *Multimedia Systems*, *2*(6), 267–279. doi:10.1007/BF01225244

Suh, S. C., Tanik, U. J., Carbone, J. N., & Eroglu, A. (2014). Applied cyber-physical systems. Springer. doi:10.1007/978-1-4614-7336-7

Sztipanovits, J., Koutsoukos, X., Karsai, G., Kottenstette, N., Antsaklis, P., Gupta, V., ... Wang, S. (2012). Toward a science of cyber–physical system integration. *Proceedings of the IEEE, 100*(1), 29–44. doi:10.1109/JPROC.2011.2161529

Youngblood, G. M., & Cook, D. J. (2007). Data mining for hierarchical model creation. *IEEE Transactions on Systems, Man and Cybernetics. Part C, Applications and Reviews, 37*(4), 561–572. doi:10.1109/TSMCC.2007.897341

Chapter 7
Autonomous Hexapod Robot With Artificial Vision and Remote Control by Myo–Electric Gestures:
The Innovative Implementation Tale of gAItano

Valentina Franzoni
La Sapienza University of Rome, Italy

ABSTRACT

The robot gAItano is an intelligent hexapod robot, able to move in an environment of unknown size and perform some autonomous actions. It uses the RoboRealm software in order to filter and recognize color blobs in its artificial vision stream, activate a script (VBScript in our case, or C or Python scripts) to compute decisions based on perception, and send the output to actuators using the PIP protocol. gAItano is thus a rational computerized agent: autonomous, or semi-autonomous when remote controlled; reactive; based on model (e.g., the line). gAItano moves in an environment which is partially observable, stochastic, semi-episodic, static, or semi-dynamic in case of human intervention, continuous both on perceptions and actions, multi-agent, because of human intervention that can have collaborative nature (e.g., when the human moves a block or the robot to increase his performance), or competitive (e.g., when the human moves a block or the robot to inhibit his performance).

DOI: 10.4018/978-1-5225-5510-0.ch007

INTRODUCTION

In this project, an autonomous robot had been developed and tested in an unknown human-centred environment. The robot is part of the system both for complex autonomous tasks, independently managed by the robot directly (e.g., keeping the order of a place, following people at a certain distance), both for interactive tasks managed by the human controlling the robot via a mobile device or Myo-electric gestures (Oskoei & Hu, 2008) (e.g., moving the robot for unpredicted tasks).

Such a system must include considerations on heterogeneous problems, such as the acceptance of the robot appearance by the humans in the work environment. The UX (usability and accessibility) (Franzoni & Gervasi, 2009; Franzoni, Gervasi, Tasso, & Pallottelli, 2008) of the robot controlling system, the performance of the autonomous vision feature and objects recognition in an unknown environment, the optimal management of physical degrees of freedom of the motion parts, and the power saving optimization should be taken into account.

In this chapter, the technical background of the gAItano project is exposed, providing all the details of the technical implementation both hardware and software. For the hardware, particular attention will be dedicated to the needed parts both for the robot and for the features (e.g. camera control, remote control), and to the power. Regarding the software, particular attention will be dedicated to autonomous vision (Bonin-Font, Ortiz, & Oliver, 2008) development, including the artificial vision system, colour and camera management, coloured-object recognition, object relocation, motion control, providing pros and cons considerations on the proposed solution.

The gAItano robot is a simple real-time implementation of basic concepts for visual recognition of coloured objects. The algorithm is a baseline for understanding how a visual recognition algorithm may look like, and has a teaching and simplifying objective, more than a performance one: besides it is performing well on appropriate light, no systematic experimentation and performance evaluation has been done on the visual recognition. In the visual recognition direction, state of the art algorithm use deep learning to recognise not only the segmented object, but the object semantics. In such an approach, it is possible to use a well-trained model to exploit the benefits of having a high number of training images. More than this, the gAItano project can be seen as a complete teaching analysis by the Artificial Intelligence point of view of the problem of the robot vision and movement, taking into account all the steps of a robotics project in a real interactive environment.

HEXAPOD TECHNICAL SPECIFICATIONS

The robot built in this project, named "gAItano" (where *AI* stands for *Artificial Intelligence*, and *Gaetano* is the Italian name that the developers chose for the robot) is a hexapod robot, created using the kit MSR-H01 Mycromagic Systems. The MSR-H01 is an aluminium-body six-legged robot structure with excellent design, available until 2012 only, in a basic kit to which additional components had been added, e.g. micro-controller, servomotors, batteries, sensors, brain. This model has some appreciable features for Robotics and Artificial Intelligence goals: it is as big as a pet, it is light but robust, it includes an excellent basic micro-controller board, well programmed to allow smooth movements for all the 6 legs and 18 grades of freedom. It supports wireless communication and Bluetooth for remote control or data exchange.

Having a good appearance and natural movements allows the robot to be accepted in human environments (Fong, Nourbakhsh, & Dautenhahn, 2003), where sensible people usually don't accept robots, especially if they look like insects or crabs. In this project, the robot had been personalised on an experimental basis, to be defined "cool and cute" like a pet.

A variety of low-cost programmable robot has also been tested for the appearance goal, and preliminary results showed that the MSR-H01 could better reach the goal compared to other "cool and scary" models, such as the excellent variety of the Lynxmotion models, which on the other hand has better support and documentation. While documentation has fundamental importance in planning and developing on existing models, in this project, the acceptation of the robot had been of primary importance, having to deal with the relationship between humans and the robot, where the robot had to move in the environment without making people feel uncomfortable. The robot had to have a "cool" look and feel, to be not only noted but also accepted and used by the humans, and a "cute" look and feel to avoid scaring the most sensible people passing by the environment.

Regarding power, the MSR-H01 can be alimented by a standard battery, starting from 1600 mAh per 6.0 V. Higher amperage facilitate the smoothness of servomotors. In this project, a 5-cell battery had been used, with 4600 mAh, which can stand up to 15 minutes of movement for 12 hours of charge, usable for demos. For an emergency charge, four standard 1.2 V. Ni-MH batteries with 2500 mAh are sufficient for few minutes. For the developing phase, the battery has been replaced with a power supply (6.0 V, 3000 mAh), more suitable for days of usage, where the rechargeable battery should be charged many times inducing a short life-span. Since the running phase can induce lags or crashes solvable with a restart, a switch is recommended to be added to the power supply cable.

gAItano, THE INTELLIGENT HEXAPOD ROBOT

The robot *gAItano* is an intelligent hexapod robot (Brooks, 1991), able to move in an environment of unknown size, and perform some autonomous actions. It uses the RoboRealm software to filter and recognise colour blobs in its artificial vision stream, activate a script (VBScript in our case, or C or Python scripts) to compute decisions based on perception, and send the output to actuators using the PIP protocol. gAItano is thus a *rational computerised agent*:

- Autonomous, or semi-autonomous when remote controlled through Android or the Myo armband;
- Reactive, since he chooses actions basing on perception;
- Based on the model, because keeps the state of some elements, e.g. the line.

gAItano moves in an *environment* which is:

- Partially observable, with the unique sensor -the webcam- providing a partial view;
- Stochastic, because in the real physical environment unexpected events can happen e.g., gAItano may accidentally hit a block while pushing another block, a human agent may move the blocks randomly during the patrol execution;
- Semi-episodic, since the agent acts on perception and not on previous ones, except for few sequential action such as coming back to the patrol side after pushing a block over the line;
- Static, or semi-dynamic in case of human intervention;

- Continuous both on *perceptions* and *actions*;
- Multi-agent, because of human intervention that can have collaborative nature (e.g. when the human moves a block or the robot to increase his performance) or competitive (e.g. when the human moves a block or the robot to inhibit his performance)

The World of gAItano

The robot gAItano is a semi-autonomous robot, able to move in an environment of unknown size, which includes a two-tone yellow/blue line, and red or green blocks (e.g. cubes, spheres, overturned glasses or general single-colour objects). If the line is not present in his view, gAItano can be remotely controlled with a mobile device or with arm/hand gestures via a wearable EMG wrist controller, and be lead to the line, which he sees through a camera mounted on his head/back and recognise through an artificial vision algorithm.

The robot can identify the line and understand where he and the blocks are concerning the line. gAItano's goal is to arrange the blocks in the environment so that the red blocks are located on the opposite side of the line concerning the side in which he stays: if any block lies on his same side, gAItano will push them on the opposite side.

At the ends of the line, two green blocks can be located. In the case, gAItano will identify them as limits of the area to be controlled: the robot will patrol the area with a crab walking between the green blocks, parallel to the line, reversing his direction any time he recognises the green block. Once scanned across the board, i.e. the third time he sees the green block, gAItano pauses some seconds before restarting to patrol the area. If anything changes in the environment during the walk, gAItano can adapt his decisions in real time.

The formal definition of the world of gAItano is therefore given in the Goal, as follows. The world of gAItano is summarised in Figure 1.

Goal: Given a real world (in a desirably limited, but potentially infinite area) where there is a two-color line (say blue and yellow), some colored blocks of two different colors (say red and green), patrol one side of the area with respect to the line, keeping it free from blocks, thus pushing eventual blocks in the opposite side of the area.

Artificial Vision of gAItano

In this subsection, the central part of the script for the artificial vision of gAItano the hexapod robot is described. The main script is a Visual Basic Script (from now on VBScript or VBS) program elaborating the input from the sensor (i.e. camera vision), later computed to exploit the robot behaviour.

Functions in the modules, referring to the application programming interface of the image processing of the software platform RoboRealm, will go in an execution pipeline and will be repeated in a loop to manage real-time modifications of the world. The same functions can be implemented manually using the OpenCV library. RoboRealm features are also based on OpenCV.

At any time, it is possible to see the preview of the image by the RoboRealm window and pause the execution of the pipeline disabling the *Run* button.

In the following paragraphs, the step-by-step construction of the pipeline modules is explained for the artificial vision of the robot. Uppercase expressions relate to RoboRealm library modules.

Figure 1. The world of gAItano. gAItano will patrol the double-colour line in the vertical direction until it finds an object in the "wrong" side of the line. When the robot identifies an object in the wrong position, it pushes it to the other side of the lines executing a push action, then the robot checks again the situation, until convergence to the positioning goal.

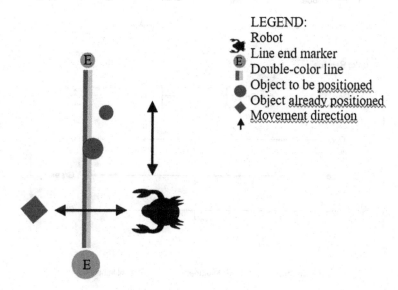

Colour Balance: Color Balance (see Figure 2) is the module for the initial balance of the colour. Setting a proper value for the primary colours in the *RGB model* (i.e. Red, Green and Blue), it is possible to adapt the vision to different lights and moments of the day. The RGB model, in fact, it is not resistant to such variations (Endres, Hess, Engelhard, & ..., 2012), and settings are needed for lighting conditions e.g. inside a room, outside, or depending on the webcam. This module is therefore instrumental to convenient on-the-go settings and avoids having to change settings in the code directly or in the blob recognition module (described later).

Camera Input: The *Set Image Marker* module (see Figure 3 (a) to create a placeholder using a personalised name, and to recall it with the defined name in a different position in the pipeline).

To create an image marker means, therefore, to reset the image to the state in which it was in the moment when the marker was created, thus ignoring subsequent steps.

In Figure 3 (b) it is shown how to directly recall the input from the webcam (or another video source). This feature is particularly useful for our pipeline to be dynamic, instead of being bonded to its serialisation.

Colour Recognition: The *Set an RGB Filter* (see Figure 4) is used for colour recognition. Other colour schemes can be used similarly.

The proposed technique is to input the video stream and then filter out colours that are not required, before recognising the desired colour. This technique allows refining the colour recognition phase on a source devoid of much of the noise, to manage shades and reflections better.

Filtering out undesired colours, in fact, prevents the creation of blobs containing noise. Each time, therefore, that it is needed to capture an RGB colour, we will capture the other two before; e.g. when it is needed to capture yellow, we firstly capture and filter out cyan and magenta.

Figure 2. Color Balance setting window

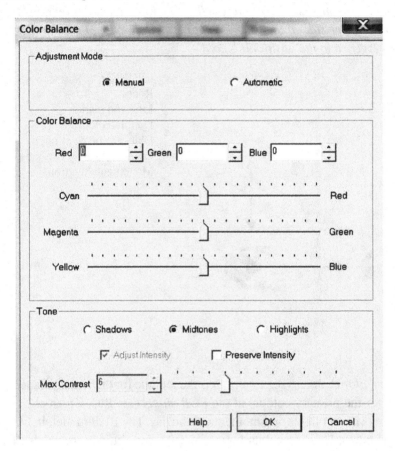

Figure 3. Set image marker setting window. (a) setting name; (b) setting the input source.

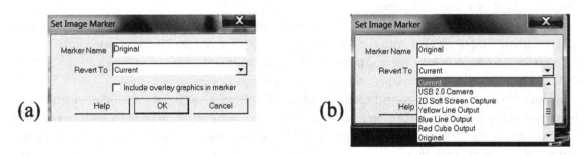

It is useful to filter out also grey, for example, if there are undesired patterns on the surface where the robot moves, or in the background. A bit of knowledge of the RGB model and colour theory is needed to understand which colours to filter out.

Aiming at capturing red colour, we will filter out green, blue and grey. It is possible to do it in a single module, but if instead the threshold is set separately (i.e. setting the intensity, hue and hysteresis), it is easier to filter all the different areas that can be visible in a complex real world. In the *Results* sector visibility modes are shown: we choose *Black Mask* to visualise the background instead of the pixels that are being filtered out, i.e. a black mask on the filtered pixels.

In Figure 4 the necessary selections for a green filter are shown: other colours will have a similar setting, where threshold values for intensity, hue and hysteresis are not general, but should be set based on the situation.

Colour Selection: With another *RGB Filter* module the primary colour to be recognised is finally selected (e.g. red). Besides the threshold values, the value that must be set up is the selection on Results: in this case, in fact, the *Color Mask* can be chosen, to colour in the selected colour the captured pixels, to create a colour blob. This procedure also needs to be repeated for each colour of interest for visual recognition.

Finally, the result will be like the one shown in Figure 5. It is worth noting that some shades are still present in the image, and some noise (see the black dots inside the red blob): a brighter image is needed, which leads us to the next filtering step.

Mean Filter and Segmentation: To get rid of the remained noise and shades, three more filters can be applied, named *Threshold*, *Mean Filter* and *Segment Colors*: such functions will result in a smooth blob, which filters out the noise.

Figure 4. Green filter settings

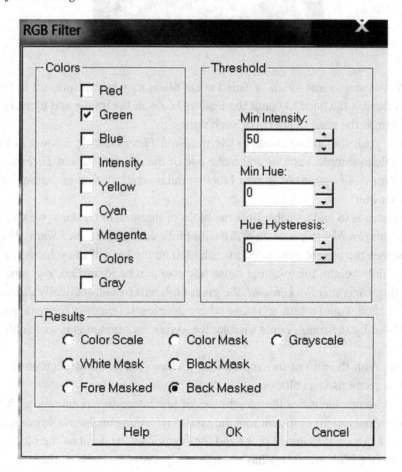

Figure 5. Resulting image after the red blob filter

Blob Filter: At this step, some small or faded noise blobs may be still present in the image. In the proposed process, there is the need to count the leading blobs in the image and identify their main features. Therefore there is the need to get rid of such noise.

To reach such a goal, the author chose to use the *Blob Filter* module, shown in Figure 6. In this module, it is possible to sample a colour and make use of the number (*Count Threshold* option) or dimension (*Weight Threshold* option) of similar blobs in the image, or of other parameters e.g. related to shape, colour, dimension.

The goal of this step is to make visible only the blobs of interest. In *Options*, we will check the voice *Create BLOBS array variable*, to create an array with blobs coordinates, *and Show Weights* if it is useful to see on the screen the weight associated to each blob on the base of the selected threshold options.

Looking at the blob weight, the eventual noise left over can be identified, e.g. small contiguous or dark blobs. Selecting *Largest is Background*, the giant blob will be automatically discarded. It is worth noting that this selection would return an image where the closest object in the real space, i.e. the closest block to be moved by the robot, is not visible; the author recommends is to double-check that this option is not on.

Block Location: With the aim of moving blocks, gAItano needs knowledge on the position of the colour blobs that he recognised as blocks.

The proposed technique identifies the coordinates of few interesting points for each blob and makes decisions considering only such points, without the need of reasoning on the whole image. In this solution, the author chose to focus on the *central* point and the *bottom lowest* point of the blob. The coordinates of the lowest point of the blob in an array have been already stocked, checking the option *Create BLOBS array variable* (see the previous paragraph about blob filtering).

Figure 6. The blob filter setting window

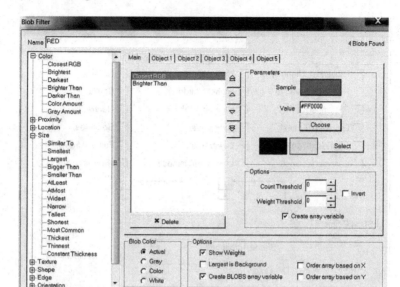

At this step, the *lowest central* point will be added, using the *Point Location* module shown in Figure 7, checking the *Lowest(Middle)* value in the *Location* section. In the *Show Points* section, it is possible to choose how to visualise the point on the graphic human interface (e.g., cross shape).

Position Coordinates: A separate *Set Variable* module is needed for each point to be memorised (see the previous paragraph about Block Location). In this way, the coordinates can be later recalled and computed in the VBScript.

It is worth noting in the figure how it is possible to recover the coordinates of the closest block, which will be first in the CLOSEST_RGB array.

Furthermore, using blocks of equal dimension in the real world, it is possible to tinker on position and distance playing on the dimension of the visible content (i.e. the bigger, the closer).

Variable Visualisation: Adding a *Watch_Variables* module, it is possible to visualise in a click the real-time values in the variables that have been created by us (or by the RoboRealm software) in the program. The image that we can expect is visible in Figure 8: something similar to Figure 5, with a refined blob and a label for the variable value. A '+' symbol for each blob (i.e. colour) will be visible on the chosen Point Location.

Recall Image Marker: When filtering more than one colour is needed, at the end of the sequence the *Set Image Marker* module can be used, as for the initial camera input (see the Camera input paragraph). With this module, it is possible to recall the original image and proceed to filter the next colour.

The sequence from *Set Image Marker* to *Variables Visualization* will be therefore repeated for each colour, i.e. four times for the primary colours in the world of gAItano (red, green, blue, yellow), plus additional optional repetitions for complementary colours, as explained in the Color Recognition paragraph.

Figure 7. The point location settings window

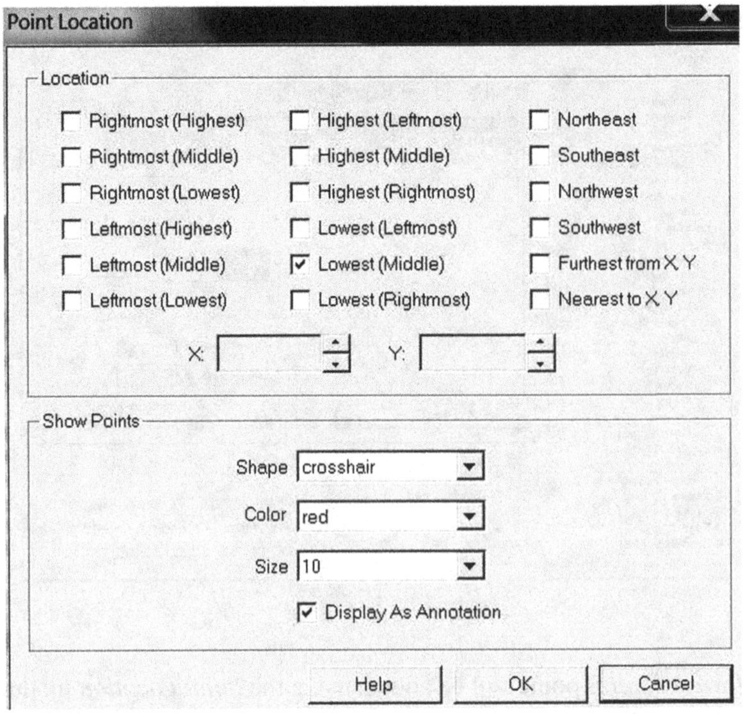

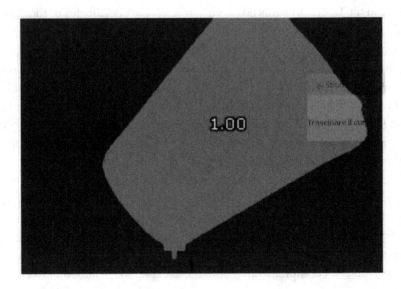

Figure 8. Resulting image after the watch variable module setting. The figure is similar to the one in Figure 5, but with clean edges and visibly identified variables for the blob (number) and the point location (cross symbol, of the same colour of the blob).

Motion With Real-Time Reactions

In this subsection, the central part of the script for the decisions and actions (i.e. motion) of gAItano the hexapod robot is described.

The main script is the same Visual Basic Script that also manages the vision, elaborating the input from the camera and returning the output to the actuators (i.e. legs and head motors) to exploit the robot behaviour. The behaviour algorithm of gAItano is resumed in the following paragraphs and is constituted by the RoboRealm script, divided in modules, that will go in an *execution pipeline*, and repeated in a *loop* to manage real-time modifications of the world. At any time, it is possible to see the preview of the image by the RoboRealm window and pause the execution of the pipeline disabling the Run button.

A RoboRealm module imports the external VBScript to the pipeline, for the artificial intelligence.

In the following paragraphs, the step-by-step construction of the pipeline modules is explained for the VBS and motion stream. It is essential for the programmer to notice again that, being a loop, it will be automatically executed from the top, if not stated, each time it finishes. Therefore, the adequate initialisation is mandatory.

The goal of the loop is to check the environment state continuously and to react in *real-time*, with adaptive behaviour.

Set Power Supply Variables: The first module in the pipeline (see Figure 9) is to *Set Variable*, where it is possible to set the variables referring to the robot power supply, which will be used later in the VBS. *POWER ON, POWER OFF* enable the robot to turn on and off the power supply, i.e. switch on and off the robot, while *WALK ENABLE* (which can be set to 0 or 1) enables the robot's capability to move, where 1 means that it can move, and 0 means standby.

The existence of such variables let stop the robot when needed without interrupting the execution flow of the pipeline VBS, for instance, to check the vision parameters in the RoboRealm graphic interface, thus being a security system.

The module can be positioned in any part of the pipeline, in this case, it is in the first part, for convenience, to have it at hand, since it is frequently used in the initial setting phase.

Figure 9. Setting window for power variables

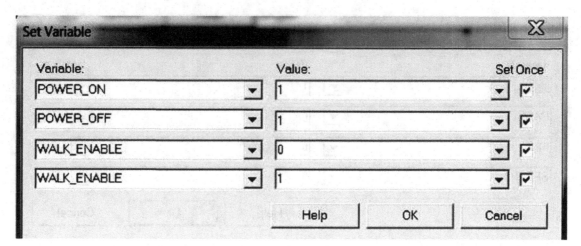

Set Motion Variables: The second module is a Set Variable, to initialise variables for the VBS and ensure that they will be reset every time the pipeline restarts: it is, therefore, essential that the module is positioned at the beginning of the program.

In RoboRealm it is possible to set at most 4 variables with this module, which means that an additional module will be necessary each time that more than four variables need to be instantiated. There is no limit on the number of Set Variable modules that can be used. In our case, we will use two modules for five variables, shown in Figure 10, i.e. direction (DIR), step (PASSO), end (FINE), pushed (SPINTO). Another variable can be set for the side of the line (LATO): in each window, four variables can be set at a time. Whenever we need to enable these variables, it will suffice to check the *Set Once* box on the right side in the figure.

In the program code, an additional description of each variable is provided in the comments.

VBS Program Module: At this step, all the variables of interested have been recovered and stored: the VBScript module can be inserted by the VBScript *Program module*, to compute the input and return in output the robot behaviour. As visible in Figure 11, It is now possible to select the VBS, edit the script and run it directly by the *Reload and Run* button, visualising in the *Messages* section of the module, as usability compliance, the messages that we printed in the execution.

Using the *Reload and Run* button will restart the pipeline. Handling robots sometimes can happen that the robot has an unexpected behaviour (e.g. walks when it should stand, or stop before expected), because of the buffer in the robot brain or controller board. In such cases, the *Reload and Run* button are not sufficient, but it is suggested to reset and restart the program.

Motion Output: Using the *Serial* module in RoboRealm, which is the final module but can be located in any point of the pipeline by the programmer, gAItano can get from the VBS the motion decisions to be sent to actuators by the artificial vision, i.e. reacting in real-time to the world.

If the COM port has been correctly set, it will be possible to see in the console the PIP text for motion commands. When connected, the console will show green text. On the right side of Figure 11, in the *Modified Variables* sub-window, it is visible the format and rate of the sequence for PIP commands, and a test function is available to test the communication before running the script.

Figure 10. Setting variables for the movement direction and step. Another variable can be created on the side of the line.

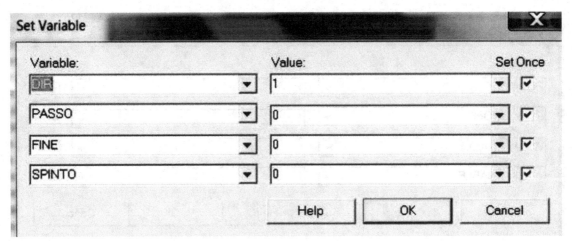

Figure 11. Setting window for the input

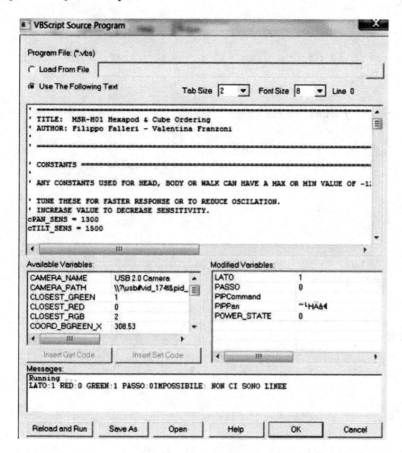

The motion output will result in walk, crab, push actions.

SOLUTIONS AND ALGORITHM

At this step, all the required settings and initialisation is done, and the algorithm for the real-time visual recognition can be discussed.

The phases of the algorithm can be summarised in five non-serial phases:

1. Identify the line and check the side.
2. Identify the object and its side.
3. Patrol the line until the end
4. Move the object (iteratively) if required, then check again.
5. Set steps for actions.

1. Side Check

```
' SIDE CHECK
' check if the robot is on the blue(=1) or yellow (=2) side of the line
lato = 0

if gLowestYellowY < gLowestBlueY then
lato=2
elseif gLowestYellowY > gLowestBlueY then
        lato=1
else
        lato=0
end if


write "SIDE:" & lato
SetVariable "SIDE", lato
```

2. Block Check

```
'---BLOCK CHECK---
'---
'***RED BLOB***

' check how many red blobs (num_red) are in view
' counting the elements of the array array gClosestRed
 num_red = 0
 for i = 0 to Ubound(gClosestRed)
     if gClosestRed(i) > 0.80 then
            num_red = num_red + 1
         end if
 next
write " RED:" & num_red

' if there are red blobs, get the coords of every red blob and put it here
if num_red <> 0 then
                gBlobRedX = getvariable("COORD_BRED_X")
                gBlobRedY = getvariable("COORD_BRED_Y")
end        if

'***END red blobs***
```

3. Setting the End and Patrol the Line

```
'---SETTING THE END

'Set the stop variable "FINE"
fine = GetVariable("FINE") ' initially 0

' STEP
spinto = GetVariable("SPINTO") ' this variable will get 1 when a block has
just been pushed
passo = GetVariable("PASSO") ' the variable "PASSO" corresponds to a movement
direzione = GetVariable("DIR") ' direction: 2 is left, 1 is right, while scan-
ning the line
fine = GetVariable("FINE")

if (fine < 3) then ' if it didn't still finish to scan the line
        if passo = 0 then ' step 0=> check for the line in the view
                write " PASSO:" & passo
                if spinto=1 then ' if a block was just pushed, then go back-
ward
                        write "Spinto=1"
                        period = 32000
                        SetVariable "PASSO", 8 ' backward
                        SetTimedVariable "PASSO", 0, period
                        write "BACKWARD"
                        SetVariable "SPINTO", 0
                end if
```

4. Push the Object If Needed

```
'---PUSH THE OBJECT

                if (gLowestBlueY <> 0) then ' The line is in view
                                if spinto=0 then ' if it did NOT just push a
block

                                        ' checks if finished
                                        if fine < 2 then
                                                write " STOP:" & fine
if num_green <> 0 then 'if a green
 block is in view

                                                        if (gBlobGreenX >
```

```
midx) then
SetVariable "DIR", 2 'CRAB
left
                                                        SetVariable
"FINE", 1

elseif          (gBlobGreenX <= midx) then
SetVariable "DIR", 1  'CRAB right
                                                        SetVariable
"FINE", 2
                                              end if
                                  end if
                        elseif fine=2 then
                              if (gBlobGreenX > midx) then
                                    SetVariable "FINE",
3
                                  end if
                        end if

if (num_red <> 0) then ' check if there are red blocks in the robot's side of
the line

' if the robot has a red block centered in the view, then PUSH ("SPINGI")
                              if (gLowestRedY < gLowest-
BlueY) then
                                          azione
gBlobRedX,midx
                              else
                                    if direzione = 2 the
n
' all the red blocks in view are ordered (in the right side of the line)
                                                period = 100
                                                SetVariable
"PASSO", 6 'crab left
SetTimedVariable "PASSO", 0, period

                                          write "CRAB
LEFT TO SCAN"
                                    elseif direzione = 1
then
                                                period = 100
                                                SetVariable
```

```
"PASSO", 5 'crab right
SetTimedVariable "PASSO", 0, period

                                                        write "CRAB
RIGHT TO SCAN"

                                              end if
                                end if

else ' the line is in view, but there are no blocks in view
                                write "NO RED BLOB"
                                if direzione = 2 then
' crab right or left, in
the                                                         direc-
tion of the line

                                        period = 100
                                        SetVariable "PASSO",
6 'crab left

"PASSO", 0, period

                                        write "CRAB LEFT TO
SCAN"

                                elseif direzione = 1 then
                                        period = 100
                                        SetVariable "PASSO",
5 'crab right

"PASSO", 0, period

                                        SetTimedVariable

                                        write "CRAB RIGHT TO
SCAN"

                                end if
                        end if

                end if

        else ' No lines in view
                write "IMPOSSIBLE TO PROCEED: I DON'T SEE LINES"
        end if

else ' if the step ("PASSO") is not 0, CHECK FOR THE ACTION TO DO AND DO IT
```

5. Actions

```
case 5 '*** CRAB RIGHT ***
        gWalk=0
        gCrab=120
        gTurn=0
        muovi gCrab,gWalk,gTurn,"CrabRight"
case 6 '*** CRAB LEFT ***
        gWalk=0
        gCrab=-120
        gTurn=0
        muovi gCrab,gWalk,gTurn,"CrabLeft"
case 7 '*** FORWARD ***
        gWalk=120
        gTurn=0
        gCrab=0
        muovi gCrab,gWalk,gTurn,"Push"
case 8 '*** BACKWARD ***
        gWalk=-120
        gTurn=0
        gCrab=0
        muovi gCrab,gWalk,gTurn,"Backward"
case 11 '*** NO OPERATION ***
        gWalk=0
        gTurn=0
        gCrab=0
        muovi gCrab,gWalk,gTurn,"STOP"
end select
```

CONCLUSION AND FUTURE RESEARCH DIRECTIONS

The gAItano project can be seen as a complete teaching analysis by the Artificial Intelligence point of view of the problem of the robot vision and movement, taking into account all the steps of a robotics project in a real interactive environment. The aim is not fine image recognition, but simple implementation of the whole process of applying visual recognition capabilities to a low-budget robot, accessible to everybody.

The innovative parts of the gAItano project include the visual recognition approach without any training and machine learning, the interaction between machine and humans, the management of movements in a GUI-based robotics platform, the real-world-centred programming for adaptive robot behaviour. The motion control using mobile platforms (i.e. Android) or myoelectric capabilities.

Any state-of-the-art algorithm on these points can enhance gAItano, given the power-saving and no-memory features.

Any new remote control interactive system can be included in the project, given the open-source, PIP-commands-based serial capabilities.

ACKNOWLEDGMENT

The author implemented such a complex system in the gAItano robot, in three different steps over a range of five academic years, at the Knowledge and Intelligent Technology Lab of University of Perugia, Italy, in the *Department of Mathematics and Computer Science*, and at the Sapienza University of Rome, *Department of Computer, Control and Management Engineering*. The project has been totally supported by the author and developed providing the robot to the laboratories for teaching and showcase purposes.

In a first step, in 2011, the gAItano robot has been built and programmed for autonomous vision by the author Valentina Franzoni together with Dr. Filippo Falleri, at the time MSc student in Computer Science at University of Perugia. In the second step, in 2015, the remote controller of gAItano had been developed with the author's professorial advice and supervision by Dr. Federico Corò and Dr. Matteo Capparucci, at the time MSc students in Computer Science, to give gAItano the features to be controlled by a mobile system (i.e. Android app) via Bluetooth. In the third and ultimate step, the author developed the free-hand Myo-electric remote control using a Myo controller (also connected via Bluetooth) in substitution of the mobile device, while in the doctoral school of Engineering in Computer Science at Sapienza University. The author acknowledges fellow researchers and the laboratories providing space and security to realise the project. A special thank has to go to Prof. Alfredo Milani, professor of Artificial Intelligence, and to Prof. Gianluca Vinti, Head of the Department of Mathematics and Computer Science, who supported the first two built of gAItano providing the lab rooms, and showcasing gAItano in several local and international events and activities on Computer Science and Artificial Intelligence in the years 2011-2015, e.g. work stand di mobile robotics Guarda che RobApp! Todi Appy Days Festival 2013 to 2015, Exhibit di Mobile Robotics Workshop for the Senato President Lanzillotta, University Orientation days 2011-2014, presentation of the new MSc course on Intelligent and Mobile Computing.

REFERENCES

Bonin-Font, F., Ortiz, A., & Oliver, G. (2008). Visual Navigation for Mobile Robots: A Survey. *Journal of Intelligent & Robotic Systems, 53*(3), 263–296. doi:10.100710846-008-9235-4

Brooks, R. A. (1991). Intelligence without representation. *Artificial Intelligence, 47*(1–3), 139–159. doi:10.1016/0004-3702(91)90053-M

Endres, F., Hess, J., & Engelhard, N. (2012). An evaluation of the RGB-D SLAM system. *Icra, 3*(c), 1691–1696. doi:10.1109/ICRA.2012.6225199

Fong, T., Nourbakhsh, I., & Dautenhahn, K. (2003). A survey of socially interactive robots. In Robotics and Autonomous Systems (Vol. 42, pp. 143–166). Academic Press. doi:10.1016/S0921-8890(02)00372-X

Franzoni, V., & Gervasi, O. (2009). Guidelines for web usability and accessibility on the Nintendo Wii. Lecture Notes in Computer Science, 5730. doi:10.1007/978-3-642-10649-1_2

Franzoni, V., Gervasi, O., Tasso, S., & Pallottelli, S. (2008). Web usability on the Nintendo Wii platform. Lecture Notes in Computer Science, 5073. doi:10.1007/978-3-540-69848-7_10

Oskoei, M., & Hu, H. H. H. (2008). Support Vector Machine-Based Classification Scheme for Myoelectric Control Applied to Upper Limb. *IEEE Transactions on Biomedical Engineering*, *55*(8), 1956–1965. doi:10.1109/TBME.2008.919734 PMID:18632358

Chapter 8
The NovaGenesis Smart Cities Model

Antonio Marcos Alberti
Inatel, Brazil

ABSTRACT

Smart cities encompass a complex, diverse, and rich ecosystem with the potential to address humanity's biggest challenges. To fully support society demands, many emerging technologies should be gracefully integrated. Current architectures and platforms frequently address specific topics, requiring intricate coordination of partial solutions. In this context, interoperability of technological solutions is mandatory. Examples include interoperability of IETF standards (e.g., 6LowPAN, RPL, CoAP to other IEEE standards, such as 802.15.4, and Bluetooth). Designs based on these protocols are being largely employed worldwide. However, they have some limitations that deserve our attention. Recent examples, such as ramsomware and DDoS attacks, are concerning many people on the suitability of our current stacks. NovaGenesis (NG) is an alternative architecture for TCP/IP that has been already proofed. In this chapter, the NG model for smart cities is explored, presenting its benefits. Recent results in NG are summarized and discussed on the proposed scope.

INTRODUCTION

Smart cities are a hot topic nowadays, with thousands of examples worldwide. They have the potential to successfully address the most important problems of our time, such as: sustainability of natural resources, energy fingerprint, global warming, public safety, transportation, pollution, etc. Large sensor networks can bring relevant information on water spend and leakage, electricity consumption, air quality, traffic condition, lighting effectiveness, among many other use cases. However, smart cities require an unprecedented level of technology integration, orchestration and synergy.

Smart city architectures encompass several layers, from physical devices up to information objects. The visible portion of a smart city includes: sensing devices (temperature, humidity, etc.), actuation devices (switches, engines, valves, etc.), Internet of things (IoT) gateways, cables, fibers, antennas, switches, routers, buildings, data centers, computers, racks, etc. Cloud or fog (edge) computing is required to support

DOI: 10.4018/978-1-5225-5510-0.ch008

IoT services and applications. A common approach is to employ service-oriented architecture (SOA) to orchestrate (coordinate) software-as-a-service (SaaS). Network function virtualization (NFV) is also required to improve flexibility, emulating hardware as services in the data center (Alberti et al., 2017c). Network programmability is another ingredient, since the quantity of networks and systems involved is very large. Scalability and elasticity of smart city services is also a pre-requisite. Scalability means to keep solution safety as scales increase, while elasticity means to increase or decrease services instances as the load changes. All these requirements and technologies should be gracefully integrated to provide future-proof solutions. A big engineering challenge!

Internet scale and role have changed considerably from its original purposes in the 1970's. Current Internet is growing in scales since it was opened to the general public, giving rise for plenty of applications. Many patch-work solutions were applied to extend its scope, e.g. IPSec, mobile IP (MIP) and IPv6, as well as the most recent ones focused on connecting constrained devices to the Internet, such as constrained application protocol (CoAP), IPv6 over low power wireless personal area network (6Low-PAN) and routing protocol for low power and lossy networks (RPL). These evolutionary extensions aim at fulfilling the IoT and smart cities vision, which can be defined as the efforts to bring billions of ordinary things to the Internet. In this context, the current Internet technologies will be inadequate to fully support these multifaceted exponential growths on the number of devices, mobility, interactivity, content, security and privacy issues.

The newspapers are full of examples were IoT solutions fail to deliver what consumers are expecting. Examples of malfunctioning and security threats are given in a daily basis. However, many smart cities projects assume current technologies are completely ready for such challenges. In the mean time, those that work in the information and communications technology (ICT) department certainly know the limitations of the current technologies. In this context, several initiatives have emerged worldwide to reshape the Internet under the banner of future Internet (FI) research (Alberti, 2013). NovaGenesis (NG) is one of them. NG is a "clean slate" FI architecture that has been developed since 2008. It considers IoT, virtualization, programmable networks, self-organization, SOA, cloud computing and many other ingredients since the beginning of its design (Alberti et al., 2017a).

In this chapter, NovaGenesis potential as a smart city architecture is explored. It starts with an overview of NovaGenesis proposal, its main concepts and current implementation. Then, a first glance discussion on a NovaGenesis smart city is provided. The advantages NovaGenesis offer for this aim are presented and illustrated. The chapter continues with a discussion on recent results for a future Internet of things (FIoT) with NovaGenesis (Alberti et al., 2017c). A concrete and scientifically proofed scenario is explored. Finally, some final remarks are given.

NovaGenesis

NovaGenesis[1] is a "clean slate" architecture aimed at integrating: packet networking, cloud computing, Internet of things, Internet of people, service-oriented architectures and self-organizing technologies. NovaGenesis means new beginning. The motto question of the project is: what if there is no Internet now? How could it be designed and deployed? This question has been motivating many research projects under the banner of "Future Internet" (FI) research (Alberti, 2013). In this context, NovaGenesis proposes a novel information architecture aimed at offering an alternative to current ones, e.g. TCP/IP,

ZigBee, etc. Figure 1 illustrates NovaGenesis (NG) scope. Its design started in 2008 and a first architecture design was envisioned in 2011.

NovaGenesis is a hybrid name-centric, service-centric, information-centric, host-centric, software-defined, self-organizing, mobile-friendly architecture. It can be seen as a future Internet architecture (FIA). Its objective is to create a "clean slate" architecture for new generation information exchanging and processing. NovaGenesis project aims at creating a new ICT environment to support the full, convergent and accelerated technology evolution we are experiencing today. NovaGenesis adopts the idea that all technologies are converging to a radical new, worldwide, overspread, convergent architecture for information exchanging and processing. The initiative believes that a "clean slate" architecture is required to create the ideal environment to continue technology evolution in a more cohesive, synergistic, efficient, flexible, and accelerated way.

NovaGenesis adopts the Internet of Information and Services (IoIS) paradigm, where information-centric and service-centric approaches are combined to integrate information treatment, storage, and exchanging. Three fundamental cornerstones have been proposed for the project: (i) naming and name resolution, (ii) entities life-cycling and (iii) physical world representatives (Alberti, 2013).

Naming and Name Resolution

Naming is related to language, i.e. to formulate a name requires a language. Thus, a better understanding of naming involves the study of language and its philosophy. According to Day, 2007, in 1892, Frege defined a name as:

A proper name (word, sign, sign combination, expression) expresses its sense, means or designates its meaning. By employing a sign we express its sense and designate its meaning.

From this definition, it is clear that a name is related to meaning - the semantics of a language. In this sense, names are used to distinguish existences (physical or virtual entities), since they can have different meanings in a language. A name is a set of symbols (a conceptual existence) that denote one or more existences. Names can be expressed in natural language, like English or Portuguese. In this case, we refer to them as natural language names (NLNs). For example, the name of a room or a device in an IoT environment.

People can also attribute mathematical generated names to existences. An example are the names generated from hash functions, i.e. hash codes. In this case, the names are said self-verifying names

Figure 1. Ingredients of NovaGenesis model

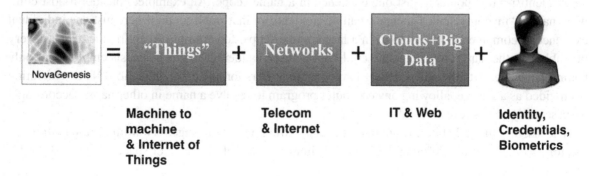

NovaGenesis =	"Things" +	Networks +	Clouds+Big Data +	(identity)
	Machine to machine & Internet of Things	Telecom & Internet	IT & Web	Identity, Credentials, Biometrics

(SVNs). They are names that can be verified anytime, proofing the uniqueness between the name and the entity being named. SVNs are typically generated using a hash function, such as message-digest algorithm 5 (MD5) or secure hash algorithm 3 (SHA-3). In this case, a variable size binary pattern is passed to the hash function to generate a fixed size hash code. The binary pattern required on the input can be the existence itself (digital patterns of computer programs or data chunks) or other patterns related to the existence being named, e.g. a digital version of existences' immutable attributes, like a person fingerprint or a unique fabrication mark inside a chip. The name is said self-certifiable because at any time the binary pattern can be hashed again to generate exactly the same SVN. For example, an SVN generated from a vehicle identification number (VIN) can be verified any time by accessing this number in a car and generating the SVN again from it. This can be implemented today by using a smartphone-based optical character recognition system. SVN proves that only a certain car could have that name generated from its unique VIN. Figure 2 provides an overview of the relationships among the concepts that will be investigated in this chapter. It will help readers towards better clarifying NovaGenesis advantages for smart cities.

Another concept related to naming, is a name binding. The linking among names has strategic importance in information architectures. A name binding can be defined as a mapping among two or more names, which represent entities. A name binding can map several names to many other names/objects. Additionally, one can expect that existences will always denote other existences by names. Therefore, name bindings can represent the relationships among named-entities. For example, a name binding can represent that one entity is contained in another one. For instance, a computer program named "A" is contained in a computer "B". Therefore, this name binding can be read as a "is contained" semantic operator, indicating a that instance "A" exists inside instance "B". Name bindings can also represent "contains" instead of "is contained". NovaGenesis (NG) creates a distributed graph of name bindings to represent relationships among any entity. This is the cornerstone of NG architecture.

The notion of a name scope (or name space) is also important. Day, 2007, defined it in his book:

The scope of a name or name space is the set of all objects to which it may be applied.

This definition can also be extended if we consider "existences" instead of "objects". Now, it is possible to define an identifier as proposed by Chun et al., 2011:

An identifier unambiguously identifies some existence from others in some name scope.

This means that an identifier needs to point to just one existence in a population. Thus, a name can be an identifier if it points to just one existence in a name scope. An example: consider a host computer named "mycomputer". This name can be an identifier in a small scope, where just one individual existence (a computer) is bound to it. In a larger name scope, for example an entire country, it is very probable that the name "mycomputer" could not be used as identifier. NovaGenesis employs not only natural language, but also self-verifying names as identifiers for any communication. Name resolution is provided as a service, allowing any computer program to resolve a name in other names accordingly to its security access level.

The last definition that is relevant to understand NovaGenesis message forwarding is the notion of a locator. However, before defining a locator, it is important to define a locator space. Chun et al., 2011, proposes:

The space of a locator is the set of all possible positions and relation defined on the positions.

Consider a computer in a certain building. The locator space is the set of all possible positions this computer can be placed on the building and the relation of this computer position with other computer positions in the same space, i.e. a notion of the distance between them. For example, assume a computer named "mycomputer" that is on a room named "II.19" at some building "II". Now, consider other computer, named "othercomputer", which is in a room named "II.17" at the same building. The locator space is all possible rooms in this building – ignoring the fact that computers can be placed elsewhere than in rooms. Note also that from the names of the rooms it is possible to derive some notion of distance. If both computers are at the same room, they are closer than in the case they are on different rooms. The space of a locator should give this notion of distance. Therefore, a locators points the position of some existence in a given locator space. NovaGenesis does not limit in the type of locators that can be used and the notion of distance can be derived from name bindings graph.

Entities Life-Cycling

Networking and computing is build over physical resources, also called substrate resources. Any hardware is a substrate resource. Examples are tablets, mobile terminals, routers, storage devices, cars, gateways, etc. A problem that is being addressed by many FIA initiatives is how to expose, negotiate, manage, and control substrate resources to create protocols. Thus, this text assumes that only one type of virtual existence is required for this purpose – a service:

Figure 2. Relationships among NovaGenesis concepts. All things, physical or virtual, are individual existences. Names can be identifiers and/or locators. Spaces limit locators range, while scopes limit the range names can be applied to individual existences. Name bindings map names to individual existences, including other names. Information and services are mutually dependent. Services are organized on layers, which combined with the other definitions support the concept of an architecture.

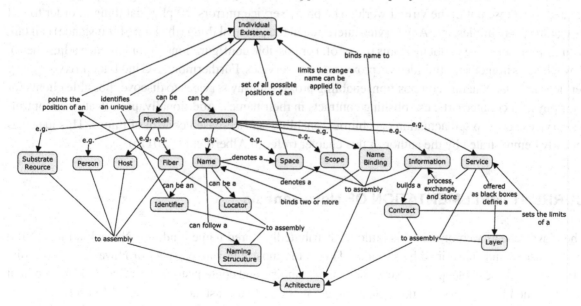

A service is an existence aimed at processing, exchanging, or storing information.

According to this definition, a computer program (or a process) is a service. Any substrate resource can be represented by named services, i.e. computer programs that represent physical entities in the virtual environment. Even protocol implementations provide services, since everything they do is exposed to other protocols as services. Therefore, NovaGenesis idea is to provide protocol-implementations-as-a-service (PIaaS).

Additionally, in the context of a service-oriented computing (SOC), it is also relevant to define a contract. Typically, services life-cycling is contract-based. That is, after peer services discovery, a contract is formulated and negotiated. Thus, a contract can be defined as:

A contract is a piece of information that sets the limits, responsibilities, clauses to be respected, as well as the criteria for completion and punishment of services that were poorly executed.

Currently, many services are performed in software without a formal contract. Consider for example an operating system (OS) and a device driver. Typically, there is no contract establishment between these services. It is assumed that the OS and the driver are mutually compatible and that both will held their jobs satisfactorily. However, resource sharing, virtualization, and the expected exponential advances in the amount of existences and their interactions are challenging this model. A possible approach for new ICT architectures is to incorporate an agreement (contract) abstraction to determine precisely how each service will perform. The combination of NovaGenesis concepts makes possible the emergence of a new class of networks: the contract-based networks (CBN). PIaaS and CBN are important innovations of NG.

Physical World Representatives

Internet of things architectures have solved the problem of heterogeneous hardware by employing software that represents physical devices at middleware platforms. This idea is called smart object. Figure 3 illustrates this powerful idea. For each physical thing, e.g. a lamp, a computer program (proxy service) is created to represent it in the virtual world. The proxy service mirrors the physical thing in order to sell its features, capabilities, etc. Any service interested in the physical thing (the lamp, for instance) can talk with its representative to obtain status (on or off) or possible configurations (luminescence adjustment). NovaGenesis implements this idea via proxy/gateway services. Furthermore, NG includes proxy/gateway services in SOA dynamic composition, enabling proxy/gateway services to discover possible clients for their physical counterparts, establishing contracts in their names. Additionally, proxy/gateway/controller services can also sell actuation capabilities, enabling service-based control of things. This idea was recently demonstrated by the author of this chapter (refer to Alberti et al., 2017c).

CURRENT IMPLEMENTATION OF NovaGenesis

The NovaGenesis web of names is build of distributedly stored name bindings. Name bindings (NBs) are published and subscribed by services. This is the most innovative aspect of NovaGenesis – a distributed, highly scalable, publish/subscribe, name binding and content storage service. NBs and content are published by any services through sending a message to an instance of a publish/subscribe service

Figure 3. Smart objects represent in software layer the physical world entities

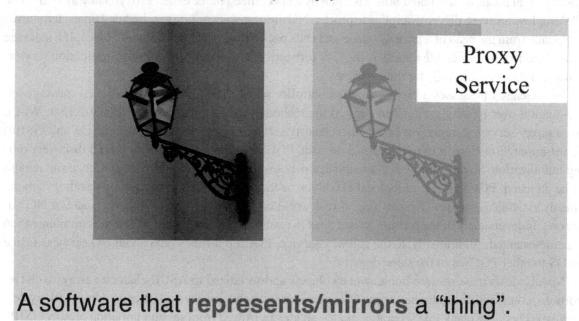

(PSS). The PSS stores which services are pre-authorized to access the published data. Also, it records a time to live (TTL) for any published data. There is also a notification functionality that enables PSS to inform other services about new publications or NB updating. However, the PSS does not store the data published. It forwards them to a generic indirection resolution service (GIRS), which selects a hash table service (HTS) to store it. Thus, published NBs and content are forwarded by GIRS to an HTS instance, in which they are stored behind a hash table data structure.

User services can expose its NBs and content to other services via PSS. Thus, other services can subscribe a services' NBs and content. PSS does the rendezvous between publishers and subscribers, enabling them to discover how published names are related each other in a secure way. Eventually, services can successively subscribe NBs to identify and locate other existences, storing these NBs in local data structures and routing information based on them.

GIRS and HTS instances form a distributed hash table (DHT). This DHT was designed from the scratch to support named-based and contract-oriented operation. Current DHTs do not employ self-certifying names to identify the DHT nodes. In addition, they relay on TCP/IP stack for communication. GIRS/HTS approach relays on NovaGenesis services to forward and route the data among DHT instances. This explains why it was decided on a "clean slate" DHT design, instead of using an already available implementation.

In the current design, an object-oriented design (OOD) approach was adopted to implement Nova-Genesis components. Every service has several internal objects called *blocks* where functionalities are implemented. *Blocks* are classified in two types: common and specialized. There are two common *blocks* that are instantiated in all services, as can be seen on Figure 4: gateway (GW) and hash table (HT). The GW provides: (i) inter *block* communication (IBC) inside a service and inter service communication (ISC) inside an OS. The IBC is a bus for communication among dynamically instantiated classes inside a service. The communication among services instantiated at different substrate resources (real world hosts, virtual hosts, or simulated hosts) is done by a specialized *block* called Proxy/Gateway (PG). The GW employs an event-driven discipline to process NG messages according to scheduled times. It removes a message from the head of a priority queue and calls back the message's destination *block*. If a message is destined to a block outside a service, the GW forwards the message to the proper destination service, using an output queue (OQ) for this purpose.

NovaGenesis possesses a proxy/gateway/controller service (PGCS) that provides: (i) message encapsulation over already established networking technologies, such Ethernet, IEEE 802.15.4, Wi-Fi; (ii) a proxy service to represent other NovaGenesis services or physical resources inside an OS; (iii) bootstrapping functionalities to initialize a domain. PGCS enables PSS, GIRS, and HTS discovery during initialization. Since an address is a name that denotes the position to where an existence can inhabit or be attached, PGCS relays on its local HT block or the domain HTS to store name-bindings among already established address formats (e.g. a real world or an emulated MAC Ethernet) and/or NG addresses. Independently of the address format used to connect PGCSes, inside NG all the communication is name-oriented. Additionally, to the gateway service, PGCS publishes NBs about NG services inside an OS to other PGCSes in the same domain.

NovaGenesis messages are implement as objects and serialized to ASCII character arrays with two portions: command lines (streamed from *CommandLine* objects) and payload (streamed from a file system archive). There is a blank line separating both – an idea borrowed from session initiation protocol (SIP). The command lines portion is composed by several textual lines, which can be dynamically expanded according to the need. The command lines are shown in Box 1.

Each command can have one or more vectorial arguments, which are structured in Box 2.

As an example, consider the message shown in Figure 5. The first command line is always related to message forwarding/routing. It has three arguments separated by < > markers. The first argument limits the space the message is allowed to follow. In this case, the space has a self-verifying name *38... D2_PGS_PID*. The substring *_PGS_PID* is attached for debugging purpose. The second argument contains message source, in this case a *block* called *223...B3_GW_BID*. The last argument is the SVN of the destination *block*. The message is transporting a name binding from a GW *block* to a hash table HT inside PGCS. The name binding to be stored on HT links the SVN *AC...B0_PSS_PID* to the NLNs: 41 and 40. The last command line is employed for message integrity verification.

Box 1.

```
         ng -command –alternative version [ vectorial arguments ]


         Where:

         -command              is the action to be done.
         –alternative          selects among alternatives the action to be done.
         version               selects the desired version of implementation.
         [vectorial arguments] are the arguments of the command.
```

Box 2.

```
< n type E1 E2 E3 E4 ... En >

    Where:

n                       is the number of elements in the argument vector.
type                    is the type of the elements in the argument vector.
E1 E2 E3 E4 ... En      are the elements of the argument vector.
```

Figure 4. Example of two applications in a simple link scenario. Underlaying software and hardware support NovaGenesis services.

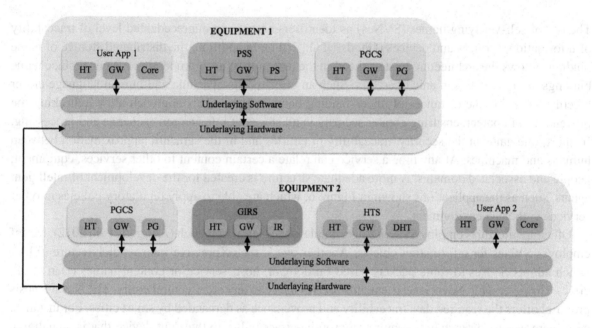

Figure 5. Example of a NovaGenesis message

```
ng -msg –cl 0.1 [ < 1 string 38...D2_PGS_PID >< 1 string 223..B3_GW_BID >< 1 string 58..AF_HT_BID > ]
ng -store –bind 0.1 [ < 1 string 0 ><1 string ACE3808CA94B7EACF0CD6D4D9327CBB0_PSS_PID >< 2 string 41 40 > ]
...
ng -scn –seq 0.1 [ < 1 string BAE12A5A0DA82BCDAA0F0165B95533B8 > ]
```

Several command lines and messages for different purposes have been developed. Interestingly, the adopted dual mode message structure (interchangeable object and text) enables the infrastructure operator to write messages from a command line interface, since the messages are human readable.

NovaGenesis ADVANTAGES FOR SMART CITIES AND RELATED WORK

NovaGenesis applications for smart cities take advantage of all link layers (e.g. Ethernet, IEEE 802.15.4, etc.) to provide a decentralized, self-organizing, contract-based and name-oriented solution to address biggest city challenges. Now, it worths to summarize the main advantages NG brings for smart cities.

Traceability and Provenience

The use of self-verifying names (SVNes) as identifiers ensures an unprecedented level of traceability of information, services and devices (Ghodsi et al., 2011). In addition, the distributed storage of name bindings allows the architecture to step ahead in the direction of accommodating meaning, since name bindings are related to semantic operators. Such an effort brings machine and human language closer together, reducing the distances of understanding between them. This approach allows checking the provenance of content, ensuring greater security in all stages of information exchange and processing. In short, one gains in the security, traceability of entities and in the semantic approximation between humans and machines. At any time a service can relate a certain content to other services, equipment, people and associated domains. A more adequate structure is created for the development of intelligent agents, such as the applications shown in Figure 6, which are able to apply regulatory policies to other services in the NG environment.

Other architectures employ SVNes. An example is the NetInf approach (Ahlgren et al., 2012). NetInf employes SVNes for information objetcs. Another one is the eXpressive Internet architecture (XIA), which adopts SVNes to route packets based on domain, host, service or content names (Dan et al., 2012). However, only NovaGenesis extends SVNes usage to any architectural entity. The NovaGenesis proposal offers the required data traceability and provenance as demanded by smart cities. For instance, a problem in a road semaphore requires appropriate traceability to the right device that is signaling a fail. There is also need that the received information is from that source. Without these guarantees, data is useless for decision making.

Semantic Orchestration

Natural-language and self-verifiable name bindings allow services to dynamically combine (orchestrate) with others, providing self-emergence of complex applications. NG employs a bottom-up approach, where decentralized self-coordination of simple services gives rise to complex applications that emerge as a result of name resolution, service offering, service discovery and dynamic contracting. Among the advantages of this new approach are the self-adaptation to changes in the physical resources and service demands. The impacts of this approach are significant, especially in the ease of creating new services and applications. In NovaGenesis, creating new applications means defining rules for aggregating existing, simple services. NovaGenesis creates a self-service environment, similar to a self-service restaurant, where the applications choose from a gigantic diversity of options the most appropriate components to the objectives set. Services are contracted according to objectives, roles, rules and high-level regulations. When applied to smart cities services, this model creates a very dynamic, extensible and trustable environment. New services can be added transparently and dynamically composed with existing ones. Service life-cycling is a client of the distributed name resolution and network cache system created by PSS, GIRS and HTS. Very importantly, smart cities services can be evolved to optimize physical resources usage while meeting high level policies/requirements. The self-organizing decentralized approach of NovaGenesis is ideal for high scale ecosystems with millions of small services as one can expect in huge smart cities with millions of nodes and services. It reduces human intervention while enabling dynamic adaptation to demand (elasticity). When compared to other architectures, neither NetInf, nor XIA implement a service-oriented design. NovaGenesis is the unique contract-based future Internet approach.

Better Utilization of Physical Resources

Physical resources such as network equipment, computers, among others, are exposed to software for use by dynamic contracting. This is done by virtual representatives of physical things – the so called smart objects. This allows for the sharing and optimization of these resources by software, reducing expenses, energy costs and creating a range of possibilities for shared use of devices, e.g. the provisioning of physical resources for virtual operators. Software orchestration brings the advantage of intelligence in the allocation of substrate (physical) resources, allowing configuration of resource slices according to the needs of clients, their services and applications.

The idea of smart objects is implemented in other smart cities architectures, such as FIWARE (Ramparany et al., 2014) and distributed Internet-like architecture for things (DIAT) (Sarkar et al., 2015). However, NovaGenesis implements smart objects as services accordingly to service-oriented architecture (SOA) paradigms. In this context, physical entities representatives can establish service contracts to interested peers.

Network Programmability

NovaGenesis proposes a new approach to software defined network (SDN), which aims to go beyond the current SDN standard called OpenFlow. In NovaGenesis, network controllers are services like any other, and can be combined and reformatted as needed. In addition, they are based on the precepts of unique identification through self-certifiable names and dynamic contracting among devices representatives and possible client services. This feature enables services to configure network devices as required by top level applications – a new concept defined as service-defined architecture (SDA) (Alberti et al., 2017c).

TinySDN (de Oliveira et al., 2015) enables software-controllers to configure IoT nodes' traffic flow tables. However, smart city requires many other important configurations, such as sensor sampling rates, node addresses, operation bandwidth, channeling, firmware updates. Only the extension of the SDN scope to these IoT functionalities can catalyze software-controllers adoption in IoT. In NovaGenesis, there is no limitation on the kind of networking functions a software-controller can configure (addressing other control and management functions expected in future smart cities).

Ease of Migration and Technological Evolution

The features discussed so far greatly facilitate the usage of NovaGenesis as alternative architecture to TCP/IP. Interoperability with the legacy is guaranteed through proxy/gateway (P/G) services. Thus, access to legacy technologies can be done via PGCSes, which represent legacy technologies within the NovaGenesis cloud network. All the particularities of access to legacy technologies as well as dynamic contracting of legacy resources can be implemented via PGCSes. Therefore, NovaGenesis contains natural mechanisms for integrating other technologies inside its ecosystem. This is very relevant in smart cities, in which heterogeneity of sensors, gateways, middleware, platforms, architectures and communication models exist. For instance, a PGCS can be developed to represent a set of IoT nodes. In this case, it is implemented at the gateway and represents nodes and physical gateway inside NG. Gateways for different technologies can be implemented, allowing interoperability to them.

Increased Efficiency and Effectiveness

One of the main problems of the current ICT infrastructures is the excessive overhead, which significantly reduces the efficiency of the network. NovaGenesis breaks protocol implementations into small functional blocks – network services – that are dynamically combined as needed by other services and applications. Flexible and unlimited protocol stacks can be created for each application on the network. Thus, naturally, efficiency increases, since only the necessary functionalities are combined dynamically. In addition, the paradigms of dynamic orchestration of services and substrate resources, combined with unlimited name spaces, increase the effectiveness of the infrastructure while providing coherent and traceable data distribution. In this regard, NovaGenesis advances state-of-the-art in two fronts: (i) it reduces protocol stack overhead to the essential for each application, and (ii) it revolutionize the architecture to make content search and distribution more secure and effective. In summary, flexible layering is enabled and software solutions are stacked from protocol implementation up to applications.

Reducing Human Interference

One of the main concerns with the current Internet is whether it will accommodate the exponential growth we are experiencing in the amount of traffic, number of nodes and terminals, increase in interactivity, quantity of services and applications, in addition to increased heterogeneity. The impact of exponential growth in the management and operation of ICT infrastructure will be one of the greatest challenges in the coming decades. Thus, solutions that reduce the degree of human interference in the systems are quite desirable. Absorbing this expected exponential growth through the hiring of IT and Telecom teams can certainly increase the high operating costs of smart cities industry. NovaGenesis architecture aims to create a hierarchy of decision-making loops (provoking stigmergy), therefore enabling self-organization, self-management and self-configuring capabilities. The goal is to create several "autopilots" that reduce human interference and optimize the architecture as a whole. This is fundamental in smart cities, since huge scales can be expected in large cities like Seul, Tokyo, São Paulo.

DIAT provides zero configuration of new devices and services, as well as self-management of data/services, including autonomic composition. semi-autonomic service composition. Future versions of NovaGenesis will include autonomic decision cycles like DIAT.

Synergistic Optimization

The autonomic and cognitive decision cycles envisioned for NovaGenesis enables the synergistic optimization of functionalities distributed in the different levels of the architecture. In other words, services can optimize their functionalities depending on successful contracts and reputation of current and previous peers. Decision-making based on information from many partners facilitates cross-layer optimization, allowing evolution of parameters and features for each possible scenario of application. This feature enables smart city services to self-optimize their practices accordingly to positive and negative feedbacks collected from established contracts. Therefore, a smart city enabled with this feature avoids excessive manual intervention, since services are capable to optimize their functions based on observed behaviors. Services can avoid working together with other services that have low reputation or verify if contracts fit on application requirements. For instance, in public transportation services that demand detailed traffic information NG services can optimize the frequency of data sampling and configure sensors accordingly, avoiding unnecessary data.

Security, Privacy and Trust

In NovaGenesis architecture, not only traditional security mechanisms, but also new mechanisms are employed from the beginning of design (2008) to address existing Internet deficiencies, as well as to improve security, privacy and trust (SPT) in future networks. Reliable networks, assymetric criptography, hash functions, social behavior, reputation-based contracting of services, self-verifiable identifiers, among other security mechanisms are intended to improve support for smart cities security.

Security and privacy start from naming and name resolution. Naming has a fundamental role in SPT (Ghodsi et al., 2011). Self-verifying naming enables services to verify content provenance and integrity. The publish/subscribe paradigm also helps on securing access to information, since receiving services only subscribe data from sources in the same trust network. Therefore, uncertain data from unknow sources are less probable to be processed. In other words, services only exchange sensible information with services in the same trust network.

The combination of SVNes and content pub/sub enables architectures to verify information being subscribed in a more secure way (Ahlgren et al., 2012). This approach is not exclusive to NovaGenesis. NetInf architecture also provides self-verifying access to information (Ahlgren et al., 2012). However, NovaGenesis extends this feature to all entities, including domains, services, operating systems, network cards, hosts, etc.

In addtion, NovaGenesis provides contract-based operation, which is an addition layer of security, since all services need to establish trustable networks in order to pub/sub contents. This feature is unique to NovaGenesis architecture. Pub/sub can employ simetric or assymetric criptography, depending on the computer power of end devices. NovaGenesis enables physical things to be represented by proxy services, which can implement assymetric criptography. Privacy is enforced based on established contracts, i.e. access to information is granted based on established trust networks. In other words, access to a certain information object is granted only if an adequate contract is signed by both sides.

In summary, in a NovaGenesis smart city all services can take advantage of these features, increasing SPT support to an adequate level. For instance, contracts established to compromised nodes can be revoked, eliminating the damage a misbehaving data source can cause. Distributed deny of service

(DDoS) can be mitigated by the formation of trust network, i.e. the extend of damage that unreliable nodes can do is limited by contract-based operation.

With all these features, NovaGenesis provides exciting possibilities for future smart cities.

NovaGenesis SMART CITY ARCHITECTURE: A FIRST GLANCE DISCUSSION

Smart cities are one of the main use cases of IoT. However, they are not limited to IoT technology. Smart cities include cloud/fog computing, big data, data analytics, semantic annotation, semantic interoperability, dynamic services composition, smart objects, security, privacy, trust, infrastructure programmability, among many others. Therefore, smart city architecture design is a quite challenging task, since it needs to integrate several topics commonly fragmented. This is exactly the reason for this chapter: to illustrate how the NG proposal organizes and tackles the various integration challenges present in a smart city. The overall vision on how NovaGenesis helps solving this problem is illustrated in Figure 6.

The bottom portion of Figure 6 represents smart cities hardware, from optical fibers and radio links up to computing nodes. This is the substrate layer of NG model. The second layer from bottom up is a fundamental software layer. In this layer, NG core runs as software in operating systems. The current prototype is a set of Linux user space programs. Meanwhile, NG hardware is in design phase and comprises a programmable switch/router for NG messages. The intermediate layer comprises NG basic services, such as PSS, GIRS, HTS and PGCS. These services provide name resolution, distributed

Figure 6. NovaGenesis model for smart cities

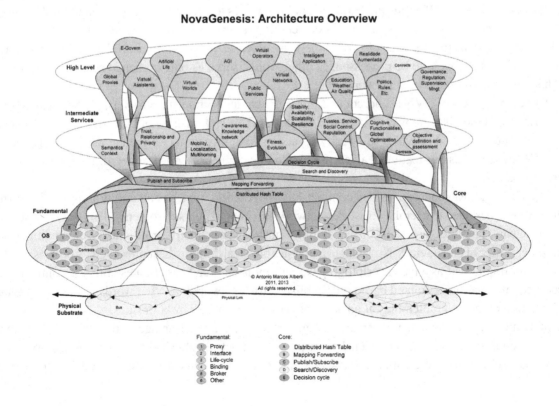

cache of NG name bindings and content, and message encapsulation/forwarding/routing among hosts. The search and discovery service proposed in the figure is not implemented yet. Even though, services can discovery each other by directly accessing the publish/subscribe interface at PSS. The autonomic system is also for future versions.

The next level comprises a diversity of distributed systems covering a broad range of topics. They aim to improve security, privacy and trust (SPT), by adding role-based access control to services and resources. They also provide: (i) semantic contextualization (annotation) to data objects; (ii) roles and regulation to guarantee beneficial and safe contract establishment; (iii) knowledge representation and exchanging; (iv) drivers for service evolution; (v) services stability, availability, scalability and resiliency; (vi) tussling, social control and reputation for solving services conflicts and evolution; (vii) cognitive functionalities as a service, e.g. basic artificial intelligence functions; (viii) goal enforcement, usability (user experience) and service fitness (ranking). These functionalities complete the service ecosystem that NG offers to its upper layer. The high-level layer 2 encompasses the top applications of a smart city. For instance, city administration, surveillance and emergency services.

Figure 7 illustrates a NG domain in a smart city. Cities can be fragmented in hierarchical domains similar to this figure scenario. It encompasses N servers and M hosts. Observe that NG hardware is still in design phase, therefore the scenario employs commodity Ethernet switches. There is no need for IP routers. Ethernet networks connect all equipment together, but other link layer technologies can be adopted. NovaGenesis messages are encapsulated by PGCSes and routed using self-verifying names (Alberti et al., 2017a). The PGCS also implements IoT gateway functionalities, such as representation of connected sensors and actuators inside NG cloud. The host computers are equipped with PGCSes to represent Wi-Fi, IEEE 802.15.4 or Bluetooth low energy (BLE) nodes. This enables IoT traffic to be contextualized by NG services.

Figure 7 also illustrates several services (S1 up to S8) that run distributedly in computers. Examples of services are the ones presented in Figure 6 high levels. For instance, a service that handles reputation of device representatives (PGCSes). If some device is not working properly, its representative service (PGCS) could be penalized, losing the related contract. A third-party service contracted to evaluate the quality of contracts in a domain can reduce the reputation of this PGCS. As a consequence, client application can reduce the interest for the PGCS in future contracts, given advantage to other PGCS. Therefore, physical resource usage becomes a reflex of their quality.

Multiple PSS, GIRS and HTS instances are allowed to improve availability. The switch connects to other NG clouds (domains) in the city. A domain of domains can be deployed in municipality data center. In this case, a domain service (DS) (not shown in Figure 7) should be implemented to allow hierarchical name resolution and seamless service contracting. Finally, it is important to mention that NovaGenesis already runs embedded at IoT sensor devices (Alberti et al., 2017c). Therefore, its model has already been proofed as an alternative to current smart cities architectures.

FUTURE INTERNET OF THINGS WITH NovaGenesis

NovaGenesis concepts for IoT and smart cities have already been demonstrated scientifically in Alberti et al., 2017c. Figure 8 illustrates the concept of a future Internet of things (FIoT) with NovaGenesis. In this scenario, an IoT client application (at NG application layer or high level 1 in Figure 6) is demanding for room temperature measurements in a certain domain. A local PGCS represents (as a smart object) a sen-

Figure 7. NovaGenesis domain in a smart city

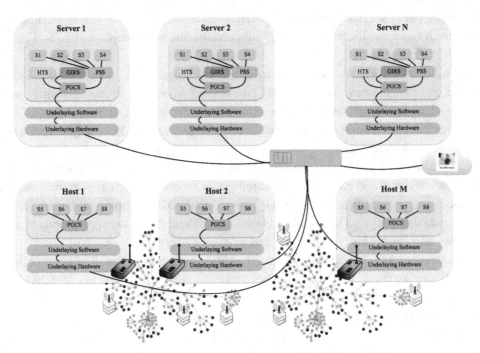

Figure 8. NovaGenesis future Internet of things scenario
Source: Alberti et al., 2017c.

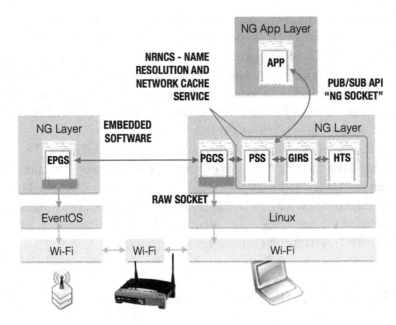

sor capable of providing temperature measurements. The IoT application discovers this PGCS and makes an offer. PGCS accepts the offer and allows the application to establish a secondary contract directly to an embedded proxy gateway service (EPGS), which in turn runs inside the IoT sensor. All communication employs only NovaGenesis and Wi-Fi. PGCS encapsulate NovaGenesis messages via a Linux raw socket. PSS, GIRS and HTS form a unique name resolution and network cache service (NRNCS) that stores name bindings and room temperature samples in JSON format. An example of a name binding is < 94BF74F8, *Measures.json* >. It is utilized to relate *Measures.json* file to its self-verifying name. Such approach provides data integrity as discussed in previous section. EPGS provides a contract offer to the IoT application, describing how frequently the temperature samples will be delivered. The IoT application accepts the contract and starts receiving the samples.

Figure 9 reproduces a Wireshark™ log containing a NG message. NovaGenesis messages are carried inside Wi-Fi frames (have the same structure than Ethernet II frames) using Ethernet type 0x1234. As can be seen, Wi-Fi frames do no have any protocol of current Internet (e.g. UDP, IP, CoAP, HTTP, 6LowPAN, etc.). The length of this Wi-Fi frame is 489 bytes. The messages are bigger than 6LowPAN, since they are ASCII text without any kind of compression. This is quite useful for debugging in this

Figure 9. Wireshark™ capture of a NovaGenesis message carrying a temperature sample (26°C)

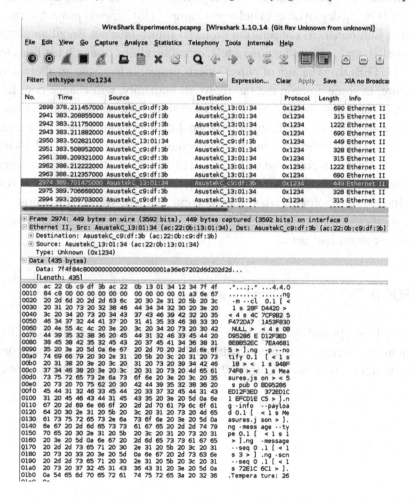

development phase. In future versions, more compact messages will be designed and source compressed versions will be employed. In addition, Alberti et al., (2017c), provides a stack efficiency comparison to 6LowPAN. It has been demonstrated that NG has smaller RAM and ROM requirements than a similar 6LowPAN implementation with CoAP. In this scenario, a 32 bits *Murmurhash* 3 have been employed to generate the self-verifying names. Finally, it is important to observe that NovaGenesis messages are routed using hash codes as node addresses, as can be verified in the Figure 9. The PSS component provides name resolution from Ethernet MAC addresses to these hash codes, such as 4C7CF9B2.

This example demonstrates NovaGenesis approach for IoT, which is ready to be extended to smart cities. Imagine an army of devices represented by PGCSes, which expose their measurement and actuating features. Think on client applications searching for these devices and establishing trustable contracts. NovaGenesis enables applications to query for adequate services, favoring evolution and quality. It provides mechanisms to optimize physical resources utilization, while meeting high level demands.

CONCLUSION

NovaGenesis is an alternative architecture for smart cities. Its development continues at the time of this writing. Scalability and performance tests are being done at ICT Lab, Inatel, Brazil. A scenario closer to a real one is being deployed at Inatel smart campus (ISCampus) project. Experiments are also being conducted at Europe/Brazil cooperation projects: future Internet Brazilian environment for experimentation (FIBRE) and federated union of telecommunications research facilities for an EU-Brazil open laboratory (FUTEBOL). The aim of NovaGenesis project is to create an alternative to the current Internet architecture. In some point in the future, we as humanity, will change core Internet protocols to new ones (replace the technologies). NovaGenesis aims to help on this step. No one wants to loose the gains we have achieved with the Internet, neither the investments done, but we need to seriously think about how to decouple policy making from underlaying technologies (TCP, UDP, IP, DNS, etc.) to enable other stacks in the Internet. No technology remains forever. Global interoperability is not an excuse to make the Internet obsolete. We need to keep the Internet working and evolving, but we also need to replace Internet technologies when they become limited. We need to allow alternatives. The risk of doing nothing can be the emergence of competing solutions that do not preserve the fantastic achievements of the current Internet.

ACKNOWLEDGMENT

This work was partially supported by Finep, with resources from Funttel, Grant No. 01.14.0231.00, under the Radiocommunication Reference Center (Centro de Referência em Radiocomunicações - CRR) project of the National Institute of Telecommunications (Instituto Nacional de Telecomunicações - Inatel), Brazil.

REFERENCES

Ahlgren, B., Dannewitz, C., Imbrenda, C., Kutscher, D., & Ohlman, B. (2012). A survey of information-centric networking. *IEEE Communications Magazine, 50*(7), 26–36. doi:10.1109/MCOM.2012.6231276

Alberti, A. M. (2013). A Conceptual-Driven Survey on Future Internet Requirements, Technologies, and Challenges. *Journal of the Brazilian Computer Society, 19*(3), 291–311. doi:10.100713173-013-0101-2

Alberti, A. M., Casaroli, M. A., Singh, D., & Righi, R. (2017a). Naming and name resolution in the future Internet: Introducing the NovaGenesis approach. *Elsevier Future Generation Computer Systems, 67*, 163–179. doi:10.1016/j.future.2016.07.015

Alberti, A. M., Mazzer, D., Bontempo, M. M., De Oliveira, L. H., Righi, R., & Sodré, A. C. Jr. (2017b). Cognitive radio in the context of Internet of things using a novel future internet architecture called NovaGenesis. *Elsevier Computers & Electrical Engineering, 57*, 147–161. doi:10.1016/j.compeleceng.2016.07.008

Alberti, A.M., Scarpioni, G. D., Magalhães, V.J., Cerqueira Sodré Jr, A., Rodrigues, J. J. P. C. & Righi, R. da R. (2017c) Advancing NovaGenesis architecture towards future Internet of things. *IEEE Internet of Things Journal, 99*, 1-1.

Chun, W., Lee, T. H., & Choi, T. (2011) *Yanail: yet another definition on names, addresses, identifiers, and locators.* Presented at the *6th International Conference on Future Internet Technologies*, Seoul, South Korea. 10.1145/2002396.2002399

Day, J. (2007). *Patterns in network architecture: A return to fundamentals* (1st ed.). Prentice Hall.

de Oliveira, B. T., Gabriel, L. B., & Margi, C. B. (2015). TinySDN: Enabling multiple controllers for software-defined wireless sensor networks. *IEEE Latin America Transactions, 13*(11), 3690–3696. doi:10.1109/TLA.2015.7387950

Ghodsi, A., Koponen, T., Rajahalme, J., Sarolahti, P., & Shenker, S. (2011). Naming in content-oriented architectures. Presented at *ACM SIGCOMM Workshop on Information-centric Networking, ICN '11*, Toronto, Canada. 10.1145/2018584.2018586

Han, D., Anand, A., Dogar, F., Li, B., Lim, H., Machado, M., ... Steenkiste, P. (2012). Xia: Efficient support for evolvable internetworking. Presented at *9th USENIX Conference on Networked Systems Design and Implementation, NSDI'12*, San Jose, CA.

Ramparany, F., Marquez, F. G., Soriano, F., & Elsaleh, T. (2014). *Handling smart environment devices, data and services at the semantic level with the FI-WARE core platform.* Presented at IEEE International Conference on Big Data (Big Data). 10.1109/BigData.2014.7004417

Sarkar, C., Akshay, A. U., Prasad, R. V., Rahim, A., Neisse, R., & Baldini, G. (2015). DIAT: A scalable distributed architecture for IoT. *IEEE Internet of Things Journal, 2*(3), 230–239. doi:10.1109/JIOT.2014.2387155

KEY TERMS AND DEFINITIONS

Contract: A piece of information that specifies how a service should be performed.

Existence: Anything that inhabits the physical or virtual worlds.

Identifier: A name that is unique in some scope.

Locator: A name that offers the notion of distance in a space.

Name: A set of natural language or engineered symbols attributed to existences.

Name Binding: A binding among names.

NovaGenesis: A novel information processing, exchanging, and storage architecture to serve as an alternative to TCP/IP internet.

Protocol: A shared language agreed among peers to communicate.

Protocol Implementation: A service that implements the actions, rules, and procedures required to support a protocol.

Service: Virtual existence aimed at exchanging, processing, and storing information in any computational substrate.

Substrate Resource: A physical thing that supports the existence of virtual ones.

ENDNOTE

[1]   www.inatel.br/novagenesis.

Chapter 9
Advances in Steam Quality Monitoring Systems in Power Plants

Mahmoud Meribout
Khalifa University, UAE

Imran Saied
University of Edinburgh, UK

Esra Al Hosani
Adco Corporation, UAE

ABSTRACT

Online and reliable monitoring of steam quality in power plants is of great importance in smart grids today since it can mitigate eventual erosions and buildups which may occur in associated metal equipment such as pipes and steam turbine. This in turn causes a substantial reduction in the amount of energy produced by the steam generator. This chapter presents state of the art online and offline sensing techniques used for steam quality monitoring in power plants. This includes optical, orifice, swirling, vortex, conductive, and PH meters. While offline monitoring techniques, such as isokinetic sampling technique are still widely deployed for steam monitoring mainly because of the relative simplicity, online monitoring techniques offer the possible to identify transient steam purity conditions. It also allows the prediction of future states of either the steam turbine or the steam quality and hence offers the possibility of effective preventive actions.

INTRODUCTION

The US Energy Information Administration (EIA) predicts that despite the wide availability of low power consuming lightbulbs and high power efficient appliances, demand for electricity will reach 351 GW over the next 25 years, mainly driven by the increasing installations of HVAC (Heat, Ventilator, and AC) equipment in homes or industrial plants in the world. Part of this energy will be provided by

DOI: 10.4018/978-1-5225-5510-0.ch009

renewable energy sources such as wind energy and solar or nuclear, but most of it is expected to be supplied by natural gas and to lower extend geothermal plants. These sources of energy usually use/ produce a high quantity of steam, the quality of which may affect considerably the output power level. Impurities carried in the steam can cause hydrogen damage and fouling of superheaters, re-heaters, and turbines. In addition, a condensation due to energy losses results in liquid droplets of sub-micrometer size carried in the steam. The size of droplets increase as the steam travels to the turbine which can cause damage to various components of the system including the turbine itself and also erosion of the internal wall of the pipe which in turn generates a stream of solid contaminants that can be even more critical to the system such as failure of the turbine blades and also deposit of solid particles at some locations of the pipeline, causing pressure drops of the steam and hence can substantially lower the output power. A thickness grow of only 3 mils can cause an increase of 1 to 2% in the fuel bill revenue. Hence, carryover of solid impurities and droplets of water in a superheated steam turbine remains a major concern for steam generators which may lead to turbine unbalance and threat of the integrity of the other plant equipment such as the condenser, heater, pumps, boilers, and turbines. This challenge is more crucial in geothermal power generation plants which contains naturally-occurring contaminants besides pure water than in other conventional steam powered power generation (e.g. coal, natural gas, and nuclear). Nevertheless, these latest technologies are also subject to substantial amount of contaminants created in the pipeline due to some mechanical causes. One way to mitigate these contaminants is to use fluid filters and separators (E. Al Hosani, 2014; M. Rehman, 2012; S. Teniou, 2012; Z. Piyushsinh, 2014). However this requires recurrent replacement of the filters and also would cause some increasing pressure drops of the steam. Another approach is to monitor the quality of the steam with or without sampling. Online monitoring has already been considered by some power plant operators (e.g. energy Development Corporation and Mercury) by measuring either a single compound (e.g. amount of sodium) or multiple variables (e.g. silica, gas content, pH, and conductive). Offline monitoring is also widely considered in power systems by acquiring isokinetic samples in a way that the sample represents the flowing steam. This book chapter presents at first a background of steam-based power plants, together with different sensors used for steam quality monitoring. This is followed by a presentation of a new hybrid device for real-time measurement and imaging of moving solid and liquid contaminants that may occur in steam generators. The device explores the fact that the dielectric of the steam is approximatively one while the one of water droplets when exposed at high temperature can range between 8 and 65 (M. Meribout, 2011a, E. Zhang, 2008). This contrast of dielectric values can help track water droplets as well as other solid contaminants. The device uses a dedicated Near Infra-Red device to determine the type of contaminants (i.e. water droplets and iron oxide particles) and a THz imaging system which measures the amount of contaminants as well as its flow rate. The NIR subsystem uses a pattern recognition method based on a combination of principal component analysis and least squares support vector machine (LS-SVM) (Fukutomo, 1997; Kothare, 2000; Jean, 2008; Lord, 1980). The usage of image processing techniques together with NIR spectrometry constitutes a new promising step in flow metering (Baker, 2003; Bunce, 2011; Meribout, 2010b; Grimmelius, 1999). This is demonstrated by the extensive experiments which have been conducted for different scenario where the NIR subsystem system could determine the concentration of water droplets and solid contaminants with a maximum uncertainty of +/- 1.45% and +/- 1.16% respectively. With the NIR subsystem, pixel-level accuracy of motion vector was achieved, while the concentration of solid contaminants showed consisted proportionality with the average pixel intensity (Meribout, 2009c; Gao, 2009; Meribout, 2002d).

STEAM-BASED POWER GENERATION

Power stations operate using different sources of energies such as fuel or renewable energy. Solar concentrator or geothermal activity constitutes the main source of producing steam. Figure 1 shows a geothermal activity occurring in one of the cities in Bolivia, which is caused by several interrelated physical-chemical mechanisms.

The first significant geothermal project was achieved in Italy (Lardarello) in 1904, after which several other projects took place all over the world (i.e. Russia, Japan, Indonesia, and Philippines) to lead to the first commercial project which was achieved in California, the Geysers in 1960 (Merman et al, 1975). The project could reach the goal of producing a good quality of superheated vapor dominated dry steam but carried with other few minor of other gases (e.g. isobutene, propane and their derivatives such as amonia), little amount of liquid water, and other impurities from dirt and rocks. As it is usually the case, the impurities enter directly the power station without mitigating treatments (e.g. chemical, ultrasonic (Mohsin, 2015a; Mohsin, 2015b), or microwave (Rehman, 2014) treatments as it is costly. In Java-Bali (Indonesia), a geothermal built in 1994 plant could generate up to 180 MW of power (Adiprana et al, 2014). As a consequence of steam contamination, the power capacity decreased from 60MW to 58.5 MW at the lowest. Increasing the steam flow to around 30T/h could successfully increase the electricity production since the turbine work, W, is proportional to both the mass flow of the steam, $\dot{m}$, and to the differential enthalpy, Δ:

$$W = \overset{\cup}{m} \times \Delta h \tag{1}$$

The cleaning of the deposits in the turbine was conducted in five days using condensed water generated form the condenser outlet.

Figure 1. A fumarole field in Laguna Colorada, Bolivia

In a more complicated and costly scenario of wet water, the hot brine can be exposed to a single or double flash power plant by adjusting the pressure drop at the surface of the plant. Figure 2 (a) shows a three-flash geothermal power plant while Figure 2(b) shows the diagram of a single flash geothermal power plant.

Figure 3 shows a cross section of a typical steam turbine. It consists of a high-pressure sand low pressure sections. High pressure steam first enters the high-pressure section inlet (denoted 1) which is then routed through the high-pressure turbine stages (denoted 2), driving he turbine blades to cause rotation of the common rotor shaft of the steam turbine. Similarly, low pressure steam enters the low-pressure section through the inlet 3 to route the low pressure steam through the low pressure turbine stages (denoted 4) to cause rotation of the common shaft of the steam turbine.

Consider an upset from the water treatment submodule which causes creating water droplets. The existence of impurities such as chloride causes the following chemical reaction:

$$Mgcl2 + 2H2O + heat \; Mg(OH)2 + 2HCL$$

Figure 2. Geothermal plants: (a) typical three flash geothermal power plant (TCI) (b) diagram of a single flash geothermal power plant

(a)

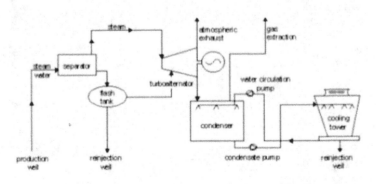

(b)

Figure 3. Block diagram of a typical steam turbine
Source: Roy et al, 2012

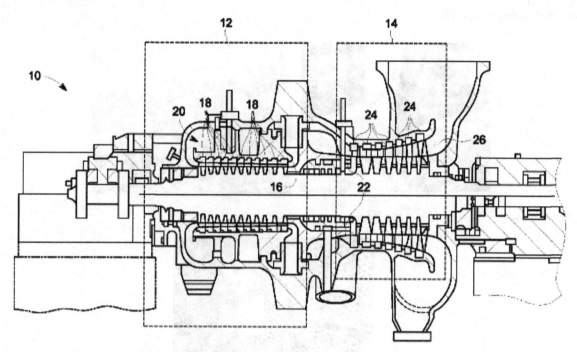

While hydrochloric acid (HCL) is a potential source of corrosion, it will also accumulate and settle down at some locations of the pipeline. This accumulation can lead to in its turn to hydrogen damage of the tubes which leads to creation of methane which then can cause corrosion of the pipeline and accumulation of solid particles at some locations of the pipeline. In (R. Adiprana et al, 2010), it was revealed a thickness of contaminants of up to 0.6 mm was observed in the pipe (Figure 4). A further X-ray analysis of the contaminants indicate the presence of sulfide, chloride, and iron.

To assess the quality of the steam, the following variable, Q, can be defined:

$$Q = \frac{m_{vapor}}{m_{Total}} \tag{2}$$

where m_{vapor} represents the mass of the vapor and m_{Total} the total mass of the contaminated steam. Another metric is the steam purity (in ppm unit) which is a measure of the total solid particles entertained in the process flow.

STEAM MONITORING SYSTEMS IN POWER STATIONS

Most of the meters used so far for steam monitoring provide the gross volumetric or mass flow rate of steam dominated fluid passing through the pipeline. Orifice meter has been used in California's geothermal plant (J. Lokevin et al, 2009) to provide both the mass flow rate and the mixture enthalpy

Figure 4. Deposit of contaminants in the pipeline of the steam power generator (a and b) and on steam strainer (c)
SourceL Adiprana et al., 2010

(a)

(b)

(c)

of the produced fluid using some orifice equations (L. Maxey et al, 1995) (Figure 5). Quality control of the steam was also estimated using some weir calculations but no indication about its performance was revealed. One of the issues which may face the accuracy of this meter is the continuous variations of the density of the process which is a key variable in the Coriolis equation. An acceptable estimation of the density is usually performed by adding few additional sensors such as line pressure sensor and temperature sensors.

Figure 6 illustrates the principle of operation of the orifice meter. The orifice plate which is inserted within the probe causes a pressure drop, *h*, which is proportional to the flow rate, Q, of the steam according to the following equation:

$$Q = CA\sqrt{2gh} \tag{3}$$

where C is the coefficient of discharge (dimensionless), A the area of the orifice, g the gravitational constant (9.8 m/s2) and h the differential pressure which can be measured using a differential pressure sensor with two tap pressure at the upstream and downstream section of the meter respectively. Even though the meter cause relatively high pressure drop to the process and provides a relatively low range of measurements since it can't handle flows with low velocities, it is still the most used meter in steam monitoring industry.

Figure 5. Interior view of James-tube pressure transducer used in the orifice plate
Source: Lokevin, 2009

ABB Corporation (Maxey et al., 1995) provides another metering technology, namely a swirl meter, which consists of three pipe diameters upstream and one downstream, eliminating the pipework modifications usually required to read low flow rates. The principle of operation of the meter consists to generate a rotational movement of input steam at the stagnation point of the inlet pipe (Figure 7 (a)). In the center of this rotation a vortex core is formed which is forced into a secondary spiral-spaced rotation by the backflow. The frequency response of this rotation is proportional to the flow and can be even linear over a wide range of measurement with a proper design of the internal geometry of the meter measuring device. This frequency is measured using a piezo sensor and the corresponding signal undergoes downstream processing in the transmitter. Figure 7 (b) shows a photograph of the meter.

The meter features zero maintenance requirement and an accuracy of 99.5% over the entire flow range and a turndown of up to 10 times that of an orifice plate. The nominal diameter of the probe is selected on the basis of the maximum operating flow, Q_{vmax}.

Another similar meter that measures the frequency of vertices downstream a bluff body was recently suggested by Endress + Hauser Company (Berman et al., 1975). The device which consists of a vortex meter (Prowirl 72Fmeter), a pressure transmitter (Cerabar PMP51) and a temperature sensor (TR14) (Figure 8) was successfully used by Arecelor Mittal Zeniuca in their hot rolled production plant. The vortex flow meter comprises some heat insulating parts to protect the electronics of the transmitter from overheating.

Figure 6. Principle of operation of an orifice flow meter

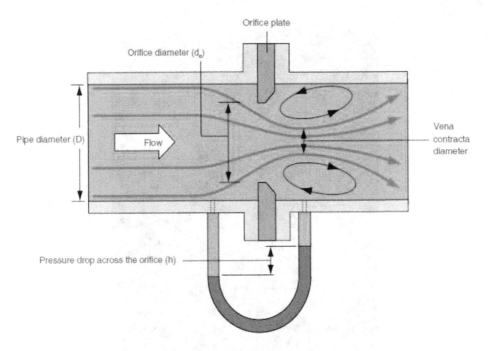

Figure 7. The ABB swirl flow meter: (a) measuring principle of the meter and (b) block diagram of the probe

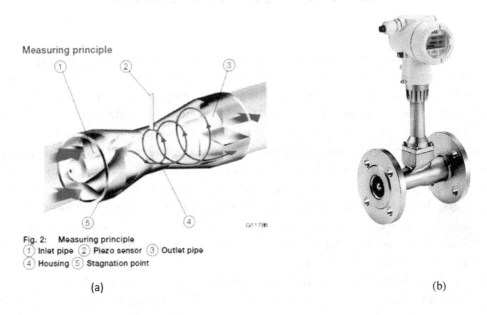

(a)

(b)

Figure 8. Vortex meter for steam monitoring from endress + Hauer
Source: Berman et al, 1975

Figure 9 shows the principle of operation of a vortex flow meter. It consists of a bluff body which is when it is heat by the steam, create vertices, the frequency of which is proportional to the velocity of the flow. Knowing the diameter of the pipeline, the volumetric flow rate can then be determined. The measurement of vertices is usually performed using an array of piezoelectric sensors placed downstream the bluff body. The meter usually provides the best accuracy (compared to orifice meter or even Coriolis meter) for the measurement of flow of steam, entrained with water droplets.

Figure 9. Principle of operation of a vortex flow meter

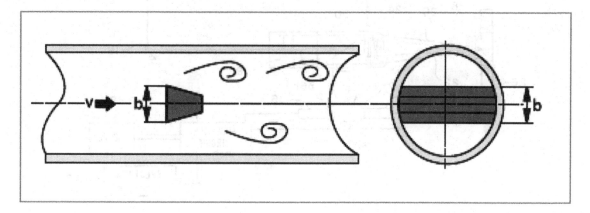

The usage of optical techniques for monitoring wet steam was revealed in (Gao et al., 2009). The sensor uses laser Doppler velocimetry (LDV) device to produce backscatter light which is then processed by a spectrum analyzer to generate a visibility waveform in the frequency domain. The waveform includes a fundamental frequency, the amplitude of which is correlated to the particles sizes and few harmonics. Figure 10 shows the overall principle of the meter. The beam splitter divides the output beam into two coherent beams of same power and of wavelengths of 488 and 514.5 nm respectively. The two generated beams (beam1 and beam 2 in the Figure) are then focused by a lens towards the process. The backscattered light is collected onto the color separator for further treatment.

Recently, General Electric has also suggested another optical sensor for steam monitoring (Grimmelius et al.,1999). The fundamental concept of the device is based on Mie scattering theory which represents the analytical solution of Maxwell's equation for the scattering of electromagnetic radiation of spherical particles. It consists to emit multiple optical waves into the steam and then collect the amount of light transmitted for each of these waves using an array of several photodetectors. The received signals are then normalized by dividing their corresponding intensity by the reference intensity in case of wet steam allows to determine the degree of purity of the steam. Thus, a small intensity ratio corresponds low quality steam. A minimum residual is then determined by solving optimization expression for each scaling factor, which leads to determine the droplet size distribution at nm scale (i.e. in the range from 100 to 5,000 nm) and consequently the steam quality.

Conductivity and pH sensors were also suggested in (Gao et al., 2009) based on the fact that the ionic solutes composing the steam affect both the conductivity and pH of the steam. Hence, since the individual conductivities and pH of all common ions are known, the conductivity can be correlated with their concentration. In case of boiler feed water for instance, the most dominant ions are ammonium and hydroxide and therefore measuring the conductivity and pH of the feed water can inform on the quality of the steam generated downstream the boiler. In Gao et al., 2009 pH and conductivity sensor were used, in addition to a corrosion potential sensor in order to predict the corrosion within the steam turbine. The

Figure 10. Optical sensor for steam monitoring using laser Doppler velocimetry (LDV)
Source: Gao et al., 2009

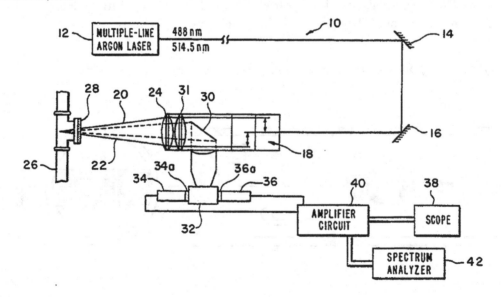

measurement is done on condensed water stored in a chamber within which the steam is pressurized. This however can't represent accurately the characteristic of the steam. The corrosion potential sensor consists of a simple member electrode made of the same material as that of the moving blade (i.e. 13% Cr steel) to operate as a reference electrode and as a structural member.

Another work done for offline steam monitoring used an isokinetic sampling method by introducing either a single-point or multi port traversing probe (Figure 11) (Gao et al., 2009). An effective sampling requires the use of a specifically nozzle installed in a precise location for a given precisely calculated sampling rate. It also requires a good proximity to the steam turbine but away from the flow disturbances (e.g. valves. bends, and changes in the pipe diameter). It should also be downstream to any cleaning filter (e.g. scrubbing system). The principle of isokinetic sampling is well described in (Baker, 2003).

The sample is then handled using a sodium analyzer (Hash 9245) from Hash company (Figure 12). The analyzer which measures the amount of sodium before entering the superheater is able to detect the amount of sodium in the range from 0.01 to 10,000 ppb.

AN INNOVATIVE IMAGING SYSTEM FOR STEAM MONITORING

Figure 13(a) shows the overall installation of the suggested monitoring system. The device which can be placed around any section of the pipeline between the boiler and the steam turbine is composed of an NIR subsystem and a THz subsystem to determine both the type, concentration and flow rate of various contaminants (Figure 13(b)). The two subsystems which can be inserted into the pipelines through flanges and are powered by a single power supply, 24 VDC consume less than 2 Amps and are simultaneously non-intrusive and non-invasive. The whole pre and post processing is done onboard by an FPGA board which then communicates the results to a microcontroller-based transmitter to transfer the data to the remote-control room (Baker, 2003). The material of the THz probe can be made of any material which is transport of THz waves (i.e. material with low dielectric value) such as Inconel 600 which can also sustain high temperatures. The next sections illustrate each of these two subsystems. The NIR receiving probe is attached to the wall of the cylindrical probe via a sapphire convex lens which has the ability to support high temperature while being transparent to NIR radiations.

Figure 11. Isokinetic sampling method for steam quality monitoring in power plant (a) single point traversing probe prepared before installation (b) fixed multiport isokinetic probe

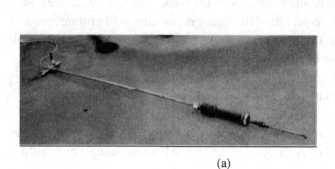

(a)   (b)

Figure 12. The 9240 multi-channel sodium analyzer
Source: Gao et al., 2009

THE NIR SUSBSYTEM

The NIR subsystem is used to complement the THz subsystem where it can provide more accurate results to determine low concentrations of contaminants (i.e. sub-mg concentrations) and also their types, while it can be almost blind for measuring higher concentrations. Figure 14 shows the cross-section of the NIR probe. It consists of a ring of eight (8) NIR receiving probes which are evenly threaded on a 2" diameter cross section of the device via ½ NPT holes. Two sources of light which consist of a 5 V switching regulator (Power trends, 78HT205HC) to feed a 6 W tungsten halogen lamp emit continuously the light by placing them in a such way that the emitted light covers the whole cross-sectional area. Such placement of NIR receivers will let the device to perform NIR tomography imaging in future research. The NIR spectrum has a range from 500 to 2500 nm, a resolution of 5 nm, and a programmable data acquisition time which depends on the number of spectrums to acquire.

In our case, three samples which were averaged within 5 ms time for the same sample showed a very good accuracy as they were enough to discriminate between water and solid contaminants as well as to determine the concentration of each of these elements at sub-mg resolution. The acquired spectrum is then transferred to an FPGA board which performs background compensation (offsets and sloped baselines elimination) to enhance the S/N ratio and PCA analysis to determine both the sample composition

Figure 13. The suggested combined THZ-NIR device (a): the overall installation of the suggested device in a power station (b): the THz and NIR subsystems interfaced to the transmitter

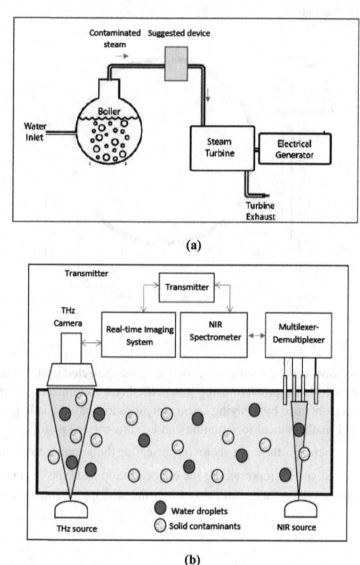

(a)

(b)

and concentration. The PCA analysis which was determined in the range from 800 to 1600 nm was used to reduce the number of variables to be considered by the pattern recognition algorithm by keeping only significant variables which are a linear combination of the original variables. This is because the NIR spectral response consists of several thousands of variables. The new variables which are uncorrelated and represent the most common variation are represented as a combination of orthogonal principal components (PC). Hence, each acquired spectrum has a score along each principal component and can be visualized in the hyper-spectral data. The pattern recognition algorithm is then developed to distinguish water droplets cluster from solid contaminants cluster and also to determine the concentration within each cluster. This latest consists of the Least squares-support vector machine (LS-SVM) which

Figure 14. Cross section of the NIR probe array

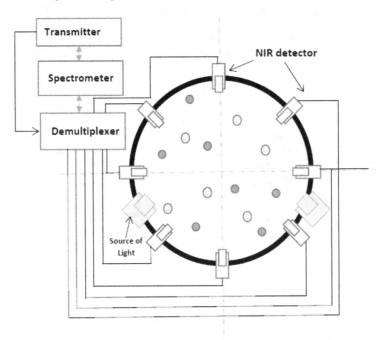

uses learning theory to solve multi-dimensional function. It was selected over the neural network algorithm since it overcomes its extra-problem using a structural risk minimization principles. Hence, the support vectors (SVs) are obtained by applying linear equations instead of quadratic programming (QP) problems. The LS-VSM mathematical formulation can be summarized as follows: Assuming that the training set $\{x_k, y_k\}_{k=1}^{N}$ where x_k is the input vector (representing the sample coordinates in the PC frame) ($x \in R^n$) and y_k the output vector (representing the concentration and type of contaminants) ($y \in R$). The following regression model is then built using a non-linear mapping function, $\Phi(.)$:

$$y(x) = \omega^T \Phi(x) + b \tag{4}$$

where $w(\in R^n)$ is the weight vector and b the bias. The corresponding new optimization problem in case a least squares support vector is used as a soft testing tool can be formulated as follows using the principal of structural risk minimization (SRM):

$$\min_{w,b,w} J\left(w,e\right) = \frac{1}{2}\left(w^T w + \alpha \sum_{k=1}^{N} e_k^2\right) \tag{5}$$

Subject to the constraints:

$$y_k = w^T \varphi\left(x_k\right) + b + e_k \tag{6}$$

with: $k = 1, \ldots, N$

where α is the regularization parameter which let the model's complexity and the training errors stable and e_k is the random error equilibrium. The Lagrange function is then adopted to solve the following optimization problem:

$$L(w,b,e,s) = J(w,e) - \sum_{k=1}^{N} s_k \left[w^T \varphi(x_k) + b + e_k - y_k \right])$$ (7)

where s_k is the Lagrange multiplier which is also named the support value. The solution of the above equation can be obtained using the following partial differential equations with respect to each variable:

$$\frac{dL}{dw} = 0 : w = \sum_{k=1}^{N} s_k \varphi(x_k)$$ (8)

$$\frac{dL}{db} = 0 : \sum_{k=1}^{N} s_k = 0$$

$$\frac{dL}{de_k} = 0 : s_k = \alpha e_k$$

$$\frac{dL}{ds_k} = 0 : w^T \varphi(x_k) + b + e_k - y_k = 0$$

The above set of equations can be expressed according to the following matrix product:

$$\begin{bmatrix} 0 & I_v^T \\ I_v & M\alpha^{-1}I \end{bmatrix} \begin{bmatrix} b \\ s \end{bmatrix} = \begin{bmatrix} 0 \\ y \end{bmatrix}$$ (9)

With the following assumptions:

$$I_v = [1,1....1] \; y = [y_1,....., y_n]$$

$$s = [s_1,....., s_n]$$

$$M = \{\varphi(x_k)^T\left(x_l\right) = K\left(x_k, x_l\right) where : k, l = 1, ..., N\}$$

where $K\left(x_k, x_l\right)$ is the vector of reference which must satisfies the Mercer's condition to perform both linear and non-linear mapping. In this paper, this function was considered as follows:

$$K\left(x_k, x_l\right) = \exp\left(-\frac{\left|\left|x_k, x_l\right|\right|^2}{2\rho^2}\right) \tag{10}$$

Consequently, the LS-SVM classification model can be expressed as:

$$y\left(x\right) = sgn\sum_{k=1}^{N}s_k K\left(x_k, x_l\right) + b \tag{11}$$

Figure 15. Photograph of the THz imaging subsystem

THE THZ IMAGING SUBSYSSTEM

The THz imaging subsystem complements the NIR subsystem by measuring high concentrations of contaminants which may not be captured by the NIR subsystem. As shown in Figure 15 below, a THz source continuously emits THz waves into the probe which are then captured by a 2D imaging system (64 x 64 pixels in this paper). The pixel intensity, which depends on the dielectric value of the object in the vicinity of the camera and the THz source, is used to determine the concentration of contaminants and its flow rate. The latter is determined by computing the motion vector at each block of the image, centered at (i_0, j_0), using block-based motion estimation algorithm (Figure 16):

$$Match\left(i_0, j_0\right) = \min_{u,v}[\sum_{i=i_0-\frac{N}{2}}^{i_0+\frac{N}{2}} \sum_{j=j_0-\frac{N}{2}}^{j_0+\frac{N}{2}} \mid I\left(i,j\right) - I^{-1}\left(i+u, j+v\right) \mid$$

for

$$u \in \left[-\frac{M}{2}, \frac{M}{2}\right]$$

and

$$v \in \left[-\frac{M}{2}, \frac{M}{2}\right] \tag{12}$$

Figure 16. Block-based motion estimation for flow measurement of contaminants

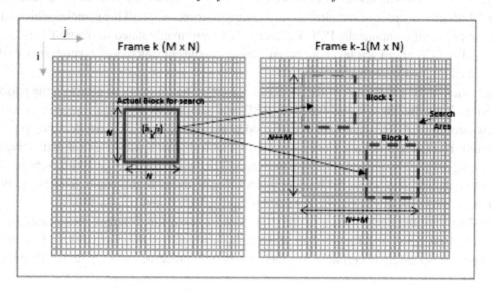

where Match(i_0, j_0) represents the best match of the block centered at pixel (i_0, j_0) in the reference image, N x N is the block size (N = 8 in this paper), and $(N+M)$ x $(N+M)$ the search area (M = 6) (Abldurhman et al., 2014). The global motion vector $V(V_x, V_y$ in the whole THz image is then determined by computing the average of individual motion vectors. This way, the total flow rate and the flow of individual contaminants can be determined.

The regular highly parallel computation structure of the above algorithm allows for the design of a dedicated parallel architecture based on Field Programmable Gate Array (FPGA) (Stratix V FPGA in this paper), where the on-chip memory array and the DSP block array which comprise floating point multipliers and adders allowed to achieve the motion estimation algorithm at the THz frame rate (i.e. 30 frames/s).

RESULTS AND DISCUSSION

The assessment of the device was conducted on a home-made 3 m-length trolley system which consists of two 1 cm width parallel belts attached to two pulleys at each end. Different concentrations of water and iron oxide particles were put on 50 mm * 20 mm microscopic slides. The water droplets were uniformly dropped on the slides using a plastic ear dropper bottle, while the black powder particles were measured using a precise microgram scaler to be then uniformly dropped on the microscopic slides. This way, the setup can help assess the accuracy of the system for very small concentrations of contaminants which is not easily done with a flow loop. NIR spectroscopy is a vibrational technique which relates to the absorbance of energy due to the excitation of molecules. This corresponds to overtones and combinations of the fundamental vibration frequencies related to specific functional groups which are dominated by O-H in case of water droplets. Figure 17 shows the absorbance spectra of 4 different concentrations of water droplets. As it was expected, the absorbance increases based on the function of the number of droplets. Similarly, Figure 18 shows that that absorbance of the solid contaminants (iron oxide) increases based on the function of their concentration. The solid contaminants were prepared using very accurate scale machine. The clear dissimilarity of the two spectrums is explored to distinguish between water droplets and solid contaminants. The results of PCA which was used to reduce the data dimensionality is shown in Figure 19. Hence, in order to visualize the clustering information of all the samples which have been tested, three principal components, PC1, PC2, and PC3 were manipulated to obtain the PC1 x PC2 x PC2 scores. The PCA graph was taken for two different samples of iron oxides taken from two different locations, in addition to water droplets samples.

The selection of the parameters of the LS-SVM algorithm has an obvious effect on the performance of the device. The radial basis kernel function (RBF) was adopted in this paper, where two parameters, ρ^2 and α, where adjusted. Too small (respectively too large) value of ρ leads to overlearning (respectively under learning) for the sample data. Hence, a two grid search approach with cross validation was adopted on the training set for obtaining optimum parameters. The two parameters ρ^2 and α were used for the assessment of algorithm to obtain the best combination of ρ^2 and α. In this paper, the best results by the grid searching and cross validation was obtained with $\alpha = 35.765$ and $\rho^2 = 24.143$.

Figure 20 shows the performance of the NIR-based system for different concentrations of solid contaminants. Hence, the linear regression of the curve resulted in 0.9905 and 1.0012 first order coefficients. The corresponding uncertainty was then +/- 1.45%, which was slightly higher than the case of

Figure 17. VIS/NIR absorbance of four different amounts of water droplets

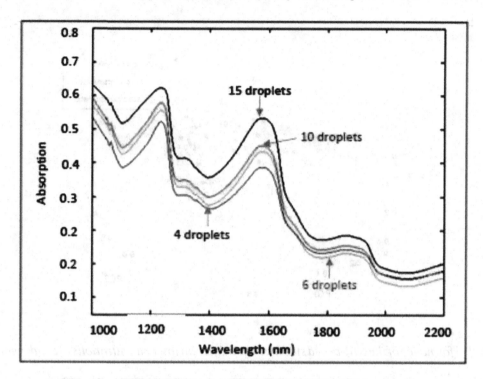

Figure 18. NIR spectra for different concentrations of solid contaminants

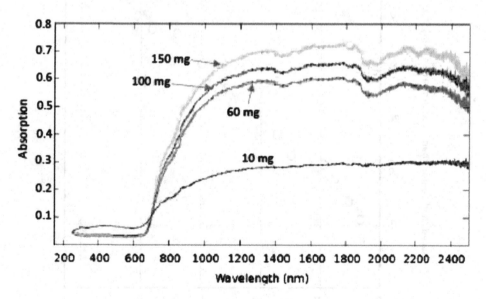

Figure 19. 3D PCA graphs for contaminants (solid and liquid contaminants)

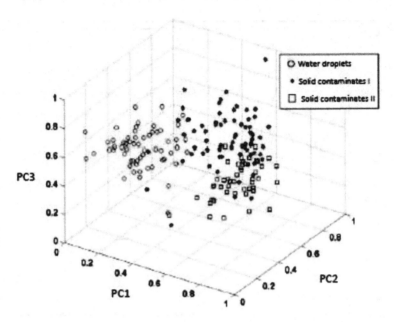

Figure 20. Performance of the NIR-based subsystem for different low concentrations of solid contaminants

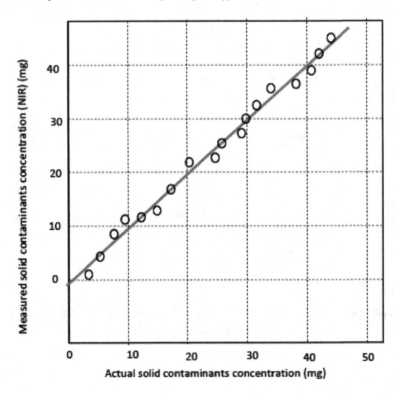

water droplets where the uncertainty was around +/-1.16%. Both results demonstrate that the NIR-based subsystem is capable to deal with low concentration of both solid contaminants and water droplets. The usage of NIR tomography technique, which constitutes our next target, can even help know the distribution of these contaminants across the section of the probe.

With the THz subsystem, the concentration was measured by counting the average pixel value which is proportional to the amount of contaminants (Figure 21). Figure 22 shows the results of motion estimation algorithm for a microscopic slide containing 100 mg of solid contaminants taken at two different

Figure 21. Normalized pixel intensity for various concentration of solid contaminants

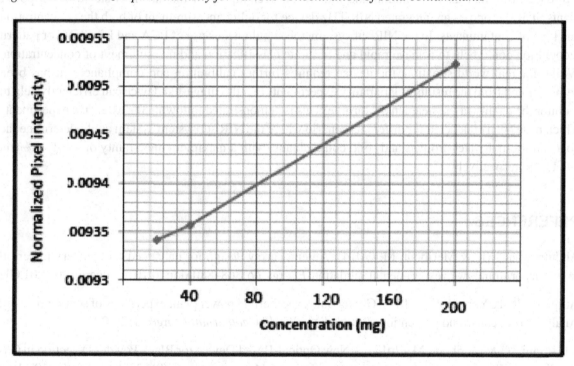

Figure 22. Motion vector fields for two THz images taken at two different time slots for the same sample containing 100 mg of solid contaminants

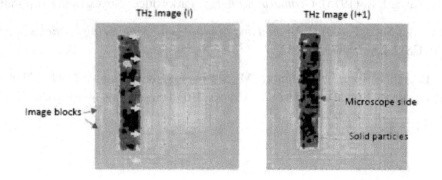

time slots. Hence, the computed motion vector matches the movement of the slide. Correct results of motion vectors were obtained for all samples carried so far.

CONCLUSION

Safe and reliable operation of steam-based power generators depends upon the quality of steam which usually carries water droplets and/or solid contaminants. Even though mitigation techniques such as mechanical filtering and chemical treatments can enhance the efficiency of the system, electronic instrumentation still plays a vital role in proper management of the power generator. This book chapter introduced different instrumentation and monitoring techniques for the steam in steam-based power plants. It also proposes an integrated NIR-THz device for online measurement of both the concentration and type of contaminants. In the NIR subsystem, the simultaneous use of PCA and LS-SVM for pattern recognition could help to achieve rapid and accurate classification and measurement of concentration. While, for real world situation, the device requires further calibration and compliances, it has been demonstrated from the results of laboratory experiments that the suggested device can efficiently help to monitor the quality of the steam in the turbine. This is demonstrated following the extensive experiments which have been conducted for different scenario where the NIR subsystem system could determine the concentration of water droplets and solid contaminants with a maximum uncertainty of +/- 1.45% and +/- 1.16% respectively.

REFERENCES

Abdulrahman, M., & Meribout, M. (2014). Antenna array design for enhanced oil recovery under oil reservoir constraints with experimental validation. *Energy*, *66*, 868–880. doi:10.1016/j.energy.2014.01.002

Adiprana, R., & Yuniarto, E. (2010). Guung Salak geothermal power plant experience of scaling/deposit: Analysis, root cause and prevention. *Proceedings World Geothermal Congress*, 25-29.

Al Hosani, E., & Meribout, M. (2014). A New Optical-Based Device for Black Powder Detection in Gas Pipelines. *IEEE Transactions on Instrumentation and Measurement*, *63*(9), 2238–2252. doi:10.1109/TIM.2014.2308985

Baker, M. (2003). *Fluid Contaminant Sensor.* US patent: US 6,549,856 B2.

Berman, B., & Edward, R. (1975). *Geothermal Energy.* Park Ridge: Noyes Data Corporation.

Bunce, R., & Dovali-Solis, F. (2011). *Method and Apparatus for Monitoring Particles in a Gas Turbine Working Fluid.* US Patent US871,237,B2.

Fukutomi, S., Takagi, T., Tani, J., Hashimoto, M., Shimone, J., & Harada, Y. (1997). Numerical Evaluation of ECT Impedance Signal due to Minute Cracks. IEE Transactions on Magnetic, 33(2).

Gao, Z., Thomas, G., & Ronald, G. (2009). A Complex Space Vector Approach to Rotor Temperature Estimation for Line-Connected Induction Machines with Impaired Cooling. IEEE Transactions on Industrial Electronics, 56(1), 239-247.

Grimmelius, H., Meiler, P. P., Maas, H., Bonnier, B., Grevink, J. S., & Van Kuilenburg, R. F. (1999). Three State-of-the-Art Methods for Condition Monitoring. IEEE Transaction on Industrial Electronics, 46(2), 407-416.

Jean, B. (2008). A Microwave sensor for steam quality. *IEEE Transactions on Instrumentation and Measurement, 57*(4), 751–754. doi:10.1109/TIM.2007.913821

Kothare, M., Metler, B., Morari, M., Bendotti, P., & Falinower, C. (2000). Level Control in the Steam Generator of a Nuclear Plant. *IEEE Transactions on Control Systems Technology, 8*(1), 55–69. doi:10.1109/87.817692

Lord, W., & Palanisamy, R. (1980). Detection and Modeling of Agneite Buildup in Steam Generators. *IEEE Transactions on Magnetics, MAG-16*(5).

Lovekin, J., & James, W. (2009). Correlation of Rig Tests and James Tube Tests in the Coso Geothermal Field. *Proceedings, Fifteenth Workshop on Geothermal Reservoir Engineering.*

Maxey, L., & Simpson, M. (1995). *Optical wet steam monitor.* US patent 5,383,024.

Meribout, M. (2011). A wireless sensor network-based infrastructure for real-time and online pipeline section. *IEEE Sensors Journal, 11*(11), 2966–2972. doi:10.1109/JSEN.2011.2155054

Meribout, M., & Al Naamany, A. (2009). A collision free data link layer protocol for wireless sensor networks and its application in intelligent transportation systems. *IEEE Wireless Telecommunications Symposium (WTS'2009)*, 1-6. 10.1109/WTS.2009.5068957

Meribout, M., Galeel, M., Al Marzouqi, M., & Aasi, M. A. (2010). A new concept for an effective leak detection in multiphase fluid pipelines. *2011 First International Conference on sensor device Technologies and Applications (SensorDevices'2010)*, 206-210.

Meribout, M., Nakanishi, M., & Ogura, T. (2002). A Parallel Algorithm for Real-time Object Recognition. Pattern Recognition Journal, 35(9).

Mohsin, M., & Meribout, M. (2015). An extended model for ultrasonic-based enhanced oil recovery with experimental validation. *Ultrasonics Sonochemistry, 23*, 413–423. doi:10.1016/j.ultsonch.2014.08.007 PMID:25219873

Mohsin, M., & Meribout, M. (2015). Oil-water de-emulsificatin using ultrasonic technology. *Ultrasonics Sonochemistry, 22*, 573–579. doi:10.1016/j.ultsonch.2014.05.014 PMID:24935027

Piyushsinh, Z. (2014). Application of Monitoring Approaches on Steam Turbine of Thermal Power Plant for Better Performance. *International Journal of Mechanical Engineering and Robotics Research, 3*(2).

Rehman, M., & Meribout, M. (2012). Conventional versus Electrical Enhanced Oil Recovery: A Review. *Journal of Petroleum Exploration and Production Technology, 2*(4), 169–179. doi:10.100713202-012-0035-9

Roy, B., & Guo, T. (2012). *Method and system for steam quality monitoring.* US Patent 2012/0123696 A1.

Teniou, S., & Meribout, M. (2012). A new Hierarchical algorithm for Electrical Capacitance Tomography. *Measurement Journal (Elsevier), 45*(4), 683–690. doi:10.1016/j.measurement.2011.12.022

Zhang, E., Zhang, H., & Xue, B. (2008). Application of Integrated Neural Network based on information Combination for fault Diagnosis in Steam Turbine Generator. *International conference on Condition Monitoring and Diagnostic*, 21-24.

Chapter 10
Secure Embedded Systems:
Concepts and Issues

Ali Ahmadinia
California State University – San Marcos, USA

Ahmed Saeed
COMSATS Institute of Information Technology, Pakistan

ABSTRACT

As computing devices have become an almost integral part of our lives, security of systems and protection of the sensitive data are emerging as very important issues. This is particularly evident for embedded systems which are often deployed in unprotected environments and at the same time being constrained by limited resources. Security and trust have also become important considerations in the design of virtually all modern embedded systems as they are utilized in critical and sensitive applications such as in transportation, national infrastructure, military equipment, banking systems, and medical devices. The increase in software content and network connectivity has made them vulnerable to fast spreading software-based attacks such as viruses and worms, which were hitherto primarily the concern of personal computers, servers, and the internet. This chapter discusses the basic concepts, security attacks types, and existing preventive measures in the field of embedded systems and multi-core systems.

1. INTRODUCTION

The modern embedded devices can execute almost all the network/internet applications that were normally designed to run on devices such as personal computer (PC) in the past. Today's embedded devices are increasingly getting involved in network communications. The safety-critical systems also require communication of sensitive data through public networks which are not fully protected from unauthorized accesses. Security has become a very serious issue as the attacks against these systems are becoming more pivotal and sophisticated. Embedded systems are used in certain application domains where traditional personal computers or servers are not suitable to use due to a limited budget, power supply, size, or weight. On the other hand, security techniques being designed for general purpose computing devices are not suitable for such embedded systems due to its limited resources.

DOI: 10.4018/978-1-5225-5510-0.ch010

In this chapter, the key characteristics of an embedded system that lead to various security exploitations are presented in Section 2 and different types of security attacks are discussed in Section 3. The overview of existing security solutions and their limitations related to generic embedded systems NoC based multi-core systems are presented in Section 4 and the critical analysis of existing security mechanisms is discussed in Section 5.

2. VULNERABILITIES IN EMBEDDED SYSTEMS

Typically, embedded systems are categorized based on the design methodology followed, processor architecture, assigned workload and other characteristics such as area, power consumption, and performance. There are two important key characteristics that make such embedded systems prone to the security attacks. Firstly, the simplified processing capabilities and limited power resources expose such systems to a number of possible security attacks. Secondly, the network connectivity to the outside world, without any inbuilt protection, also leaves such systems vulnerable to security attacks. Overall, these characteristics lead to the following vulnerabilities.

Due to *constrained computational resources* of an embedded system, typical security solutions cannot be deployed that are used to prevent security attacks in conventional computer systems (e.g., firewalls, anti-virus, intrusion detection system).

Due to the *limited power supply*, the embedded systems can only allocate limited resources in terms of power consumption to provide system security. For example, it is not feasible to implement complex encryption algorithms as security features, which are computationally intensive and consequently consume more power.

Embedded systems being deployed at *remote locations* (e.g., public location, remote field location), cannot be monitored all the time. Therefore, such embedded systems are more vulnerable to physical attacks. Examples of sensitive data that should be protected are cryptographic keys or information stored on a smart card.

For embedded systems, the *network connectivity*, either wireless or wired, has become usual. Such network access is essential for remote configuration, information collection and applying updates. Specifically, where the embedded system is connected to the public network, vulnerabilities in the system can be exploited remotely from anywhere. For example, in a video surveillance system, an altered video feed can be attached to a security camera. Similarly, in an electricity meter, the data can be overwritten through unauthorized access.

Peripherals or sensor devices attached to the embedded systems are also vulnerable to attacks. Damaging the peripherals may also cause incorrect operation of the system such as tampering with the calibration of a sensor may lead to erroneous output.

Typically, embedded systems are designed to work in good operating conditions. As such systems may be installed in a *hostile environment*, the attacker can overheat the system in order to stop it from working properly or even cause other environmental damages.

These kinds of vulnerabilities in the embedded systems can be exploited by an attacker to steal private data, drain the power supply, destroy the system, or modify the system behavior for other than its designed purpose. Therefore, security-awareness is becoming a primary design objective to be considered at each level of the software and hardware platforms design for future SoC embedded devices. In fact, it is very likely that an attacker might choose weak points of the system instead of using complex methods (e.g. brute force attacks) in order to get access to the protected information.

3. ATTACKS ON EMBEDDED SYSTEMS

Embedded systems are attacked mainly, either to get access to the sensitive information or to slow down the system. Security attacks on embedded systems, depending on the functional objectives of the attack, are more commonly categorized as data confidentiality attacks, data integrity attacks, and availability attacks.

3.1. Nature of Attacks

3.1.1. Data Modification Attacks

Such attacks target integrity of the secure data. These types of attacks get illegal access to write in the secure area of the systems in order to modify behavior or configuration of the system. It also includes execution of malicious code in addition to the normal tasks. For instance, during a data transfer, the sensitive information can be modified by the attacker without the knowledge of the sender or receiver. Even if the communication link is secured, the data can be modified such as through buffer overflow attacks. The overflow attacks may cause writing at unwanted addresses memory, consequently modifying the data. After gaining the illegitimate access, the attacker can either modify or delete the sensitive data. Moreover, the attacker might change the database or alter the application data so that it can perform extra operations.

3.1.2. Data Extraction Attacks

Such attacks target confidentiality of the secure data and are based on getting illegal access to read sensitive data stored in secure targets. The stolen information can be sensitive data (e.g. encryption keys and passwords), instructions from critical programs, configuration registers and so on. Similar to code modification attacks, the sensitive information can be extracted through a buffer overflow or similar techniques exploiting vulnerabilities in the system hardware or software.

3.1.3. Performance Degradation Attacks

These kinds of attacks more formally known as a denial of service (DOS) attacks. The main objective of these attacks is to bring down the system performance by overloading computing and communications resources. The unnecessary resource utilization downgrades the operability of the system and may implicate real-time behaviors of the system. Embedded systems operating on the battery are the target of these types of attacks. Such attacks may also involve continuous sending of requests to the victim embedded system, in order to force execution of power-hungry tasks. Such type of attacks also targets communication medium of the system in order to reduce throughput which may result in failure to meet specific deadlines especially in the case of real-time systems.

In a shared memory environment, unauthorized access to the data and instructions of the program running on the system can compromise its integrity, which may lead to system crash or unexpected behavior. Therefore, protection of sensitive data is very critical, specifically in multi-core systems where memory blocks are often shared among different processing cores.

Depending on the nature of agent being used, attacks on embedded systems can be either software based (e.g., viruses, malware) or physical in nature(e.g., chip cutting or chemical attacks (Ravi, Raghunathan, Kocher, & Hattangady, 2004) and might involve side channel analysis (e.g., power consumption analysis (Kocher, Jaffe, & Jun, 1999), timing analyses (Song, Wagner, & Tian, 2001). One or more of these types of agents can be used by an attacker in order to breach confidentiality and integrity of data and availability of the system.

3.2. Physical Attacks

Physical attacks require direct access to the target device and are based on intruding into the system either through physical tampering or observing the state of the system. These types of attacks require an understanding of the characteristic implementation of the system or some of its properties in order to break into the security of the device. Physical attacks are more commonly categorized as invasive (or active) and non-invasive (or passive) attacks.

3.2.1. Invasive Attacks

Invasive or *active attacks* require direct access to the components present within the system and this may be achieved by breaking its packaging. For instance, if a system is being implemented on a printed circuit board (PCB) comprising of various components then by means of probes the communication among different components can be eavesdropped to get the desired information. For SoCs, access to the internal information is achieved through advanced techniques by disintegrating the chip. Micro-probes are used to observe the internal structure and detect values on buses, memories, and interfaces. A probing station, consisting of a microscope and micromanipulators for positioning micro-probes on the surface of the chip, can be used to launch a typical micro-probing attack. Such probing stations are commonly used during manufacturing phase of the ICs in order to verify their functionality. Normally, the chip is disintegrated carefully by dissolving the protecting layers through different chemical solutions. Micro-probes or electron microscopes are therefore used to detect values inside the IC. Such attacks are difficult to conduct due to expensive infrastructure and skills required. However, physical attacks can be employed to get useful information, such as the internal layout of the chip and the allocation of its main components, which can be further used to perform other types of passive attacks.

3.2.2. Non-Invasive Attacks

Non-invasive or *passive attacks*, which are more commonly known as side-channel attacks, do not damage the target IC and are based on external analysis of the system. In order to conduct these kinds of attacks, the expert knowledge of the internal implementation of a system is required. Examples of side-channel attacks include simple power analysis (SPA) (Mangard, 2003), differential power analysis (DPA) (Kocher et al., 1999), timing analysis (Song et al., 2001) and electromagnetic analysis (EMA) attacks (Rao & Rohatgi, 2001).

In timing analysis attacks, the time required by the system to process a set of known inputs is observed with the aim to recover the secret information (e.g., cryptographic keys). For instance, to get the encryption key through timing analysis attack, the attacker must have complete knowledge of the implementation of a cryptographic algorithm and access to the system. Specific hardware blocks dedicated to the cryptographic algorithm are targeted and the time required to generate output against different input combinations is observed.

Power analysis attacks are based on observing the power dissipated by the device while performing the specific task. Gate switching activity and the parasitic capacitance of the interconnect wires play major roles in dynamic power consumption. These kinds of attacks were first introduced by Kocher et al. (Kocher et al., 1999) by successfully extracting the secret keys being used in an encryption program by analyzing the power consumption of a chip. Power analysis attacks can be categorized as simple power analysis (SPA) and differential power analysis (DPA). SPA attacks are based on direct analysis of power consumption measurements gathered during the execution of a cryptographic task whereas DPA attacks are based on the use of error correction techniques and statistical analysis of power being dissipated during given cryptographic operation.

Electromagnetic analysis attacks are based on analyzing the electromagnetic radiations emitted by the system. This is normally achieved by placing coils within the range of the chip and interpreting the measured electromagnetic field values.

These measurements can be analyzed either directly, using simple analysis, or just like DPA more advanced correlation techniques can be used. As compared to the power analysis attacks, EMA attacks are more flexible and measurements can be made at a notable distance from the device. Moreover, indepth knowledge of the device layout can be used to conduct the attack more effectively.

3.3. Software Attacks

Vulnerabilities in the embedded systems can also be manipulated through software attacks using malware such as Trojan horses, viruses, and worms. Malware is a term used for any malicious piece of software that gets installed on the target system without the consent of the valid user and performs undesirable tasks. These kinds of attacks exploit weaknesses in the application code, such as in the case of using buffer overflow or similar techniques. Example of software attacks include code-reuse techniques, injection of malware through heap-based buffer overflows, stack-based buffer overflows, exploitation of dangling pointers (also known as use-after-free) and format strings vulnerabilities. Once the malware is installed, it can steal confidential data, modify the behavior of the system or even disable it completely.

As the embedded systems software increase in functionality and complexity, they are well expected to become an ideal target for security attacks. The network connectivity of embedded devices has increased the number of attacks that may target the system as the physical access to the device is no longer required (Studnia et al., 2013). For instance, upgrading system software and downloading new applications over public network increase the chances allowing attackers to launch a malicious code. Various malware for smartphones have been reported in recent years and such attacks are likely to target embedded devices utilizing network connectivity. Software attacks can be launched using a low cost and simple platform set-up as compared to the physical attacks; they represent a major challenge in securing embedded systems. More recently, Checkoway et al., (2011) have successfully demonstrated that various security attacks can be launched through remote access by uncovering and exploiting vulnerabilities in embedded devices deployed inside a car.

Buffer overflow-based software attacks are one of the major causes of security outbreaks. These types of attacks are mainly caused due to unsafe programming languages like C/C++ and poor programming practices. These attacks occur when a program takes input from the user by storing data into a buffer using unprotected library functions. While accessing memory locations various library functions (e.g., *strcpy, memcpy*) in C and C++ do not check buffer bounds and can be therefore easily manipulated to overwrite the allocated bounds of the buffers. Even bounded functions such as *strcpy* can cause vulnerabilities when used incorrectly. According to a report published by Sourcefire (Younan et al., 2010), buffer overflow-based attacks are responsible for 14% of all vulnerabilities and 35% of critical vulnerabilities over the past 25 years.

Buffers allocated on the stack are most commonly exploited to execute malicious code. Before going into the details, it is important to understand how a program data is organized in memory. Every program has its own memory space to store user data and can be categorized as a stack, heap, and a data region. The stack is used to store statically allocated local variables and function return addresses. Heap is used for storing dynamically allocated variables whereas *data region* is used to store globally declared initialized and uninitialized variables.

Stack smashing (One, 1996) is a classic example of buffer overflow-based attacks. During attack execution, the return address of a function on the stack is replaced through a buffer overflow. In case of unprotected execution, on function return, the control may be switched to the specific location where malicious code is placed as shown in Figure 1. In order to conduct this kind of attack, an unprotected

Figure 1. Typical buffer overflow leading to a stack smashing attack

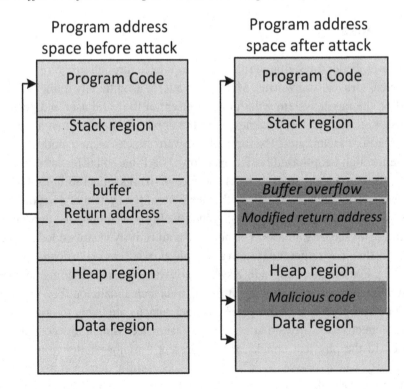

buffer variable is located in the program and then it is loaded with a special input value so that its stack frame is overflown and the return address changed to jump to a new location. In a similar fashion, the buffers, allocated either dynamically in the *heap region* or globally in the *data region* of the memory, can be also overflown and exploited by the attackers.

Return-into-lib(c) (RILC) (Wojtczuk, 2001) is the simplest form of code-reuse attack and it also depends on buffer overflow. In a RILC attack, the return address of a function is overwritten with the address of another function, from a shared library, that is already present in the program's memory. For programs being written in C language, shared library *libc* is always linked to the final executable being generated by any standard compiler (such as GNU Compiler Collection, *gcc*). As *libc* is the standard C library which provides functions required to perform important operations as input/output, memory management, and string manipulation, it is the most likely target of an attacker in order to achieve required outcome. Moreover, different functions can be connected together which permit an attacker to execute a sequence of random function calls. Such methods can be used to degrade the system performance.

Similarly, return-oriented programming (ROP) is a refined and generalized form of RILC attack. It is relatively a new way to accomplish security exploits without injecting any malicious piece of code. In this kind of attack, the control flow of the program is redirected through buffer overflow and then different blocks of instructions from the existing program code are executed to create new functionality and achieve desired results. ROP attack was first introduced by Shacham (Shacham, 2007) and he called the group of instructions a *gadget*. These gadgets can be connected together to achieve a specific task. In this way, a malicious activity can be performed by using different gadgets such as to load and store data from one memory location to another.

Memory can be allocated dynamically and accessed through pointers. The allocated memory can also be got freed when it is no longer required. Dangling pointers emerge when the given memory is deallocated and it can still be accessed through the pointer. Dangling pointers may lead to use-after-free vulnerabilities as attackers can locate such pointers in the program and then launch malicious code by injecting it at the memory location being pointed by the dangling pointer. Such attacks based on dangling pointers have become more prevalent among attackers. For instance, CVE-2014-1776 ("NVD - CVE-2014-1776," 2014) is one of the most recent user-after vulnerabilities exploited by the attackers.

4. EXISTING SECURITY SOLUTIONS

For the last couple of decades, different security solutions for embedded systems have been proposed depending on the nature of attacks, system configurations, functional characteristics and performance requirements. Various security mechanisms (Bayrak, Velickovic, Ienne, & Burleson, 2012; Yang et al., 2012) exist to address physical attacks. Recent technological advancements at the chip manufacturing level have improved the physical security of the SoC embedded devices in terms of increased design complexity, higher cost of the attack infrastructure and advanced skills required to launch a physical attack. At the same time, software-based attacks do not require tampering with the device and can be launched remotely without the need of any sophisticated or expensive platform as compared to the physical attacks. Therefore, the main focus here is the handling of software-based attacks and the relevant security solutions have been elaborated and discussed in detail in this section. There are various security solutions that have been proposed in the literature for embedded systems. Based on the implementation level, these solutions can be categorized as follows.

4.1. Hardware-Assisted Countermeasures

Currently, for embedded systems, different hardware-assisted secure processing techniques have been presented in the literature such as reference monitors, secure memory architecture, cryptographic algorithms, dynamic information flow tracking (DIFT) and hardware virtualization.

Software-based attacks that target confidentiality and integrity of the data can be avoided by encrypting the data. Various security technologies and mechanisms have been designed around cryptographic algorithms in order to provide specific security services. For example, secure communication protocols provide ways of ensuring secure communication channels. Internet Protocol Security (IPSec) and Transport Layer Security (TLS) ("IETF Datatracker," 2017) are popular examples of such security protocols being used nowadays by modern server machines to secure communication over the Internet. Cryptographic algorithms such as Advanced Encryption Standard (AES) and RSA ("IETF Datatracker," 2017) have been used in embedded systems to establish the integrity of data within the system. Milenkovic et.al (Milenković, Milenković, & Jovanov, 2005) presented a solution to ensure the integrity of software running on the system using AES to encrypt instruction blocks of the program using special hardware keys at the time of secure software configuration. The encrypted signatures for each block are stored along with the program code. During program execution, signatures are decrypted from instructions and verified with the stored signatures to detect any invalid changes in the program instructions. Similarly, Huffmire et al., (2008) presented a complete security solution for a reconfigurable multi-core embedded system where a separate processing core is dedicated to handling AES operations.

Protection against code injection attacks can be achieved by implementing secure memory architectures such as execute-only memory (XOM). The main purpose of XOM is to mark and use certain areas of the memory for executable instructions. The memory can be divided into executable and non-executable regions. For example, Intel's x86 architecture ("AMD, Intel put antivirus tech into chips | ZDNet," 2004) has a non-executable bit that prevents the execution of code in the specified area of the memory, thereby averting some buffer overflow attacks. Lie et al., (2000) presented hardware implementation of a XOM restricting unauthorized read/write operations to the memory and only allowing instructions to be fetched for execution. The required protection is provided by encrypting the program instructions using a combination of symmetric and asymmetric cryptography.

Hardware virtualization security solutions are based on isolating such processing cores that require a higher level of security. In such techniques, the components are partitioned into two separate regions. Different access rules can be defined which can be used to configure a specific component as trusted or un-trusted unit. Such access rules are normally configured through dedicated and secured software, which is commonly known as a hypervisor. Yan et al. in (Yan, Li, Li, & Deng, 2009) have presented a concept of hardware isolation for embedded systems such as mobile devices. It is based on deactivating the vulnerable components (such as Bluetooth and WiFi) when sensitive applications are executing on the system. Such hardware isolation can achieve a basic protection level even when the software running on the system has been compromised by malware. In the field of embedded systems, similar techniques have been presented recently such as ARM's TrustZone technology (ARM, 2017), where the system components are divided into secure and non-secure where the system resources are separated into trusted and un-trusted regions. This security mechanism also involves ARM AMBA bus architecture and I/O devices interfaces to be altered and a dedicated software module in order to support the required security features.

Present hardware based reference monitors (Arora, Ravi, Raghunathan, & Jha, 2005; Mao & Wolf, 2010; Rahmatian, Kooti, Harris, & Bozorgzadeh, 2012; Yoon, Mohan, Choi, Kim, & Sha, 2013) in the embedded systems, are based on observing the state of program being executed by the processor and comparing it with a predefined static model. Typically, such reference monitors emphasize on the detection of code modification attacks and are implemented to operate in parallel with the other processing cores. The static models are normally obtained through static analysis and profiling of the programs to be loaded on the system. For example, Arora et al., (2005) presented a hierarchical hardware-assisted monitoring architecture to check program behavior at the basic block level and validate the integrity of the instruction stream using cryptographic hash tables for secure program execution in embedded systems. The program properties are extracted at compile time through static program analysis in a hierarchical manner through inter and intraprocedural control flow analysis for each program. Mao et al. (Mao & Wolf, 2010) suggested a hardware-assisted security monitoring component in embedded systems to detect execution of malicious program or modification in the actual program. The idea is to match the data stream coming out of the processor with the anticipated behavior. At design time, the behavior of the actual program is derived in the form of a graph from the off-line analysis of the binary file. A hashed pattern and control flow pattern is used in particular for that purpose.

Rahmatian et al., (2012) presented a hardware-based solution to detect deviations in a program execution at runtime, as a result of code injection attacks in embedded systems. Primarily, it is based on monitoring of system calls generated by programs at runtime. The behavior of the genuine system is modeled at design time by characterizing the legal sequence of system calls. A separate FSM is associated with each executing program. Similarly, the security solution presented in Yoon et al., (2013) is based on observing and interpreting the basic properties of the real-time system to detect any malicious activity.

Hardware-based Dynamic Information Flow Tracking (DIFT) (Doudalis, Clause, Venkataramani, Prvulovic, & Orso, 2012) is another effective technique to ensure protection against software-based attacks. The basic idea is to mark certain input sources that are untrusted and track the flow of information that is being supplied to the program through these input sources. All data values that are dependent on the marked input value are also get marked (more commonly known as tainted values). If the tainted value leads to any un-tainted data value during program execution then an alert signal is generated reflecting an unauthorized access. Most recently Doudalis et al., (2012) have presented a hardware-assisted solution for embedded systems to detect illegal memory accesses (IMAs) in the C/C++ based applications when a pointer is used to access memory outside the bounds of the allocated memory area. It is based on associating unique taint marks with each pointer and its allocated memory block. These taint marks are then propagated and verified through taint checking instructions, whenever memory is accessed. The binary executable is instrumented by tainting the pointer variables and a hardware module is implemented to propagate taints along with the pointers and to perform taint checking whenever memory is accessed.

4.2. Software-Assisted Countermeasures

Different software-assisted security techniques have been presented so far depending on the resources of the target which include compile-time instrumentation, binary-level instrumentation, secure operating systems, static analysis of source code.

Various software-assisted solutions have been presented based on compile-time instrumentation of the program source code for the run-time detection of out-of-bounds memory accesses. Programming languages such as C and C++ are more commonly used by the designers to implement applications in the field of embedded systems. These languages are not type safe as they provide direct memory access through pointer variables and also allow pointer arithmetic operations without any bounds checking. Such pointer variables can be exploited by the attackers to corrupt the memory contents to inject their own code. Typically, a memory object (i.e., allocated block of memory) is accessed through a pointer variable and it must always point within the range of its referent memory object. Compile-time instrumentation based security techniques convert the program source code into a compiler intermediate representation, find the lower and upper of each memory object and then insert extra instructions for the bound verification whenever particular memory object is accessed. Bounds checking solutions as presented in (Nagarakatte, Zhao, Martin, & Zdancewic, 2009; Younan et al., 2010) are based on storing bound information (start and end address of each memory object) in a table (specialized data structure) which is used at run-time by their inserted check instructions to perform address verification against each memory access (such as LOAD and STORE operations). Other compiler based techniques such as (Hasabnis, Misra, & Sekar, 2012; Serebryany, Bruening, Potapenko, & Vyukov, 2012) track bounds of memory objects and use shadow memory to insert guard zones (extra memory blocks) around them. Extra check instructions are inserted to detect any overflow or underflow by finding any memory access pointing to guard zones.

Among different techniques (Doudalis et al., 2012; Hastings & Joyce, 1991; Nethercote & Seward, 2007) that operate at the binary level, Purify (Hastings & Joyce, 1991) is one of the early solutions in this area. It enforces the insertion of extra checking instructions directly into the application's object code and verifies every memory read and write operation performed by the application under execution. Valgrind (Nethercote & Seward, 2007) is an openly available instrumentation framework for building dynamic analysis tools. The Valgrind's MemCheck tool uses shadow memory to keep track of which memory areas have been allocated and pinpoints illegal accesses to uninitialized memory. However, accesses to memory areas that have been initialized and temporal memory errors cannot be detected by Valgrind. Another approach presented in Doudalis et al., (2012) associates unique taint marks with each pointer and its allocated memory block. These taint marks are then propagated and verified through taint checking instructions, whenever memory is accessed. This approach works at binary level but requires modification in run-time libraries to generate taint marks properly.

Operating systems-based security solutions are designed with the consideration that the integrity of sensitive data is compromised when malware is being injected by the attacker. Such solutions prevent the execution of the malicious code by splitting the actual program memory into a code region and a data region. The code region is marked as read-only whereas the data region is marked as a non-executable region. For example, an important security feature, data execution prevention (DEP) is available in many operating systems through hardware support. Address space layout randomization (ASLR) is another vital security feature offered by many OS which makes it difficult to find target blocks of code for buffer overflow attacks. It is based on randomly arranging the address space of important data areas of a program such as the base address of the program executable and the position of the stack, heap and shared libraries.

Static code analysis tools e.g. (Xie, Chou, & Engler, 2003; Heine & Lam, 2003) are used to detect any vulnerability or programming bug in the program without actually running it on the target system. These kinds of tools are based on various types of techniques such as data flow analysis, control flow graphs and taint analysis. Typically, static code analysis is used during the development phase and in most cases, partial source code or some time complete code is used to perform such type of analysis. These tools may generate false positive results, due to unavailability of real input sets to test the integrity and security of data as it flows through the program. Language-based approaches such as (Dhurjati, Kowshik, Adve, & Lattner, 2003; Necula, Condit, Harren, McPeak, & Weimer, 2005) are also static in nature as these solutions aim to reduce the probability of illegal memory accesses by converting unsafe languages (e.g., C,C++) into safe variants.

5. CONCLUSION

Existing solutions addressing software-based attacks have many constraining factors and thus do not represent generic and scalable security solutions for the forthcoming multi-core based SoC devices. For instance, operating system based techniques such as data execution prevention, address space layout randomization and non-executable memory have made it difficult for traditional buffer overflow based attacks to inject and execute malicious code but the recent attack techniques such as return-oriented programming and return-into-libc can still exploit buffer overflow and execute code in the presence of such security mechanisms.

Furthermore, software-based solutions (as discussed in the previous section) have not been tested for multi-core embedded systems executing multi-threaded applications. Compile-time instrumentation-based techniques such as in (Doudalis et al., 2012; Serebryany et al., 2012; Younan et al., 2010) require either modified run-time memory allocators or a dedicated compiler driver while other solutions e.g. (Austin, Breach, & Sohi, 1994; Hasabnis et al., 2012) require modifications in the source code which may result in compatibility issues. Some of these compiler-based techniques such as (Akritidis, Costa, Castro, & Hand, 2009) do not cover all memory safety violations while others provide complete protection at the cost of notable performance overhead. Moreover, tools performing analysis at binary level do not require source code and recompilation but they increase the memory utilization and execution time overhead largely as the tool is first loaded into the memory and main application runs on the top of it.

Hardware-assisted techniques (Huffmire et al., 2008; Milenković et al., 2005; Suh, O'Donnell, Sachdev, & Devadas, 2005) based on cryptography are not realistic for multi-core based SoC devices due to resource constraints and large power consumption and performance overheads. Hardware security solutions such as (Arora et al., 2005; Mao & Wolf, 2010; Rahmatian et al., 2012; Yoon et al., 2013) are based on system monitoring to ensure code integrity, require static behavior model of the applications that are to be installed on the system. These techniques are not suitable for embedded systems where applications can be downloaded and installed on the fly. Moreover, these techniques either require dedicated processing core or customized processor architecture to perform monitoring which is not feasible for modern multi-core systems.

Since existing security solutions are not designed to confront present-day attacks and cannot cater for security requirements and performance constraints for new multi-core systems, therefore new solutions are needed to enable the embedded systems to process date securely. The new security solutions for SoC embedded systems must be energy efficient, flexible, effective, and robust in nature and meet performance requirements.

REFERENCES

Akritidis, P., Costa, M., Castro, M., & Hand, S. (2009). Baggy Bounds Checking: An Efficient and Backwards-Compatible Defense against Out-of-Bounds Errors. In *USENIX Security Symposium* (pp. 51–66). Academic Press.

AMD. (2004). *Intel put antivirus tech into chips | ZDNet*. Retrieved September 13, 2017, from http://www.zdnet.com/article/amd-intel-put-antivirus-tech-into-chips/

ARM. (2017). *TrustZone-ARM*. Retrieved from http://www.arm.com/products/processors/technologies/trustzone/index.php

Arora, D., Ravi, S., Raghunathan, A., & Jha, N. K. (2005). Secure embedded processing through hardware-assisted run-time monitoring. In *Design, Automation and Test in Europe* (pp. 178–183). Proceedings. doi:10.1109/DATE.2005.266

Austin, T. M., Breach, S. E., & Sohi, G. S. (1994). Efficient Detection of All Pointer and Array Access Errors. In *ACM Conference on Programming Language Design and Implementation (PLDI)* (pp. 290–301). ACM. 10.1145/178243.178446

Bayrak, A. G., Velickovic, N., Ienne, P., & Burleson, W. (2012). An Architecture-independent Instruction Shuffler to Protect Against Side-channel Attacks. *ACM Trans. Archit. Code Optim., 8*(4), 20:1–20:19.

Checkoway, S., McCoy, D., Kantor, B., Anderson, D., Shacham, H., & Savage, S., … others. (2011). Comprehensive Experimental Analyses of Automotive Attack Surfaces. In *USENIX Security Symposium*. San Francisco: USENIX.

Dhurjati, D., Kowshik, S., Adve, V., & Lattner, C. (2003). Memory Safety Without Runtime Checks or Garbage Collection. In *ACM Conference on Language, Compiler, and Tool for Embedded Systems* (pp. 69–80). ACM. 10.1145/780732.780743

Doudalis, I., Clause, J., Venkataramani, G., Prvulovic, M., & Orso, A. (2012). Effective and Efficient Memory Protection Using Dynamic Tainting. *Computers. IEEE Transactions on, 61*(1), 87–100.

Hasabnis, N., Misra, A., & Sekar, R. (2012). Light-weight Bounds Checking. In *International Symposium on Code Generation and Optimization* (pp. 135–144). Academic Press.

Hastings, R., & Joyce, B. (1991). Purify: Fast detection of memory leaks and access errors. *Proc. of USENIX Conference.*

Heine, D. L., & Lam, M. S. (2003). A Practical Flow-sensitive and Context-sensitive C and C++ Memory Leak Detector. *SIGPLAN Notices, 38*(5), 168–181. doi:10.1145/780822.781150

Huffmire, T., Brotherton, B., Sherwood, T., Kastner, R., Levin, T., Nguyen, T. D., & Irvine, C. (2008). Managing Security in FPGA-Based Embedded Systems. *Design Test of Computers, IEEE, 25*(6), 590–598. doi:10.1109/MDT.2008.166

IETF Datatracker. (2017). Retrieved September 12, 2017, from https://datatracker.ietf.org/

Kocher, P., Jaffe, J., & Jun, B. (1999). Differential power analysis. In Advances in Cryptology—CRYPTO'99 (pp. 388–397). Springer. doi:10.1007/3-540-48405-1_25

Lie, D., Thekkath, C., Mitchell, M., Lincoln, P., Boneh, D., Mitchell, J., & Horowitz, M. (2000). Architectural Support for Copy and Tamper Resistant Software. *SIGPLAN Notices, 35*(11), 168–177. doi:10.1145/356989.357005

Mangard, S. (2003). A simple power-analysis (SPA) attack on implementations of the AES key expansion. In Information Security and Cryptology—ICISC 2002 (pp. 343–358). Springer.

Mao, S., & Wolf, T. (2010). Hardware Support for Secure Processing in Embedded Systems. *Computers. IEEE Transactions on, 59*(6), 847–854.

Milenković, M., Milenković, A., & Jovanov, E. (2005). Hardware Support for Code Integrity in Embedded Processors. In *Intl. Conf. on Compilers, Architectures and Synthesis for Embedded Systems* (pp. 55–65). Academic Press. 10.1145/1086297.1086306

Nagarakatte, S., Zhao, J., Martin, M. M., & Zdancewic, S. (2009). SoftBound: Highly compatible and complete spatial memory safety for c. *ACM SIGPLAN Notices, 44*(6), 245–258. doi:10.1145/1543135.1542504

Necula, G. C., Condit, J., Harren, M., McPeak, S., & Weimer, W. (2005). CCured: Type-safe retrofitting of legacy software. *ACM Transactions on Programming Languages and Systems, 27*(3), 477–526. doi:10.1145/1065887.1065892

Nethercote, N., & Seward, J. (2007). Valgrind: A framework for heavyweight dynamic binary instrumentation. *ACM SIGPLAN Notices, 42*(6), 89–100. doi:10.1145/1273442.1250746

NVD - CVE-2014-1776. (2014). Retrieved September 12, 2017, from https://nvd.nist.gov/vuln/detail/CVE-2014-1776

One, A. (1996). Smashing the stack for fun and profit. *Phrack Magazine, 7*(49), 14–16.

Rahmatian, M., Kooti, H., Harris, I. G., & Bozorgzadeh, E. (2012). Hardware-Assisted Detection of Malicious Software in Embedded Systems. *Embedded Systems Letters, IEEE, 4*(4), 94–97. doi:10.1109/LES.2012.2218630

Rao, J. R., & Rohatgi, P. (2001). EMpowering Side-Channel Attacks. *IACR Cryptology ePrint Archive, 2001*, 37.

Ravi, S., Raghunathan, A., Kocher, P., & Hattangady, S. (2004). Security in embedded systems: Design challenges. *ACM Transactions on Embedded Computing Systems, 3*(3), 461–491. doi:10.1145/1015047.1015049

Serebryany, K., Bruening, D., Potapenko, A., & Vyukov, D. (2012). AddressSanitizer: A fast address sanity checker. In USENIX ATC (Vol. 2012). USENIX.

Shacham, H. (2007). The geometry of innocent flesh on the bone: Return-into-libc without function calls (on the x86). In *Proc. of ACM conference on Computer and communications security* (pp. 552–561). ACM. 10.1145/1315245.1315313

Song, D. X., Wagner, D., & Tian, X. (2001). Timing Analysis of Keystrokes and Timing Attacks on SSH. In *USENIX Security Symposium* (*Vol. 2001*). USENIX.

Studnia, I., Nicomette, V., Alata, E., Deswarte, Y., Kaaniche, M., & Laarouchi, Y. (2013). Survey on security threats and protection mechanisms in embedded automotive networks. In *Dependable Systems and Networks Workshop (DSN-W), IEEE/IFIP Conference on* (pp. 1–12). IEEE. 10.1109/DSNW.2013.6615528

Suh, G. E., O'Donnell, C. W., Sachdev, I., & Devadas, S. (2005). Design and implementation of the AEGIS single-chip secure processor using physical random functions. In *International Symposium on Computer Architecture* (pp. 25–36). Academic Press. 10.1109/ISCA.2005.22

Wojtczuk, R. (2001). The advanced return-into-lib (c) exploits: PaX case study. *Phrack Magazine, 11*(58).

Xie, Y., Chou, A., & Engler, D. (2003). ARCHER: Using Symbolic, Path-sensitive Analysis to Detect Memory Access Errors. *SIGSOFT Softw. Eng. Notes, 28*(5), 327–336. doi:10.1145/949952.940115

Yan, Q., Li, Y., Li, T., & Deng, R. (2009). Insights into malware detection and prevention on mobile phones. In Security Technology (pp. 242–249). Academic Press. doi:10.1007/978-3-642-10847-1_30

Yang, S., Gupta, P., Wolf, M., Serpanos, D., Narayanan, V., & Xie, Y. (2012). Power Analysis Attack Resistance Engineering by Dynamic Voltage and Frequency Scaling. *ACM Trans. Embed. Comput. Syst., 11*(3), 62:1–62:16.

Yoon, M.-K., Mohan, S., Choi, J., Kim, J.-E., & Sha, L. (2013). SecureCore: A multicore-based intrusion detection architecture for real-time embedded systems. In *Real-Time and Embedded Technology and Applications Symposium (RTAS), 2013 IEEE 19th* (pp. 21–32). IEEE. 10.1109/RTAS.2013.6531076

Younan, Y., Philippaerts, P., Cavallaro, L., Sekar, R., Piessens, F., & Joosen, W. (2010). PAriCheck: an efficient pointer arithmetic checker for C programs. In *Proceedings of the 5th ACM Symposium on Information, Computer and Communications Security* (pp. 145–156). ACM. 10.1145/1755688.1755707

Chapter 11
Preferences, Machine Learning, and Decision Support With Cyber-Physical Systems

Yuri P. Pavlov
Institute of Information and Communication Technologies, Bulgarian Academy of Sciences, Bulgaria

Evgeniy Ivanov Marinov
Institute of Biophysics and Biomedical Engineering, Bulgarian Academy of Sciences, Bulgaria

ABSTRACT

Modeling of complex processes with human participations causes difficulties due to the lack of precise measurement coming from the qualitative nature of the human notions. This provokes the need of utilization of empirical knowledge expressed cardinally. An approach for solution of these problems is utility theory. As cyber-physical systems are integrations of computation, networking, and physical processes in interaction with the user is needed feedback loops, the aim of the chapter is to demonstrate the possibility to describe quantitatively complex processes with human participation. This approach permits analytical representations of the users' preferences as objective utility functions and modeling of the complex system "human-process." The mathematical technique allows CPS users dialog and is demonstrated by two case studies, portfolio allocation, and modeling of a competitive trade by a finite game and utility preference representation of the trader. The presented formulations could serve as foundation of development of decision support tools and decision control.

INTRODUCTION

The principles of rationality in the human behavior and the determination of the best decision solutions require a meaningful mathematical approach relevant to the problems under consideration. The meaning of best varies from problem to problem (Keeney & Raiffa, 1999; Keeney, 1988). The variety of the complex processes with human participations as social obligations, financial and engineering problems e.g. causes difficulties due to the inherent time variant properties and the lack of precise measurement coming from the qualitative nature of the human notions. This complexity of problems pose in question

DOI: 10.4018/978-1-5225-5510-0.ch011

the needs of development of decision support methods and tools for design of advanced contemporary systems as Cyber-Physical Systems (Lee, 2008; Bradley & Atkins, 2015; Hahn & Kuhn, 2012).

Cyber-Physical Systems (CPS) are integrations of computation, networking, and physical processes in interaction with the user. In fact, such kind of systems are information and computer based systems supporting processes of control, management, decision making with supporting organizational, managing and/or business information and decisions (Lee, 2008; Bradley & Atkins, 2015). These systems maintain operational levels in which the human interaction and decisions could be crucial for the final result. In general, CPS are interactive software systems with the purpose of supporting the decision-maker with information and accompanying optimal solutions. In such kind of systems empirical knowledge can be taken into account, introduced in a convenient way even in cardinal form. Additionally, CPS could maintain data bases, sorting of sequential data, monitoring of dynamical processes, mathematical analysis etc. Such design needs feedback loops and interaction with the human (user) participating in the process. Physical and software components and the dialog with the users are deeply intertwined, each operating on different special mathematical scales (Keeney, 1988; Lee, 2008; Pfanzagl, 1971).

The incomplete human acquired information could be compensated by expressions of qualitative human preferences in dialog with the users. The preferences are expressed in regard to the main purpose and the related sub-objectives to the problem under consideration and are external manifestations of the human estimations (Keeney & Raiffa, 1999; Keeney, 1988; Pavlov & Andreev, 2013; Pavlov, 2005). Possible approach for solution of these problems is the Theory of measurement, the Utility theory and the Stochastic programming (Keeney & Raiffa, 1999; Pfanzagl, 1971; Fishburn, 1970, 1978). The Utility theory basically deals with the expressed subjective user preferences. Possible criteria for "the meaning of *best*" can be an expert (decision maker-DM) utility function (Keeney, 1988; Pavlov & Andreev, 2013; Fishburn, 1978).

The aim of this chapter is to demonstrate an analytical mathematical technique and the possibility to describe quantitatively complex social, ecological, biological and other processes. Such an approach provides analytical representations of the user's preferences as objective utility functions and mathematical description of the complex system „human-process". In fact, the approach is a value driven design and control of complex processes where the human choice is decisive for the final solution (Pavlov & Andreev, 2013; Pavlov, 2005; Collopy & Hollingsworth, 2009). The human preferences are usually of cardinal type and contain uncertainty. This uncertainty of the preference expressions points to the stochastic approximation theory. The utility function evaluations are based on the recurrent stochastic procedures and are in fact machine-learning of the same preferences as those of the decision maker. The suggested approach can be regarded as a realization of the *prescriptive decision making* and allows practitioners to take advantage of individual application of the achievements of decision making theory in various fields of human activities and CPS users dialog integrated in different networks and even with the internet.

The approach is demonstrated by two case studies. The first one is portfolio allocation with Wiener process and portfolio allocation in the case of financial process with colored noise both modeled by Black-Scholes stochastic differential equation (Pavlov, 2015, 2017). The second case study is modeling of a competitive trade of small store by a finite game and minmax determination of the „saddle-point" as equilibrium of the trade (Pavlov, Terzieva & Kademova-Katzarova, 2014). The presented formulations could serve as foundation of development of decision support tools for design of management/control in Cyber-Physical Systems. This value-oriented modeling leads to the development of preferences-based decision support in machine learning environment and control/management value-based design.

VALUE BASED DESIGN, PREFERENCES, UTILITY FUNCTION

In the chapter we direct our attention to a complex, mathematically well-founded method in which the user is presented through his preference representation as value or utility function. Value-based design is an engineering strategy based on system analyses which enables multidisciplinary design optimization. Value-driven design creates an environment that enables optimization providing designers with an objective function that takes as input all the important attributes of the system being designed and outputs a score (Keeney, 1988; Collopy & Hollingsworth, 2009; Biffl, Aurum, Boehm, Erdoginus & Grunbacher, 2006; Yin, Zhao, Li & Chengbin, 2015; Pavlov, 2016). The well-grounded and precise mathematical approach to this subject requires the usage of the achievements of the Measurement theory (scaling), Utility theory, Decision-making theory (normative and prescriptive approaches), Probability theory and some results from optimal control theory (Pfanzagl, 1971; Fishburn, 1970; Krantz, Luce, Suppes & Tversky, 1971, 1989, 1990). On such informational level the basic notions are sets, relations, measurement, scales. When the alternatives are arranged by preferences we talk about the *ordering scale*. The relation is axiomatically anti-symmetric and transitive.

1. $x < y \Rightarrow \neg(y < x)$
2. $(x < y \,\&\, y < z) \Rightarrow x < z$

Here the empirical relation $(x \succ y)$ means x is more preferable than y. If there are incomparable alternatives then the relation is a partial ordering. In case of existence of a value function, the equivalence relation ($\approx$) is defined based on the preference relation ($\succ$).

3. $x \approx y \Leftrightarrow \neg x < y \,\&\, \neg y < x$

And the following axioms hold (Pfanzagl, 1971; Fishburn, 1970):

4. $x \approx x$
5. $x \approx y \Rightarrow y \approx x$
6. $\neg x < x \,\&\, (x < y \Rightarrow \neg y < x)$

One of the most popular examples of such kind of ordering is the Morses scale of rigidity. We say that the mineral M_1 is more rigid (harder) than the mineral M_2, if the first one scratches the surface of the second one. The validity of the six axioms bears the definition of the value function $u(.)$ total relation. For the value function the following holds:

$$(\forall x, y \in X)(x > y \Rightarrow u(x) > u(y) \,\&\, (\neg x \approx y \Rightarrow y > x \lor x > y)) \tag{1}$$

Such value function can be sufficient to determine an extreme value. It cannot be applied in problems with mathematical expectation, such as in the problems of decision-making under risk and uncertainty.

If through the help of the ordering we can numerically evaluate the difference between the alternatives, we talk about *interval scale*. In this case are admissible mathematical operations such as central moment and variation. This scale is determined up to a positive linear map $l(.)$:

$$(\forall x \in X)(\forall a, b \in R: a>0)(l(x) = ax + b) \tag{2}$$

Such is the scale in which the temperature is measured. In this scale is defined the utility function evaluated on the base of the decision-makers preferences by the gambling approach (Keeney & Raiffa, 1999; Raiffa, 1968). A stronger scale is the *ratio scale*. In this scale the starting measuring point is fixed and only the measurement units could be changed. Such is the scale in which the weight is measured. Here the following axioms hold:

7. $(x=y \wedge z>0) \Rightarrow ((x+z)>y)$;
8. $x+y=y+x$;
9. $(x=y \wedge z=q) \Rightarrow (x+z=y+q)$;
10. $q+(x+y)=(q+y)+x$.

Such kind of scale is the scale in which the weight is measured.

By the normalization of the utility function between 0 and 1 is achieved the measurement of utility in the *ratio scale*. The usage of mathematical expectation in processes under risk and uncertainty is admissible in that scale. In the end could be noted that mathematically infinite number of intermediate scales are possible (Pfanzagl, 1971).

In the case of decision making under certainty, to every Decision maker's (DM) choice corresponds only one outcome (alternative x, x∈X). With X is noted the set of alternatives, possible outcomes provoked by the DM's actions.

Let us consider a more general scheme of interaction between the DM and the real world. Assuming that for every choice of the DM there are (i) possible outcomes (alternatives), ($i=1\div n$), each of which occurring with probability p_i, ($\sum_{i=1}^{n} p_i = 1$). That is, to every decision corresponds as final outcome one possibility distribution (p) (Fishburn, 1970, 1978). Following the Bayesian approach it is reasonable to maximise the mathematical expectation $\sum_{i=1}^{n} p_i u(x_i)$ (Keeney & Raiffa, 1999; Keeney, 1988). In this formula the function $u(x)$ is a utility function, by which the different final alternatives x∈X are evaluated.

The so called normative (axiomatic) approach considers the conditions for existence of utility function u(.) (Pfanzagl, 1971; Fishburn, 1978). Let X be the set of alternatives and P be a set of probability distributions over X. A utility function $u(.)$ will be defined any function for which the following is fulfilled:

$$(p \succ q, (p,q) \in P^2) \Rightarrow (\int u(.)dp \succ \int u(.)dq).$$

In keeping with Von Neumann's axiomatic and theory described in (Fishburn, 1970) the interpretation of the above formula provides that, the integral of the utility function $u(.)$ is a measure for comparison of the probability distributions p and q defined over X. The notation $(p \succ q)$ expresses the preferences of DM over P including those over X ($X \subseteq P$). Standard description of the utility function application in the case of finite probability distribution is presented in Figure 1.

It is clear that the assumption of existence of a utility function $u(.)$ leads to the "negatively transitive" ($\neg(p \succ t) \wedge \neg(t \succ q)) \Rightarrow \neg(p \succ q)$) and "asymmetric" relation ($\succ$). These properties imply the existence of

Figure 1. Utility function application

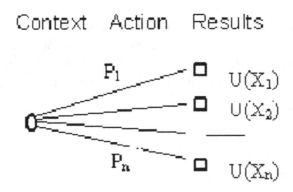

asymmetry $((x \succ y) \Rightarrow (\neg(y \succ x)))$, transitivity $((x \succ y) \wedge (y \succ z) \Rightarrow (x \succ z))$ and transitivity of the "indifference" relation $(\approx)$ (axioms 1÷6).The transitivity of the relations $(\succ)$ and $(\approx)$ is violated very often in practice. The violation of the transitivity of the relation $(\succ)$ could be interpreted as a lack of information, or as a DM's subjective mistake. The violation of the transitivity of the relation $(\approx)$ is due to the natural "uncertainty" of the human's preference and to the qualitative nature of expressions of the subjective notions and evaluations (Allais, 1953; Kahneman & Tversky, 1979; Cohen & Jaffray, 1988; Shmeidler, 1989). There are diverse empirical methods for utility evaluation and all of them are necessarily based on the "lottery" approach (gambling approach) (Keeney & Raiffa, 1999; Raiffa, 1968).

A "lottery" is called every discrete finite probability distribution over X. We denote as $<x, y, \alpha>$ the lottery: here α is the probability of the appearance of the alternative x and $(1- \alpha)$ - the probability of the alternative y. The most widely used evaluation approach is the assessment: $z \approx <x, y, \alpha>$, where $x, y, z \in$ X, $(x \succ z \succ y)$ and $\alpha \in [0,1]$ (Keeney & Raiffa, 1999; Raiffa, 1968). The bottleneck of this approach is the violations of the transitivity of the relations and the so called "certainty effect" and "probability distortion" (Kahneman & Tversky, 1979; Cohen & Jaffray, 1988; Shmeidler, 1989). In complex situations, it is difficult to determine the alternatives x (the best) and y (the worst) under the condition that $(x \succ z \succ y)$, where z is the analyzed alternative.

The measurement scale of the utility function $u(.)$ originates from the previous mathematical formulation of the relations $(\succ)$ and $(\approx)$ and on the fact that the set of the probability distributions P, $(X \subseteq P)$ is a convex set $((q, p) \in P^2 \Rightarrow (\alpha q + (1-\alpha)p) \in P,$ for $\forall \alpha \in [0,1])$. These conditions determine the utility function $u(.)$ over X up to an affine transformation (i.e. the interval scale) (Fishburn, 1970).

The Utility function is build-up (evaluated) by pattern recognition of two sets, which represent comparisons between lotteries (Pavlov & Andreev, 2013; Pavlov, 2005):

$Au = \{(\alpha, x, y, z) \, / \, (\alpha u(x) + (1-\alpha)u(y)) > u(z)\}$,
$Bu = \{(\alpha, x, y, z) \, / \, (\alpha u(x) + (1-\alpha)u(y)) < u(z)\}$.

The notations x, y, z mean elements of X and α is a random value occurring in the lotteries $<x, y, \alpha>$. The evaluation process is a machine-learning one based on the DM's preferences and is a probabilistic pattern recognition procedure because $(Au \cap Bu \neq \varnothing)$ and means in fact that the utility evaluation is a stochastic approximation with noise (uncertainty) elimination (Pavlov, 2005; Aizerman, Braverman, & RozonoerL, 1970). The following recurrent procedure represents the evaluation (Pavlov & Andreev, 2013):

DM compares the "lottery" <x, y,α> with the simple alternative z, z$\in$X ("better-$\succ$, f(x, y, z,α)=1", "worse-$\succ$, f(x, y, z,α)=(-1)" or "can't answer or equivalent- $\sim$, f(x, y, z,α)=0". The discrete function f(.) denotes the qualitative DM's answer expressed as preference. This determine a learning point ((x, y, z,α), f(x, y, z,α)).

The DM or expert compares the lottery <x, y,α> with the simple alternative z (a learning point ((x, y, z,α), f(x, y, z,α))), and with a subjective probability $D_1(x, y, z,\alpha)$ is referred to A_u (f(x, y, z,α) =1) or with subjective probability $D_2(x, y, z,\alpha)$ is referred to B_u (f(x, y, z,α) =-1). Every point (x, y, z,α), is referred to the following function: f(x, y, z,α) =1 for ($\succ$), f(x, y, z,α)=-1 for ($\succ$) и f(x, y, z,α)=0 for ($\approx$) (this collation is a subjective characteristic, representing the intuition or the empirical knowledge of the DM) (Pavlov & Andreev, 2013). In the DM's answers the subjective and probability uncertainties are taken into account too. It is assumed that the ''learning points'' (x, y, z,α)are given by the probability distribution F(x, y, z,α). Then the probabilities $D_1(x, y, z,\alpha)$ and$D_2(x, y, z,\alpha)$ are the conditional mathematical expectations of f(.) over the sets A_u and B_u respectively (Pavlov, 2005; Aizerman, Braverman & RozonoerL, 1970):

$D_1(x, y, z,\alpha)= \mathbf{M}(f/x, y, z,\alpha), \mathbf{M}(f/x, y, z,\alpha)>0;$

$D_2(x, y, z,\alpha)=-\mathbf{M}(f/x, y, z,\alpha), \mathbf{M}(f/x, y, z,\alpha)<0.$

By $\mathbf{M}$ is denoted the mathematical expectation, in our case the conditional mathematical expectation of the function f(.) in the point (x, y, z,α). By $D'(x, y, z,\alpha)$ is denoted the random variable:

$= D_1(x, y, z,\alpha),$ if $\mathbf{M}(f/x, y, z,\alpha)>0;$

$D'(x, y, z,\alpha) = -D_2(x, y, z,\alpha),$ if $\mathbf{M}(f/x, y, z,\alpha)<0;$

$= 0,$ if $\mathbf{M}(f/x, y, z,\alpha)=0.$

The measurable function $D'(x, y, z,\alpha)$ over the σ-algebra, generated by the probability distribution F(x, y, z,α), is approximated by a function of this kind:

$G(x, y, z,\alpha) = (\alpha g(x) + (1-\alpha)g(y)-g(z)).$

The function $G(x, y, z,\alpha)$ is positive over the set A_u and negative over B_u depending on the degree/precision of the approximation of D'(x, y, z,α). In this case g(x) can be taken as an approximation of the utility u(.) based on the evaluation of the function f(.):

f(.): $f=D'+\xi, \mathbf{M}(\xi/x, y, z,\alpha)=0, \mathbf{M}(\xi^2/x, y, z,\alpha)<d, d\in\mathbf{R}.$

It is admissible the utility u(.) to be square integrable function: $\int u^2(x)dF_x < +\infty,$, where F_x is the conditional probability distribution over X. Let $\{\Phi_i()\}$ be a family of functions defined over X (*orthogonal family of Chebyshev polynomials or Legendre polynomials), for which the following decomposition holds*:

$$u(x) \underset{L_2}{=} \sum_i r_i \Phi_i(x), \, r_i \in R$$

We denote t=(x, y, z,α) and depending on the structure of the set A_u is assumed that:

$\psi_i(t) = \psi_i(x, y, z, \alpha) = \alpha\Phi_i(x) + (1-\alpha)\Phi_i(y) - \Phi_i(z)$.

It is assumed also that $g(x)$ can be decomposed in the series:

$$g(x) = \sum_i c_i \Phi_i(x).$$

The learning points are used in the following recurrent algorithm (Pavlov & Andreev, 2013):

$$c_i^{n+1} = c_i^n + \gamma_n \left[D'(t^{n+1}) + \xi^{n+1} - \overline{(c^n, \Psi(t^{n+1}))} \right] \Psi_i(t^{n+1}) \tag{3}$$

$$\sum_n \gamma_n = +\infty, \, \sum_n \gamma_n^2 < +\infty, \, \forall n, \, \gamma_n \geq 0$$

Rewritten in another notation it looks like this:

$$c_i^{n+1} = c_i^n + \gamma_n \left[f(t^{n+1}) - \overline{(c^n, \Psi(t^{n+1}))} \right] \Psi_i(t^{n+1}) \tag{4}$$

$$\sum_n \gamma_n = +\infty, \, \sum_n \gamma_n^2 < +\infty, \, \forall n, \, \gamma_n \geq 0$$

The coefficients c_i^n are used in the decomposition of the function $g^n(x)$ over the family of base $\Phi_i(x)$:

$$g^n(x) = \sum_{i=1}^{N} c_i^n \Phi_i(x).$$

In the above stated formulas we substitute:

$(c^n, \Psi(t)) = \alpha g^n(x) + (1-\alpha)g^n(y) - g^n(z) = G^n(x, y, z, \alpha)$.

The ''bar'' on the top $\overline{y} = (c^n, \Psi(t))$ means:

$\overline{y} = 1$, if y>1, $\overline{y} = -1$, if y<-1, $\overline{y} = y$ if (1<y<1).

The proposed procedure is machine learning. It trains the computer on the DM's preferences (Aizerman, Braverman & RozonoerL, 1970). At the same time it is a procedure of recognizing the sets of the positive and negative DM's answers (preferences) over the lotteries, defined as points $((x, y, z, \alpha), f(x, y, z, \alpha))$ in the five dimensional space $H^5=[0,1] \times [-1, 1]^4$. In Figure 2 are given three dimensional projections of pattern recognition of the sets Au and Bu, (Au∩Bu≠∅), a real world example. The learning points are given numerically by a uniformed distribution modeled through L_{pr} - the Sobol's pseudo-random sequence (Sobol, 979; Joe & Kuo, 2008). The relatively dense interfusion in Figure 2 is due to the fact that the fourth coordinate cannot be depicted. With the darker color are depicted the expert's answers ''greater than (1)'' and with the clearer one ''less than (-1)''. On the right hand side of the figure the sets Au and Bu, (Au∩Bu≠∅) are separated. The recognition of the positive and negative DM's answers is more complicated than the classical stochastic pattern recognition; since theoretically only a part of the pattern recognition function G^n is an approximation of the DM's utility function and the DM's answers are cardinals. The powerful Aizerman's theory of the potential functions method allows such stochastic pattern recognition (Pavlov & Andreev, 2013; Aizerman, Braverman & RozonoerL, 1970):

In reality the training DM's answers (learning points) are a finite number. Because of the use of the L_{pr} pseudorandom series, the number of the N_m learning points is of the form $N_m =2^p$, where p is an integer (5, 6, 7 or 8) (Sobol, 1979). In practice the learning N_m number points are located in circle by the recurrent stochastic approximation procedure in order to be evaluated the coefficients (c_i) in the polynomial representation of the utility function u(.). On Figure 3 is shown an example of such an evaluation of a utility function.

The seesaw line takes part in the function G^n which is a pattern recognition function of the positive and negative DM's preferences and the smooth one is an approximation of the von Neuman's utility function.

Frequently occurring case in practice are the multiattribute problems. According to the psychological research 7 is the maximal number of attributes which can be simultaneously comprehended by a human. It is well known that this number of attributes is on the limits of the human's capabilities for perception (Larichev & Morgoev, 1991). The multiattribute problems need multiattribute utility functions and this

Figure 2. Three dimensional projections of the sets A and B

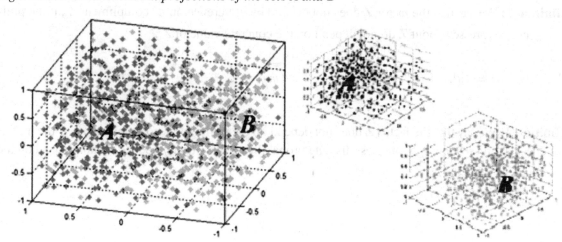

Figure 3. Pattern recognition and utility evaluation

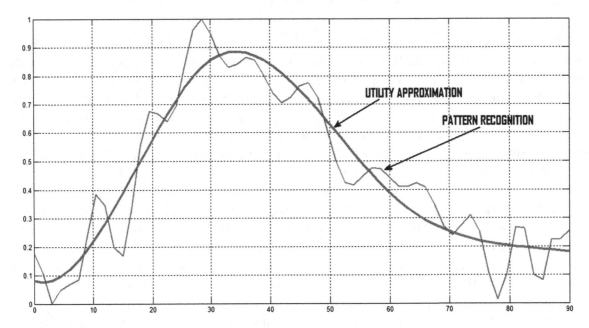

is a much more complicated problem. We face the need of utilization of the achievements of the Multiattribute utility theory allowing the decomposition of the multiattribute utility to more simple functions (Keeney & Raiffa, 1999; Pandey, Nikolaidis, & Mourelatos, 2011). In the best case this decomposition leads to descriptions by single attribute functions.

Let us give a couple of theorems, allowing the decomposition of the utility functions to single attribute functions. This theory is stated in details in (Keeney & Raiffa, 1999). Let $X = \prod_{i=1}^{n} X_i$ be a Cartesian product of (n) single factor spaces. Let us represent the set X as a Cartesian product of two of its subsets, which are complement of each other, $X = Z \times \overline{Z}$ and we state two very important from practical point of view notions.

Definition 1: We say that the factor **Z** does not depend by preference on its compliment $\overline{Z}$, if the preferences expressed about **Z** do not depend on the concrete value of $\overline{Z}$:

$$(y', \overline{\overline{y}}) \succsim_{\approx} (y'', \overline{\overline{y}}) \Leftrightarrow (y', \overline{\overline{y}}) \succsim_{\approx} (y'', \overline{\overline{y}}), \forall (y', y'') \in Z^2, \forall (\overline{y}, \overline{y}) \in \overline{Z}.$$

Definition 2: We say that the factor **Z** does not depend on the utility of its complement $\overline{Z}$, if the preferences expressed through lotteries (discrete probability distributions) upon **Z** do not depend on the concrete value of $\overline{Z}$:

$$< (x,z),(y,z),\alpha > \underset{\approx}{\succ} < (x',z),(y',z),\alpha > \Leftrightarrow$$
$$\Leftrightarrow < (x,z'),(y,z'),\alpha > \underset{\approx}{\succ} < (x',z'),(y',z'),\alpha >,$$
$$\forall (x,y,x',y') \in Z \times Z \times Z \times Z, \forall (z,z') \in \overline{Z} \times \overline{Z}.$$

We state three basic theorems, giving the most general decompositions of the multiattribute utility into simpler utility functions (Keeney & Raiffa, 1999).

Theorem 1: Let the set X be a Cartesian product of (n) attributes $X = \prod\limits_{i=1}^{n} X_i$. Let us assume that every subset of these attributes does not depend on the utility of its complement. Then, if the following conditions of existence of a utility function hold, it will looks like this:

$$u(x) = \sum_{i=1}^{n} k_i u_i(x_i) + k \sum_{i=1,j>i}^{n} k_i k_j u_i(x_i) u_j(x_j) + .. + k^{n-1} k_1 k_2 .. k_n u_1(x_1) u_2(x_2) .. u_n(x_n),$$
$$x = (x_1, x_2, .., x_n).$$

In the above formula $k, k_1, k_2, .., k_n$ are coefficients, $u_1(x_1), u_2(x_2), .., u_n(x_n)$ are single attribute utilities. This result follows from the fact that the utility functions are determined up to a positive affine map. Utility functions of such type are called *multiplicative utility functions*.

Theorem 2: Let the set X be a Cartesian product of (n) attributes $X = \prod\limits_{i=1}^{n} X_i$. Let us assume that every attribute X_i does not depend on the utility of its complement on the other (n-1) attributes. Then, if the following conditions of existence of a perfect utility function hold, it will look like this:

$$u(x) = \sum_{i=1}^{n} k_i u_i(x_i) + \sum_{i=1}^{n} \sum_{j>i} k_{ij} u_i(x_i) u_j(x_j) + .. + k_{12..n} u_1(x_1) u_2(x_2) .. u_n(x_n),$$
$$x = (x_1, x_2, .., x_n)$$

The utility function of such type is called a *polylinear utility function*.

Theorem 3: Let the set X be a Cartesian product of (n) attributes $X = \prod\limits_{i=1}^{n} X_i$. If the preferences of the lotteries defined over $X_1, X_2, .., X_n$ depend on the marginal distributions only, then the perfect utility function will look like this:

$$u(x) = \sum_{i=1}^{n} k_i u_i(x_i), \ x = (x_1, x_2, .., x_n).$$

The case of an *additive utility function* is discussed in detail in (Fishburn, 1970). Theorem 3 implies that the application of an additive function in practice requires very strict conditions. These conditions can be restated as inter-independence between the different attributes. Is this a frequently observed case? A contra-example is that the heavy industry does not depend upon the raw materials? This theorem shows that the utilization of additive functions as an objective criterion for the choice of decision in complex social, economical and other problems is often irrelevant.

The utility of the above stated theorems is obvious. For the construction of the multiattribute utilities is required the construction of one dimensional utility functions and the corresponding coefficients to be determined. If we norm the multiattribute utility as $u(\overline{x_1}, \overline{x_2}, .., \overline{x_n}) = 1$ and $u(\overline{\overline{x_1}}, \overline{\overline{x_2}}, .., \overline{\overline{x_n}}) = 0$, then every basis function $u_i(x_i)$ is of the following form $u_i(x_i) = u(\overline{x_1}, \overline{x_2}, .., x_i, .., \overline{x_n})$. Because the utility functions are determined in the interval scale, one can assume a second normalization for every single-attribute utility, $u_i(\overline{x_i}) = 1$ and $u_i(\overline{\overline{x_i}}) = 0$. After the second assumption we are in the ratio scale because the zero is fixed [6, 7]. After the expression of the preferences and the comparison of the single-attribute functions in different values, one determines the values of the coefficients in the polylinear, multiplicative and additive utility functions. These questions are discussed in detail in the book (Keeney & Raiffa, 1999). A thoroughgoing explanation of the considered problems can be found in the prominent books (Keeney & Raiffa, 1999; Pfanzagl, 1971; Fishburn, 1970; Raiffa, 1968).

The authors propose the following procedure for evaluation of the coefficients in the multiattribute utility function, which is equivalent to the procedure for the evaluation of the subjective uncertainty or the subjective probability of the DM described by Raiffa in his famous book (Raiffa, 1968). The multiattribute utility and the single attribute utility functions are normed between 0 and 1 and are measured in the interval scale. These facts permit determination of coefficients in the decomposition of the multiattribute utility function by comparisons, an easy procedure. The coefficients are determined by comparisons of lotteries of the following simple way (Pavlov & Andreev, 2013):

$$
\left.
\begin{cases}
U(x_1) \times \alpha \\
+ \\
U(x_2) \times (1-\alpha)
\end{cases}
\begin{matrix} \succ \\ \approx \\ \prec \end{matrix}
\right\}
\approx \quad U(x_3).
$$

In the formula x_1, x_2 and x_3 are fixed and preliminarily is fulfilled $(x_1 \succ x_3 \succ x_2)$. The questions to the decision maker are like lotteries in which we vary only the values by $\alpha \in [0,1]$. Two of them $U(x_1)$ and $U(x_2)$ are with fixed values (utilities) and the aim is to determine the third value $U(x_3)$. The stochastic procedure is of the type of Robins-Monro but the convergence is much quicker. The procedure is the following (Pavlov & Andreev, 2013). Let α is a uniformly distributed random value in $[0, 1]$. We define the following random vector $\chi = (\eta_1, \eta_2, \eta_3)$, where:

1. If $(\succ) \Rightarrow \chi = (\eta_1 = 1, \eta_2 = 0, \eta_3 = 0)$;
2. If $(\succ) \Rightarrow \chi = (\eta_1 = 0, \eta_2 = 0, \eta_3 = 1)$;
3. If indiscernibility $(\approx) \Rightarrow \chi = (\eta_1 = 0, \eta_2 = 1, \eta_3 = 0)$.

Let χ^n is a learning sequence of independent random values with equal to χ distribution. The stochastic recurrent procedure is as follows:

$$(\lambda_1^{n+1}, \lambda_2^{n+1}, \lambda_3^{n+1}) = \Pr_P \left[(\lambda_1^n, \lambda_2^n, \lambda_3^n) - \gamma_n ((\eta_1^n, \eta_2^n, \eta_3^n) - (\lambda_1^n, \lambda_2^n, \lambda_3^n)) \right],$$

$$\sum_1^\infty \gamma_n = \infty, \sum_1^\infty \gamma_n^2 < \infty, \gamma_n \geq 0, \forall n \in N. \tag{5}$$

The notation $\Pr_p$ has the meaning of projection over the set:

$$P = \{ (\lambda_1, \lambda_2, \lambda_3) \, / \, \lambda_1 \geq 0, \lambda_2 \geq 0, \lambda_3 \geq 0, \lambda_1 + \lambda_2 + \lambda_3 = 1 \}.$$

The searched subjective probability $U(x_3)$ (coefficient (c) in the multiattribute decomposition) is determined in the end as follows:

$$U(x_3) = U(x_2) + ((\lambda_1 + \lambda_2) \, / \, 2)(U(x_1) - U(x_2)), \, c = (\lambda_1 + \lambda_2)/2).$$

The proposed procedure and its modifications are machine learning (Pavlov & Andreev, 2013; Aizerman, Braverman & RozonoerL, 1970). The DM is comparatively fast in learning to operate with the procedure. A session with 128 questions (learning points) takes approximately 30 minutes and requires only qualitative answers "yes", "no" or "equivalent ". The learning points $((x, y, z, \alpha), f(x, y, z, \alpha))$ could also be set with a Sobol's pseudo random sequence (Sobol, 1979).

The described algorithms for stochastic approximation and theorems for decomposition of the utility functions provide a unified approach and methods for evaluation of the expert knowledge by expressed on cardinal level expert preferences in the framework of the lottery approach.

PREFERENCES PORTFOLIO ALLOCATION, WIENER AND COLORED NOISE PROCESS

Mathematical economics allows economists to create models to predict economic activity and to conduct quantitative tests. Its fields are applications of mathematics for economic analyses. The optimal portfolio allocation is one of the basic problems of mathematical finance and the construction of utility function in concordance costumers' preferences is a now a day trend of scientific investigation (Ekeland, 1979; Neumann, Goldie & Milton, 2000). Consider a non-risky asset S^0 and risky one S. Following the presentations in (Touzi & Tourin, 2012) the Black-Scholes stochastic differential equation is determined by:

$$dS_t^0 = S_t^0 r dt \text{ and } dS_t = S_t \mu dt + \sigma dW_t$$

In notations r, μ and σ mean constants ($r = 0.03$, $\mu = 0.05$ and $\sigma = 0.3$) and W is a one dimensional Brownian motion. By X_t is denoted the state space vector of the controlled time continuous financial market. The investment policy is defined by a progressively adapted process $\pi = \{\pi_t, t \in [0,T]\}$ where π_t represents the amount $(X_t \pi_t)$ $(\pi_t \in [0,1])$ invested in the risky process at moment t. The remaining wealth $(X_t - \pi_t X_t)$ at the same moment t is invested in the non-risky process. The time period T is 25 weeks. The dynamic of the liquidation value X_t of a self-financing strategy satisfies is given by the stochastic differential equation (SDE):

$$dX_t^{\pi} = \pi_t X_t^{\pi} \frac{dS_t}{S_t} dt + (X_t^{\pi} - \pi_t X_t^{\pi}) \frac{dS_t^0}{S_t^0} = (rX_t^{\pi} + (\mu - r)\pi_t X_t^{\pi})dt + \sigma \pi_t X_t^{\pi} dW_t$$

It is obvious that in these conditions and parameters is true

$$\mathrm{E} \int_0^T (\pi_t X_t^{\pi})^2 dt < \infty.$$

Here E denote mathematical expectation defined in the initial filtered probability space $(\Omega, \mathcal{F}, F, P)$ with canonical filtration $F = \{F_t, t \geq 0\}$ of the Brownian motion defined over the probability space $(\Omega, \mathcal{F}, P)$. More precisely, E denotes the mathematical expectation over the probability space $(\Omega, \mathcal{F}, P)$. The objective of the investor (decision maker-DM) is to choose the control (the amount π_t invested in the risky process) so as to maximize the expected utility of his final wealth at moment T, i.e.:

$$V(t, x) := \sup_{\pi \in [0,1]} \mathrm{E}[U(X_T^{t, x, \pi})],$$

where $X^{t, x, \pi}$ is the solution of the controlled stochastic differential equation with initial condition (initial wealth) x at time t [12, 13, 28]. It is supposed that if the state space vector (the liquidation value) is zero in a moment t then it remains zero until the end T ($X_T^{t, x, \pi} = 0$).

We assume that the outcome set X is a two-attribute product set V×W, with generic element x= (v, w). The sets V and W are attribute sets where V designates the first attribute- π_t, (the amount $X_t \pi_t$, $\pi_t \in [0,1]$) invested in the risky process and W designates the second attribute, quantity of money in BGN's. When the utility function over the consequences is known, it is easy to exploit it using a computer. However, in practice, the effective construction of function raises numerous problems. A multiattribute utility function is usually hard to perform due to the cognitive limitations of decision makers (Keeney & Raiffa, 1999; Shmeidler, 1989). Hence, the usual requirement is that they be decomposable as a simple combination of single-attribute more easily constructed utility functions. The aggregation of the two attributes in a multiattribute utility function needs investigation of *Utility independence* in between the risky investment and the quantity of money (see definition 2) (Keeney & Raiffa, 1999; Pavlov, 2015, 2017). We mark as (v, w_1)£(v, w_2) the lottery <(v, w_1), (v, w_2),α>: α is the probability of the appearance of the alternative (v, w_1) and (1-α) - the probability of the appearance of the alternative (v, w_2). The subjective or objective probability α describes the uncertainty with one risky investment event £. It is said that the second attribute w is utility independent if:

$$(v, w_1)£(v, w_2)\{(v, w_3)£(v, w_4) \Leftrightarrow (v', w_1)£(v', w_2)\{(v', w_3)£(v', w_4)$$

for all v, v' $\in$V and for all w_1, w_2, w_3, $w_4 \in$W. That is, preferences on W do not depend on the particular deterministic level at which v$\in$V is fixed. A convenient implication of the described utility independence is that changing v does not affect rank-ordering in W. The following theorem describes a well-known result (see theorems 1 and 2) (Keeney & Raiffa, 1999).

Theorem 4: Assume that the image of the function $F(w) \rightarrow U(v, w)$ is an interval for all v, where U(v, w) is the two attribute utility function. Then w is utility independent if and only if $U(v, w) = f(v) p(w) + g(v)$ for some functions f, p, g with f positive function.

Let W be relevant over a range w° to w^*, let V be relevant over a range v° to v^* and assume that U(v, w^*)>U(v, w°) for all v and U(v^*,w)>U(v°, w) for all w. We may rewrite this independency condition as:

$$U(v, w) = U(v, w^\circ) + [U(v, w^*) - U(v, w^\circ)] . U(v^\circ, w).$$

It is supposed that the preferences over the set W (the amount X_t at any moment t - quantity of money) do not depend on the particular deterministic level at which the risky investment π_t (v∈V) is fixed at moment t. In other words, *it is supposed that the preferences associated with the quantity of BGN's (set W) are utility independent from the level of risky investment π (set V)*. For description of the objective function is needed evaluation of the single-attribute utility functions U(v, w^*), U(v, w°) and U(v°, w) following the conclusions of the theorem. This multiattribute utility is relevant with the decision maker's preferences and permits optimal control design in agreement with the intuition and the empirical knowledge of the of the decision maker. The DM's objective utility function is shown on the Figure 4.

The control input is π_t and determines the partition amount $(X_t\pi_t)$ invested in the risky process at any moment t. The optimal control could be determined step by step from the Hamilton-Jacobi-Bellman partial differential equation in agreement with the dynamical programming principle [28]:

$$\frac{\partial B}{\partial t}(t, X) + \sup_{\pi \in [0,1]} [(rX + (\mu - r)\pi X)\frac{\partial B}{\partial X}(t, X) + \frac{1}{2}\sigma^2\pi^2 x^2 \frac{\partial^2 B}{\partial^2 X}(t, X)] = 0.$$

Figure 4. Utility:1≈1000000BGN's

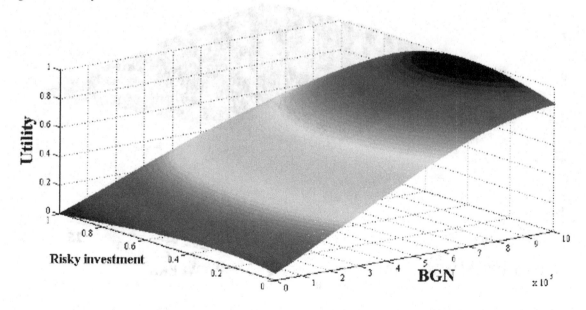

235

We underline that the coefficients in the stochastic differential equation are continuous, the objective function U(.) is continuous and that the optimal control is continuous by parts. These conditions determine that there is a smooth by parts solution of the HJB partial differential equation (Touzi & Tourin, 2012). Following the presentations in (Krylov, 1980) and passing through generalized solution of the Black-Scholes stochastic differential equation we found polynomial approximations of the Hamilton-Jacobi-Bellman (HJB) function $B(t, X)$ and of the control manifold $\pi(t,X)$ (Pavlov, 2015, 2017). They are shown in Figures 5 and 6.

The stochastic process is started in 30 different initial points; from 1000 BGN's to 30000 BGN's and the optimal control solutions could be seen in Figure 8. In Figure 7 is shown the optimal solution whit final wealth X_T evaluated in BGN's. The black seesaw line under the objective utility function in Figure 8 is a sample of stochastic optimal control process flow.

The Wiener process is an abstraction, sometimes far away from the reality because the white noise assumption is too strong. In the rest of the paragraph will be investigated the optimal portfolio control allocation in the case of a financial process with colored noise. Data from a real process (available in internet) are used: „*GNP in 1982 Dollars, discount rate on 91-day treasury bills, yield on long term treasury bonds, 1954Q1-1987Q4; source: Business Conditions Digest*". The noise of the real financial process (Figure 9) is far away from the white noise as could be seen by the correlation function in Figure 10. The approximation of the real correlation function is shown also in the same figure.

The problem of colored noise modeling and optimal filtering in linear control theory is repeatedly discussed and has practical significance (Kwakernaak & Sivan, 1972). The real financial process noise could be approximated by colored noise as is shown in Figure 10. This assumption permits modifications in the Black-Scholes model. The stochastic differential equation is appended to a three dimensional differential equation (Pavlov, 2017):

Figure 5. HJB function

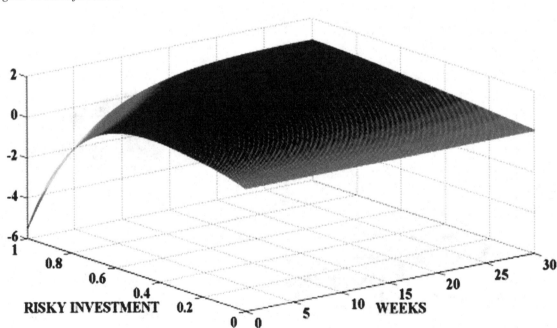

Figure 6. Optimal control manifold

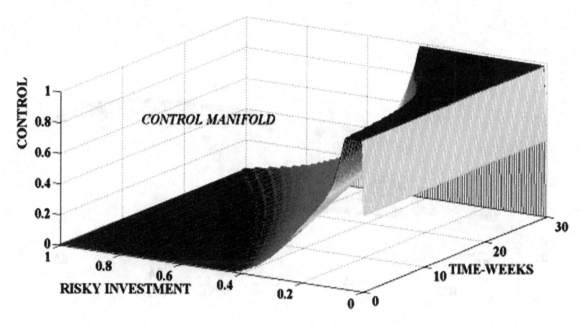

Figure 7. Scale in BGN's

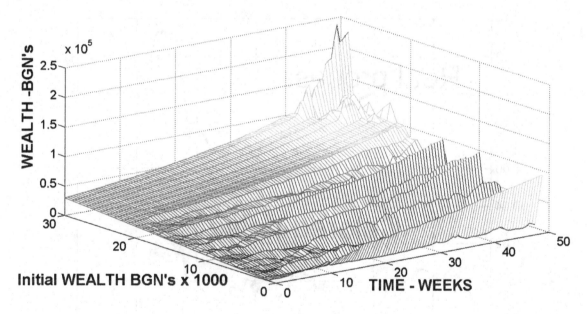

Figure 8. Utility:1≈1000000 BGN's

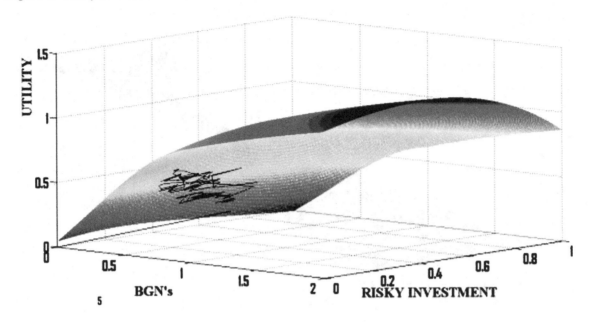

Figure 9. Experimental data

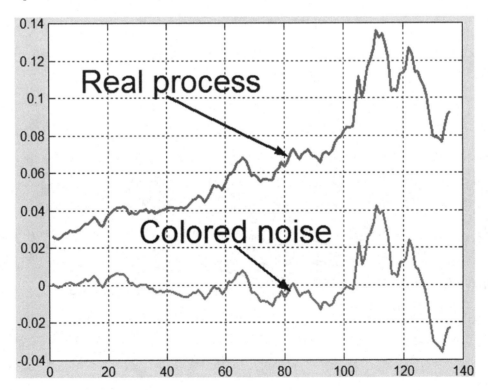

Figure 10. Correlation functions

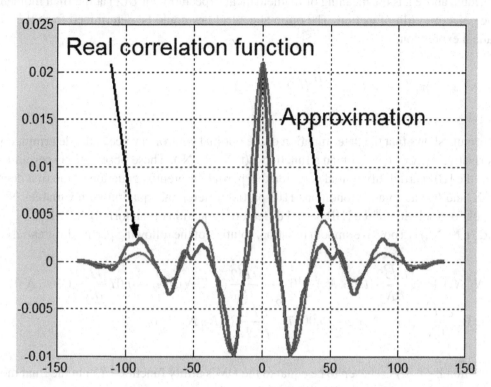

$$dX_t^{\pi} = (rX_t^{\pi} + (\mu - r)\pi_t X_t^{\pi})dt + \pi X_t^{\pi} N_1$$
$$dN_1 = N_2 dt + 0.0028 dW_t$$
$$dN_2 = -(0.135 N_1 + 0.07 N_2)dt + 0.0047 dW_t$$

It is obvious that the noise N appears autonomously in the second and the third row and that this is a description of a linear system. The wealth X_t appears only with its first derivative in the Hamilton-Jacobi-Bellman (HJB) partial differential equation.

$$\frac{\partial B}{\partial t}(t, X, N_1, N_2) + \sup_{\pi \in [0,1]} [(rX + (\mu - r)\pi X) + \pi X N_1]\frac{\partial B}{\partial X}(t, X, N_1, N_2)$$
$$+ N_2 \frac{\partial B}{\partial N_1}(t, X, N_1, N_2) - (0.135\frac{\partial B}{\partial N_1}(t, X, N_1, N_2) + 0.07\frac{\partial B}{\partial N_2}(t, X, N_1, N_2)) +$$
$$+ \frac{1}{2}(0.0028)^2 \frac{\partial^2 B}{\partial^2 N_1}(t, X, N_1, N_2) + \frac{1}{2}(0.0047)^2 \frac{\partial^2 B}{\partial^2 N_2}(t, X, N_1, N_2) = 0.$$

The main objective of the DM is again maximization of the expected DM's utility $U(X)$ at the final moment T:

$$V(t, x) := \sup_{\pi \in [0,1]} E[U(X_T^{t, x, \pi})].$$

The formula above has the meaning of mathematical expectation of $U(X)$ at the final moment where $U(.)$ is the objective utility function. The optimal control law could be determined from the following mathematical expression:

$$\sup_{\pi \in [0,1]} [(rX_t + (\mu - r)\pi_t X_t) + \pi X_t N_{1_t}] \frac{\partial B}{\partial X}(t, X, N_1, N_2)$$

This formula shows that the determination of the optimal control law needs the determination of the partial derivative on X of the Bellman's function $B(t, X, N_1, N_2)$. These observations permit a decomposition of the HJB partial differential equation to a partial differential equation of the first degree with variables X_t and (t) and to an autonomous HJB partial differential equation with variables N_1 and N_2. We will look for a solution of the HJB partial differential equation of the form $B_1(t, X)B_2(t, N_1, N_2)$. The function $B_2(t, N_1, N_2,)$ is a positive smooth function, solution of the following partial differential equation:

$$\frac{\partial B_2}{\partial t}(t, N_1, N_2) + N_2 \frac{\partial B_2}{\partial N_1}(t, N_1, N_2) - [0.135 \frac{\partial B_2}{\partial N_1}(t, X, N_1, N_2) + 0.07 \frac{\partial B_2}{\partial N_2}(t, N_1, N_2)] +$$
$$+ \frac{1}{2}(0.0028)^2 \frac{\partial^2 B_2}{\partial^2 N_1}(t, N_1, N_2) + \frac{1}{2}(0.0047)^2 \frac{\partial^2 B_2}{\partial^2 N_2}(t, N_1, N_2) = 0.$$

The function $B_1(T, X)$ is chosen to be equal to the DM's utility function $U(X)$ in the final moment T. This function is solution of the partial differential equation:

$$\frac{\partial B_1}{\partial t}(t, X, N_1, N_2) + \sup_{\pi \in [0,1]} [(rX + (\mu - r)\pi X) + \pi X N_1] \frac{\partial B_1}{\partial X}(t, X, N_1, N_2) = 0$$

The decomposition permits determination of the partial derivative on X of the Belman's function $B(t, X, N_1, N_2)$ as follows:

$$\frac{\partial B}{\partial X}(t, X, N_1, N_2) = \frac{\partial U}{\partial X}(t, X)e^{\int_t^T (r + (\mu - r)\pi_s + \pi_s E(N_{1(s)}))ds} B_2(t, N_1, N_2),$$

In the formula π_t, $t \in [0,T]$ is the optimal control policy and $E(N_1(t))$ is the mathematical expectation of the colored noise at moment t. We remind that the color noise is generated by the linear system with Gauss white noise as input as could be seen in the formulae as stated above. Now it is clear that the two partial derivatives have the same sign and the formula of the optimal control law becomes:

$$\sup_{\pi \in [0,1]} [(rX_t + (\mu - r)\pi_t X_t) + \pi_t X_t N_{1_t}] sign(\frac{\partial U}{\partial X}(t, X))$$

The stochastic process is started in 30 different initial points; from 1000 BGN's to 30000 BGN's.

The solutions are shown in Figure 11. In the next Figure 12 are shown the same solutions but with the classical control law in the case of Wiener process. We underline that in Figure 11 and Figure 12 are shown two different optimal solutions of the final wealth evaluated as utilities U(X). It is well seen that the solution that renders an account of the colored noise gives much better results.

The noise in the numerical modeling is approximated by colored noise as output of a linear system with Gauss white noise input (Kwakernaak & Sivan, 1972). A sample of the colored noise and its cor-

Figure 11. Utility:1≈1000000 BGN's

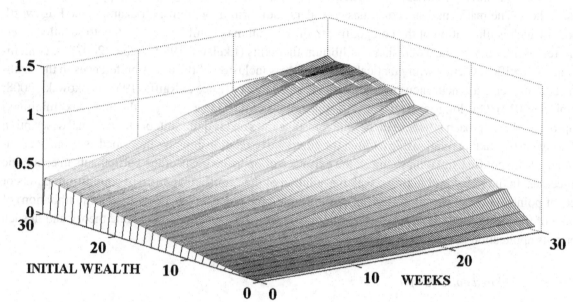

Figure 12. Utility: 1≈1000000 BGN's

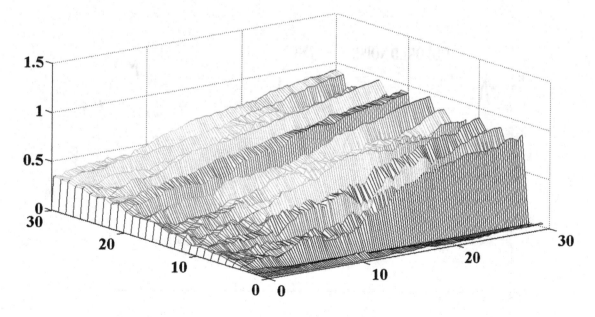

relation function are shown in Figure 13 and Figure 14. The linear system is constructed based on the approximation of the correlation function shown in Figure 10. The approach described by this example is in fact is a value driven design and control (Pavlov, 2016).

SMALL STORE MODELLING: GAME, PREFERENCES, UTILITY

The theoretical basis of Game theory and its applications in the mathematical economics attract permanently scientific interest. The applied aspects of the Game theory are of interest for applications of many researchers. The mathematical economics considers equilibrium theorems, for example the Edgeworth model which is illustration of the competitive trading in minmax equilibrium; the Pareto set allocations and representations of the Walrasian equilibrium theorems (Ekeland, 1979; Aubin, 2007). A contemporary scientific tendency with practical applicability is inclusion of the user's preferences in the mathematical model in a synchronous manner with the game theory (Luce & Raiffa, 1957; Laskowski, 2008; Jamison, 2012). One long-term tendency in applications of the Game theory is the min-max (minimax) approach. This approach is central in the antagonistic games and is quite suitable for a formal description of competitive trading relationships. Often the competitive relationships are described as "conflict situations". With conflict situation we mean the existence of opposite goals of the participants in economic processes. In the stated problems we seek the solution of the "conflict" in form of equilibrium points or sets of points (contract curve), reflecting equilibrium in the processes, not destruction (annihilation) of some of the participants. That is how the minimax approach is understood in Game theory and in such form its application in practice is sought.

Figure 13. Colored noise sample

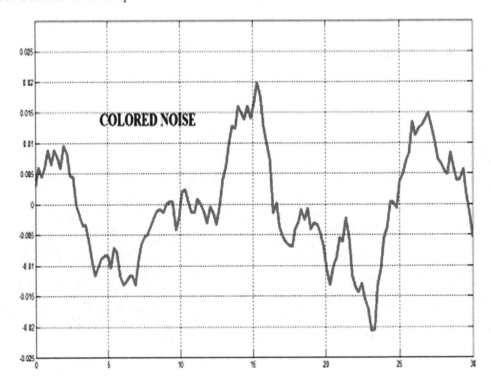

Figure 14. Correlation function

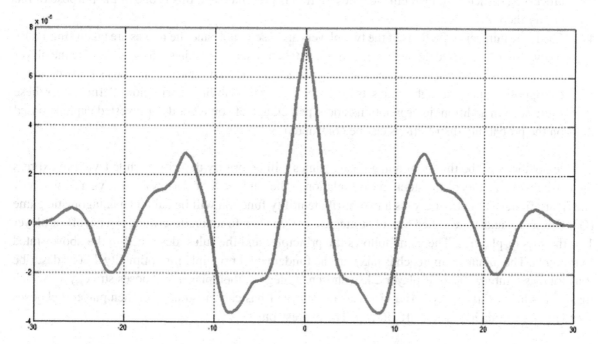

In this example we demonstrate applications of the antagonistic games through the achievements of Utility and Measurement theory (Pavlov, Terzieva, & Kademova-Katzarova, 2014). Briefly will be discussed the basic principles, underlying the theory of antagonistic games:

1. The relationships are determined by opposed interests of the participants in the process; let us call it a competitive market. There are two sides, competing for the same resource and a finite number of possibilities for actions (strategies). The finite antagonistic games are relevant for common purpose and well understood by the common user. In the infinite antagonistic games, we incorporate situations, described by sets with the cardinality of Z (the set of integers) and more generally by sets with the cardinality of the continuum.

2. The actions of the two players are undertaken independently of each other, with no mutual awareness. The result of the sections is evaluated by pay-off reflected by a utility function of the first player and the loss or dissatisfaction of the second player. So far in the theory and practice are mainly employed objective or material data, such as amount of money or quantity of goods, etc. Our approach allows the incorporation of the Utility theory for the assessment of the two participants in the conflict in a broader perspective. For example, seeking the equilibrium besides the gain of money, one can take into account factors like „convenience" from some situation, ecological effects, physiological influence, etc. The Utility function as description of both conflict parties (players) in the antagonistic game could be a key factor for the relevant mathematical modeling and the successful application of the minimax approach.

3. In terms of Utility objective function each of the two participating sides assesses itself and the opposite side. The utilization of the multiattribute Utility theory for description of the antagonistic interaction is natural and fits well in Game theory. By this way a quantitative expression of complex

processes, difficult for mathematical description is presented and this is one of the purpose of the Utility theory.

4. The finite numbers of actions of the two players are inseparable and the moves are taken simultaneously. What amounts to the same thing, they are taken in succession in such a manner that the player who moves second does not know the choice made by the first player. This allows to be modeled the opposing sides through finite sets of strategies and probability distributions defined over these finite sets. In addition, interpretations about percentage of some goods or invested capitals based on the probability distributions can be considered.

The notations of the theory of antagonistic games will be briefly described while trying to express the fundamental factors of the stock market relations. The triple $< X, Y, U(x, y)/ x \in X, y \in Y>$, where X and Y are finite sets, and U(x, y) is a two-attribute utility function will be called an antagonistic game (G). The sets X and Y are called sets of strategies. $U(x, y)$ is a function describing the payoff of player 1 or the loss of player 2. The game follows the principles and the rules, described in the above stated four points. The minimax approach is taken as the fundamental principle for optimality. Let us describe it as follows (Aubin, 2007). If player 2 has chosen strategy y, then player 1 chooses strategy x_0, which maximizes his payoff $U(x_0,y)$. And vice versa, if player 1 has chosen strategy y, then player 2 chooses strategy y_0, maximizing his payoff $U(x,y_0)$. The expression

$$\min_{y \in Y} U(x_0, y) = \max_{x \in X} \min_{y \in Y} U(x, y) = v_d(\Gamma) \tag{6}$$

is called lower price of the game G. It is a guaranteed payoff of the first player if it chooses strategy x_0. Analogically, for the second player the minimal loss is determined by

$$\max_{x \in X} U(x, y_0) = \min_{y \in Y} \max_{x \in X} U(x, y) = v_g(\Gamma)$$

Obviously the inequality

$$v_g(G) \geq v_d(G) \tag{7}$$

is always valid. In the case of equality

$$v_g(G) = v_d(G) \tag{8}$$

in the above expression, the discrete game is in equilibrium and it can be assumed that both players are satisfied by this solution. Actually this minimax principle guarantees payoff value $v_d(G)$ in any case and it could be taken as the principle of the cautious trader.

In general the equilibrium solution does not exist. One decision would be: the set of finite strategies to be expanded comprising all discrete finite probability distributions-mixed strategies. These probability distributions are defined on the finite sets X and Y. In this setting the choice is between discrete probability distributions over X (mixed strategies) $X(x)$ and over Y - respectively $Y(y)$. The semantic interpretations of these distributions are based (determined) on the semantic of the concrete problem to be solved. For example, such interpretation can be some percentage of allocated funds for one or another economical domain or some number of customers of some product in percentage, etc. The mixed strategy $X(x)$ (the discrete probability distribution) can be stated in the following way,

$$X = (\lambda_1, \lambda_2, ..., \lambda_m), \; \lambda_i \geq 0, \sum_{i=1}^{m} \lambda_i = 1$$

Similarly, the mixed strategy $Y(y)$ is represented as follows,

$$Y = (\eta_1, \eta_2, ..., \eta_n), \; \eta_i \geq 0, \sum_{j=1}^{n} \eta_j = 1$$

The von Neumann theorem provides that for the finite game the mixed minimax equilibrium solution always exists [33]:

$$v_g(\Gamma) = v_d(\Gamma) = \sum_{i-1}^{m} \sum_{j=1}^{n} U(x_i, y_j) \lambda_i \eta_j \qquad (9)$$

In another notation the above expression can be restated as,

$$\min_{Y(y)} U(X(x_0), Y(y)) = \max_{X(x)} \min_{Y(y)} U(X(x), Y(y)) =$$
$$= \max_{X(x)} U(X(x), Y(y_0)) = U(X(x_0), Y(y_0))$$

In the formula the mixed strategies $X(x_0)$ and $Y(y_0)$ are the searched equilibrium, the solution of the finite antagonistic game, determined by the minimax approach. There are number of theorems considering this result in detail. An interesting result from practical perspective is the following. If $X(x_0)$ and $Y(y_0)$ are such solutions, then

$$v_g(\Gamma) = v_d(\Gamma) = \sum_{i-1}^{m} \sum_{j=1}^{n} U(x_i, y_j) \lambda_i \eta_j = U(X(x_0), Y(y_0)) =$$
$$= U(X(x_0), y_j) = U(x_i, Y(y_0))$$

The element y_j as element of $Y(y_0)$ appears as possible outcome with probability η_j. The same applies to the second player in regard to the strategy of the first player. The discrete variable x_i belongs to the initial set of alternatives $X(x_0)$ as possible outcome with probability λ_i.

From the brief description of the notions so far, it follows that firstly a direct solution (8) of the finite game is sought. If such equality (solution) does not exist, a solution in mixed strategies is sought. Key factor in every application of the Game theory is the determination of semantically justified objective function $U(x,y)$. In the market relations this can be a utility function, representing the preferences of the players. By this way, the human's preferences represented by a Utility function are naturally embedded mathematically in the considered problem.

Let us discuss the following example from the competitive market domain as application of the so far exposed theoretical results and methods. In this problem the methods of Game and Utility theory are combined. The problem represents planning and forecasting based on the minimax method of the stock's availability of a small store. The aim is to obtain a forecasting of the income of the store as a guarantee against bankrupt in any distribution of the opposite player. In this problem the opposite player is the competitive market (the Nature). This solution shows the guaranteed minimal income of the store in the worst for the Shopkeeper distribution of the purchases of the different products. It could be called the *solution of the cautious seller*. Similar forecasting and analyzes could be convenient at the beginning of an e-business, when it is not sure if it will be successful. Another convenient case would be when the shop is threatened with bankruptcy and an adequate estimate of the guaranteed minimal income is needed. As objective function is used the Utility function of the seller versus the different products for sells. The products used in the example are selected in an arbitrary manner and for the sake of demonstration only. The following products are chosen:

1. Sweets, bonbons, cafe 1 – 2 BGN;
2. Bread and bakery products 2 – 3 BGN;
3. Fruits and vegetables up to 3 BGN;
4. Cheap cheese and dairy products up to 5 BGN;
5. Expensive cheese and dairy products 12 – 13 BGN;
6. Sausage and salami;
7. Expensive meat products, fish up to 20 BGN;
8. Expensive candies and sweets up to20 – 30 BGN;
9. Bio fruits and vegetables;
10. Expensive wine and alcoholic drinks.

The main goal of the discussed problem is to be estimated a relevant distribution for the schedule of the store supply (in regard to the above stated products) such that the best income to be ensured in case of the worst distribution of the purchases in regard to the products (worst market status). In other words, the aim is the best income to be ensured in the worst situation of the market for the Shopkeeper in accordance with the minimax approach. The meaning of this solution is the allocation of the money in an optimal way in regard to the ten products.

More detailed description and the essence of the methodology is as follows: from all the purchased goods from the previous months are estimated how much of the purchases count to the first family of products. If we take the number of the first product's purchase and divide it by the number of all the purchased products for the considered time period, we determine the probability of purchasing the first product. By the same way are determined the probabilities for purchasing the rest of the products. This is the probability distribution is the appearance of the competitive market (Nature) as player in the antagonistic game. Actually, it means that the market is the second player with the mixed strategy $Y(y)$. Then the determined above finite probability distribution describes the current state of the market. Namely, the distribution $Y(\eta)$ is the distribution, by which the second player - the market participates in the game.

$$Y = (\eta_1, \eta_2, ..., \eta_n), \ \eta_i \geq 0, \ \sum_{j=1}^{n} \eta_j = 1 \tag{10}$$

As assumed, the Shopkeeper is player 1 and his/her participation is described by the mixed strategy $X(\lambda)$

$$X = (\lambda_1, \lambda_2, ..., \lambda_m), \ \lambda_i \geq 0, \ \sum_{i=1}^{m} \lambda_i = 1 \tag{11}$$

This probability distribution semantically means the allocated money by percent age for the next period of the shop activity, for the first product.

Actually, we plan the future activity of the shop through the distribution $X(\lambda)$, ac- cording to the worst possible situation of the market $Y(\eta)$. This is the guaranteed income from the sales for the next period. If we keep the strategy of the allocation of the funds for the support of the shop $X(\lambda)$, we would have incomes always better or equal to the price of the game:

$$v_g(\Gamma) = v_d(\Gamma) = \sum_{i-1}^{m} \sum_{j=1}^{n} U(x_i, y_j) \lambda_i \eta_j$$

This result should be considered as mathematical expectation, because the market is manifested stochastically by discrete distributions. The distribution $Y(\eta)$ is a statistical estimate of the distribution of the market and that is why the conclusions from the result of game, the solution will manifest itself averaged in the following periods of the shop's activity. The solution itself requires two main computations. The first one is the utility evaluation of the two attribute objective function $U(x,y)$ based on the Shopkeeper's preferences. By this way the objective function takes into account the two players (the Shopkeeper and the competitive market). The payoff matrix of the antagonistic game is determined by the Shopkeeper's preferences in respect to the products for sell.

On the diagonal of the matrix $U(x, y)$ of the game $G = <X,Y,U(x, y) \mid x \in X, y \in Y >$ we put the utilities (the payoffs from the sale of the product s_i), and in the other positions we put zeros since they do not contribute to the payoff in the presented game. Of course, some penalty values outside the diagonal can be put instead of zeros and this would change the semantic of the problem in consideration and it is an additional possibility. The Utility of the Shopkeeper is evaluated through the sale of every single product. On the diagonal of the matrix this utility is set, which means that if we allocate λ_1 amount of money for the first product and accomplish η_1 percent sales from it, then the income from it would be

$$U(\lambda_1, \eta_1) = \lambda_{1*} V(s_1) * \eta_1.$$

In the above formula we denoted by $V(s)$ the Utility function of the Shopkeeper in respect to the products s. Therefore, the first important point of this solution is the construction of this Utility function. We assume that the scale of the products S is the ratio scale over which we construct $V(s)$. This is achieved by semantically charging the products with the Shopkeeper's utility of the product's price or ease of the sale. In that way we arrange the list with the products. For determination of the scale we compute the utility of product number 10 by the algorithm (5) and obtain 0.33. The Shopkeeper's utility function is shown on Figure 15.

The second important point is the computation of the mixed game- the minimax solution. This happens after the problem is brought to a linear programming task (Bazara & Shetty, 1979). The solution is chosen as "saddle-point" of mixed strategies determined as finite probability distribution over each row and column of the matrix (Aubin, 2007). It is known from the theory that the meaning of the game equals the smallest number θ, for which exists a distribution:

$$Y = (\eta_1, \eta_2, \ldots, \eta_n), \ \eta_i \geq 0, \ \sum_{j=1}^{n} \eta_j = 1, \quad \eta_i \geq 0.$$

The following inequality is valid

$$\sum_{i-1}^{m} \sum_{j=1}^{n} U(x, y_j)\eta_j = U(x, Y(y)) \leq \theta, \ \forall x \in X.$$

If we denote by (h_{ij}) the matrix of the finite game, the above inequality takes the form

$$\sum_{i=1}^{n} h_{iy}\lambda_i \geq \theta, \ \forall y \in Y.$$

This inequality is brought to the following problem of the linear programming

Figure 15. Utility evaluation

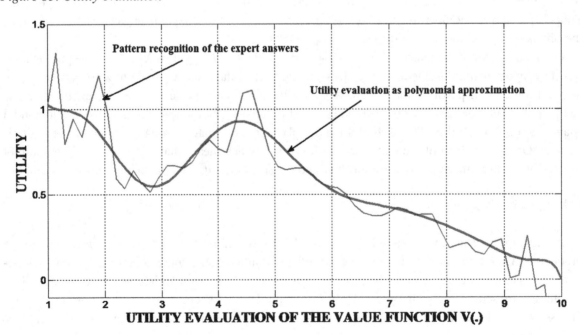

$$\sum_{i=1}^{n} h_{iy} u_i \geq 1, \ y = (1 \div 10), \ u_i \geq 0.$$

For the optimal solution (u*) we obtain

$$\theta = \frac{1}{\left(\sum_{i=1}^{10} u_i^* \right)}.$$

The optimal solution of the game for the second player (the Nature) is

$$X = (\lambda_1, \lambda_2, ..., \lambda_n), \ \lambda_i \geq 0, \ \lambda_i = \frac{u_i^*}{\sum_{i=1}^{10} u_i^*}.$$

The optimal distribution (minmax saddle-point) over the ten types of products for the first player (Shopkeeper) is the following vector:

Product1 → 0.0566006
Product2 → 0.0666184
Product3 → 0.0855441
Product4 → 0.0526425
Product5 → 0.0519164
Product6 → 0.0855441
Product7 → 0.1003717
Product8 → 0.1158135
Product9 → 0.1568308
Product10 → 0.2281176

If these values are multiplied by 100%, we get the percentages of the common amount of money (funds), allocated for every product for the support of the shop. This distribution of the funds guarantees a minimax equilibrium by the worst distribution of the competitive market and better incomes by every other distribution. For the solution of the problem are needed two main computation procedures. The first one is the determination of the Utility function of the Shopkeeper and the computation of the elements of the matrix of the game. The second procedure is the determination of the optimal solutions for the Nature (the worst market situation) and optimal solutions for the Shopkeeper (the best distribution of the quantities of the different products in the shop).

This approach and methods could provide supporting solutions related to other complex problems. In this problem's solution are stressed the possibilities of the Utility theory and its application in the domain of antagonistic Games.

CONCLUSION

The aim of the chapter was to demonstrate an analytical mathematical technique and the possibility to describe quantitatively complex social, ecological, biological and other processes and to show a possibility for mathematical construction of complex human- process models. This approach in fact is a value driven design and control of complex processes where the human choice is decisive for the final solution.

Cyber-Physical Systems (CPS) are integrations of computation, networking, and physical processes in interaction with the user. An embedded computer, management or control needs feedback loops and interaction with the human participating in the process. Physical and software components and the dialog with the users are deeply intertwined, each operating on different special mathematical scales. Starting from the previous the inclusion of a value model as part of an CPS system can be done in different ways. At the first level, in the development of such a system, it may be useful to carefully obtain a 'good' objective function. Such a good objective function could provide carefully thought advises and judgments built implicitly into the CPS system. But the human notations and preferences have in general qualitative expressions and uncertainty. At this level arises the need of stochastic algorithms and stochastic machine–learning.

The CPS system could include a value model that offered the user choice of an objective function (human-process model). For instance, a value model connected to a system designed to aid personal financial investment may allow the user to provide value judgments about an appropriate risk attitude and appropriate value tradeoffs for income in different time periods.

The third level of a value model for a CPS system would offer the users a menu for flexible and easy dialog for selection of the form of the objective utility function at the level of the qualitative preferences. It may also provide for easy sensitivity analysis with different objective functions and additionally would allow the user to completely assess his/her objective function as part of the concrete CPS system related to the considered problem.

Such a flexible system has to be based on a given set of objectives and attributes. Users may focus on different sets of fundamental objectives for their specific purposes. This option is not too different from having a separate system to assess (evaluate) an individual's utility function. The suggested approach can be regarded as a realization of the *prescriptive decision making approach*. The utility function is an abstraction presented in the limits of the normative approach, the axiomatic systems of von Neumann. The mathematical expectation measured in the interval scale on the base of the DM's preferences over lotteries is an approximation of the von Neumann-Morgenstren utility function.

The presented formulations could serve as foundation of development of decision support tools for design of management/control in Cyber-Physical Systems. This value-oriented modeling leads to the development of preferences-based decision support in machine learning environment and control/management value-based design.

REFERENCES

Aizerman, M., Braverman, A., & Rozonoer, L. E. (1970). *Potential Function Method in the Theory of Machine Learning*. Moscow: Nauka. (in Russian)

Allais, M. (1953). Le comportement de l'homme rationnel devant le risque: Critique des postulats et axiomes de l'école américaine. *Econometrica, 21*(4), 503–546. doi:10.2307/1907921

Aubin, J.-P. (2007). Mathematical Methods of Game and Economic Theory. North-Holland.

Bazara, M., & Shetty, C. (1979). *Nonlinear Programming: Theory and Algorithms*. New York: Wiley.

Biffl, S., Aurum, A., Boehm, B., Erdoginus, H., & Grunbacher, P. (Eds.). (2006). Value-Based Software Engineering. Springer-Verlag. doi:10.1007/3-540-29263-2

Bradley, J. M., & Atkins, E. M. (2015). Optimization and Control of Cyber-Physical Vehicle Systems. *Sensors (Basel), 15*(12), 23020–23049. doi:10.3390150923020 PMID:26378541

Cohen, M., & Jaffray, J. Y. (1988). Certainty Effects versus Probability Distortion: An Experimental Analysis of Decision Making Under Risk. *Journal of Experimental Psychology. Human Perception and Performance, 14*(4), 554–560. doi:10.1037/0096-1523.14.4.554

Collopy, P., & Hollingsworth, P. (2009). *Value-driven design. AIAA Paper 2009-7099*. Reston, VA: American Institute of Aeronautics and Astronautics.

Ekeland, I. (1979). *Elements d'économie mathématique*. Hermann. (in Russian)

Fishburn, P. (1970). *Utility theory for decision-making*. New York: Wiley. doi:10.21236/AD0708563

Fishburn, P. (1978). Utility Theory. In J. Moder & S. Elmaghraby (Eds.), *Handbook of Operations Research: Foundations and Fundamentals*. New York: Van Nostrand Reinhold Company.

Hahn, G. J., & Kuhn, H. (2012). Designing Decision Support Systems for Value-Based Management: A Survey and an Architecture. *Decision Support Systems-DSS, 53*(3), 591–598. doi:10.1016/j.dss.2012.02.016

Jamison, J. (2012). Games with Synergistic Preferences. *Games, 3*(1), 41–55. doi:10.3390/g3010041

Joe, S., & Kuo, F. (2008). Constructing Sobol' sequences with better two-dimensional projections. *SIAM Journal on Scientific Computing, 30*(5), 2635–2654. doi:10.1137/070709359

Kahneman, D., & Tversky, A. (1979). Prospect theory: An analysis of decision under risk. *Econometrica, 47*(2), 263–291. doi:10.2307/1914185

Keeney, R. L. (1988). Value-driven Expert Systems for Decision Support. *Decision Support Systems, 4*(4), 405–412. doi:10.1016/0167-9236(88)90003-6

Keeney, R. L., & Raiffa, H. (1999). *Decision with multiple objectives: Preferences and value trade-offs*. Cambridge, UK: Cambridge University Press.

Krantz, D. H., Luce, R. D., Suppes, P., & Tversky, A. (Eds.). (1990). Foundations of Measurement (Vols. 1-3). New York: Academic Press.

Krylov, N. V. (1980). *Controlled Diffusion Processes*. New York: Springer-Verlag. doi:10.1007/978-1-4612-6051-6

Kwakernaak, H., & Sivan, R. (1972). *Linear optimal control systems*. New York: Wiley.

Larichev, O. & Morgoev V. (1991). Problems, Methods and Systems of Extracting Expert Knowledge. *Automation and Telemechanics*, 6. (in Russian)

Laskowski, S. (2008). Cooperative and Non-cooperative, Integrative and Distributive Market Games with Antagonistic and Altruistic, Malicious and Kind Ways of Playing. *Journal of Telecommunications and Information Technology*, *4*, 88–96.

Lee, E. A. (2008). Cyber Physical Systems: Design Challenges. *ISORC '08 Proceedings of the 2008 11th IEEE Symposium on Object Oriented Real-Time Distributed Computing*, 363-369.

Luce, D., & Raiffa, H. (1957). *Games and decisions: Introduction and critical survey*. New York: Wiley.

Neumann, P., Goldie, S., & Milton, W. (2000). Preference-based Measures in Economic Evaluationin Health Care. *Annual Review of Public Health*, *21*(1), 587–611. doi:10.1146/annurev.publhealth.21.1.587 PMID:10884966

Pandey, V., Nikolaidis, E., & Mourelatos, Z. (2011). Multi-objective decision making under uncertainty and incomplete knowledge of designer preferences. *SAE International Journal of Materials and Manufacturing*, *4*(1), 1155–1168. doi:10.4271/2011-01-1080

Pavlov, Y. (2016). Value Based Decision Control for Complex Systems. Encyclopedia: Artificial Intelligence: Concepts, Methodologies, Tools, and Applications, Information Resources Management Association (IRMA-USA), 50, 1253-1268.

Pavlov, Y. P. (2005). Subjective preferences, values and decisions. Stochastic Approximation Approach. *Proceedings of Bulgarian Academy of Sciences*, *58*(4), 367–372.

Pavlov, Y. P. (2015). Rational Portfolio Investment Based on Consumer's Preferences: Black-Scholes Model and Stochastic Control. *Journal of Communication and Computer*, 262-271.

Pavlov, Y. P. (2017). Value Based Decision Control: Preferences Portfolio Allocation, Wiener and Color Noise Cases. *IOSR Journal of Computer Engineering*, *19*(1), 53–60.

Pavlov, Y. P., & Andreev, D. R. (2013). Decision Control, Management, and Support in Adaptive and Complex Systems: Quantitative Models. IGI Global. doi:10.4018/978-1-4666-2967-7

Pavlov, Y. P., Terzieva, V., & Kademova-Katzarova, P. (2014). Optimal Financial Allocation Of Starting Small Factory Resources: Preferences Based Approach. In *4ᵗʰ International Conference On Application of Information and Communication Technology and Statistics in Economy and Education (ICAICT-SEE-2014)*. Sofia University Of National And World Economy (UNWE).

Pfanzagl, J. (1971). *Theory of Measurement*. Wurzburg: Physical-Verlag. doi:10.1007/978-3-662-41488-0

Raiffa, H. (1968). *Decision Analysis*. New York: Addison-Wesley Reading Mass.

Shmeidler, D. (1989). Subjective probability and expected utility without additivity. *Econometrica*, *57*(3), 571–587. doi:10.2307/1911053

Sobol, I. M. (1979). On the systematic search in a hypercube. *SIAM Journal on Numerical Analysis*, *16*(5), 790–793. doi:10.1137/0716058

Touzi, N. & Tourin, A. (2012). *Optimal Stochastic Control, Stochastic Target Problems and Backward SDEs*. Springer- Business & Economics.

Yin, H., Zhao, C., Li, M., & Chengbin, M. (2015). Utility Function-Based Real-Time Control of a Battery Ultracapacitor Hybrid Energy System. *IEEE Transactions on Industrial Informatics*, *11*(1), 220–231. doi:10.1109/TII.2014.2378596

Compilation of References

Abdullah, J. (2014). *Chapter: Radio Propagation Model For Wireless Sensor Network Simulation. In Advances in wireless Network Research.* Nova Publisher.

Abdullah, J., & Parish, D. J. (2007). Node connectivity index as mobility metric for GA based QoS routing in MANET. *Proceedings of the 4th international Conference on Mobile Technology, Applications, and Systems*, 104-111. 10.1145/1378063.1378082

Abdulrahman, M., & Meribout, M. (2014). Antenna array design for enhanced oil recovery under oil reservoir constraints with experimental validation. *Energy*, *66*, 868–880. doi:10.1016/j.energy.2014.01.002

Adiprana, R., & Yuniarto, E. (2010). Guung Salak geothermal power plant experience of scaling/deposit: Analysis, root cause and prevention. *Proceedings World Geothermal Congress*, 25-29.

Agrawal, R. a. (2000). *Privacy-preserving data mining* (Vol. 29). ACM.

Ahlgren, B., Dannewitz, C., Imbrenda, C., Kutscher, D., & Ohlman, B. (2012). A survey of information-centric networking. *IEEE Communications Magazine*, *50*(7), 26–36. doi:10.1109/MCOM.2012.6231276

Ahmadi, H., Pham, N., Ganti, R., Abdelzaher, T., Nath, S., & Han, J. (2010). Privacy-aware regression modeling of participatory sensing data. *Int'l Conf. Embedded Networked Sensor Systems*, 99–112. 10.1145/1869983.1869994

Aizerman, M., Braverman, A., & Rozonoer, L. E. (1970). *Potential Function Method in the Theory of Machine Learning.* Moscow: Nauka. (in Russian)

Akella, R., & McMillin, B. M. (2009). Model-Checking BNDC Properties in Cyber-Physical Systems. *Proceedings of the 33rd Annual IEEE International Computer Software and Applications Conference.*

Akkaya, K. A. S. (2015). Software defined net- working for wireless local networks in smart grid. SoftwarLocal Computer Networks Conference Workshops (LCN Workshops), 2015 IEEE 40th, 826–831.

Akkaya, K., & Younis, M. (2005). A survey on routing protocols for wireless sensor networks. *Ad Hoc Networks*, *3*(3), 325–349. doi:10.1016/j.adhoc.2003.09.010

Akritidis, P., Costa, M., Castro, M., & Hand, S. (2009). Baggy Bounds Checking: An Efficient and Backwards-Compatible Defense against Out-of-Bounds Errors. In *USENIX Security Symposium* (pp. 51–66). Academic Press.

Akyildiz, I. F., & Kasimoglu, I. H. (2004). Wireless sensor and actor networks: Research challenges. *Ad Hoc Networks*, 2(4), 351–367. doi:10.1016/j.adhoc.2004.04.003

Akyildiz, I. F., Su, W., Sankarasubramaniam, Y., & Cayirci, E. (2002). Wireless Sensor Networks: A Survey. *IEEE Comput. J.*, 38, 393–422.

Al Hosani, E., & Meribout, M. (2014). A New Optical-Based Device for Black Powder Detection in Gas Pipelines. *IEEE Transactions on Instrumentation and Measurement*, 63(9), 2238–2252. doi:10.1109/TIM.2014.2308985

Alberti, A.M., Scarpioni, G. D., Magalhães, V.J., Cerqueira Sodré Jr, A., Rodrigues, J. J. P. C. & Righi, R. da R. (2017c) Advancing NovaGenesis architecture towards future Internet of things. *IEEE Internet of Things Journal*, 99, 1-1.

Alberti, A. M. (2013). A Conceptual-Driven Survey on Future Internet Requirements, Technologies, and Challenges. *Journal of the Brazilian Computer Society*, 19(3), 291–311. doi:10.100713173-013-0101-2

Alberti, A. M., Casaroli, M. A., Singh, D., & Righi, R. (2017a). Naming and name resolution in the future Internet: Introducing the NovaGenesis approach. *Elsevier Future Generation Computer Systems*, 67, 163–179. doi:10.1016/j.future.2016.07.015

Alberti, A. M., Mazzer, D., Bontempo, M. M., De Oliveira, L. H., Righi, R., & Sodré, A. C. Jr. (2017b). Cognitive radio in the context of Internet of things using a novel future internet architecture called NovaGenesis. *Elsevier Computers & Electrical Engineering*, 57, 147–161. doi:10.1016/j.compeleceng.2016.07.008

Alhafidh, B. M., & Allen, W. (2016). Design and simulation of a smart home managed by an intelligent self-adaptive system. *International Journal of Engineering Research and Applications*, 6(8), 64–90.

Alhafidh, B., Khzaali, H., Mahmood, A., & Allen, W. (2016). *Smart homes based on smart cities design patterns*. United Scholars Publishing.

Alho, P. (2015). *Service-Based Fault Tolerance for Cyber-Physical Systems : A Systems Engineering Approach*. Tampere University of Technology. Retrieved from http://www.tut.fi/tutcris

Alho, P. (2017). *Service-based Fault Tolerance for Cyber-Physical Systems*. Tampere University of Technology.

Allais, M. (1953). Le comportement de l'homme rationnel devant le risque: Critique des postulats et axiomes de l'école américaine. *Econometrica*, 21(4), 503–546. doi:10.2307/1907921

AMD. (2004). *Intel put antivirus tech into chips | ZDNet*. Retrieved September 13, 2017, from http://www.zdnet.com/article/amd-intel-put-antivirus-tech-into-chips/

Ammari, H. M., & Das, S. K. (2008). Integrated coverage and connectivity in wireless sensor networks: A two-dimensional percolation problem. *IEEE Transactions on Computers*, *57*(10), 1423–1433. doi:10.1109/TC.2008.68

Ammari, H. M., & Das, S. K. (2009). Critical density for coverage and connectivity in three-dimensional wireless sensor networks using continuum percolation. *IEEE Transactions on Parallel and Distributed Systems*, *20*(6), 872–885. doi:10.1109/TPDS.2008.146

Ancillotti, E., Bruno, R., & Conti, M. (2013). The role of communication systems in smart grids: Architectures, technical solutions and research challenges. *Computer Communications*, *36*(17–18), 1665–1697. doi:10.1016/j.comcom.2013.09.004

Ansar, S., Ansar, W., Ansar, K., Mehmood, M. H., Raja, M. Z. U., & Javaid, N. (2017). Demand side management using meta-heuristic techniques and ToU in smart grid. In L. Barolli, T. Enokido, & M. Takizawa (Eds.), *Advances in Network-Based Information Systems. NBiS 2017. Lecture Notes on Data Engineering and Communications Technologies* (Vol. 7, pp. 203–217). Cham: Springer.

Antsaklis, P. (2014). Goals and Challenges in Cyber-Physical Systems Research Editorial of the Editor in Chief. *IEEE Transactions on Automatic Control*, *59*(12), 3117–3119. doi:10.1109/TAC.2014.2363897

Arampatzis, T., Lygeros, J., & Manesis, S. (2005). A survey of applications of wireless sensors and wireless sensor networks. *Proceedings of the 20th IEEE International Symposium on Intelligent Control*, 719–724. 10.1109/.2005.1467103

ARM. (2017). *TrustZone-ARM*. Retrieved from http://www.arm.com/products/processors/technologies/trustzone/index.php

Armstrong, J. (2003). *Making reliable distributed systems in the presence of sodware errors*. Mikroelektronik och informationsteknik. Retrieved from http://citeseerx.ist.psu.edu/viewdoc/download?doi=10.1.1.3.408&rep=rep1&type=pdf

Arora, D., Ravi, S., Raghunathan, A., & Jha, N. K. (2005). Secure embedded processing through hardware-assisted run-time monitoring. In *Design, Automation and Test in Europe* (pp. 178–183). Proceedings. doi:10.1109/DATE.2005.266

Asare, P., Broman, D., Lee, E. A., Prinsloo, G., Torngren, M., & Sunder, S. S. (2017). *A Cyber Physical Systems- a concept map*. Retrieved September 5, 2017, from http://cyberphysicalsystems.org

Aubin, J.-P. (2007). Mathematical Methods of Game and Economic Theory. North-Holland.

Austin, T. M., Breach, S. E., & Sohi, G. S. (1994). Efficient Detection of All Pointer and Array Access Errors. In *ACM Conference on Programming Language Design and Implementation (PLDI)* (pp. 290–301). ACM. 10.1145/178243.178446

Avizienis, A. (1985). The N-version approach to fault-tolerant software. *IEEE Transactions on Software Engineering, SE-11*(12), 1491–1501. doi:10.1109/TSE.1985.231893

Avizienis, A., & Chen, L. (1977). On the Implementation of N-Version programming for software fault tolerance during execution. *Ieee Compsac, 77*, 149–155.

Avižienis, A., Laprie, J. C., Randell, B., & Landwehr, C. (2004). Basic concepts and taxonomy of dependable and secure computing. *IEEE Transactions on Dependable and Secure Computing, 1*(1), 11–33. doi:10.1109/TDSC.2004.2

Ayari, N., Barbaron, D., Lefevre, L., & Primet, P. (2008). Fault tolerance for highly available internet services: Concepts, approaches, and issues. *IEEE Communications Surveys and Tutorials, 10*(2), 34–46. doi:10.1109/COMST.2008.4564478

Aydeger, A. K. A. (2015). Sdn-based resilience for smart grid communication. *Network Function Virtualization and Software Defined Network (NFV-SDN), 2015 IEEE Conference on*, 31-33.

Aydeger, A., Akkaya, K., & Uluagac, A. S. (2015). Sdn-based resilience for smart grid communication. *Network Function Virtualization and Software Defined Network (NFV-SDN), 2015 IEEE Conference on*, 31-33.

Bagheri, B., Yang, S., Kao, H. A., & Lee, J. (2015). Cyber-physical systems architecture for self-aware machines in industry 4.0 environment. *IFAC-PapersOnLine, 48*(3), 1622–1627. doi:10.1016/j.ifacol.2015.06.318

Baker, M. (2003). *Fluid Contaminant Sensor.* US patent: US 6,549,856 B2.

Bakken, D. (2002). Paradigms for Distributed Fault Tolerance. *Verssimo & Rodrigues Book*, 1–57.

Balasch, J., Munts, V., & Nin, J. (2014). Using genetic algorithms for attribute grouping in multivariate microaggregation. *Intelligent Data Analysis, 18*(5), 819–836.

Baronti, P., Pillai, P., Chook, V. W., Chessa, S., Gotta, A., & Hu, Y. F. (2007). Wireless sensor networks: A survey on the state of the art and the 802.15.4 and ZigBee standards. *Computer Communications, 30*(7), 1655–1695. doi:10.1016/j.comcom.2006.12.020

Başar, T., & Olsder, G. J. (1999). *Dynamic noncooperative game theory.* Society for Industrial and Applied Mathematics, Classics in Applied Mathematics.

Bass, L., Clements, P., & Kazman, R. (2012). *Software Architecture in Practice.* Pearson Education India. doi:10.1024/0301-1526.32.1.54

Basu, A. K., Panigrahi, T. K., Chowdhury, S., Chowdhury, S. P., Chakraborty, N., Sinha, A., & Song, Y. H. (2007). Key energy management issues of setting market clearing price (MCP) in micro-grid scenario. In *2007 42nd International Universities Power Engineering Conference* (pp. 854–860). Academic Press.

Bayrak, A. G., Velickovic, N., Ienne, P., & Burleson, W. (2012). An Architecture-independent Instruction Shuffler to Protect Against Side-channel Attacks. *ACM Trans. Archit. Code Optim., 8*(4), 20:1–20:19.

Bazara, M., & Shetty, C. (1979). *Nonlinear Programming: Theory and Algorithms*. New York: Wiley.

Berman, B., & Edward, R. (1975). *Geothermal Energy*. Park Ridge: Noyes Data Corporation.

Bhandari, G. P., & Gupta, R. (2017). Fault Repairing Strategy Selector for Service-Oriented Architecture. *I.J. Modern Education and Computer Science Modern Education and Computer Science, 6*(6), 32–39. doi:10.5815/ijmecs.2017.06.05

Bhandari, G. P., & Gupta, R. (2018). Extended Fault Taxonomy of SOA-Based Systems. *CIT. Journal of Computing and Information Technology, 25*(4), 237–257. doi:10.20532/cit.2017.1003569

Biffl, S., Aurum, A., Boehm, B., Erdoginus, H., & Grunbacher, P. (Eds.). (2006). Value-Based Software Engineering. Springer-Verlag. doi:10.1007/3-540-29263-2

Bonin-Font, F., Ortiz, A., & Oliver, G. (2008). Visual Navigation for Mobile Robots: A Survey. *Journal of Intelligent & Robotic Systems, 53*(3), 263–296. doi:10.100710846-008-9235-4

Bradley, J. M., & Atkins, E. M. (2015). Optimization and Control of Cyber-Physical Vehicle Systems. *Sensors (Basel), 15*(12), 23020–23049. doi:10.3390150923020 PMID:26378541

Bredereck, R., Nichterlein, A., Niederm, R., & Philip, G. (2011). The effect of homogeneity on the complexity of kanonymity. *18th international conference on Fundamentals of computation theory* (pp. 53-64). Berlin: Springer-Verlag.

Breivold, H. P., & Sandstrom, K. (2015). Internet of Things for Industrial Automation-Challenges and Technical Solutions. *Proceedings - 2015 IEEE International Conference on Data Science and Data Intensive Systems; 8th IEEE International Conference Cyber, Physical and Social Computing; 11th IEEE International Conference on Green Computing and Communications and 8th IEEE Inte*. 10.1109/DSDIS.2015.11

Bretas, A. S., Bretas, N. G., Carvalho, B., Baeyens, E., & Khargonekar, P. P. (2017). Smart grids cyber-physical security as a malicious data attack: An innovation approach. *Electric Power Systems Research, 149*(August), 210–219. doi:10.1016/j.epsr.2017.04.018

Brooks, R. A. (1991). Intelligence without representation. *Artificial Intelligence, 47*(1–3), 139–159. doi:10.1016/0004-3702(91)90053-M

Bunce, R., & Dovali-Solis, F. (2011). *Method and Apparatus for Monitoring Particles in a Gas Turbine Working Fluid*. US Patent US871,237,B2.

Cahn, A., Hoyos, J., Hulse, M., & Keller, E. (2013). Software-defined energy communication networks: From substation automation to future smart grids. IEEE SmartGridComm, 558–563.

Caliebe, P., Lauer, C., & German, R. (2011). Flexible integration testing of automotive ECUs by combining AUTOSAR and XCP. In *ICCAIE 2011 - 2011 IEEE Conference on Computer Applications and Industrial Electronics* (pp. 67–72). IEEE. 10.1109/ICCAIE.2011.6162106

Capers Jones. (2012). Software Quality in 2012: a Survey of the State of the Art. *White Paper, Software Productivity Research*, 1–25. Retrieved from http://sqgne.org/presentations/2012-13/Jones-Sep-2012.pdf

Carl, G., Kesidis, G., Brooks, R. R., & Suresh Rai. (2006). Denial-of-service attack-detection techniques. *IEEE Internet Computing*, *10*(1), 82–89. doi:10.1109/MIC.2006.5

Cataliotti, A., Cosentino, V., Di Cara, D., Russotto, P., & Tine, G. (2012). On the use of narrow band power line as communication technology for medium and low voltage smart grids. In *2012 IEEE International Instrumentation and Measurement Technology Conference Proceedings* (pp. 619–623). IEEE. 10.1109/I2MTC.2012.6229503

Cesena, E., Ramunno, G., & Vernizzi, D. (2008). Secure storage using a sealing proxy. In *Proceedings of the 1st European workshop on system security - EUROSEC '08* (p. 27). New York: ACM Press. 10.1145/1355284.1355290

Checkoway, S., McCoy, D., Kantor, B., Anderson, D., Shacham, H., & Savage, S., ... others. (2011). Comprehensive Experimental Analyses of Automotive Attack Surfaces. In *USENIX Security Symposium*. San Francisco: USENIX.

Chettri, S. K., Paul, B., & Dutta, A. K. (2013). Statistical Disclosure Control for Data Privacy Preservation. *International Journal of Computers and Applications*, *80*(10).

Chiaradonna, S., Bondavalli, A., & Strigini, L. (1994). On Performability Modeling and Evaluation of Software Fault Tolerant Structures. *Proceedings of the First European Dependable Computing Conference on Dependable Computing*, 97–114. Retrieved from http://0-dl.acm.org.wam.city.ac.uk/citation.cfm?id=645330.650098

Choi, H., Wang, J., & Hughes, E. A. (2009). Scheduling for information gathering on sensor network. *Wireless Networks*, *15*(1), 127–140. doi:10.100711276-007-0050-9

Choi, W., & Das, S. K. (2009). CROSS: A probabilistic constrained random sensor selection scheme in wireless sensor networks. *Performance Evaluation*, *66*(12), 754–772. doi:10.1016/j.peva.2009.08.004

Chun, W., Lee, T. H., & Choi, T. (2011) *Yanail: yet another definition on names, addresses, identifiers, and locators*. Presented at the *6th International Conference on Future Internet Technologies*, Seoul, South Korea. 10.1145/2002396.2002399

Cohen, M., & Jaffray, J. Y. (1988). Certainty Effects versus Probability Distortion: An Experimental Analysis of Decision Making Under Risk. *Journal of Experimental Psychology. Human Perception and Performance, 14*(4), 554–560. doi:10.1037/0096-1523.14.4.554

Collopy, P., & Hollingsworth, P. (2009). *Value-driven design. AIAA Paper 2009-7099*. Reston, VA: American Institute of Aeronautics and Astronautics.

Constandache, I., Bao, X., Azizyan, M., & Choudhury, R. R. (2010). Did you see Bob?: Human localization using mobile phones. *MobiCom, 2010*, 149–160.

Cormen, T. H., Stein, C., Rivest, R. L., & Leiserson, C. E. (2001). *Introduction to Algorithms* (2nd ed.). McGraw-Hill Higher Education.

Cristescu, R., Beferull-Lozano, B., Vetterli, M., & Wattenhofer, R. (2010). Network correlated data gathering with explicit communication: NP-completeness and algorithms. *IEEE/ACM Transactions on Networking, 14*(1), 41–54. doi:10.1109/TNET.2005.863711

Cuomo, F., Cipollone, E., & Abbagnale, A. (2009). Performance analysis of IEEE 802.15.4 wireless sensor networks: An insight into the topology formation process. *Computer Networks, 53*(18), 3057–3075. doi:10.1016/j.comnet.2009.07.016

Dang, T., & Ringland, K. (2012). Optimal load scheduling for residential renewable energy integration. In *2012 IEEE Third International Conference on Smart Grid Communications (SmartGridComm)* (pp. 516–521). IEEE. 10.1109/SmartGridComm.2012.6486037

Dargie, W., & Poellabauer, C. (2010). *Fundamentals of Wireless Sensor Networks: Theory and Practice* (Vol. 191). New York: John Wiley & Sons, Ltd. doi:10.1002/9780470666388

Das, S. K., Datta, A. K., Potop-Butucaru, M. G., Patel, R., & Yamazaki, A. (2009). Self-stabilizing minimum connected covers of query regions in sensor networks. *Wireless Communications and Mobile Computing*.

Day, J. (2007). *Patterns in network architecture: A return to fundamentals* (1st ed.). Prentice Hall.

de Oliveira, B. T., Gabriel, L. B., & Margi, C. B. (2015). TinySDN: Enabling multiple controllers for software-defined wireless sensor networks. *IEEE Latin America Transactions, 13*(11), 3690–3696. doi:10.1109/TLA.2015.7387950

Dhurjati, D., Kowshik, S., Adve, V., & Lattner, C. (2003). Memory Safety Without Runtime Checks or Garbage Collection. In *ACM Conference on Language, Compiler, and Tool for Embedded Systems* (pp. 69–80). ACM. 10.1145/780732.780743

Domingo-Ferrer, J. (2005). Microaggregation for protecting individual data. *Proceso de Toma de Decisiones, Modelado y Agregaci´on de*, 171–178.

Domingo-Ferrer, J. (2008, March). A critique of k-anonymity and some of its enhancements. In *Availability, Reliability and Security, 2008. ARES 08. Third International Conference on* (pp. 990-993). IEEE.

Domingo-Ferrer, J. a. (2001). A quantitative comparison of disclosure control methods for microdata. *Confidentiality, disclosure and data access: theory and practical applications for statistical agencies*, 111-134.

Domingo-Ferrer, J., Solanas, A., & Martinez-Balleste, A. (2006). Privacy in statistical databases: k-anonymity through microaggregation. *GrC*, 774-777.

Domingo-Ferrer, V. T. (2003). Record linkage methods for multidatabase data mining. Information Fusion in Data Mining, 101-132.

Domingo-Ferrer, J., Mart'ınez-Ballest'e, A., Mateo-Sanz, J., & Seb'e, F. (2006). Efficient multivariate data-oriented microaggregation. *The VLDB Journal, 15*(4), 355–369. doi:10.100700778-006-0007-0

Domingo-Ferrer, J., & Mateo-Sanz, J. M. (2002). Practical data-oriented microaggregation for statistical disclosure control. *IEEE Transactions on Knowledge and Data Engineering, 14*(1), 189–201. doi:10.1109/69.979982

Domingo-Ferrer, J., Sánchez, D., & Rufian-Torrell, G. (2013). Anonymization of nominal data based on semantic marginality. *Information Sciences, 242*, 35–48. doi:10.1016/j.ins.2013.04.021

Domingo-Ferrer, J., & Torra, V. (2005). Ordinal, continuous and heterogeneous k-anonymity through microaggregation. *Data Mining and Knowledge Discovery, 11*(2), 195–212. doi:10.100710618-005-0007-5

Dong, X., Lin, H., Tan, R., Iyer, R. K., & Kalbarczyk, Z. Software- defined networking for smart grid resilience: Opportunities and challenges. *1st ACM Workshop on CPSS 2015.*

Dorsch, N., Kurtz, F., Georg, H., Hagerling, C., & Wietfeld, C. (2014). Software- defined networking for smart grid communications: Applications, challenges and advantages. *IEEE SmartGridComm, 2014.*

Doudalis, I., Clause, J., Venkataramani, G., Prvulovic, M., & Orso, A. (2012). Effective and Efficient Memory Protection Using Dynamic Tainting. *Computers. IEEE Transactions on, 61*(1), 87–100.

Douglass, B. P. (2002). *Real-Time Design Patterns: Robust Scalable Architecture for Real-Time Systems* (Vol. 1). Addison-Wesley Professional.

Douglass, B. P. (2010). Design Patterns for Embedded Systems in C. *Embedded, 384*. doi:10.1016/B978-1-85617-707-8.00006-6

Dunn, W. R. (2003). Designing safety-critical computer systems. *Computer, 36*(11), 40–46. doi:10.1109/MC.2003.1244533

Efthymiou, C., & Kalogridis, G. (2010). Smart Grid Privacy via Anonymization of Smart Metering Data. In *2010 First IEEE International Conference on Smart Grid Communications* (pp. 238–243). IEEE. 10.1109/SMARTGRID.2010.5622050

Ekeland, I. (1979). *Elements d'économie mathématique*. Hermann. (in Russian)

Elson, J., & Estrin, D. (2004). Sensor Networks: A bridge to the Physical World. *Wireless Sensor Network*, 3–20.

Endres, F., Hess, J., & Engelhard, N. (2012). An evaluation of the RGB-D SLAM system. *Icra*, *3*(c), 1691–1696. doi:10.1109/ICRA.2012.6225199

Energy Agency, I. (n.d.). *International Energy Agency: Executive Summary, An energy system under stress*. Author.

Engell, S. (2014). *Cyber-physical Systems of Systems Definition and core research and innovation areas Systems of Systems*. TU Dortmund.

Esmalifalak, M., Nguyen, H., Zheng, R., & Han, Z. (2011). Stealth false data injection using independent component analysis in smart grid. In *2011 IEEE International Conference on Smart Grid Communications (SmartGridComm)* (pp. 244–248). IEEE. 10.1109/SmartGridComm.2011.6102326

Falkenauer, E. (1998). *Genetic Algorithms and Grouping Problems*. New York: John Wiley & Sons, Inc.

Fang, X., Misra, S., Xue, G., & Yang, D. (2012). Smart Grid – The New and Improved Power Grid. *IEEE Communications Surveys and Tutorials*, *14*(4), 944–980. doi:10.1109/SURV.2011.101911.00087

Fan, K. W., Liu, S., & Sinha, P. (2007). Structure-free data aggregation in sensor networks. *IEEE Transactions on Mobile Computing*, *6*(8), 929–942. doi:10.1109/TMC.2007.1011

Fan, Z., Kulkarni, P., Gormus, S., Efthymiou, C., Kalogridis, G., Sooriyabandara, M., & Chin, W. H. (2013). Smart Grid Communications: Overview of Research Challenges, Solutions, and Standardization Activities. *IEEE Communications Surveys and Tutorials*, *15*(1), 21–38. doi:10.1109/SURV.2011.122211.00021

Farmad, H. S., & Biglar, S. (2012). Integration of demand side management, distributed generation, renewable energy sources and energy storages. In *Integration of Renewables into the Distribution Grid, CIRED 2012 Workshop* (pp. 1–4). Academic Press. 10.1049/cp.2012.0784

Fasolo, E., Rossi, M., Widmer, J., & Zorzi, M. (2007). In-network aggregation techniques for wireless sensor networks: A survey. *IEEE Wireless Communications*, *14*(2), 70–87. doi:10.1109/MWC.2007.358967

Fishburn, P. (1970). *Utility theory for decision-making*. New York: Wiley. doi:10.21236/AD0708563

Fishburn, P. (1978). Utility Theory. In J. Moder & S. Elmaghraby (Eds.), *Handbook of Operations Research: Foundations and Fundamentals*. New York: Van Nostrand Reinhold Company.

Fong, T., Nourbakhsh, I., & Dautenhahn, K. (2003). A survey of socially interactive robots. In Robotics and Autonomous Systems (Vol. 42, pp. 143–166). Academic Press. doi:10.1016/S0921-8890(02)00372-X

Franzoni, V., & Gervasi, O. (2009). Guidelines for web usability and accessibility on the Nintendo Wii. Lecture Notes in Computer Science, 5730. doi:10.1007/978-3-642-10649-1_2

Franzoni, V., Gervasi, O., Tasso, S., & Pallottelli, S. (2008). Web usability on the Nintendo Wii platform. Lecture Notes in Computer Science, 5073. doi:10.1007/978-3-540-69848-7_10

Frey, S., Rashid, A., Zanutto, A., Busby, J., & Follis, K. (2016). On the role of latent design conditions in cyber-physical systems security. In *Software Engineering for Smart Cyber-Physical Systems (SEsCPS), 2016 IEEE/ACM 2nd International Workshop on* (pp. 43-46). IEEE.

Fudenberg, D., & Levine, D. K. (1998). *The theory of learning in games*. MIT Press.

Fukutomi, S., Takagi, T., Tani, J., Hashimoto, M., Shimone, J., & Harada, Y. (1997). Numerical Evaluation of ECT Impedance Signal due to Minute Cracks. IEE Transactions on Magnetic, 33(2).

Funabashi, T., Tanabe, T., Nagata, T., & Yokoyama, R. (2008). An autonomous agent for reliable operation of power market and systems including microgrids. In *2008 Third International Conference on Electric Utility Deregulation and Restructuring and Power Technologies* (pp. 173–177). Academic Press. 10.1109/DRPT.2008.4523397

Galli, S., Scaglione, A., & Wang, Z. (2010). Power Line Communications and the Smart Grid. In *2010 First IEEE International Conference on Smart Grid Communications* (pp. 303–308). IEEE. 10.1109/SMARTGRID.2010.5622060

Ganesan, D., Greenstein, B., Estrin, D., Heidemann, J., & Govindan, R. (2005). Multiresolution storage and search in sensor networks. *ACM Transactions on Storage, 1*(3), 277–315. doi:10.1145/1084779.1084780

Gao, Z., Thomas, G., & Ronald, G. (2009). A Complex Space Vector Approach to Rotor Temperature Estimation for Line-Connected Induction Machines with Impaired Cooling. IEEE Transactions on Industrial Electronics, 56(1), 239-247.

Gellings, C. W., & Chamberlin, J. H. (1987). *Demand-Side Management: Concepts and Methods*. Academic Press.

Ghodsi, A., Koponen, T., Rajahalme, J., Sarolahti, P., & Shenker, S. (2011). Naming in content-oriented architectures. Presented at *ACM SIGCOMM Workshop on Information-centric Networking, ICN '11*, Toronto, Canada. 10.1145/2018584.2018586

Ghosh, U., & Datta, R. (2015). A secure addressing scheme for large-scale managed manets. *IEEE eTransactions on Network and Service Management, 12*(3), 483–495. doi:10.1109/TNSM.2015.2452292

Ghosh, U., Dong, X., Tan, R., Kalbarczyk, Z., Yau, D. K., & Iyer, R. K. (2016). A simulation study on smart grid resilience under software- defined networking controller failures. *Proceedings of the 2nd ACM International Workshop on Cyber-Physical System Security, CPSS 2016*, 52-58. 10.1145/2899015.2899020

Goodney, A., Kumar, S., Ravi, A., & Cho, Y. H. (2013). Efficient pmu networking with software defined networks. *IEEE SmartGridComm, 2013*.

Goodney, S. K. (2013). Efficient pmu networking with software defined networks. *IEEE SmartGrid-Comm, 2013.*

Goudarzi, H., Hatami, S., & Pedram, M. (2011). Demand-side load scheduling incentivized by dynamic energy prices. In *2011 IEEE International Conference on Smart Grid Communications (SmartGridComm)* (pp. 351–356). IEEE. 10.1109/SmartGridComm.2011.6102346

Grimmelius, H., Meiler, P. P., Maas, H., Bonnier, B., Grevink, J. S., & Van Kuilenburg, R. F. (1999). Three State-of-the-Art Methods for Condition Monitoring. IEEE Transaction on Industrial Electronics, 46(2), 407-416.

Gungor, V. C., & Lambert, F. C. (2006). A survey on communication networks for electric system automation. *Computer Networks*, *50*(7), 877–897. doi:10.1016/j.comnet.2006.01.005

Guo, J., Chen, I. R., Tsai, J. J. P., & Al-Hamadi, H. (2017). A hierarchical cloud architecture for integrated mobility, service, and trust management of service-oriented IoT systems. In *2016 6th International Conference on Innovative Computing Technology, INTECH 2016* (pp. 72–77). Academic Press. 10.1109/INTECH.2016.7845021

Gyllstrom, D. N. B. (2014). Recovery from link failures in a smart grid communication network using openflow. IEEE SmartGridComm, 254–259.

Gyllstrom, D., Braga, N., & Kurose, J. (2014). Recovery from link failures in a smart grid communication network using openflow. IEEE SmartGridComm, 254–259.

Hahn, G. J., & Kuhn, H. (2012). Designing Decision Support Systems for Value-Based Management: A Survey and an Architecture. *Decision Support Systems-DSS*, *53*(3), 591–598. doi:10.1016/j.dss.2012.02.016

Han, D., Anand, A., Dogar, F., Li, B., Lim, H., Machado, M., ... Steenkiste, P. (2012). Xia: Efficient support for evolvable internetworking. Presented at *9th USENIX Conference on Networked Systems Design and Implementation, NSDI'12*, San Jose, CA.

Han, L., Potter, S., Beckett, G., Pringle, G., Welch, S., Koo, S.-H., ... Tate, A. (2010). FireGrid: An e-infrastructure for next-generation emergency response support. *Journal of Parallel and Distributed Computing*, *70*(11), 1128–1141. doi:10.1016/j.jpdc.2010.06.005

Hao, J., Piechocki, R. J., Kaleshi, D., Chin, W. H., & Fan, Z. (2015). Sparse Malicious False Data Injection Attacks and Defense Mechanisms in Smart Grids. *IEEE Transactions on Industrial Informatics*, *11*(5), 1–12. doi:10.1109/TII.2015.2475695

Hargrave, B. J., & Kriens, P. (2007). *OSGi Best Practices! IBM Lotus OSGi Best Practices*. London: Event.

Hasabnis, N., Misra, A., & Sekar, R. (2012). Light-weight Bounds Checking. In *International Symposium on Code Generation and Optimization* (pp. 135–144). Academic Press.

Hastings, R., & Joyce, B. (1991). Purify: Fast detection of memory leaks and access errors. *Proc. of USENIX Conference.*

He, H., & Yan, J. (2016). Cyber-Physical Attacks and Defenses in the Smart Grid: A Survey. *IET Cyber-Physical Systems: Theory & Applications, 1*, 13–27.

Heine, D. L., & Lam, M. S. (2003). A Practical Flow-sensitive and Context-sensitive C and C++ Memory Leak Detector. *SIGPLAN Notices, 38*(5), 168–181. doi:10.1145/780822.781150

Heinzelman, W. B., Chandrakasan, A. P., & Balakrishnan, H. (2002). An application-specific protocol architecture for wireless microsensor networks. *IEEE Wireless Communications, 1*(4), 660–670. doi:10.1109/TWC.2002.804190

Heinzelman, W. R., Chandrakasan, A. P., & Balakrishnan, H. (2000). *Energy-efficient communication protocol for wireless microsensor networks.* Hawaii Intl Conf. on System Sciences. doi:10.1109/HICSS.2000.926982

Herrmann, D. (1999). *Software Safety and Reliability.* Institute of Electrical & Electronics Engineers.

Hiller, M. (1998). *Software Fault-Tolerance Techniques from a Real-Time Systems Point of View.* Technical Report No.98-16, Department of Computer Engineering, Chalmers University of Technology.

Horvath, I., & Gerritsen, B. H. (2012). Cyber-physical systems: Concepts, technologies and implementation principles. In Proceedings of tmce (Vol. 1, pp. 7–11). Academic Press.

Huang, C. F., & Tseng, Y. C. (2005). The coverage problem in a wireless sensor network. *Mobile Networks and Applications, 10*(4), 519–528. doi:10.100711036-005-1564-y

Huang, C. F., Tseng, Y. C., & Wu, H. L. (2007). Distributed protocols for ensuring both coverage and connectivity of a wireless sensor network. *ACM Transactions on Sensor Networks, 3*(1), 5, es. doi:10.1145/1210669.1210674

Hu, F. (2013). *Cyber-physical systems: Integrated computing and engineering design.* CRC Press. doi:10.1201/b15552

Huffmire, T., Brotherton, B., Sherwood, T., Kastner, R., Levin, T., Nguyen, T. D., & Irvine, C. (2008). Managing Security in FPGA-Based Embedded Systems. *Design Test of Computers, IEEE, 25*(6), 590–598. doi:10.1109/MDT.2008.166

IEC. (2005). IEC 61508:2005 Functional safety of electrical-electronic-programmable electronic safety related systems. *IEC 61508.*

IEEE 802.15.4-2006. (2006). *Wireless MAC and PHY Specifications for Low Rate Wireless Personal Area Networks (WPANs).* IEEE Computer Society.

IEEE SA - 2030-2011 - IEEE Guide for Smart Grid Interoperability of Energy Technology and Information Technology Operation with the Electric Power System (EPS), End-Use Applications, and Loads. (n.d.).

IEEE Standard 802.15.4d. (2009). *Low-power Wireless Network technology.* IEEE Computer Society.

IEEE standard for IT. (2006). *Telecommunication and information exchange between systems; local and metropolitan area networks specific requirements part 15.4: wireless MAC and PHY layer specifications for low-rate wireless personal area networks (LR-WPANs) (rev. of IEEE Std 802.15.4-2003), 2006.* IEEE.

IETF Datatracker. (2017). Retrieved September 12, 2017, from https://datatracker.ietf.org/

Intanagonwiwat, C., Govindan, R., & Estrin, D. (2000). Directed diffusion: A scalable and robust communication paradigm for sensor networks. *MobiCom, 2000,* 56–67. doi:10.1145/345910.345920

Jackson, D. (2009). A direct path to dependable software. *Communications of the ACM, 52*(4), 78. doi:10.1145/1498765.1498787

Jackson, D., Thomas, M., & Millett, L. (2007). *Software for Dependable Systems.* National Academies Press; doi:10.17226/11923

Jamison, J. (2012). Games with Synergistic Preferences. *Games, 3*(1), 41–55. doi:10.3390/g3010041

Jaro, M. A. (1989). Advances in record-linkage methodology as applied to matching the 1985 census of Tampa, Florida. *Journal of the American Statistical Association, 84*(406), 414–420. doi:10.1080/01621459.1989.10478785

Jaskolka, J., & Villasenor, J. (2017). *Identifying implicit component interactions in distributed cyber-physical systems.* Academic Press.

Javaid, N., Javaid, S., Abdul, W., Ahmed, I., Almogren, A., Alamri, A., & Niaz, I. (2017). A Hybrid Genetic Wind Driven Heuristic Optimization Algorithm for Demand Side Management in Smart Grid. *Energies, 10*(3), 319–363. doi:10.3390/en10030319

Jean, B. (2008). A Microwave sensor for steam quality. *IEEE Transactions on Instrumentation and Measurement, 57*(4), 751–754. doi:10.1109/TIM.2007.913821

Jennic JN5121. (2010). Retrieved from http://www.jennic.com/

Jeon, S. Y., Ahn, J. H., & Lee, T. J. (2016). Data distribution in IoT networks with estimation of packet error rate. In *International Conference on Next Generation Mobile Applications, Services, and Technologies* (pp. 94–98). Academic Press. 10.1109/NGMAST.2016.25

Joe, S., & Kuo, F. (2008). Constructing Sobol' sequences with better two-dimensional projections. *SIAM Journal on Scientific Computing, 30*(5), 2635–2654. doi:10.1137/070709359

Kabalci, Y. (2016). A survey on smart metering and smart grid communication. *Renewable & Sustainable Energy Reviews, 57*(May), 302–318. doi:10.1016/j.rser.2015.12.114

Kabashkin, I., & Kundler, J. (2017). *Reliability of Sensor Nodes in Wireless Sensor Networks of Cyber Physical Systems.* Academic Press. 10.1016/j.procs.2017.01.149

Kabir, M. E., & Wang, H. (2011). Microdata protection method through microaggregation: A median-based approach. *Inf. Sec. J.: A Global Perspective, 20*(1), 1-8.

Kahneman, D., & Tversky, A. (1979). Prospect theory: An analysis of decision under risk. *Econometrica, 47*(2), 263–291. doi:10.2307/1914185

Kalogridis, G., Efthymiou, C., Denic, S. Z., Lewis, T. a., & Cepeda, R. (2010). Privacy for Smart Meters: Towards Undetectable Appliance Load Signatures. *Smart Grid Communications (SmartGridComm), 2010 First IEEE International Conference on*, 232–237.

Kao, H.-A., Jin, W., Siegel, D., & Lee, J. (2015). A cyber physical interface for automation systems—methodology and examples. *Machines, 3*(2), 93–106. doi:10.3390/machines3020093

Karnouskos, S. (2011). Cyber-physical systems in the SmartGrid. *IEEE International Conference on Industrial Informatics (INDIN)*, 20–23.

Keeney, R. L. (1988). Value-driven Expert Systems for Decision Support. *Decision Support Systems, 4*(4), 405–412. doi:10.1016/0167-9236(88)90003-6

Keeney, R. L., & Raiffa, H. (1999). *Decision with multiple objectives: Preferences and value trade-offs.* Cambridge, UK: Cambridge University Press.

Khalifa, T., Naik, K., & Nayak, A. (2011). A Survey of Communication Protocols for Automatic Meter Reading Applications. *IEEE Communications Surveys and Tutorials, 13*(2), 168–182. doi:10.1109/SURV.2011.041110.00058

Khan, M. T., Serpanos, D., & Shrobe, H. (2017). A rigorous and efficient run-time security monitor for real-time critical embedded system applications. In *2016 IEEE 3rd World Forum on Internet of Things, WF-IoT 2016* (pp. 100–105). IEEE. 10.1109/WF-IoT.2016.7845510

Khan, H. N., Iftikhar, H., Asif, S., Javaid, N., Maroof, R., & Ambreen, K. (2017). Demand Side Management using Strawberry Algorithm and Bacterial Foraging Optimization Algorithm in Smart Grid. In L. Barolli, T. Enokido, & M. Takizawa (Eds.), *Advances in Network-Based Information Systems. NBiS 2017. Lecture Notes on Data Engineering and Communications Technologies* (Vol. 7, pp. 191–202). Cham: Springer.

Khan, R. H., & Khan, J. Y. (2013). A comprehensive review of the application characteristics and traffic requirements of a smart grid communications network. *Computer Networks, 57*(3), 825–845. doi:10.1016/j.comnet.2012.11.002

Kim, H.-M., & Kinoshita, T. (2009). Multiagent system for Microgrid operation based on power market environment. In *INTELEC 2009 - 31st International Telecommunications Energy Conference* (pp. 1–5). Academic Press. 10.1109/INTLEC.2009.5351771

Kim, Y.-J., He, K., Thottan, M., & Deshpande, J. G. (2014). Virtualized and self-configurable utility communications enabled by software-defined networks. IEEE SmartGridComm, 416–421.

Kim, T. T., & Poor, H. V. (2011). Strategic Protection Against Data Injection Attacks on Power Grids. *IEEE Transactions on Smart Grid, 2*(2), 326–333. doi:10.1109/TSG.2011.2119336

Knight, J. C., & Leveson, N. G. (1986). An Experimental Evaluation of the Assumption of Independence in Multiversion Programming. *IEEE Transactions on Software Engineering, SE, 12*(1), 96–109. doi:10.1109/TSE.1986.6312924

Koçak, D. (2014). Thinking Embedded, Designing Cyber-Physical: Is it Possible? In *Applied Cyber-Physical Systems* (pp. 241–253). New York, NY: Springer. doi:10.1007/978-1-4614-7336-7_18

Kocher, P., Jaffe, J., & Jun, B. (1999). Differential power analysis. In Advances in Cryptology—CRYP-TO'99 (pp. 388–397). Springer. doi:10.1007/3-540-48405-1_25

Konemann, J., Levin, A., & Sinha, A. (2004). A. Sinha, Approximating the degree-bounded minimum diameter spanning tree problem. *Algorithmica, 41*(2), 117–129. doi:10.100700453-004-1121-2

Kosut, O., Jia, L., Thomas, R. J., & Tong, L. (2011). Malicious Data Attacks on the Smart Grid. *IEEE Transactions on Smart Grid, 2*(4), 645–658. doi:10.1109/TSG.2011.2163807

Kothare, M., Metler, B., Morari, M., Bendotti, P., & Falinower, C. (2000). Level Control in the Steam Generator of a Nuclear Plant. *IEEE Transactions on Control Systems Technology, 8*(1), 55–69. doi:10.1109/87.817692

Krantz, D. H., Luce, R. D., Suppes, P., & Tversky, A. (Eds.). (1990). Foundations of Measurement (Vols. 1-3). New York: Academic Press.

Krishna, K., & Murty, M. N. (1999). Genetic k-means algorithm. *Trans. Sys. Man Cyber. Part B, 29*(3), 433–439. doi:10.1109/3477.764879 PMID:18252317

Krylov, N. V. (1980). *Controlled Diffusion Processes*. New York: Springer-Verlag. doi:10.1007/978-1-4612-6051-6

Kühn, U., & Stüble, C. (2009). User-Friendly and Secure TPM-based Hard Disk Key Management. In Future of Trust in Computing (pp. 171–177). Wiesbaden: Vieweg+Teubner. doi:10.1007/978-3-8348-9324-6_18

Kühn, U., Selhorst, M., & Stüble, C. (2007). Realizing property-based attestation and sealing with commonly available hard- and software. In *Proceedings of the 2007 ACM workshop on Scalable trusted computing - STC '07* (p. 50). New York: ACM Press. 10.1145/1314354.1314368

Kulasekera, A. L., Gopura, R. A. R. C., Hemapala, K. T. M. U., & Perera, N. (2011). A review on multi-agent systems in microgrid applications. *2011 IEEE PES International Conference on Innovative Smart Grid Technologies-India, ISGT India 2011*, 173–177. 10.1109/ISET-India.2011.6145377

Kuntze, N., Rudolph, C., Cupelli, M., Liu, J., & Monti, A. (2010). Trust infrastructures for future energy networks. In *IEEE PES General Meeting* (pp. 1–7). IEEE. 10.1109/PES.2010.5589609

Kuzlu, M., & Pipattanasomporn, M. (2013). Assessment of communication technologies and network requirements for different smart grid applications. In Innovative Smart Grid Technologies (ISGT), 2013 IEEE PES (pp. 1–6). IEEE. doi:10.1109/ISGT.2013.6497873

Kuzlu, M., Pipattanasomporn, M., & Rahman, S. (2014). Communication network requirements for major smart grid applications in HAN, NAN and WAN. *Computer Networks*, *67*, 74–88. doi:10.1016/j.comnet.2014.03.029

Kwakernaak, H., & Sivan, R. (1972). *Linear optimal control systems*. New York: Wiley.

Laprie, J.-C., Arlat, J., Beounes, C., & Kanoun, K. (1990). Definition and analysis of hardware-and software-fault-tolerant architectures. *Computer*, *23*(7), 39–51. doi:10.1109/2.56851

Larichev, O. & Morgoev V. (1991). Problems, Methods and Systems of Extracting Expert Knowledge. *Automation and Telemechanics*, 6. (in Russian)

Laskowski, S. (2008). Cooperative and Non-cooperative, Integrative and Distributive Market Games with Antagonistic and Altruistic, Malicious and Kind Ways of Playing. *Journal of Telecommunications and Information Technology*, *4*, 88–96.

Lee, E. A. (2008). Cyber Physical Systems: Design Challenges. *ISORC '08 Proceedings of the 2008 11th IEEE Symposium on Object Oriented Real-Time Distributed Computing*, 363-369.

Lee, E. A. (2008, May). Cyber physical systems: Design challenges. In *Object oriented real-time distributed computing (isorc), 2008 11th ieee international symposium on* (pp. 363-369). IEEE.

Lee, J., Jung, D.-K., Kim, Y., Lee, Y.-W., & Kim, Y.-M. (2010). Smart grid solutions, services, and business models focused on telco. IEEE/IFIP Network Operations and Management Symp. Workshops, 323–326.

Lee. (2006). *Cyber-Physical Systems - Are Computing Foundations Adequate?* Position Paper for NSF Workshop On Cyber-Physical Systems: Research Motivation, Techniques and Roadmap, Austin, TX.

Lee, H. C., Banerjee, A., Fang, Y. M., Lee, B. J., & King, C. T. (2010). Design of a multifunctional wireless sensor for in-situ monitoring of debris flows. *IEEE Transactions on Mobile Computing*, *59*(11), 2958–2967.

Lee, J., Ardakani, H. D., Yang, S., & Bagheri, B. (2015). Industrial big data analytics and cyber-physical systems for future maintenance & service innovation. *Procedia CIRP*, *38*, 3–7. doi:10.1016/j.procir.2015.08.026

Lehman, M. M. (1980). Programs, Life Cycles, and Laws of Software Evolution. *Proceedings of the IEEE*, *68*(9), 1060–1076. doi:10.1109/PROC.1980.11805

Li, N. L. (2007, April). t-closeness: Privacy beyond k-anonymity and l-diversity. In *ICDE 2007. IEEE 23rd International Conference on* (pp. 106-115). IEEE.

Liang, G., Zhao, J., Luo, F., Weller, S. R., & Dong, Z. Y. (2017). A Review of False Data Injection Attacks Against Modern Power Systems. *IEEE Transactions on Smart Grid*, *8*(4), 1630–1638. doi:10.1109/TSG.2015.2495133

Lie, D., Thekkath, C., Mitchell, M., Lincoln, P., Boneh, D., Mitchell, J., & Horowitz, M. (2000). Architectural Support for Copy and Tamper Resistant Software. *SIGPLAN Notices*, *35*(11), 168–177. doi:10.1145/356989.357005

Li, F., Qiao, W., Sun, H., Wan, H., Wang, J., Xia, Y., ... Zhang, P. (2010). Smart Transmission Grid: Vision and Framework. *IEEE Transactions on Smart Grid*, *1*(2), 168–177. doi:10.1109/TSG.2010.2053726

Li, H., Mao, R., Lai, L., & Qiu, R. C. (2010). Compressed Meter Reading for Delay-Sensitive and Secure Load Report in Smart Grid. In *2010 First IEEE International Conference on Smart Grid Communications* (pp. 114–119). IEEE. 10.1109/SMARTGRID.2010.5622027

Li, N., Chen, L., & Low, S. H. (2011). *Optimal demand response based on utility maximization in power networks*. IEEE Power and Energy Society General Meeting.

Lin, H., Slagell, A., Kalbarczyk, Z., Sauer, P., & Iyer, R. (2016). Runtime semantic security analysis to detect and mitigate control-related attacks in power grids. *IEEE Transactions on Smart Grid*.

Liu, R.-S. (2016). An Algorithmic Game Approach for Demand Side Management in Smart Grid with Distributed Renewable Power Generation and Storage. *Energies*, *9*(8), 654.

Liu, S., Liu, X. P., & El Saddik, A. (2013). Denial-of-Service (dos) attacks on load frequency control in smart grids. In 2013 IEEE PES Innovative Smart Grid Technologies Conference (ISGT) (pp. 1–6). IEEE.

Liu, Y., Ning, P., & Reiter, M. K. (2009). False data injection attacks against state estimation in electric power grid. *16th ACM Conference on Computer and Communications Security ccs. Mininet: An instant virtual network on your laptop (or other pc)*. Retrieved from http://mininet.org/

Liu, Y., Ning, P., Dai, H., & Liu, A. (2010). Randomized Differential DSSS: Jamming-Resistant Wireless Broadcast Communication. In 2010 Proceedings IEEE INFOCOM (pp. 1–9). IEEE.

Liu, Y., Peng, Y., Wang, B., Yao, S., Liu, Z., & Concept, A. (2017). Review on Cyber-physical Systems. *IEEE/CAA Journal of Automatica Sinica, 4*(1), 27–40.

Liu, L., Esmalifalak, M., Ding, Q., Emesih, V. A., & Han, Z. (2014). Detecting False Data Injection Attacks on Power Grid by Sparse Optimization. *IEEE Transactions on Smart Grid, 5*(2), 612–621. doi:10.1109/TSG.2013.2284438

Liu, Y., Reiter, M. K., & Ning, P. (2009). False data injection attacks against state estimation in electric power grids. In *Proceedings of the 16th ACM conference on Computer and communications security - CCS '09* (pp. 21-32). New York: ACM Press. 10.1145/1653662.1653666

Li, W., & Zhang, X. (2014). Simulation of the smart grid communications: Challenges, techniques, and future trends. *Computers & Electrical Engineering, 40*(1), 270–288. doi:10.1016/j.compeleceng.2013.11.022

Logenthiran, T., Srinivasan, D., & Shun, T. Z. (2011). Multi-Agent System for Demand Side Management in smart grid. *2011 IEEE Ninth International Conference on Power Electronics and Drive Systems*, 424–429. 10.1109/PEDS.2011.6147283

Logenthiran, T., Srinivasan, D., & Shun, T. Z. (2012). Demand Side Management in Smart Grid Using Heuristic Optimization. *Smart Grid. IEEE Transactions on, 3*(3), 1244–1252.

Lopez, M. A., De La Torre, S., Martin, S., & Aguado, J. A. (2015). Demand-side management in smart grid operation considering electric vehicles load shifting and vehicle-to-grid support. *International Journal of Electrical Power and Energy Systems, 64*, 689–698.

Lord, W., & Palanisamy, R. (1980). Detection and Modeling of Agneite Buildup in Steam Generators. *IEEE Transactions on Magnetics, MAG-16*(5).

Lovekin, J., & James, W. (2009). Correlation of Rig Tests and James Tube Tests in the Coso Geothermal Field. *Proceedings, Fifteenth Workshop on Geothermal Reservoir Engineering*.

Lu, Y., Lu, S., Fotouhi, F., Deng, Y., & Brown, S. J. (2004). Fgka: a fast genetic k-means clustering algorithm. In *Proceedings of the 2004 ACM symposium on Applied computing* (pp. 622-623). New York, NY: ACM.

Luce, D., & Raiffa, H. (1957). *Games and decisions: Introduction and critical survey*. New York: Wiley.

Lu, G., Krishnamachari, B., & Raghavendra, C. S. (2004). An adaptive energy-efficient and low-latency MAC for data gathering in wireless sensor networks. *Intl. Parallel and Distributed Processing Symp.*

Lu, Y., & Cecil, J. (2016). An internet of things (IoT)-based collaborative framework for advanced manufacturing. *International Journal of Advanced Manufacturing Technology, 84*(5-8), 1141–1152.

Lynch, J.P. (2007). *An Overview of Wireless Structural Health Monitoring for Civil Structures*. Academic Press.

Lyu, M. R. (1996). Handbook of software reliability engineering. Academic Press.

Machanavajjhala, A. G., Kifer, D., Gehrke, J., & Venkitasubramaniam, M. (2007). l-diversity: Privacy beyond k-anonymity. *ACM Transactions on Knowledge Discovery from Data*, *1*(1), 3, es. doi:10.1145/1217299.1217302

Maharjan, I. (2010). *Demand Side Management: Load Management, Load Profiling, Load Shifting, Residential And Industrial Consumer, Energy Audit, Reliability, Urban, Semi-urban And Rural Setting.* LAP LAMBERT Academic Publishing.

Ma, M., & Yang, Y. (2007). SenCar: An energy-efficient data gathering mechanism for large-scale multihop sensor networks. *IEEE Transactions on Parallel and Distributed Systems*, *18*(10), 1476–1488. doi:10.1109/TPDS.2007.1070

Mangard, S. (2003). A simple power-analysis (SPA) attack on implementations of the AES key expansion. In Information Security and Cryptology—ICISC 2002 (pp. 343–358). Springer.

Mao, S., & Wolf, T. (2010). Hardware Support for Secure Processing in Embedded Systems. *Computers. IEEE Transactions on*, *59*(6), 847–854.

Martínez, S., Sánchez, D., & Valls, A. (2012). Semantic adaptive microaggregation of categorical microdata. *Computers & Security*, *31*(5), 653–672. doi:10.1016/j.cose.2012.04.003

Marufuzzaman, M., & Reaz, M. B. I. (2013). Hardware simulation of pattern matching and reinforcement learning to predict the user next action of smart home device usage. *World Applied Sciences Journal*, *22*(9), 1302–1309.

Maxey, L., & Simpson, M. (1995). *Optical wet steam monitor.* US patent 5,383,024.

McDaniel, P., & McLaughlin, S. (2009). Security and Privacy Challenges in the Smart Grid. *IEEE Security & Privacy Magazine*, *7*(3), 75–77. doi:10.1109/MSP.2009.76

Medrano-E'Vers, A., Morales-Hernández, A. E., Valencia-López, R., & Hernández-Salcedo, D. R. (2017). *Enfermedad granulomatosa crónica* (Vol. 33). Medicina Interna de Mexico. doi:10.100713398-014-0173-7.2

Melodia, T., Pompili, D., & Akyildiz, I. F. (2006). A communication architecture for mobile wireless sensor and actor networks. *Sensor and Ad Hoc Communications and Networks Conf.*, 109–118. 10.1109/SAHCN.2006.288415

Melodia, T., Pompili, D., Gungor, V. C., & Akyildiz, I. F. (2005). *A distributed coordination framework for wireless sensor and actor networks.* Intl Symp. Mobile Ad Hoc Networking and Computing. doi:10.1145/1062689.1062704

Meng, F.-L., & Zeng, X.-J. (2016). A Profit Maximization Approach to Demand Response Management with Customers Behavior Learning in Smart Grid. *IEEE Transactions on Smart Grid, 7*(3), 1516–1529. doi:10.1109/TSG.2015.2462083

Meribout, M., & Al Naamany, A. (2009). A collision free data link layer protocol for wireless sensor networks and its application in intelligent transportation systems. *IEEE Wireless Telecommunications Symposium (WTS'2009)*, 1-6. 10.1109/WTS.2009.5068957

Meribout, M., Galeel, M., Al Marzouqi, M., & Aasi, M. A. (2010). A new concept for an effective leak detection in multiphase fluid pipelines. *2011 First International Conference on sensor device Technologies and Applications (SensorDevices'2010)*, 206-210.

Meribout, M., Nakanishi, M., & Ogura, T. (2002). A Parallel Algorithm for Real-time Object Recognition. Pattern Recognition Journal, 35(9).

Meribout, M. (2011). A wireless sensor network-based infrastructure for real-time and online pipeline section. *IEEE Sensors Journal, 11*(11), 2966–2972. doi:10.1109/JSEN.2011.2155054

Milenković, M., Milenković, A., & Jovanov, E. (2005). Hardware Support for Code Integrity in Embedded Processors. In *Intl. Conf. on Compilers, Architectures and Synthesis for Embedded Systems* (pp. 55–65). Academic Press. 10.1145/1086297.1086306

Miluzzo, E., Lane, N. D., Fodor, K., Peterson, R., Lu, H., Musolesi, M., ... Campbell, A. T. (2008). Sensing meets mobile social networks: the design, implementation and evaluation of the CenceMe application. *Int'l Conf. Embedded Networked Sensor Systems*, 337–350. 10.1145/1460412.1460445

Misra, P. K., Mottola, L., Raza, S., Duquennoy, S., Tsiftes, N., Hoglund, J., & Voigt, T. (2013). Supporting cyber-physical systems with wireless sensor networks: An outlook of software and services. *Journal of the Indian Institute of Science, 93*, 441–462.

Mohsenian-Rad, A.-H., Wong, V. W. S., Jatskevich, J., Schober, R., & Leon-Garcia, A. (2010). Autonomous Demand Side Management Based on Game-Theoretic Energy Consumption Scheduling for the Future Smart Grid. *IEEE Transactions on Smart Grid, 1*(3), 320–331. doi:10.1109/TSG.2010.2089069

Mohsin, M., & Meribout, M. (2015). An extended model for ultrasonic-based enhanced oil recovery with experimental validation. *Ultrasonics Sonochemistry, 23*, 413–423. doi:10.1016/j.ultsonch.2014.08.007 PMID:25219873

Mohsin, M., & Meribout, M. (2015). Oil-water de-emulsificatin using ultrasonic technology. *Ultrasonics Sonochemistry, 22*, 573–579. doi:10.1016/j.ultsonch.2014.05.014 PMID:24935027

Molina, E., Jacob, E., Matias, J., Moreira, N., & Astarloa, A. (2015). Using software defined networking to manage and control iec 61850-based systems. *Computers & Electrical Engineering, 43*, 142–154. doi:10.1016/j.compeleceng.2014.10.016

Mottola, L., & Picco, G.P. (2011). Programming wireless sensor networks: Fundamental concepts and state of the art. *ACM Comput. Survey, 43*.

Muccini, H., & Weyns, D. (2016). *Self-Adaptation for Cyber-Physical Systems: A Systematic Literature Review*. Academic Press. 10.1145/1235

Nagarakatte, S., Zhao, J., Martin, M. M., & Zdancewic, S. (2009). SoftBound: Highly compatible and complete spatial memory safety for c. *ACM SIGPLAN Notices, 44*(6), 245–258. doi:10.1145/1543135.1542504

NASA. (2004). *NASA Software Safety Guidebook. National Aeronautics and Space Administration*. Retrieved from http://www.hq.nasa.gov/office/codeq/doctree/871913.pdf

National Energy Technology Laboratory for the U.S. Department of Energy. (2008). *Advanced Metering Infrastructure. NETL Modern Grid Strategy*. Author.

National Institute of Standards and Technology. (2010). NIST Special Publication 1108 NIST Framework and Roadmap for Smart Grid Interoperability Standards. *NIST Special Publication*, 1–90.

Necula, G. C., Condit, J., Harren, M., McPeak, S., & Weimer, W. (2005). CCured: Type-safe retrofitting of legacy software. *ACM Transactions on Programming Languages and Systems, 27*(3), 477–526. doi:10.1145/1065887.1065892

Nethercote, N., & Seward, J. (2007). Valgrind: A framework for heavyweight dynamic binary instrumentation. *ACM SIGPLAN Notices, 42*(6), 89–100. doi:10.1145/1273442.1250746

Neumann, P., Goldie, S., & Milton, W. (2000). Preference-based Measures in Economic Evaluation in Health Care. *Annual Review of Public Health, 21*(1), 587–611. doi:10.1146/annurev.publhealth.21.1.587 PMID:10884966

Nguyen, H. K., Song, J., Bin, & Han, Z. (2012). Demand side management to reduce Peak-to-Average Ratio using game theory in smart grid. In *2012 Proceedings IEEE INFOCOM Workshops* (pp. 91–96). IEEE.

Nisan, N. (2007). *Tim Roughgarden, ´C Eva Tardos, V. V. V* (1st ed.). Algorithmic Game Theory.

NSF. (2006). *National Science Foundation- Call for Position Papers*. Retrieved August 2, 2017, from http://varma.ece.cmu.edu/CPS/

NVD - CVE-2014-1776. (2014). Retrieved September 12, 2017, from https://nvd.nist.gov/vuln/detail/CVE-2014-1776

Oganian, A., & Domingo-ferrer, J. (2001). On the complexity of optimal microaggregation for statistical disclosure control. *Statistical Journal of the United Nations Economic Commission for Europe, 18*, 345–354.

One, A. (1996). Smashing the stack for fun and profit. *Phrack Magazine, 7*(49), 14–16.

Openflow switch specification. (n.d.). Retrieved from http://www.openflow.org/documents/ openflow-spec-v1.0.0.pdf

Oskoei, M., & Hu, H. H. H. (2008). Support Vector Machine-Based Classification Scheme for Myoelectric Control Applied to Upper Limb. *IEEE Transactions on Biomedical Engineering, 55*(8), 1956–1965. doi:10.1109/TBME.2008.919734 PMID:18632358

Ould-Ahmed-Vall, E., Blough, D. M., Heck, B. S., & Riley, G. F. (2005). Intl Conf. Mobile Ad Hoc and Sensor Systems. Academic Press.

Pandey, V., Nikolaidis, E., & Mourelatos, Z. (2011). Multi-objective decision making under uncertainty and incomplete knowledge of designer preferences. *SAE International Journal of Materials and Manufacturing, 4*(1), 1155–1168. doi:10.4271/2011-01-1080

Pan, M. S., Fang, H. W., Liu, Y. C., & Tseng, Y. C. (2008). Address assignment and routing schemes for ZigBee-based long-thin wireless sensor networks. *Vehicular Tech. Conf.*, 173–177. 10.1109/VETECS.2008.48

Pan, M. S., Tsai, C. H., & Tseng, Y. C. (2009). The orphan problem in ZigBee wireless networks. *IEEE Transactions on Mobile Computing, 8*(11), 1573–1584. doi:10.1109/TMC.2009.60

Parisini, T. (2016). *TC 6.4. Fault Detection*. Supervision & Safety of Technical Processes-SAFEPROCESS.

Pavlov, Y. (2016). Value Based Decision Control for Complex Systems. Encyclopedia: Artificial Intelligence: Concepts, Methodologies, Tools, and Applications, Information Resources Management Association (IRMA-USA), 50, 1253-1268.

Pavlov, Y. P. (2015). Rational Portfolio Investment Based on Consumer's Preferences: Black-Scholes Model and Stochastic Control. *Journal of Communication and Computer*, 262-271.

Pavlov, Y. P., & Andreev, D. R. (2013). Decision Control, Management, and Support in Adaptive and Complex Systems: Quantitative Models. IGI Global. doi:10.4018/978-1-4666-2967-7

Pavlov, Y. P., Terzieva, V., & Kademova-Katzarova, P. (2014). Optimal Financial Allocation Of Starting Small Factory Resources: Preferences Based Approach. In *4ᵗʰ International Conference On Application of Information and Communication Technology and Statistics in Economy and Education (ICAICT-SEE-2014)*. Sofia University Of National And World Economy (UNWE).

Pavlov, Y. P. (2005). Subjective preferences, values and decisions. Stochastic Approximation Approach. *Proceedings of Bulgarian Academy of Sciences, 58*(4), 367–372.

Pavlov, Y. P. (2017). Value Based Decision Control: Preferences Portfolio Allocation, Wiener and Color Noise Cases. *IOSR Journal of Computer Engineering, 19*(1), 53–60.

Pfanzagl, J. (1971). *Theory of Measurement*. Wurzburg: Physical-Verlag. doi:10.1007/978-3-662-41488-0

Piyushsinh, Z. (2014). Application of Monitoring Approaches on Steam Turbine of Thermal Power Plant for Better Performance. *International Journal of Mechanical Engineering and Robotics Research, 3*(2).

Pullum, L. L. (2001). *Software Fault Tolerance - Techniques and Implementation*. Artech House. Retrieved from http://books.google.com/books?hl=en&lr=&id=hqXvxsO5xz8C&oi=fnd&pg=PR11&dq=Software+Fault+Tolerance+Techniques+and+Implementation&ots=Db4NT-35tv&sig=HP7s49bjFlS9YQF3Q5DUSO7p2rQ

Qian, J., Gao, F., Wang, G., Jin, S., & Zhu, H. (2017). Noncoherent Detections for Ambient Backscatter System. *IEEE Transactions on Wireless Communications, 16*(3), 1412–1422. doi:10.1109/TWC.2016.2635654

Rahim, S., Javaid, N., Ahmad, A., Khan, S. A., Khan, Z. A., Alrajeh, N., & Qasim, U. (2016). Exploiting heuristic algorithms to efficiently utilize energy management controllers with renewable energy sources. *Energy and Building, 129*, 452–470. doi:10.1016/j.enbuild.2016.08.008

Rahman, M. A., & Mohsenian-Rad, H. (2012). False data injection attacks with incomplete information against smart power grids. In *2012 IEEE Global Communications Conference (GLOBECOM)* (pp. 3153–3158). IEEE. 10.1109/GLOCOM.2012.6503599

Rahmatian, M., Kooti, H., Harris, I. G., & Bozorgzadeh, E. (2012). Hardware-Assisted Detection of Malicious Software in Embedded Systems. *Embedded Systems Letters, IEEE, 4*(4), 94–97. doi:10.1109/LES.2012.2218630

Raiffa, H. (1968). *Decision Analysis*. New York: Addison-Wesley Reading Mass.

Ramparany, F., Marquez, F. G., Soriano, F., & Elsaleh, T. (2014). *Handling smart environment devices, data and services at the semantic level with the FI-WARE core platform*. Presented at IEEE International Conference on Big Data (Big Data). 10.1109/BigData.2014.7004417

Rao, J. R., & Rohatgi, P. (2001). EMpowering Side-Channel Attacks. *IACR Cryptology ePrint Archive, 2001*, 37.

Ratnasamy, S., Karp, B., Yin, L., Yu, F., Estrin, D., Govindan, R., & Shenker, S. (2002). GHT; a geographic hash-table for data-centric storage. *ACM 2002 Intl Workshop on WSN and their Applications*, 78–87.

Ravi, S., Raghunathan, A., Kocher, P., & Hattangady, S. (2004). Security in embedded systems: Design challenges. *ACM Transactions on Embedded Computing Systems, 3*(3), 461–491. doi:10.1145/1015047.1015049

Rehman, M., & Meribout, M. (2012). Conventional versus Electrical Enhanced Oil Recovery: A Review. *Journal of Petroleum Exploration and Production Technology, 2*(4), 169–179. doi:10.100713202-012-0035-9

Roth, K., & Brodrick, J. (2008). Energy Harvesting for Wireless Sensors. *ASHRAE Journal, 50*(5), 84–90.

Roy, B., & Guo, T. (2012). *Method and system for steam quality monitoring.* US Patent 2012/0123696 A1.

Roy, D. K., & Sharma, L. K. (2010). Genetic k-means clustering algorithm for mixed numeric and categorical data sets. *International Journal of Artificial Intelligence & Applications, 1*(2), 23–28. doi:10.5121/ijaia.2010.1203

Ryu sdn framework. (n.d.). Retrieved from https://osrg.github.io/ryu/

S, S. R., & Ramesh, V. (2015). A Novel Integrated Approach of Energy Consumption Scheduling in Smart Grid Environment With The Penetration of Renewable Energy. *International Journal of Renewable Energy Research, 5*(4), 1196–1205.

Saad, W., Han, Z., Poor, H. V., & Basar, T. (2012). Game-theoretic methods for the smart grid: An overview of microgrid systems, demand-side management, and smart grid communications. *IEEE Signal Processing Magazine, 29*(5), 86–105. doi:10.1109/MSP.2012.2186410

Sajid, A., Abbas, H., & Saleem, K. (2016). Cloud-Assisted IoT-Based SCADA Systems Security: A Review of the State of the Art and Future Challenges. *IEEE Access: Practical Innovations, Open Solutions, 4*, 1375–1384. doi:10.1109/ACCESS.2016.2549047

Samadi, P., Mohsenian-Rad, H., Wong, V. W. S., & Schober, R. (2014). Real-Time Pricing for Demand Response Based on Stochastic Approximation. *IEEE Transactions on Smart Grid, 5*(2), 789–798. doi:10.1109/TSG.2013.2293131

Sarkar, C., Akshay, A. U., Prasad, R. V., Rahim, A., Neisse, R., & Baldini, G. (2015). DIAT: A scalable distributed architecture for IoT. *IEEE Internet of Things Journal, 2*(3), 230–239. doi:10.1109/JIOT.2014.2387155

Schuba, C. L., Krsul, I. V., Kuhn, M. G., Spafford, E. H., Sundaram, A., & Zamboni, D. (n.d.). Analysis of a denial of service attack on TCP. In *Proceedings. 1997 IEEE Symposium on Security and Privacy (Cat. No.97CB36097)* (pp. 208–223). IEEE Comput. Soc. Press. 10.1109/SECPRI.1997.601338

Serebryany, K., Bruening, D., Potapenko, A., & Vyukov, D. (2012). AddressSanitizer: A fast address sanity checker. In USENIX ATC (Vol. 2012). USENIX.

Shacham, H. (2007). The geometry of innocent flesh on the bone: Return-into-libc without function calls (on the x86). In *Proc. of ACM conference on Computer and communications security* (pp. 552–561). ACM. 10.1145/1315245.1315313

Shmeidler, D. (1989). Subjective probability and expected utility without additivity. *Econometrica*, *57*(3), 571–587. doi:10.2307/1911053

Shwartz, L., Rosu, D., Loewenstern, D., Buco, M. J., Guo, S., Lavrado, R., ... Singh, J. K. (2010). Quality of IT service delivery #x2014; Analysis and framework for human error prevention. *Service-Oriented Computing and Applications (SOCA), 2010 IEEE International Conference on*, 1–8. 10.1109/SOCA.2010.5707161

Siano, P. (2014). Demand response and smart grids - A survey. *Renewable & Sustainable Energy Reviews*, *30*, 461–478. doi:10.1016/j.rser.2013.10.022

Sidhu, T. S., & Yin, Y. (2007). Modelling and Simulation for Performance Evaluation of IEC61850-Based Substation Communication Systems. *IEEE Transactions on Power Delivery*, *22*(3), 1482–1489. doi:10.1109/TPWRD.2006.886788

Simo Fhom, H., Kuntze, N., Rudolph, C., Cupelli, M., Liu, J., & Monti, A. (2010). A user-centric privacy manager for future energy systems. In *2010 International Conference on Power System Technology* (pp. 1–7). Academic Press. 10.1109/POWERCON.2010.5666447

Slijepcevic, S., & Potkonjak, M. (2001). *Power efficient organization of wireless sensor networks*. Intl Conf. Communications. doi:10.1109/ICC.2001.936985

Sobol, I. M. (1979). On the systematic search in a hypercube. *SIAM Journal on Numerical Analysis*, *16*(5), 790–793. doi:10.1137/0716058

Solanas, A., & Martinez-Balleste, A. (2006). V-mdav: a multivariate microaggregation with variable group size. *17th COMPSTAT Symposium of the IASC*.

Solanas, A., Seb'e, F., & Domingo-Ferrer, J. (2008). *Microaggregation-based heuristics for p-sensitive k-anonymity: one step beyond. In 2008 international workshop on Privacy* (pp. 61–69). New York: ACM.

Somani, A. K., & Vaidya, N. H. (1997). Understanding Fault Tolerance And Reliability - Guest Editors' Indroduction. *Computer*, *30*(4), 45–50. doi:10.1109/MC.1997.585153

Song, D. X., Wagner, D., & Tian, X. (2001). Timing Analysis of Keystrokes and Timing Attacks on SSH. In *USENIX Security Symposium (Vol. 2001)*. USENIX.

Soria-Comas, J. D.-F., Domingo-Ferrer, J., Sánchez, D., & Martínez, S. (2014). Enhancing data utility in differential privacy via microaggregation-based k-anonymity. *The VLDB Journal*, *23*(5), 771–794. doi:10.100700778-014-0351-4

Soria-Comas, J., & Domingo-Ferrer, J. (2012). Probabilistic k-anonymity through microaggregation and data swapping. *2012 IEEE International Conference on Fuzzy Systems*, (pp. 1-8). Brisbane, QLD: IEEE. 10.1109/FUZZ-IEEE.2012.6251280

Sotirovski, D. (2001). Towards fault-tolerant software architectures. In *Software Architecture, 2001. Proceedings. Working IEEE/IFIP Conference on* (pp. 7–13). IEEE. 10.1109/WICSA.2001.948399

Srinivas, H. (2017). *What is a green or sustainable building?* GDRC Research Output E-029. Kobe, Japan: Global Development Research Center. Retrieved from http://www.gdrc.org/uem/green-const/1-whatis.html

Stone, D. L., & Jeffay, K. (1995). An empirical study of delay jitter management policies. *Multimedia Systems*, *2*(6), 267–279. doi:10.1007/BF01225244

Storn, R., & Price, K. (1997, December). Differential evolution; a simple and efficient heuristic for global optimization over continuous spaces. *Journal of Global Optimization*, *11*(4), 341–359. doi:10.1023/A:1008202821328

Strasser, M., Popper, C., Capkun, S., & Cagalj, M. (2008). Jamming-resistant Key Establishment using Uncoordinated Frequency Hopping. In *2008 IEEE Symposium on Security and Privacy (sp 2008)* (pp. 64–78). IEEE. 10.1109/SP.2008.9

Studnia, I., Nicomette, V., Alata, E., Deswarte, Y., Kaaniche, M., & Laarouchi, Y. (2013). Survey on security threats and protection mechanisms in embedded automotive networks. In *Dependable Systems and Networks Workshop (DSN-W), IEEE/IFIP Conference on* (pp. 1–12). IEEE. 10.1109/DSNW.2013.6615528

Suh, G. E., O'Donnell, C. W., Sachdev, I., & Devadas, S. (2005). Design and implementation of the AEGIS single-chip secure processor using physical random functions. In *International Symposium on Computer Architecture* (pp. 25–36). Academic Press. 10.1109/ISCA.2005.22

Suh, S. C., Tanik, U. J., Carbone, J. N., & Eroglu, A. (2014). Applied cyber-physical systems. Springer. doi:10.1007/978-1-4614-7336-7

Sweeney, L. (2002). k-anonymity: A model for protecting privacy. *International Journal of Uncertainty, Fuzziness and Knowledge-based Systems*, *10*(5), 557–570. doi:10.1142/S0218488502001648

Szominski, S., Gadek, K., Konarski, M., Blaszczyk, B., Anielski, P., & Turek, W., … Intel. (2013). Development of a cyber-physical system for mobile robot control using Erlang. In *2013 Federated Conference on Computer Science and Information Systems, FedCSIS 2013* (pp. 1441–1448). IEEE. 10.1109/DeSE.2015.33

Sztipanovits, J., Koutsoukos, X., Karsai, G., Kottenstette, N., Antsaklis, P., Gupta, V., ... Wang, S. (2012). Toward a science of cyber–physical system integration. *Proceedings of the IEEE*, *100*(1), 29–44. doi:10.1109/JPROC.2011.2161529

Tang, S., Huang, Q., Li, X.-Y., & Wu, D. (2013). *Smoothing the energy consumption: Peak demand reduction in smart grid.* Proceedings IEEE INFOCOM.

Teniou, S., & Meribout, M. (2012). A new Hierarchical algorithm for Electrical Capacitance Tomography. *Measurement Journal (Elsevier)*, *45*(4), 683–690. doi:10.1016/j.measurement.2011.12.022

TEOS. (2010). *Terrestrial ecology observing systems, center for embedded networked sensing.* UCLA. Retrieved from http://research.cens.ucla.edu/

Texas Instruments CC2431. (2010). Retrieved from http://www.ti.com/

Thakur, A., Chaudhary, N., Tilokani, P., & Machado, J. (2017). A cyber-physical system based collaborative distributed manufacturing system architecture for intelligent manufacturing. In A cyber-physical system based collaborative distributed manufacturing system architecture for intelligent manufacturing. Academic Press.

The NETL Modern Grid Initiative. (2007, January). The NETL Modern Grid Initiative: A systems view of the modern grid. *Technology.*

Tonni, S. M., Rahman, M. Z., Parvin, S., & Gawanmeh, A. (2017). Securing Big Data Efficiently through Microaggregation Technique. In *Distributed Computing Systems Workshops (ICDCSW), 2017 IEEE 37th International Conference on* (pp. 125-130). IEEE.

Torra, V., & Domingo-Ferrer, J. (2001). *Disclosure control methods and information loss for microdata.* Elsevier.

Torres-pomales, W., & Langley, W. (2000). Software Fault Tolerance : A Tutorial. *October.*

Touzi, N. & Tourin, A. (2012). *Optimal Stochastic Control, Stochastic Target Problems and Backward SDEs.* Springer- Business & Economics.

Tricaud, C., & Chen, Y.Q. (2009). Optimal mobile actuator/sensor network motion strategy for parameter estimation in a class of CPS. *Proc of the American Control Conference*, 367–372.

Tseng, Y. C., & Pan, M. S. (2008). Quick convergecast in ZigBee beacon-enabled tree-based wireless sensor networks. *Computer Communications*, *31*(5), 999–1011. doi:10.1016/j.comcom.2007.12.015

Upadhyayula, S., Annamalai, V., & Gupta, S. K. S. (2003). A low-latency and energy-efficient algorithm for convergecast in wireless sensor networks. *Global Telecommunications Conf.*, 3525–3530. 10.1109/GLOCOM.2003.1258890

Usman, A., & Shami, S. H. (2013). Evolution of communication technologies for smart grid applications. *Renewable & Sustainable Energy Reviews*, *19*(January), 191–199. doi:10.1016/j.rser.2012.11.002

USNS Foundation. (2008). *Cyber-Physical Systems (CPS)*. Retrieved from https://www.nsf.gov/pubs/2014/nsf14542/nsf14542.htm

Vermesan, O., & Friess, P. (2014). Internet of Things Applications - From Research and Innovation to Market Deployment (O. Vermesan & P. Friess, Eds.). Academic Press. doi:10.100711036-012-0415-x

Vito, S. D. (2016, March 23). Retrieved September 10, 2017, from UCI Machine Learning Repository: https://archive.ics.uci.edu/ml/datasets/Air+Quality

Wan, C., Eisenman, S., Campbell, A., & Crowcroft, J. (2005). *Siphon: overload traffic management using multi-radio virtual sinks in sensor networks*. Intl Conf. Embedded Networked Sensor Systems. doi:10.1145/1098918.1098931

Wang, W., & Lu, Z. (2013). Cyber security in the Smart Grid: Survey and challenges. *Computer Networks*, *57*(5), 1344–1371. doi:10.1016/j.comnet.2012.12.017

Wang, X., Xing, G., Zhang, Y., Lu, C., Pless, R., & Gill, C. (2003). Integrated coverage and connectivity configuration in wireless sensor networks. *Intl Conf. Embedded Networked Sensor Systems*, 28–39.

Wang, X., Xing, G., Zhang, Y., Lu, C., Pless, R., & Gill, C. (2003). *Integrated coverage and connectivity configuration in wireless sensor networks*. Intl Conf. Embedded Networked Sensor Systems. doi:10.1145/958491.958496

Wikipedia.org. (n.d.a). *SCADA*. Retrieved September 10, 2017, from https://en.wikipedia.org/wiki/SCADA

Wikipedia.org. (n.d.b). *Stuxnet*. Retrieved September 10, 2017, from https://en.wikipedia.org/wiki/Stuxnet

Wojtczuk, R. (2001). The advanced return-into-lib (c) exploits: PaX case study. *Phrack Magazine, 11*(58).

Wolf, W. (2009). *Cyber-physical systems*. Academic Press. 10.1109/MC.2009.81

Wu, C., Mohsenian-Rad, H., Huang, J., & Wang, A. Y. (2011). Demand side management for Wind Power Integration in microgrid using dynamic potential game theory. In 2011 IEEE GLOBECOM Workshops (GC Wkshps) (pp. 1199–1204). IEEE. doi:10.1109/GLOCOMW.2011.6162371

Wua, F. J., Koab, Y. F., & Tseng, Y. C. (2011). From WSN towards cyber physical systems. *Pervasive and Mobile Computing*, *7*, 397–413. doi:10.1016/j.pmcj.2011.03.003

Wu, D., Chatzigeorgiou, D., Youcef-Toumi, K., Mekid, S., & Ben-Mansour, R. (2014). Channel-aware relay node placement in wireless sensor networks for pipeline inspection. *IEEE Transactions on Wireless Communications*, *13*(7), 3510–3523. doi:10.1109/TWC.2014.2314120

Xia, F., Tian, Y. C., Li, Y., & Sung, Y. (2007). Wireless Sensor/Actuator Network Design for Mobile Control Applications. *IEEE Sensor*, *7*(10), 2157–2173. doi:10.33907102157 PMID:28903220

Xie, Y., Chou, A., & Engler, D. (2003). ARCHER: Using Symbolic, Path-sensitive Analysis to Detect Memory Access Errors. *SIGSOFT Softw. Eng. Notes*, *28*(5), 327–336. doi:10.1145/949952.940115

Xu, K., Hassanein, H., Takahara, G., & Wang, Q. (2010). Relay node deployment strategies in heterogeneous wireless sensor networks. *IEEE Transactions on Mobile Computing*, *9*(2), 145–159. doi:10.1109/TMC.2009.105

Xu, Y., & Liu, W. (2011). Novel Multiagent Based Load Restoration Algorithm for Microgrids. *IEEE Transactions on Smart Grid*, *2*(1), 152–161. doi:10.1109/TSG.2010.2099675

Xu, Y., & Wang, W. (2013). Wireless Mesh Network in Smart Grid: Modeling and Analysis for Time Critical Communications. *IEEE Transactions on Wireless Communications*, *12*(7), 3360–3371. doi:10.1109/TWC.2013.061713.121545

Yaar, A., Perrig, A., & Song, D. (n.d.). Pi: a path identification mechanism to defend against DDoS attacks. In *Proceedings 19th International Conference on Data Engineering (Cat. No.03CH37405)* (pp. 93–107). IEEE Comput. Soc.

Yan, Q., Li, Y., Li, T., & Deng, R. (2009). Insights into malware detection and prevention on mobile phones. In Security Technology (pp. 242–249). Academic Press. doi:10.1007/978-3-642-10847-1_30

Yang, S., Gupta, P., Wolf, M., Serpanos, D., Narayanan, V., & Xie, Y. (2012). Power Analysis Attack Resistance Engineering by Dynamic Voltage and Frequency Scaling. *ACM Trans. Embed. Comput. Syst.*, *11*(3), 62:1–62:16.

Yan, Y., Qian, Y., Sharif, H., & Tipper, D. (2012). A Survey on Cyber Security for Smart Grid Communications. *IEEE Communications Surveys and Tutorials*, *14*(4), 998–1010. doi:10.1109/SURV.2012.010912.00035

Ye, F., Zhong, G., Cheng, J., Lu, S., & Zhang, L. (2003). *PEAS: a robust energy conserving protocol for long-lived sensor networks*. Intl Conf. Distributed Computing Systems.

Yin, H., Zhao, C., Li, M., & Chengbin, M. (2015). Utility Function-Based Real-Time Control of a Battery Ultracapacitor Hybrid Energy System. *IEEE Transactions on Industrial Informatics*, *11*(1), 220–231. doi:10.1109/TII.2014.2378596

Yoon, M.-K., Mohan, S., Choi, J., Kim, J.-E., & Sha, L. (2013). SecureCore: A multicore-based intrusion detection architecture for real-time embedded systems. In *Real-Time and Embedded Technology and Applications Symposium (RTAS), 2013 IEEE 19th* (pp. 21–32). IEEE. 10.1109/RTAS.2013.6531076

Younan, Y., Philippaerts, P., Cavallaro, L., Sekar, R., Piessens, F., & Joosen, W. (2010). PAriCheck: an efficient pointer arithmetic checker for C programs. In *Proceedings of the 5th ACM Symposium on Information, Computer and Communications Security* (pp. 145–156). ACM. 10.1145/1755688.1755707

Youngblood, G. M., & Cook, D. J. (2007). Data mining for hierarchical model creation. *IEEE Transactions on Systems, Man and Cybernetics. Part C, Applications and Reviews, 37*(4), 561–572. doi:10.1109/TSMCC.2007.897341

Younis, O., & Fahmy, S. (2004). HEED: A hybrid, energy-efficient, distributed clustering approach for ad hoc sensor networks. *IEEE Transactions on Mobile Computing, 3*(4), 366–379. doi:10.1109/TMC.2004.41

Yu, Krishnamachari, & Prasanna. (2004). Energy-latency tradeoffs for data gathering in wireless sensor networks. *INFOCOM2004*.

Yu, Z.-H., & Chin, W.-L. (2015). Blind False Data Injection Attack Using PCA Approximation Method in Smart Grid. *IEEE Transactions on Smart Grid, 6*(3), 1219–1226. doi:10.1109/TSG.2014.2382714

Zhang, E., Zhang, H., & Xue, B. (2008). Application of Integrated Neural Network based on information Combination for fault Diagnosis in Steam Turbine Generator. *International conference on Condition Monitoring and Diagnostic*, 21-24.

Zhang, Y., Qiu, M., Tsai, C., Hassan, M. M., & Alamri, A. (2017). Health-CPS: Healthcare cyber-physical system assisted by cloud and big data. *IEEE Systems Journal, 11*(1), 88–95. doi:10.1109/JSYST.2015.2460747

Zhang, Y., Wang, L., Sun, W. II, Green, R. C. II, & Alam, M. (2011). Distributed intrusion detection system in a multi-layer network architecture of smart grids. *IEEE Transactions on Smart Grid, 2*(4), 796–808. doi:10.1109/TSG.2011.2159818

Zhang, Z., Ma, M., & Yang, Y. (2008). Energy-efficient multihop polling in clusters of two-layered heterogeneous sensor networks. *IEEE Transactions on Computers, 57*(2), 231–245. doi:10.1109/TC.2007.70774

Zhao, E. H. (2016). *Network-Aware QoS Routing for Smart Grids Using Software Defined Networks*. Academic Press.

Zhao, J., Hammad, E., & Farraj, A. (2016). *Network-Aware QoS Routing for Smart Grids Using Software Defined Networks*. Academic Press.

Zhao, L., Hong, X., & Liang, Q. (2004). Energy-efficient self-organization for wireless sensor networks: a fully distributed approach. *Global Telecommunications Conf.*, 2728–2732.

Zhao, Z., Lee, W. C., Shin, Y., & Song, K.-B. (2013). An Optimal Power Scheduling Method for Demand Response in Home Energy Management System. *IEEE Transactions on Smart Grid, 4*(3), 1391–1400. doi:10.1109/TSG.2013.2251018

Zhu, Z., & Lambotharan, S. (2012). Overview of demand management in smart grid and enabling wireless communication technologies. *IEEE Wireless Communications*, *19*(3), 48–56. doi:10.1109/MWC.2012.6231159

Zhu, Z., Lambotharan, S., Chin, W. H., & Fan, Z. (2015). A Game Theoretic Optimization Framework for Home Demand Management Incorporating Local Energy Resources. *IEEE Transactions on Industrial Informatics*, *11*(2), 353–362.

ZigBee. (2006). *ZigBee document 064112. IEEE standard for IT(2003), Telecommunications and information exchange between systems; local and metropolitan area networks specific requirements part; 15.4:wireless medium access control (MAC) and physical layer (PHY) specifications for low-rate wireless personal area networks (LR-WPANs)*, Zigbee Alliance 2003. Author.

Zipperer, A., Aloise-Young, P. A., Suryanarayanan, S., Zimmerle, D., Roche, R., Earle, L., ... Zimmerle, D. (2013). Electric Energy Management in the Smart Home: Perspectives on Enabling Technologies and Consumer Behavior. *Proceedings of the IEEE*, *101*(11), 2397–2408. doi:10.1109/JPROC.2013.2270172

About the Contributors

Joel J. P. C. Rodrigues is a professor and senior researcher at the Inatel, Brazil, and senior researcher at the Instituto de Telecomunicações, Portugal. Prof. Rodrigues is the leader of the Internet of Things research group (CNPq) and of the NetGNA Research Group, Director for Conference Development - IEEE ComSoc Board of Governors, IEEE Distinguished Lecturer, the President of the scientific council at ParkUrbis – Covilhã Science and Technology Park, the Past-Chair of the IEEE ComSoc TCs on eHealth and on Communications Software, Steering Committee member of the IEEE Life Sciences Technical Community. He is the editor-in-chief of 3 international journals, including the International Journal of E-Health and Medical Communications, from IGI-Global, and editorial board member of several journals. He has authored or coauthored over 550 papers in refereed international journals and conferences, 3 books, and 2 patents. He had been awarded several Outstanding Leadership and Outstanding Service Awards by IEEE Communications Society and several best papers awards. Prof. Rodrigues is a licensed professional engineer (as senior member), member of the Internet Society, and a senior member ACM and IEEE.

Amjad Gawanmeh, SM IEEE, is an assistant professor, Khalifa University, UAE and affiliate Assistant professor, Concordia University Montreal, Canada. He is an assistant professor at the Department of Electrical and Computer Engineering at Khalifa University since 2010. He received the M.S. and the Ph.D degrees from Concordia University, Montreal, Canada, 2003 and 2008. He worked as a researcher for the Hardware Verification Group at Concordia University between 2000 and 2008. He worked for Applied Science University in Jordan from 2008 until 2010 as an assistant professor. His research interests are verification of hardware systems, security systems, and healthcare systems, modeling and analysis of complex systems such as CPS, performance analysis of complex systems, reliability of as medical system, and reliability of CPS. He is reviewer for several journals in IEEE, Elsevier, and Wiley. He has co-chaired several conferences such as WiMob 2015, and workshops organized in conferences such as ICC, NetSoft, LCN, Healthcom, WiMob. Has served on the TPC for key conference such as Globecom, ICC, PIMRC, ICCVE, WCNC, LCN, and Infocom workshops. He is an IEEE senior member.

* * *

Areej Abdelaal earned a bachelor's degree in Computer Engineering from Kuwait University. Interested in cutting-edge technologies and applications.

Jiwa Abdullah received his Bachelor of Engineering degree from Liverpool University, United Kingdom, in Electronic Engineering. He obtained his Master of Science degree (1990) and PhD from Loughborough University (2007), United Kingdom. His PhD thesis is on QoS for Mobile Ad Hoc Networks. Currently he is attached to the Faculty of Electrical and Electronic Engineering, Universiti Tun Hussein Onn Malaysia, Batu Pahat, Johor, Malaysia. His main interests are wireless sensor networks, underwater wireless sensor networks, mobile ad hoc networks, wireless communications, networking, application of computational intelligence to communication systems, integration of WSN and IoT, Cyberphysical Systems and also in the area of engineering educations. He authored more than 60 publications in journals, conferences and book chapters. Assoc Prof. Dr Jiwa Abdullah is a member of IEEE and Board of Engineers Malaysia.

Sa'ed Abed received his B.Sc. and M.Sc. in Computer Engineering from Jordan University of Science and Technology, Jordan in 1994 and 1996, respectively. In 2008, he received his Ph.D. in Computer Engineering from Concordia University, Canada. He has previously worked at King Faisal University in Saudi Arabia from 1997-2003. He joined Hashemite University, Jordan, as an Assistant Professor from 2008-2014. Currently, Dr. Abed is an assistant professor in the Department of Computer Engineering at Kuwait University. His research interests include Formal Methods, VLSI Design and Image Processing. Dr. Abed also served as a reviewer for various international conferences and journals.

Ali Ahmadinia received his Ph.D. degree from University of Erlangen-Nuremberg, Germany, in 2006. In 2004-2005, he worked as a research associate in Electronic imaging group, Fraunhofer Institute - Integrated Circuits (IIS), Erlangen, Germany. In 2006-2008, he was a research fellow in the School of Engineering and Electronics, University of Edinburgh, Edinburgh, UK. In 2008, he joined GCU, Glasgow, UK, where he was a senior lecturer in embedded systems. He is currently a faculty member of Department of Computer Science in California State University San Marcos, US. His research has resulted more than 100 international journal and conference publications in the areas of embedded systems and system-on-chip design, wireless and security applications.

Antônio Marcos Alberti received the degree in Electrical Engineering from Santa Maria Federal University (UFSM), Santa Maria, RS, Brazil, in 1986, and the M.Sc. and Ph.D. degrees in Electrical Engineering from Campinas State University (Unicamp), Campinas, SP, Brazil, in 1998 and 2003, respectively. In February 2004, he joined National Institute of Telecommunications (INATEL), Brazil, as an Adjunct Professor. He was a visiting researcher at Future Internet Department at Electronics and Telecommunications Research Institute (ETRI), South Korea, from March 2012 up to February 2013. He is the head of ICT Lab and chief architect of NovaGenesis convergent ICT project. He is a researcher on information architectures, including smart places, cyber infrastructures and new Internet architectures. Author of several technical and scientific articles. Contributor to the Brazilian IoT/M2M National Plan and Future Internet Forum of South Korea. Observer of emerging technologies and enthusiastic of technological evolution and its disruptions. Trend hacker and tech content writer and curator.

Nayef Abdulwahab Mohammed Alduais is currently a PhD researcher in the Internet of Things and Wireless Sensor Networks in the Faculty of Electrical and Electronic Engineering, Universiti Tun Hussein Onn Malaysia, having previously worked as an Assistant Lecturer within the Faculty of Computer Science and Engineering at Hodeidah University, Yemen, from 2007 until 2013. He has been awarded numerous medals and Scientific Excellence certificates, and has authored numerous papers for journals and conference proceedings. His main areas of research interest are in Wireless Sensor Networks and Internet of Things (IoT).

Basman Alhafidh joins Florida Institute of Technology as a Ph.D. Student in 2013 at the Department of Electrical and Computer Engineering. He was awarded his Ph.D. Scholarship from the Ministry of Higher Education in Iraq. Prior to coming to Florida Tech, he was an assistant lecturer at the University of Mosul. Basman received both his B.Sc. and M.Sc. in Computer Engineering from the University of Mosul. Currently, he is a Ph.D. Candidate at Florida Institute of Technology. Basman's teaching interests include Embedded System, Software Engineering, and Automation System. He has been the advisor for senior students at Mosul University for several years and won the Ministry of Higher Education awards in 2010 and 2011. His primary research interests are in the field of automation systems. Specifically, he is interested in the smart home, autonomous system, and IoT design and implementation system. Basman resides with his family in the city of Melbourne, Florida. In his free time, he travels with his family to another state to explore new places and visits big cities in other states to get more knowledge about people and their social life.

William Allen is currently an Associate Professor of Computer Sciences at the Florida Institute of Technology. He served as an Assistant Professor in the Computer Sciences Department from 2003 to 2010, teaching a range of undergraduate and graduate courses, conducting both funded and unfunded research and advising Master and Ph.D. students. From 1995 to 2003, Dr. Allen was a Lecturer of Computer Science at the University of Central Florida, teaching a wide range of undergraduate courses for Computer Science and Information Technology majors. His current research includes Balancing usability with security and privacy, Forensic analysis of digital data, Improving software design methodologies to develop more secure software and automation systems.

Guru Prasad Bhandari received his BCA (Bachelor of Computer Application) from Pokhara University, Nepal in 2011. In 2014, he received his MCA (Master of Computer Applications) from Banaras Hindu University, India. He is currently a research scholar, pursuing Ph.D. in Computer Applications at DST-CIMS in Banaras Hindu University since 2015. His research interests include fault-tolerance, service-oriented architecture, embedded systems and intelligent systems. His Ph.D. research topic is 'Fault Analysis of Distributed Systems'. He is a student member of IEEE. He has published several research papers in International Journals and in conference proceedings.

Valentina Franzoni obtained her Ph.D. in Engineering for Computer Science at the Department of Computer, Control, and Management Engineering at La Sapienza University of Rome. She has been a senior research assistant at the Department of Computer Science, Hong Kong Baptist University (2012) and at the Department of Mathematics and Computer Science, University of Perugia, Italy (2011–2015). She received her BSc degree and MSc (cum laude - honours) from the Department of Mathematics and Computer Science, University of Perugia, then worked as a Contract Professor for the Master in Systems and Technologies for Information and Communication Security, and Assistant Professor for Multimedia Systems and Computer Science. Her research interests include artificial intelligence, broadening from emotion recognition to network semantics, usability and web learning, in which she has a record of invited international speeches, publications and awards since 2008.

Uttam Ghosh is an Instructor of Computer Science, Tennessee State University, Nashville, TN. Earlier he worked as a Postdoctoral Research Associate in Electrical and Computer Engineering, TSU, Nashville, TN. Dr. Ghosh was a Postdoctoral Teaching Fellow in the Department of Computer and Information Science at the Fordham University. Prior joining to Fordham University, he was a postdoctoral research fellow at ADSC, Illinois at Singapore Pte. Ltd (A unit of UIUC, IL, USA). As part of his research he focused on SDN applicability on Resilient Smart Grid design and implemented SDN network for smart girds based on IEEE 37-bus system in Mininet and Testbed. Earlier he worked in several projects funded by DIT, MHRD and DRDO, Govt. of India. Dr. Ghosh has a number of publications in International Journals and Conferences in the areas of wireless networks, cyber physical system security and software defined networking. Uttam completed his MS (by Research) and PhD both from the Department of Electronics and Electrical Engineering, Indian Institute of Technology, Kharagpur, India in 2009 and 2013 respectively. Uttam received his BTech in Information Technology from Govt. College of Engineering and Textile Technology, Serampore, WB, India in 2005.

Ratneshwer Gupta did his Ph.D. in Component Based Software Engineering from Indian Institute of Technology, Banaras Hindu University, Varanasi (IIT-BHU), India. His research area is CBSE and SOA. He is serving as an Assistant Professor in School of Computer & Systems Sciences, JNU, New Delhi – 110067, India. He is actively involved in teaching and research for last 8 years. He has 16 research papers in International Journals and 26 research papers in international/national conference proceedings in his credit.

Joanna Jackson is the Manager of Information Technology at Melbourne Polytechnic, Victoria, Australia.

Evgeniy Marinov graduated Mathematics from Sofia University, Bulgaria and has two master specializations: in Mathematical Physics from Sofia University and Algebraic Geometry from University "Strasbourg I", France, PhD thesis in the area of Topology and Intuitionistic fuzzy sets. He published a Chapter in the book "Imprecision and Uncertainty in Information Representation and Processing" - Springer and several papers in International conferences: IEEE Conf. of Intelligent Systems, Conference of the European Society for Fuzzy Logic and Technology (EUSFLAT). His interests are mainly in the fields of Statistical machine learning and its applications in Decision making and Game theory. Experienced software engineer, working in the industry for several years and member of the Union of Bulgarian Mathematicians.

Mahmoud Meribout (M'91) received the B.Eng. degree in 1985 and the Ph.D. degree in electronics engineering from the University of Technology of Compiegne, Compiegne, France, in January 1995. He was with Nippon Telegraph and Telephone Corporation, Tokyo, Japan, and NEC Corporation, Tokyo, from 1995 to 2000, where he was involved in several projects related to embedded systems design. In 1998, he received the NTT Best Award for his research and development efforts in the areas of embedded systems design and imaging systems. In 2008, he joined the Electrical Engineering Department, Petroleum Institute, where he is currently an Associate Professor. His current research interests focusses on embedded systems, imaging systems (THz, MPI, optical, electrical, and magnetic tomography), instrumentation, and multiphase flow metering, and enhanced oil recovery using electrical mean.

Yuri Pavlov is associate professor in the Institute of Information and Communication Technologies, Bulgarian Academy of Sciences. He has received DUES from Paris VI - France, MSc degree in Automation from Technical University of Sofia and holds PhD from the Bulgarian Academy of Sciences. His research has been published in international journals Proceedings of Bulgarian Academy of Sciences, International online journal Bioautomation, European Journal of OR, E-learning III and the knowledge society-Belgium, Proceedings in Manufacturing Systems – Romania, Global Journals Inc. (USA), IOSR Journal of Computer Engineering etc. He is author of the monograph Pavlov, Yuri P. & Rumen D. Andreev. "Decision Control, Management, and Support in Adaptive and Complex Systems: Quantitative Models. Hershey, PA, IGI Global, 2013 and author of the monograph "Pavlov Yuri P. & Marinov E. I. (2018), VALUE BASED MODELING AND CONTROL: preferences, utility, stochastic control, LAP LAMBERT Academic Publishing, Berlin, Germany" and several chapters in "Encyclopedia of Business Analytics and Optimization" - IGI Global, Encyclopedia "Artificial Intelligence: Concepts, Methodologies, Tools and Applications" - IRMA USA, Encyclopedia of Information Science and Technology, Fourth Edition (IGI Global). He has both research and practical expertise in innovative and creative decision-making, optimal control, control design of complex systems. He has interests in the fields of decision making and decision support systems, utility theory, theory of measurement, stochastic approximation, machine learning, methods and algorithms for mathematical modeling, optimization and control of biotechnological processes and systems, different approaches for stabilization and control, reduction and equivalent transformation of nonlinear mathematical models, optimization of continuous and fed-batch cultivation processes are also of current interest. He is also member of International Institute of Informatics and Systemics (IIIS).

Ahmed Saeed received his B.S degree in Computer Engineering from COMSATS Institute of Information Technology in 2006 and his M.S, focusing on Microelectronics and System-on-Chip engineering, from Lancaster University, UK in 2008. He received the PhD degree in Computer Engineering from the Glasgow Caledonian University, UK in 2016. Currently, he is serving as an Assistant Professor in the Department of Electrical Engineering at CIIT Lahore. His research interests include but not limited to security-aware communications in multi-core systems, Network-on-Chip architecture, system security, embedded systems, and machine Learning.

Imran Saied completed his B.Sc. in Electrical Engineering from Georgia Institute of Technology and M.Sc. in Electrical Engineering from California State University in Fullerton. He had gained experience working in software and power generation companies, before embarking on a research project at The Petroleum Institute in Abu Dhabi, UAE. His research during that time focused in the area of tomography and its applications to multiphase flow metering and solid contaminant detection in oil and gas pipelines. Currently, Imran is pursuing his PhD at the University of Edinburgh where his research focuses on developing tomographic and sensor applications for medical diagnosis.

Shakila Mahjabin Tonni works as a Lecturer in the Department of Computer Science and Engineering, East West University, Dhaka. Research interests include data security, big data and data analytics. Completed MSc and BSc in Computer Science and Engineering from the Department of CSE, Jahangirnagar University, Bangladesh. Beside working as a university faculty for more than 4 years, has previous experiences of working as a Technical Writer & Software Engineer. Also, involved with Bangladesh Open Source Network (BDOSN) as a Mentor of National High School Programming.

Index

U

V

W

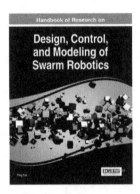

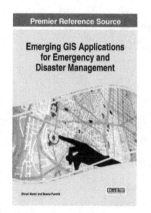 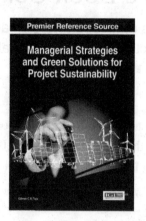  

Printed in the United States
By Bookmasters